FRAGMENTARY
REPUBLICAN LATIN
III

LCL 540

FRAGMENTARY REPUBLICAN LATIN

ORATORY

PART 1

EDITED AND TRANSLATED BY

GESINE MANUWALD

HARVARD UNIVERSITY PRESS

CAMBRIDGE, MASSACHUSETTS

LONDON, ENGLAND

2019

First published 2019

LOEB CLASSICAL LIBRARY® is a registered trademark
of the President and Fellows of Harvard College

Library of Congress Control Number 2018962593
CIP data available from the Library of Congress

ISBN 978-0-674-99723-3

*Composed in ZephGreek and ZephText by
Technologies 'N Typography, Merrimac, Massachusetts.
Printed on acid-free paper and bound by
Maple Press, York, Pennsylvania*

CONTENTS

CONTENTS

CONTENTS

CONTENTS

ORATORY, PART 2 [LCL 541]

CONTENTS

CONTENTS

CONTENTS

INDEX OF ORATORS

GENERAL INTRODUCTION

ORATORY AT ROME

Public speaking must have existed at Rome since at least the beginning of the Republican period: speeches and discussions are an obvious element of organized political interaction. In retrospect, Greek and Roman historians presenting the early history of Rome could not imagine social, political, and military procedures without the involvement of oratory and thus include speeches put into the mouth of Republican heroes in their narratives. A famous example of these early speeches is the oration allegedly given by Agrippa Menenius Lanatus (cos. 503 BC), when he persuaded the plebs to end their secession in 494 BC by telling them the story of the belly and the other parts of the body (Liv. 2.32.8–12; for a similar intervention ascribed to M. Popillius Laenas, see Cic. *Brut.* 56). For the same period, Dionysius of Halicarnassus reports a sequence of orations in the Senate in the course of a debate, followed by addresses to the People in the Forum (Dion. Hal. *Ant. Rom.* 6.35–45). These texts obviously do not reproduce the authentic words of the respective speakers (even when the delivery of a speech may be attested), and the envisaged procedures have probably been modeled on

the conventions of later historical phases. Therefore, such passages cannot be taken as "historical evidence" for particular orations; still, they indicate that public speaking was regarded as such a central element of political interaction in Rome that writers active from the late Republic onward assumed that it had always taken place.

More detailed and more reliable information about Roman oratory is available for the period from the third century BC onward (coinciding with the "beginnings of Roman literature" in about 240 BC) since fragments of speeches and eventually entire speeches survive and testimonia on the lives of some of the orators, on their speaking style, and on occasions for public speaking are extant.

The most comprehensive source for the development of oratory at Rome is the dialogic treatise *Brutus* (46 BC) by M. Tullius Cicero (106–43 BC).[1] In that work the interlocutor "Cicero," in conversation with his friends M. Iunius Brutus (**158**) and T. Pomponius Atticus (**103**),[2] provides an overview of Roman orators from the beginnings of oratory in Rome until his own time; he discusses their chronology, their characteristic features in his view, and their respective qualities and shortcomings.

---

[1] For details on the orators mentioned, see the commentaries by Douglas (1966) and Marchese (2011) and also the prosopographical study by Sumner (1973). For some more recent discussions of Cicero's *Brutus*, see, for example, Gowing 2000; Vogt-Spira 2000; Steel 2003; Dugan 2012; Aubert-Baillot and Guérin 2014; Hall 2014.

[2] Numbers in brackets after an orator's name (in bold) give their number and position in *FRL*: see "Abbreviations and Symbols."

The survey in *Brutus* starts with L. Iunius Brutus, the founder of the Roman Republic, though even for Cicero the assumption that L. Iunius Brutus had oratorical abilities is based on inference (Cic. *Brut.* 53). Other influential men from early Rome are added on the same basis (Cic. *Brut.* 53–57). The first Roman for whose eloquence there is a record is identified as M. Cornelius Cethegus (**7**) since he is mentioned by the Republican poet Ennius (Cic. *Brut.* 57–60). The earliest Roman orator whose writings are partially extant, since his speeches were published, and whose eloquence can therefore still be assessed, is defined as M. Porcius Cato (**8**) (Cic. *Brut.* 61–69).

The discussion goes on to review the main public speakers in Rome up to Cicero's time, arranged chronologically in groups. Accordingly, *Brutus* provides a great deal of information about the existence of these individuals—their political attitudes, their preferred venues for oratorical appearances, their styles of speaking—as well as occasions and examples of their speeches.

While this treatise thus offers copious valuable details, it has to be borne in mind that Cicero did not compile this material as a scholarly exercise, but rather as a statement in the debate about different styles of oratory (Atticism vs. Asianism), on the development of public speaking at Rome, and as a description of his own oratory in the contemporary context; therefore, his judgments cannot be regarded as neutral and unbiased. Accordingly, when Cicero offers assessments of his subjects' political views and their quality as orators (e.g., Cic. *Brut.* 137, 222, 305), these opinions may not have been shared by all his contemporaries and need not be adopted by modern scholars.

At the same time, when Cicero mentions that someone appeared as an orator, this piece of information is likely to be trustworthy.

As Cicero's overview implies, oratory was not originally a literary genre at Rome but instead an element of public life, essential for organizing political affairs and for the career of individuals in the public sphere. This function is the reason why oratory assumed such an important role at Rome. Only once orators decided to write up and circulate written versions of utterances after their delivery did oratory acquire a literary dimension. The written record is the precondition for the survival of traces of oratory of the past even though the edited versions probably do not match the delivered versions exactly, and most aspects of the performance situation at the point of delivery have been lost and can hardly be recovered.

In line with the professionalization of oratory over time, rhetorical training, under the influence of Greek rhetoric, emerged in Rome from the second century BC, for which Cicero stresses the combination of studying with teachers and practice (Cic. *De or.* 1.14). The introduction of Greek rhetoric, however, was not uncontroversial in Rome: a senatorial decree of 161 BC and a censorial edict of 92 BC against rhetors are recorded (Suet. *Gram. et rhet.* 25; Cic. *De or.* 3.93–95). Yet these initiatives do not seem to have stopped the progress of oratory and rhetoric significantly. Rhetorical training later developed into the practice of declamation, which started to appear in Cicero's time, according to Seneca the Elder (Sen. *Controv.* 1, *praef.* 12: **165** F 34).

Matching the increasing sophistication of the practice, rhetorical handbooks and treatises started to be produced.

According to the imperial writer Quintilian (Quint. *Inst.* 3.1.19), M. Porcius Cato (**8**) was the first to write on oratory, followed later by M. Antonius (**65** F 37–40). Texts from the Republican period surviving in full are the anonymous *Rhetorica ad Herennium* (ca. 80s BC), Cicero's youthful *De inventione rhetorica* (80s BC), from which he later distanced himself (Cic. *De or.* 1.5), and the treatises *De oratore* (55 BC), *Brutus* (46 BC), and *Orator* (46 BC) by the mature Cicero. In different ways, all these writings are atypical examples of the genre of the rhetorical textbook, which would provide a summary of the main rules. Still, they indicate the standard rhetorical categories that were discussed in Rome, as they had been in Greece, such as the tasks and duties of the orator, the levels of style, the different types of speeches, and the forms of argument. These theoretical works are supplemented in the early imperial period by the collection of practice speeches (*controversiae* and *suasoriae*) compiled by Seneca the Elder (ca. 55 BC–39 AD), the treatise *Institutio oratoria*, on the orator's education, by Quintilian (ca. 35–100 AD), who opened a public school of rhetoric and was Rome's first professional teacher of this subject, and the discussion in the *Dialogus de oratoribus* by Tacitus (ca. 55–120 AD) on the state of oratory at the time and its potential decline.

Regarding the types of speeches, the rhetorical tradition distinguished between three different categories. Of these, two were particularly prominent in public speaking at Rome: political and judicial. The former subgenre covers speeches in the Senate and to the People at public meetings (*contiones*) on political issues, including the proposal of bills for new laws. The latter covers speeches in public and private court cases. Following the establish-

ment of so-called *quaestiones perpetuae*, standing courts for major crimes, from 149 BC (cf. introduction to **37**), along with the expansion of political offices and correspondingly of (alleged) misbehavior or politically controversial activities, there was a regular sequence of trials in the late second century and especially in the first century BC. Since the accused did not normally speak on their own behalf in Rome, but were defended by advocates, often by several, there were numerous opportunities for delivering speeches. Appearing in a prominent court case was seen as a good way for a young man to start a career before turning to politics. In addition, there are a few examples of the third type, the epideictic genre of speeches, in Rome, such as funeral orations.[3]

Cicero's comments suggest that forensic oratory was seen as requiring a higher level of accomplishment than political oratory, and that in politics speaking before the People was regarded as more challenging than speaking among one's peers in the Senate. Moreover, for the assessment of someone's oratory, the five tasks of an orator (*inventio, dispositio, elocutio, memoria, actio*—invention, arrangement, style, memory, delivery), are taken into account: only a few speakers are identified as outstanding in all areas.

SOURCES AND EVIDENCE

Out of the large number of political and judicial speeches that must have been made over the centuries of the Ro-

---

[3] On Roman funeral speeches, see Flach 1975; Kierdorf 1980.

man Republic, only some of Cicero's speeches survive in full. This reduction is due to two main reasons: first, Roman orators (including Cicero) did not write up all their speeches. Instead, they made decisions on whether they wished to edit delivered orations, and they merely published a selection of important and/or successful speeches (after producing written versions had become standard). Only in the case of published speeches can more than references to the occasions remain. Second, later generations were interested in specific historical incidents, in particular speakers, or in certain stylistic features; therefore, not all material that had reached written form was preserved in equal measure.

While the reduction over the course of transmission is similar to what can be observed for other Roman literary genres, there is hardly any other genre in Rome that is so dominated by a single figure as Republican oratory is by Cicero: his works not only furnish the only complete examples of texts of this genre but also provide much of the information about other speakers and oratorical occasions. So as not to succumb to a one-sided view of the subject determined by Cicero, it is vital to collect and consider whatever material exists about other speakers in Republican Rome from outside his corpus.

The orators and their oratorical appearances covered in these volumes, therefore, open up a wider perspective on Roman Republican oratory; they give an insight into potential forms and themes as well as into the wide variety of occasions and styles. The picture is still determined, however, by the available sources as well as by the assessments and preferences of the transmitting authors. Nev-

ertheless, the fact that this overview includes orators from different phases within the Republican period as well as men given high or low rankings by contemporaries and by later ancient authors can contribute to providing a fuller panorama of Roman Republican oratory.

In addition to Cicero's remarks and quotations, the majority of references to oratorical occasions can be found in the commentators on Cicero, in Valerius Maximus, Quintilian, Tacitus, Fronto, and historiographers, while proper fragments have mainly been preserved in the archaist Aulus Gellius and the works of lexicographers, grammarians, and rhetoricians interested in particular words, phrases, or stylistic figures. The material available for individual orators varies accordingly.

What emerges is a sense of which orators were more "prolific" and/or more "famous" than others, but this is an impression shaped by the sources.[4]

"FRAGMENTS" OF ROMAN ORATORY

Editing the "fragments" of Roman Republican oratory is in many ways more complex than editing some of the other writers or literary genres represented in *Fragmentary Republican Latin* (*FRL*). In addition to the standard difficulties created by any fragmentary corpus (for instance, problems of transmission and attribution), the task of presenting the remains of Roman Republican oratory is confronted from the start with the essential and difficult question of whom and what to include or not to include.

---

[4] On the sources (and their problems) for the "lost orators of Rome," see Steel 2007.

In the case of M. Tullius Cicero, the only orator from the Roman Republican period for whom entire speeches remain, it is fairly obvious that he was an "orator" and what a "speech" of his constitutes.[5] As regards other individuals, if "orator" is understood to be anyone who ever voiced an utterance in a formal or semiformal context, the list of Republican orators would have to include every known magistrate, since anyone who ever proposed a law would have spoken to present it to the Senate and/or the People, and every magistrate would have given an inaugural speech and/or made a statement on some matter in the Senate at least once. For most Republican politicians, however, the fact that they must have spoken in public can be inferred only from what is known about their public careers and the standard political procedures; there is no specific evidence confirming that they did so or giving details about occasion, content, or style of any utterance.

In light of this situation, the present edition focuses on those orators for whom there is some specific evidence for their oratory and/or for individual speeches and remarks made by them; and it provides the necessary contextual information for the passages given. The project *Fragments of the Republican Roman Orators* to be published by Oxford University Press (*FRRO*: http://www.frro.gla.ac.uk) attempts a wider coverage of material, including lists of events at which speeches were made and notices of all kinds of speeches. Such an extensive database will not be replicated here. Lists of Republican magistrates have been compiled in *MRR*; overviews of proposals of laws

---

[5] For speeches of Cicero not transmitted in full, see Crawford 1984 and 1994.

presented and passed are provided in *LPPR* and Elster 2003; surveys of identifiable civil and military *contiones* are given in *CCMR* (App. A–D). Full information about known trials is available in *TLRR*.[6] Such works can be consulted for further historical details.

Even with a more limited focus on individuals for whom speech-making is attested and on evidence specifically on oratory, decisions remain difficult; this situation is connected with the issue of defining "fragments" and "testimonia" and of distinguishing between them.

What can be set off fairly clearly from notices about specific speeches is information about a person's life and oratory more generally. Passages illustrating these aspects have been included and are given separately as testimonia (T + number) before the documentation on individual speeches. These passages also provide insight into oratorical values and rhetorical terminology in use in ancient Rome.

If one applies a narrow definition for material on individual speeches, one would accept only pieces quoted as verbatim fragments. While this might be most correct in philological terms (and in view of the title of this series), it would give a skewed impression of the scope of Republican oratory, for a great deal of relevant information is conveyed by indirect quotations and comments. Thus, this edition has adopted what is hopefully a happy medium: it does not include every mention of politicians who are likely to have made speeches or of occasions at which

[6] For details of standard reference works quoted with abbreviated titles, see "Bibliography" and "Abbreviations and Symbols."

speeches must have been made; instead, it limits itself to more concrete instances where the sources provide an indication of the context and/or the content of speeches made and/or identify individuals as frequent speakers or as known for a particular style, even though this information can take a variety of forms and does not always include "fragments."[7]

Accordingly, since all these varieties are taken into account, this edition covers material of the following types with regard to individual speeches: phrases defined in the sources as verbatim utterances of a specific orator (as well as some where the attribution is doubtful, but possible), passages described as extracts from speeches, summaries of speeches or parts of speeches in indirect discourse, speeches put into the mouth of historical orators in historiographical works, and references to the context and content of speeches. Only the first category could unambiguously be defined as "fragments" and only the last as "testimonia" about speeches; the others are somewhere in between. Therefore, no attempt has been made to distinguish between "fragments" and "testimonia" of utterances in the presentation: all the relevant passages documenting specific utterances in one way or another are given in the context of the source authors with continuous numbering; what may be a verbatim fragment is marked by quotation marks. For the sake of simplicity and consistency, all passages documenting orations are referred to as "F + number," although most of them are not actual "fragments."

Even the apparently verbatim fragments, though, are

[7] For comments on defining "fragments" with reference to orators, see, for example, *ORF*[4] II, pp. vi–viii; Balbo 2004, 11–14.

not unambiguous, because of the originally oral nature of oratory: in many cases it is unknown whether orators published a written version of their speeches and the "fragments" come from those versions, or whether there was oral or informal transmission of key phrases (including other agents than the orators themselves) and these were written down at some point (records of Senate meetings were kept only from the time of Caesar onward). Obviously, even if the fragments derive from versions produced by the orators, there is the question (debated with respect to Cicero's speeches) as to what extent the written texts resemble what was said at the original point of delivery, which included not only set speeches but also verbal exchanges and impromptu remarks provoked by the situation. The original words spoken cannot be fully recovered for any Republican orator; what can be compiled is only what entered the written transmission. This situation makes it questionable whether one can speak of "verbatim fragments of Roman oratory" at all, and is another reason not to try to introduce a rigid artificial distinction between "fragments" and "testimonia" of speeches of Republican orators.

For speeches given in historiographical works (e.g., Livy, Sallust, Appian, Cassius Dio, Plutarch), it is well known that these do not report the actual words spoken by the historical figures (particularly if the orations are given in the Greek language) and are rather speeches put into their mouths as the historiographers envisage them or as they suit the writers' aims. Nonetheless, beyond being revealing elements of the historians' narratives, these texts still indicate the occasions and topics of such speeches and provide information about how the respec-

tive orators were seen.[8] Therefore, as evidence (testimonia), these passages (even Greek ones) can helpfully be included to complement the portrayal of individuals also attested otherwise as speakers. Accordingly, speeches transmitted in ancient historiographers have been given where they seemed to illustrate an oratorical occasion otherwise attested, or to complement other evidence on a specific orator (though, due to their dubious nature, they are presented as summaries and not printed in full).

In addition to these principles, in drawing the line between what should and should not be included, this edition has been inspired by the valuable edition of *Oratorum Romanorum Fragmenta* (*ORF*) by Enrica Malcovati, even though her editorial decisions have not escaped criticism, particularly the fact that she does not clarify her principles in detail in the edition.[9]

Malcovati's edition first appeared in three volumes in 1930. A much-revised edition was published in 1955 (reprinted with additions and corrections, but with the same numbering, in 1967 and 1976): this version consisted of a single volume with a different layout and distribution of the material, and it included a larger number of orators and texts. The fourth edition saw the addition of a separate index volume, compiled by a team of scholars in Graz (Austria). In several articles and notices, Malcovati ex-

[8] For considerations on the role of speeches in Roman historiography, see Miller 1975; on the status of speeches in Cassius Dio see e.g. Fomin 2016; Burden-Strevens 2016; 2018; Kemezis 2016.

[9] See especially Badian 1956 and 1968.

plained some of her principles and justified some of her decisions, partly in response to comments made by reviewers of earlier editions.[10]

Malcovati's implicit and explicit methods as well as reviewers' comments[11] were taken on board when it was decided to base this edition on Malcovati. On reflection, this seemed to be the best compromise, since thereby her numbering of orators and texts could be kept. A complete departure from Malcovati would lead to a new numbering of orators, testimonia, and fragments. This would have the advantage that additional orators could be properly inserted into the sequence, the chronological ordering could be adjusted, and separate numerical sequences for testimonia and "fragments" could be introduced. Since, however, Malcovati's numbers are still the standard system of reference, it seemed more convenient and user-friendly to retain Malcovati's numbers and add only a few further orators and passages, signaled by a combination of numbers and capital letters.

This edition thus includes all orators recognized by Malcovati from the second edition onward (with the addenda, supplemented in later editions in an appendix, put into the sequence), with the exception of M. Porcius Cato (**8**), because of the amount of material that survives for his oratory; this will be included in a separate volume of the Loeb Classical Library, along with the other works of Cato. Obviously, the only other well-known orator from

[10] See Malcovati 1955 and also 1965, 1967, 1973, 1976.

[11] Reviews of all editions are listed under "Malcovati" in the Bibliography.

the Republican period who is missing from this edition is M. Tullius Cicero: his (complete) speeches can be found elsewhere in the LCL.

Beyond the orators identified by Malcovati, a few additional ones have been inserted into the sequence, with separate numbering (numbers with a capital letter as a suffix), also to fill identified gaps.[12] While Malcovati is right to point out that an edition of oratorical fragments should not be a reproduction of Cicero's *Brutus*, those speakers for whom specific interventions are noted or who are identified as well-known speakers or displaying a particular style in this treatise have been included;[13] the selection should not be affected by value judgments based on Cicero's assessment.[14]

In the case of some of the orators found in Malcovati, there are testimonia pointing to further oratorical appearances, not documented by Malcovati with numbered passages or titles of speeches: these are identified with full references in the introductions to the respective orators. In a few instances, where the additional sources are extensive, revealing, and/or similar to others given, it was felt that, beyond more detailed documentation, the portrait of an orator would benefit from some of them being printed

[12] See especially Badian 1956.

[13] Calculations vary; according to one view, only for fifty-three individuals out of the almost three hundred orators mentioned in the *Brutus* are more details given (Vogt-Spira 2000, 209, based on Kytzler 1970, 270, 286).

[14] For a list of orators in Cicero's time, see Bardon 1952, 212–14; for a list of speeches delivered between 81 and 42 BC, see Bardon 1952, 214–17.

as additional texts; therefore, such texts have been added. To avoid interfering with the existing numeration adopted from Malcovati, they have been put within the sequence of "fragments," identified by capital letters added as a suffix to the respective numbers (F 1A, F 3B, etc.).

Ap. Claudius Caecus (**1**) has been retained as the starting point of the collection, despite references to earlier oratorical appearances mentioned above, because he seems to be the first man to have been recognized as eloquent in the Roman tradition and for whose oratory evidence was available in Cicero's time. The sequence concludes with M. Valerius Messalla Corvinus (**176**), although some speeches of the last few men listed date to a time after the "Republican period"; their dates of birth, however, and the bulk of their literary activity associate them with Republican times, in contrast to Octavian / Augustus, who can be regarded as inaugurating the "Imperial period" and who therefore has not been included.

Since oratory in Rome was so closely connected with public life, almost all orators represented are male, except for Hortensia (**93**), the daughter of the famous orator Q. Hortensius Hortalus (**92**). Valerius Maximus devotes a section of his work (8.3) to female pleaders: in addition to Hortensia (**93**), he mentions Maesia of Sentinum (8.3.1; *TLRR* 384) and Carfania (d. 48 BC), wife of the senator Licinius Buccio (8.3.2), but there is little detailed information about their oratorical activity. Understandably, there is no record of a large number of female speakers in Republican Rome.

With public speaking focused on Rome, orators from the allied and Latin communities around Italy, to whom Cicero devotes a brief section in the Brutus (Cic. *Brut.*

169–72), have been included only when they are known to have spoken at Rome (L. Papirius Fregellanus [11]; T. Betutius Barrus Asculanus [84]).

Like Malcovati (and other editions of similar material), this edition errs on the side of providing more rather than less. Therefore, since it comprises "fragments of oratory," and not just "fragments of speeches", it includes utterances by orators that were probably not made in set speeches, yet are transmitted as uttered by them (along with some apparently deriving from verbal exchanges in court or in the Senate) and that thus complement the portrait of their speaking. For orators who were also active in other literary genres, it is not always clear whether a fragment transmitted without attribution to a specific work comes from a speech or, for instance, a historiographical work. Where a connection with oratory is possible, these texts have been presented with an appropriate note. Malcovati even includes the rhetorical treatise by M. Antonius (65), edicts of M. Calpurnius Bibulus (122), and the eulogy of Cato by M. Iunius Brutus (158). Since one could argue that all these items are instances of formal speech similar to and/ or connected with oratory, they have been retained so as to provide the fullest picture possible.

Malcovati provides a Latin title for each speech, mostly developed from one of the ancient sources for the speech. These titles have been replaced by English descriptions (on both the Latin and the English sides), to avoid the impression that there are transmitted and established designations.

In Malcovati's edition each speech is given a Roman numeral, and the title is followed by a date wherever possible. The numbers for orations have not been taken over:

it was deemed that the numbering of the source texts was sufficient to identify particular oratorical occasions and to enable cross-references, while the numbering of orations might convey a false sense of completeness in terms of the overall number of speeches known for each orator and of their sequence. Potential dates for speeches for which there is sufficient evidence are discussed in the introductions to each orator or speech. As Malcovati's numbering has been kept, her order of speeches is followed (according to the chronology established by her, with speeches of unknown date at the end, followed by unplaced fragments).

EDITORIAL PRACTICE

The texts for the "fragments" and "testimonia" have not been taken from Malcovati's edition, but rather from the most recent and/or most reliable editions of the source authors (listed in the Bibliography), giving precise indications of the locations of the passages printed.[15] For all pieces of evidence, as much of the context is given as is necessary for a full understanding and evaluation of the information on an orator or an oration. The textual apparatus has not been reproduced in full; it includes only brief notes on major issues affecting the sense and/or the attribution. Because of the wide range of source authors, no specific *sigla* have been used to identify individual manu-

---

[15] Where references are to the page numbers of a particular edition, the abbreviated last name of the editor is supplied for identification; full details are given in the Bibliography.

scripts; instead, they are referred to as *"cod."* or *"codd.,"* as appropriate.

For source authors who are represented elsewhere in the Loeb Classical Library, those existing English translations have provided starting points (with thanks to their respective translators), though they have all been updated and adapted for the purposes of this edition. The texts from source authors not (yet) included in the LCL have been newly translated.

This edition, like that of Malcovati, gives at the beginning of each entry general testimonia on the life or the assessment of a person's oratory. In contrast to testimonia on individual speeches (subsumed under "fragments": "F + number"), these are marked as Testimonia by "T + number." This distinction is made clearer here than in Malcovati, who numbered all passages illustrating a given orator sequentially, just printing the testimonia in smaller font. The adoption of Malcovati's numbering, however, means that the sequences of "fragments" do not always begin with F 1, but rather with various numbers, depending on the amount of testimonia.

The section on each orator starts with a brief introduction, including references both to the general testimonia printed and to other pieces of evidence. These introductions identify each orator by their *RE* number, the highest political offices they reached (if any) and other prosopographical data where relevant, and, where details are known, provide brief summaries of their biographies, focusing on key events characterizing the respective men and/or relevant to their oratory. These introductions also survey the general assessment of each person's oratory in

antiquity and other literary activity (if any). Further, brief introductions to the individual speeches provide the necessary context for these if it is not obvious from the source texts. Notes on the individual texts confine themselves to points of detail.

For cross-references to other orators and speeches, the names of orators, their numbers (in bold), and the numbers of the texts ("T or F + number") are used.

A number of orators appear frequently in a variety of contexts, and they are identified by their full name and number each time they are mentioned in the sources, to indicate the multiple connections between orators of each period. These cross-references should be followed up for more information about the individuals, since details of their careers or the cases they were involved in are not typically repeated outside their own entries. This is especially the case if several orators spoke on the same political or forensic issues: more detailed background information tends to be given in connection with the first orator involved (occasionally the most prominent), which can be found via these cross-references. If the same testimonium gives information about several orators, it is typically printed only once, with cross-references given in the other places where it is relevant. For cases in which Cicero was involved, details are not always provided, as they can easily be found in biographies of Cicero or introductions to editions of the orations he delivered on those occasions.

Doubtful attribution of passages to a particular orator or a specific speech is discussed in the relevant introductions and notes.

In the Latin text, { } indicates deletions, < > marks additions (by modern scholars), ⌊ ⌋ denotes supplements

from a secondary tradition, and [ ] encloses explanations. Words to be deleted are rarely translated; if so, they are also enclosed in { } in the English version. Meaningful additions to the Latin (beyond individual letters to create a grammatical text) have also been marked in the English by < > (apart from very corrupt texts discussed in notes). Substantial additions to the English version for the sake of clarity have been enclosed in [ ], and square [ ] brackets are again used for explanations.

The dating of Cicero's letters follows that given in D. R. Shackleton Bailey's editions (including those in the Loeb Classical Library).

NOTE ON TRANSLATIONS

Most of the material in these volumes consists of "testimonia" or similar texts; thus translation for the most part is straightforward, in the sense that one mainly has to deal with complete texts rather than with true fragments that may not even consist of a complete clause. However, because some entries comprise longer texts from different periods, by different authors, in different languages (Latin and Greek), and in different genres, they represent a wide range of writing styles. Hence, the translations try to reproduce the nature of each text as far as is feasible. Overall, they aim at providing a reliable guide to the Latin or the Greek text, thus staying close to the original while offering readable English.

Since so few "fragments" (in the narrow sense) survive for Roman Republican oratory, it is almost impossible in most cases to get a sense of the style of individual orators and imitate that in the English translation. For a few indi-

viduals, however, enough material is extant to suggest that they used particular rhetorical features or specific types of prose rhythm.[16]

Because an overview of Roman Republican oratory is closely linked with Roman Republican politics, the source texts exhibit a number of key technical terms that are notoriously difficult to translate. For those the following solutions have been adopted: *senatus* and *populus Romanus* have been translated as (capitalized) "Senate" and "Roman People" to indicate the official roles of these bodies and to avoid confusion with more general uses of "people." *res publica* has been rendered as "Republic," although this transliteration, as it were, is not without its problems. The capitalization is meant to define it as a Roman political term (rather than a "republic" in the modern sense) and thus to convey its connotations. *contio* is translated as "meeting of the People" or "public meeting" to indicate the openness of such an assembly in contrast to *comitia*. *curia* is rendered as "Senate house," while *forum* and *rostra* are not translated (just capitalized as "Forum" and "Rostra"), as there is no proper equivalent in English, and a paraphrase seemed unnecessarily clumsy. The addresses *patres conscripti* and *Quirites* are reproduced as "Members of the Senate" and "Romans," respectively. *iudices* is given as "judges" to mark the decision-making role of these individuals. Of the main charges brought against politicians in the late Republic, *de (pecuniis) repetundis* is generally rendered as "extortion / extortion of money / recovery of extorted money," and *de ma-*

---

16 For comments on style and prose rhythm of "minor" Republican orators, see Bardon 1952, *passim*.

iestate as "treason." As regards general legal terminology, for *ius civile*, "civil law" is used, implying a contrast to "public law."

FURTHER READING

Since Roman oratory is not only a literary but also a political and forensic genre, background reading in a variety of areas can contribute to a fuller appreciation of the context.

Useful reference works therefore include overviews of Roman oratory (e.g., Clarke 1953 and 1996; Dominik and Hall 2007; Kennedy 1972; Porter 1997; Cavarzere 2000 [with discussion of fragmentary orators]; Steel 2006); recent collections of case studies of individual orators and speeches (Steel and van der Blom 2013; van der Blom 2016; Gray, Balbo, Marshall, and Steel 2018); studies and commentaries on Cicero's rhetorical treatises (for *Brutus* see n. 1; for *De oratore* see the five volumes of Leeman and Pinkster 1981–2008); introductions to the Roman judicial system or discussions of aspects thereof (e.g., Greenidge 1901; Jones 1972; Kunkel 1973; du Plessis, Ando, and Tuori 2016; see also Bauman 1967; Gruen 1968a; Bauman 1996; Lintott 1999a) and of the Roman law-making process (e.g., Williamson 2005); descriptions of the workings of the political system and the Roman Senate (e.g., Bonnefond-Coudry 1989 [with a list of attested meetings of the Senate]; Lintott 1999b) as well as of the *contio* in Republican Rome (e.g., Pina Polo 1989 [with a list of attested *contiones*]; 1996; Millar 1998; Mouritsen 2001 and 2013; Morstein-Marx 2004).

Some of the orators in these volumes are not well known as individuals and have not received any major

studies, beyond being mentioned in general works on Roman oratory, on Roman history and politics, or on the texts in which they appear (brief comments on many of them, though, are offered in Bardon 1952). The more famous orators, such as Cn. Pompeius Magnus (**111**), L. Sergius Catilina (**112**), C. Iulius Caesar (**121**), and M. Antonius triumvir (**159**), have been the focus of much modern scholarship, and some recent works are listed in the introductions to each of them.

Malcovati's notes in her edition (not specifically quoted here) provide further information on the historical context of each orator and each speech (and have been gratefully used, with some updates and clarifications). For particularly important or controversial matters, articles on questions of detail are quoted at the appropriate points; a full record of all secondary literature discussing various (mainly historical) problems relating to each item has not been attempted.

ABBREVIATIONS AND SYMBOLS

NUMBERING AND REFERENCING

number in bold (e.g., **1**): sequential number of an orator in *FRL* and Malcovati

number + lowercase letter in bold (e.g., **58b**): sequential number of an orator in *FRL* and Malcovati, added in Malcovati's later editions

number + capital letter in bold (e.g., **19A**): sequential number of an orator in *FRL*, added to those covered in Malcovati

T + number in bold (e.g., **T 1**): general testimonium on life and/or works of an orator

F + number in bold (e.g., **F 4**): "fragment" of an utterance of an orator

F + number + lowercase letter in bold (e.g., **F 1b**): "fragment" of an utterance of an orator, added in Malcovati's later editions

F + number + capital letter in bold (e.g., **F 2A**): "fragment" of an utterance of an orator in *FRL*, added to those covered in Malcovati

number in bold + T/F + number (e.g., **25** T 5 or **58** F 4

or **159** F 7C): cross-reference to a passage quoted as
T or F for the orator with this number

Since Malcovati's numbering has been retained as the basis, testimonia and "fragments" are numbered sequentially, so that the first fragment may have various numbers, depending on the amount of testimonia.

REFERENCE WORKS

CCMR   Pina Polo, Francisco. *Las contiones civiles y militares en Roma*. Zaragoza, 1989.

FRL   *Fragmentary Republican Latin*. Loeb Classical Library. Cambridge, MA, 2018ff.

LPPR   Rotondi, Giovanni. *Leges publicae populi Romani. Elenco cronologico con una introduzione sull'attività legislativa dei comizi romani. Estratto dalla Enciclopedia Giuridica Italiana*. Milano, 1912 (repr., Hildesheim, 1966: with supplement from: Giovanni Rotondi. *Scritti Giuridici I*. Milano, 1922).

MRR   Broughton, T.R.S. *The Magistrates of the Roman Republic*. 3 vols. Philological Monographs XV, vols. I–III. New York, 1951–1986.

RE   Pauly, August Friedrich, Georg Wissowa et al., eds. *Real-Encyclopädie der classischen Altertumswissenschaft*. Stuttgart, 1893–1980.

TLRR   Alexander, Michael C. *Trials in the Late Roman Republic, 149 BC to 50 BC*. Phoenix Suppl. XXVI. Toronto / Buffalo / London, 1990.

COLLECTIONS OF FRAGMENTS

FPL[4] *Fragmenta poetarum Latinorum epicorum et
lyricorum praeter Enni Annales et Ciceronis
Germanicique Aratea, post W. Morel et K.
Büchner editionem quartam auctam curavit*
Jürgen Blänsdorf. Berlin, 2011.

FRHist *The Fragments of the Roman Historians*, ed.
by T. J. Cornell. 3 vols. Oxford, 2013.

GL *Grammatici Latini*, ex recensione Henrici
Keilii. 7 vols. Leipzig, 1855–1880.

GRF Funaioli, Hyginus, ed. *Grammaticae Romanae
Fragmenta. Collegit recensuit. Editio stereotypa editionis anni MCMVII*. Stuttgart,
1969.

HRR *Historicorum Romanorum reliquiae, iteratis
curis collegit, disposuit, recensuit, praefatus
est* Hermannus Peter. 2 vols. Leipzig, 1914–
1916.

ORF[4] *Oratorum Romanorum Fragmenta liberae rei
publicae quartum edidit* H. Malcovati. *I–
Textus*. Aug. Taurinorum / Mediolani /
Patavii / Bononiae / Florentiae / Aterni /
Romae / Neapoli / Barii / Panormi, 1976
(Corpus Scriptorum Latinorum Paravia-
num).

RLM *Rhetores Latini minores. Ex codicibus maximam partem primum adhibitis emendabat*
Carolus Halm. Leipzig, 1863.

TrGF *Tragicorum Graecorum fragmenta*. Vols. I–V.
Göttingen, 1971–2004.

TrRF *Tragicorum Romanorum fragmenta*. Vols. I–
II. Göttingen, 2012.

BRACKETS

{ }	deletions (by modern scholars)
⟨ ⟩	additions (by modern scholars)
⌊ ⌋	supplements from a secondary tradition
[ ]	explanations and substantial additions to the English version

BIBLIOGRAPHY

1. EDITIONS OF TRANSMITTING AUTHORS

1.1. Aelian (Ael.)

García Valdés, Manuela, Luis Alfonso Llera Fueyo, and Lucia Rodríguez-Noriego Guillén, eds. *Claudius Aelianus. De natura animalium.* Berlin, 2009.

1.2. Appian (App.)

Mendelssohn, Ludwig, and Paul Viereck, eds. *Appiani Historia Romana. Ex recensione Ludovici Mendelssohnii.* 2 vols. Leipzig, 1879–1881. *Editio altera correctior curante Paulo Viereck. Volumen alterum.* Leipzig, 1905.

1.3. Apuleius (Apul.)

Helm, Rudolf, ed. *Apulei Platonici Madaurensis opera quae supersunt.* Vol. II, Fasc. 1. *Pro se de magia liber (apologia).* Editio stereotypa editionis alterius cum addendis. Leipzig, 1959 [^{1}1912, ^{4}1963, ^{5}1972, repr.].

1.4. Aquila Romanus (Aquila Rom.)

Halm, Carolus, ed. *Rhetores Latini minores. Ex codicibus maximam partem primum adhibitis emendabat*. Leipzig, 1863.

1.5. Arusianus (Arus.)

Keil, Heinrich, ed. *Grammatici Latini. Vol. VII. Scriptores de orthographia: Terentius Scaurus, Velius Longus, Caper Agroecius, Cassiodorius Martyrius, Beda Albinus, Audacis Excerpta Dosithei, Ars grammatica Arusiani Messii, Exempla elocutionum Cornelii Frontonis, Liber de differentiis, Fragmenta grammatica*. Leipzig, 1880 [repr. Hildesheim, 1961].

1.6. Asconius (Asc.)

Clark, Albertus Curtis, ed. *Q. Asconii Pediani Orationum Ciceronis quinque enarratio. Recognovit brevique adnotatione critica instruxit*. Oxford, 1907.

1.7. Ps.-Asconius (Ps.-Asc.)

Stangl, Thomas, ed. *Ciceronis Orationum Scholiastae. Asconius. Scholia Bobiensia. Scholia Pseudasconii Sangallensia. Scholia Cluniacensia et recentiora Ambrosiana ac Vaticana. Scholia Lugdunensia sive Gronoviana et eorum excerpta Lugdunensia. Volumen II: Commentarios continens*. Wien / Leipzig, 1912.

BIBLIOGRAPHY

1.8. Caesar (Caes.)

Damon, Cynthia, ed. *C. Iulii Caesaris commentariorum libri III de bello civili. Recognovit brevique adnotatione critica instruxit.* Oxford, 2015.

1.9. Cassius Dio (Cass. Dio)

Boissevain, Ursulus Philippus, ed. *Cassii Dionis Cocceiani Historiarum Romanarum quae supersunt.* Edidit. 5 vols. Berlin, 1895–1931 (repr.).

1.10. Catullus (Catull.)

Mynors, R. A. B., ed. *C. Valerii Catulli carmina. Recognovit brevique adnotatione critica instruxit.* Oxford, 1958.

1.11. Charisius (Char.)

Barwick, Karl [B.], ed. *Flavii Sosipatri Charisii artis grammaticae libri V.* Edidit C. B. Addenda et corrigenda collegit et adiecit F. Kühnert. Leipzig, 1964 [repr. Stuttgart / Leipzig, 1997].

Keil, Heinrich, ed. *Grammatici Latini. Vol. I. Flavii Sosipatri Charisii Artis grammaticae libri V, Diomedis Artis grammaticae libri III, ex Charisii arte grammatica excerpta.* Leipzig, 1857 [repr. Hildesheim, 1961].

1.12. Chirius Fortunatianus (Chir. Fortun.)

Halm, Carolus, ed. *Rhetores Latini minores. Ex codicibus maximam partem primum adhibitis emendabat.* Leipzig, 1863.

1.13. Cicero (Cic.)

Clark, Albertus Curtis, ed. *M. Tulli Ciceronis orationes [I]. Pro Sex. Roscio, De imperio Cn. Pompei, Pro Cluentio, In Catilinam, Pro Murena, Pro Caelio. Recognovit brevique adnotatione critica instruxit.* Oxford, 1905.

———. *M. Tulli Ciceronis orationes [II]. Pro Milone, Pro Marcello, Pro Ligario, Pro rege Deiotaro, Philippicae I–XIV. Recognovit brevique adnotatione critica instruxit. Editio alterius impressio nova paucis locis correcta.* Oxford, 1918.

———. *M. Tulli Ciceronis orationes [IV]. Pro P. Quinctio, Pro Q. Roscio comoedo, Pro A. Caecina, De lege agraria contra Rullum, Pro C. Rabirio perduellionis reo, Pro L. Flacco, In L. Pisonem, Pro C. Rabirio Postumo. Recognovit brevique adnotatione critica instruxit.* Oxford, 1909.

———. *M. Tulli Ciceronis orationes [VI]. Pro Tullio, Pro Fonteio, Pro Sulla, Pro Archia, Pro Plancio, Pro Scauro. Recognovit brevique adnotatione critica instruxit.* Oxford, 1911.

Crawford, Jane W. *M. Tullius Cicero. The Fragmentary Speeches. An Edition with Commentary.* 2nd ed. American Classical Studies 37. Atlanta, 1994.

Douglas, A. E., ed. *M. Tulli Ciceronis Brutus.* Oxford, 1966.

Giusta, Michelangelus, ed. *M. Tulli Ciceronis Tusculanae disputationes.* Torino, 1984.

Kumaniecki, Kazimierz F., ed. *M. Tulli Ciceronis scripta quae manserunt omnia. Fasc. 3. De oratore.* Leipzig, 1969.

BIBLIOGRAPHY

Molger, Jean, ed. *Cicéron. Les paradoxes des Stoïciens. Texte établi et traduit.* CUF. Paris, 1971.

Peterson, Gulielmus, ed. *M. Tulli Ciceronis [III]. Divinatio in Q. Caecilium, In C. Verrem. Recognovit brevique adnotatione critica instruxit. Editio altera recognita et emendata.* Oxford, 1917.

———. *M. Tulli Ciceronis [V]. Cum senatui gratias egit, Cum populo gratias egit, De domo sua, De haruspicum responso, Pro Sestio, In Vatinium, De provinciis consularibus, Pro Balbo. Recognovit brevique adnotatione critica instruxit. Editio altera recognita et emendata.* Oxford, 1911.

Plasberg, Otto, ed. *M. Tulli Ciceronis scripta quae manserunt omnia. Fasc. 42. Academicorum reliquiae cum Lucullo. Recognovit O. Plasberg. Editio stereotypa editionis prioris (MCMXXII).* Stuttgart / Leipzig, 1996.

———. *M. Tulli Ciceronis scripta quae manserunt omnia. Fasc. 45. De natura deorum. Recognovit O. Plasberg. Iterum edidit appendicem adiecit W. Ax.* Leipzig, 1933 [[1]1917].

Powell, J. G. F., ed. *M. Tulli Ciceronis De re publica, De legibus, Cato maior de senectute, Laelius de amicitia. Recognovit brevique adnotatione critica instruxit.* Oxford, 2006.

Puccioni, Giulio, ed. *Marco Tullio Cicerone. Frammenti delle orazioni perdute.* Milano, 1971.

Reynolds, L. D., ed. *M. Tulli Ciceronis De finibus bonorum et malorum libri quinque. Recognovit brevique adnotatione critica instruxit.* Oxford, 1998.

Shackleton Bailey, D. R., ed. *M. Tulli Ciceronis Epistulae ad Atticum.* 2 vols. Stuttgart, 1987.

————. *M. Tulli Ciceronis Epistulae ad familiares libri I–XVI.* Stuttgart, 1988.

————. *M. Tulli Ciceronis Epistulae ad Quintum fratrem, Epistulae ad M. Brutum, accedunt Commentariolum petitionis, fragmenta epistularum.* Stuttgart, 1988.

Stroebel, Eduard, ed., *M. Tulli Ciceronis scripta quae manserunt omnia. Fasc. 2. Rhetorici libri duo qui vocantur de inventione.* Leipzig, 1915.

Westman, Rolf, ed. *M. Tulli Ciceronis scripta quae manserunt omnia. Fasc. 5. Orator.* Leipzig, 1980.

Wilkins, A. S., ed. *M. Tulli Ciceronis Rhetorica. Recognovit brevique adnotatione critica instruxit.* 2 vols. Oxford, 1902 / 1903.

Winterbottom, Michael, ed. *M. Tulli Ciceronis De officiis. Recognovit brevique adnotatione critica instruxit.* Oxford, 1994.

1.14. Columella (Columella)

Rodgers, R. H., ed. *L. Iuni Moderati Columellae Res rustica. Incerti auctoris liber de arboribus. Recognovit brevique adnotatione critica instruxit.* Oxford, 2010.

1.15. Cruquius (Comm. Cruq.)

Q. Horatius Flaccus, ex antiquissimis undecim lib. ms. et schedis aliquot emendatus, & plurimis locis cum Commentariis antiquis expurgatus & editus, opera IACOBI CRUQUII *Messenij apud Bruganos politioris litteraturæ professoris publici. Eiusdem in eundem enarrationes, observationes, & variæ lectiones, cum aliis quibusdam & indice locupletissimo.* Antverpiae, M. D. LXXVIII.

1.16. Diodorus Siculus (Diod. Sic.)

Fischer, C. T., ed. *Diodori Bibliotheca Historica. Post I. Bekker et L. Dindorf recognovit. Vol. VI. Ex recensione Ludovici Dindorfii. Editio stereotypa editionis annorum MDCCCLXVII / MDCCCLXVIII*. Stuttgart, 1969.

1.17. Diomedes (Diom.)

Keil, Heinrich, ed. *Grammatici Latini. Vol. I. Flavii Sosipatri Charisii Artis grammaticae libri V, Diomedis Artis grammaticae libri III, ex Charisii arte grammatica excerpta*. Leipzig, 1857 [repr. Hildesheim, 1961].

1.18. Donatus (Donat.)

Wessner, Paulus, ed. *Aeli Donati quod fertur Commentum Terenti, accedunt Eugraphi Commentum et Scholia Bembina*. Recensuit. Vol. 1. Leipzig, 1902.

1.19. Festus (Fest.) / Paulus (Paul. *Fest.*)

Lindsay, Wallace M. [L.], ed. *Sexti Pompei Festi De verborum significatu quae supersunt cum Pauli Epitome*. Leipzig, 1913 [repr. Hildesheim / New York, 1965].

1.20. Firmicus Maternus (Firm. Mat.)

Kroll, W., and F. Skutsch, eds. *Iulii Firmici Materni Matheseos Libri VIII. Ediderunt W. Kroll et F. Skutsch. Fasciculus prior. Libros IV priores continens. Editio stereotypa editionis anni MDCCCXCVII*. Stuttgart, 1968.
Kroll, W., F. Skutsch, and K. Ziegler, eds. *Iulii Firmici Ma-*

terni Matheseos Libri VIII. Ediderunt W. Kroll et F. Skutsch in operis societatem assumpto K. Ziegler. Fasciculus alter. Libros IV posteriores cum praefatione et indicibus continens. Editio stereotypa editionis anni MCMXIII addenda addendis subiunxit K. Ziegler. Stuttgart, 1968.

1.21. Florus (Flor.)

Malcovati, Henrica, ed. *L. Annaei Flori quae exstant. Iterum edidit.* Scriptores Graeci et Latini consilio Academiae Lynceorum editi. Roma, 1972.

1.22. Frontinus (Frontin.)

Rodgers, R. H., ed. *Frontinus De aquaeductu urbis Romae. Edited with introduction and commentary.* Cambridge Classical Texts and Commentaries. Cambridge, 2004.

1.23. Fronto (Fronto)

van den Hout, Michael J. P., ed. *M. Cornelii Frontonis epistulae schedis tam editis quam ineditis Emundi Hauleri usus iterum edidit.* Leipzig, 1988.

1.24. Gellius (Gell.)

Marshall, P. K., ed. *A. Gellii Noctes Atticae. Recognovit brevique adnotatione critica instruxit.* 2 vols. Oxford, 1968 [ed. corr. 1990].

BIBLIOGRAPHY

1.25. Grammatici incerti

Keil, Heinrich, ed. *Grammatici Latini. Vol. V. Artium scriptores minores: Cledonius Pompeius Iulianus, Excerpta ex commentariis in Donatum, Consentius, Phocas, Eutychus, Augustinus, Palaemon Asper, De nomine et pronomine, De dubiis nominibus*. Leipzig, 1923 [repr. Hildesheim, 1961].

1.26. Granius Licinianus (Gran. Licin.)

Criniti, Nicola, ed. *Grani Liciniani reliquiae*. Edidit. Leipzig, 1981.

1.27. Hieronymus / Jerome (Hieron.)

Helm, Rudolf, ed. *Eusebius, Werke. Siebenter Band. Die Chronik des Hieronymus. Hieronymi Chronicon. Herausgegeben und in 2. Auflage bearbeitet von Rudolf Helm. 3., unveränderte Auflage mit einer Vorbemerkung von Ursula Treu*. Die griechischen Schriftsteller der ersten Jahrhunderte, Eusebius, Siebenter Band. Berlin, 1984.

1.28. Horace (Hor.)

Shackleton Bailey, D. R., ed., *Q. Horati Flacci opera. Edidit*. Stuttgart, 1985.

1.29. Isidore (Isid.)

Lindsay, W. M., ed. *Isidori Hispalensis Episcopi Etymologiarum sive originum libri XX. Recognovit brevique adnotatione critica instruxit*. 2 vols. Oxford, 1911.

1.30. Iulius Exuperantius (Iul. Exup.)

Zorzetti, Naevius, ed. *Iulii Exuperantii Opusculum*. Leipzig, 1982.

1.31. Iulius Rufinianus (Iul. Rufin.)

Halm, Carolus, ed. *Rhetores Latini minores. Ex codicibus maximam partem primum adhibitis emendabat*. Leipzig, 1863.

1.32. Iulius Severianus (Iul. Severian.)

Halm, Carolus, ed. *Rhetores Latini minores. Ex codicibus maximam partem primum adhibitis emendabat*. Leipzig, 1863.

1.33. Iulius Victor (Iul. Vict.)

Giomini, Remo, and Maria Silvana Celentano, eds. *C. Iulii Victoris Ars rhetorica*. Leipzig, 1980.
Halm, Carolus, ed. *Rhetores Latini minores. Ex codicibus maximam partem primum adhibitis emendabat*. Leipzig, 1863.

1.34. Josephus (Joseph.)

Niese, Benedictus, ed. *Flavii Iosephi opera. Edidit et apparatu critico instruxit*. Berlin, 1887–1895.

1.35. Lactantius Placidus (Lactant.)

Brandt, Samuel, ed. *L. Caeli Firmiani Lactanti Opera omnia, accedunt carmina eius quae feruntur et L. Caecilii*

qui inscriptus est de mortibus persecutorum liber, re-censuerunt Samuel Brandt et Georgius Laubmann. Pars I: Divinae institutiones et Epitome divinarum institutio-num recensuit S. B. Prag / Wien / Leipzig, 1890.

1.36. Livius (Liv.)

Briscoe, John, ed. *Titi Livi ab urbe condita. Libri XLI–XLV. Edidit.* Stuttgart, 1986.

———. *Titi Livi ab urbe condita. Libri XXXI–XL. Tomus II. Libri XXXVI–XL. Edidit.* Stuttgart, 1991.

Jal, Paul, ed. *Abrégés des livres de l'histoire romaine de Tite-Live. Tome XXXIV. Texte établi et traduit.* 2 vols. CUF. Paris, 1984.

Rossbach, Otto, ed. *T. Livi Periochae omnium librorum, fragmenta Oxyrhynchi reperta, Iulii Obsequentis pro-digiorum liber. Edidit.* Leipzig, 1910.

Walsh, P. G. *Titi Livi ab urbe condita libri XXVI–XXVII.* Leipzig, 1982.

1.37. Macrobius (Macrob.)

Kaster, R. A., ed. *Ambrosii Theodosii Macrobii Saturnalia. Recognovit brevique adnotatione critica instruxit.* Oxford, 2011.

1.38. Marius Victorinus (Mar. Vict.)

Keil, Heinrich, ed. *Grammatici Latini. Vol. VI. Scripto-res artis metricae. Marius Victorinus, Maximus Victori-nus, Caesius Bassus, Atilius Fortunatianus, Terentianus Maurus, Marius Plotius Sacerdos, Rufinus, Mallius The-*

odorus, Fragmenta et excerpta metrica. Leipzig, 1874 [repr. Hildesheim, 1961].

1.39. Cornelius Nepos (Nep.)

Ruch, Michel, ed. *Cornelius Nepos. Vies d'Hannibal, de Caton et d'Atticus. Édition, introduction et commentaire*. Érasme 21. Paris, 1968.

1.40. Nonius Marcellus (Non.)

Lindsay, Wallace M. [L.], ed. *Nonii Marcelli De conpendiosa doctrina libros XX, Onionsianis copiis usus edidit*. 3 vols. Leipzig, 1903.

1.41. Orosius (Oros.)

Arnaud-Lindet, Marie-Pierre, ed. *Orose. Histoires (Contre les Païens). Tome I. Livres I–III. Texte établi et traduit*. CUF. Paris, 1990.

1.42. Pliny the Elder (Plin.)

Mayhoff, Carolus, ed. *C. Plini Secundi Naturalis Historiae libri XXXVII post Ludovici Iani obitum recognovit et scripturae discrepantia adiecta edidit*. 6 vols. Stuttgart, 1892–1909.

1.43. Pliny the Younger (Plin.)

Mynors, R. A. B., ed. *C. Plini Caecili Secundi Epistularum libri decem. Recognovit brevique adnotatione critica instruxit*. Oxford, 1963.

1.44. Plotius Sacerdos (Sacerd.)

Keil, Heinrich, ed. *Grammatici Latini. Vol. VI. Scriptores artis metricae. Marius Victorinus, Maximus Victorinus, Caesius Bassus, Atilius Fortunatianus, Terentianus Maurus, Marius Plotius Sacerdos, Rufinus, Mallius Theodorus, Fragmenta et excerpta metrica.* Leipzig, 1874 [repr. Hildesheim, 1961].

1.45. Plutarch (Plut.)

Bernardakis, Gregorius N., ed. *Plutarchi Chaeronensis Moralia. Recognovit. Vol. II.* Leipzig, 1889.

Gärtner, Hans, ed. *Plutarchus, Vitae parallelae. Vol. I, Fasc. I. Quartum recensuit Konrat Ziegler. Editionem quintam curavit Hans Gärtner.* München / Leipzig, 2000.

———. *Plutarchi Vitae parallelae. Recognoverunt Cl. Lindskog et K. Ziegler. Vol. I, Fasc. 2. Tertium recensuit Konrat Ziegler. Editionem correctiorem cum addendis curavit Hans Gärtner.* Stuttgart / Leipzig, 1994.

———. *Plutarchi Vitae parallelae. Recognoverunt Cl. Lindskog et K. Ziegler. Vol. II, Fasc. 2. Iterum recensuit Konrat Ziegler. Editionem correctiorem cum addendis curavit Hans Gärtner.* Stuttgart / Leipzig, 1994.

Ziegler, Konrat, ed. *Plutarchi Vitae parallelae. Recognoverunt Cl. Lindskog et K. Ziegler. Vol. II, Fasc. 1. Iterum recensuit K. Ziegler.* Leipzig, 1964.

———. *Plutarchi Vitae parallelae. Recognoverunt Cl. Lindskog et K. Ziegler. Vol. III, Fasc. 1. Iterum recensuit K. Ziegler.* Leipzig, 1971.

———. *Plutarchi Vitae parallelae. Recognoverunt Cl.*

Lindskog et K. Ziegler. Vol. III, Fasc. 2. Iterum recensuit K. Ziegler. Leipzig, 1973.

1.46. Polybius (Polyb.)

Büttner-Wobst, Theodorus, ed. *Polybii Historiae. Editionem a Ludovico Dindorfio curatam retractavit et instrumentum criticum addidit. Vol. IV.* Leipzig, 1904.

1.47. Pomponius (Pomp.)

Behrends, Okko, Rolf Knütel, Berthold Kupisch, and Hans Hermann Seiler, eds. *Corpus Iuris Civilis. Text und Übersetzung. II. Digesten 1–10. Gemeinschaftlich übersetzt und herausgegeben.* Corpus Iuris Civilis. Text und Übersetzung. Auf der Grundlage der von Theodor Mommsen und Paul Krüger besorgen Textausgaben. Heidelberg, 1995.

1.48. Porphyrio (Porph. in Hor.)

Meyer, Gulielmus, ed. *Pomponii Porphyrionis commentarii in Q. Horatium Flaccum. Recensuit.* Leipzig, 1874.

1.49. Priscian (Prisc.)

Hertz, Martin, ed. *Grammatici Latini. Vol. II / III. Prisciani grammatici Caesariensis Institutionum grammaticarum libri XVIII.* Leipzig, 1855 / 1859 [repr. Hildesheim, 1961].

Keil, Heinrich, ed. *Grammatici Latini. Vol. III. Prisciani grammatici Caesariensis De figuris numerorum, De metris Terentii, De praeexercitamentis rhetoricis libri, In-*

stitutio de nomine et pronomine et verbo, Partitiones duodecim versuum Aeneidos principalium. Accedit Prisciani qui dicitur liber de accentibus. Leipzig, 1859 [repr. Hildesheim, 1961].

1.50. Quintilian (Quint.)

Winterbottom, Michael, ed. *M. Fabi Quintiliani Institutionis oratoriae libri duodecim. Recognovit brevique adnotatione critica instruxit.* 2 vols. Oxford, 1970.

1.51. *Rhetorica ad Herennium (Rhet. Her.)*

Marx, Fridericus, ed. *M. Tulli Ciceronis scripta quae manserunt omnia. Fasc. 1. Incerti auctoris de ratione dicendi ad C. Herennium lib. IV. Iterum recensuit Fridericus Marx. Editionem stereotypam correctiorem cum addendis curavit Winfried Trillitzsch.* Leipzig, 1964.

1.52. Sallust (Sall.)

Reynolds, L. D., ed. *C. Sallusti Crispi Catilina, Iugurtha, Historiarum fragmenta selecta, Appendix Sallustiana. Recognovit brevique adnotatione critica instruxit.* Oxford, 1991.

1.53. Scholia Ciceronis (Schol. ad Cic.)

Stangl, Thomas, ed. *Ciceronis Orationum Scholiastae. Asconius. Scholia Bobiensia. Scholia Pseudasconii Sangallensia. Scholia Cluniacensia et recentiora Ambrosiana ac Vaticana. Scholia Lugdunensia sive Gronoviana et*

eorum excerpta Lugdunensia. Volumen II: Commentarios continens. Wien / Leipzig, 1912.

1.54. Seneca the Elder (Sen.)

Håkanson, Lennart, ed. *L. Annaeus Seneca maior. Oratorum et rhetorum sententiae, divisiones, colores. Recensuit.* Leipzig, 1989.

1.55. Seneca the Younger (Sen.)

Reynolds, L. D., ed. *L. Annaei Seneca ad Lucilium Epistulae morales. Recognovit et adnotatione critica instruxit.* 2 vols. Oxford, 1965.

———. *L. Annaei Seneca Dialogorum libri duodecim. Recognovit brevique adnotatione critica instruxit.* Oxford, 1977.

Roncali, Renata, ed. *L. Annai Senecae Ἀποκολοκύντωσις. Edidit.* Leipzig, 1990.

1.56. Servius (Serv.)

Thilo, Georgius, ed. *Servii grammatici qui feruntur in Vergilii carmina commentarii. Vol. I. Aeneidos librorum I–V commentarii.* Leipzig / Berlin, 1881 [repr. Leipzig / Berlin, 1923].

———. *Servii grammatici qui feruntur in Vergilii carmina commentarii. Vol. II. Aeneidos librorum VI–XII commentarii.* Leipzig / Berlin, 1884 [repr. Leipzig / Berlin, 1923].

———. *Servii grammatici qui feruntur in Vergilii carmina commentarii. Vol. III, Fasc. 1. In Bucolica et Georgica commentarii.* Leipzig, 1887 [repr. Leipzig, 1927; Hildesheim, 1961].

1.57. Suetonius (Suet.)

Kaster, R. A., ed. *C. Suetoni Tranquilli De vita Caesarum libros VIII et De grammaticis et rhetoribus librum recognovit brevique adnotatione critica instruxit*. Oxford, 2016.

Reifferscheid, Augustus, ed. *C. Suetoni Tranquilli praeter Caesarum libros reliquiae. Edidit. Inest Vita Terenti a Friderico Ritschelio emendata atque enarrata*. Leipzig, 1860.

1.58. Tacitus (Tac.)

Heubner, Henricus, ed. *P. Cornelii Taciti libri qui supersunt. Tom. I. Ab excessu Divi Augusti. Edidit*. Stuttgart, 1983.

———. *P. Cornelii Taciti libri qui supersunt. Tom. II, Fasc. 4. Dialogus de oratoribus. Edidit*. Stuttgart, 1983.

1.59. Terentianus Maurus (Terent. Maur.)

Keil, Heinrich, ed. *Grammatici Latini. Vol. VI. Scriptores artis metricae. Marius Victorinus, Maximus Victorinus, Caesius Bassus, Atilius Fortunatianus, Terentianus Maurus, Marius Plotius Sacerdos, Rufinus, Mallius Theodorus, Fragmenta et excerpta metrica*. Leipzig, 1874 [repr. Hildesheim, 1961].

1.60. Valerius Maximus (Val. Max.)

Briscoe, John, ed. *Valeri Maximi Facta et dicta memorabilia*. 2 vols. Stuttgart, 1998.

1.61. Varro (Varro)

Flach, Dieter, ed. and trans. *Marcus Terentius Varro. Gespräche über die Landwirtschaft. Herausgegeben, übersetzt und erläutert.* 3 vols. Texte zur Forschung 65–67. Darmstadt, 1996–2002.

1.62. Velleius Paterculus (Vell. Pat.)

Watt, W. S., ed. *Velleii Paterculi Historiarum ad M. Vinicium consulem libri duo. Recognovit. Editio correctior editionis primae (MCMLXXXVIII).* Stuttgart / Leipzig, 1998.

1.63. *De viris illustribus* ([Aurel. Vict.] *Vir. ill.*)

Pichlmayr, Fr., ed. *Sexti Aurelii Victoris Liber de Caesaribus. Praecedunt Origo gentis Romanae et Liber de viris illustribus urbis Romae, subsequitur Epitome de Caesaribus. Recensuit Fr. Pichlmayr. Editio stereotypa correctior editionis primae, addenda et corrigenda iterum collegit et adiecit R. Gruendel.* Leipzig, 1966.

2. EDITIONS OF FRAGMENTS OF ORATORS

Balbo, A., ed. *I frammenti degli oratori romani dell'età augustea e tiberiana. Parte prima: Età augustea.* Minima Philologica, Serie latina 1. Alessandria, 2004.
Fragments of the Republican Roman Orators (FRRO): http://www.frro.gla.ac.uk.
Malcovati, H. (E.), ed. *Oratorum Romanorum Fragmenta liberae rei publicae, iteratis curis recensuit collegit.*

Corpus Scriptorum Latinorum Paravianum. Aug. Taurinorum / Mediolani / Patavii / Florentiae / Aterni / Romae / Neapoli / Catinae / Panormi, 1955 [*ORF²*].

―――. *Oratorum Romanorum Fragmenta liberae rei publicae quartum edidit. I—Textus.* Corpus Scriptorum Latinorum Paravianum. Aug. Taurinorum / Mediolani / Patavii / Bononiae / Florentiae / Aterni / Romae / Neapoli / Barii / Panormi, 1976 [*ORF⁴*].

―――. *Oratorum Romanorum Fragmenta liberae rei publicae quartum edidit. II—Index verborum, e scidulis ab † Helmut Gugel collectis compositus ab Helmuth Vretska adiuvante Carolo Vretska.* Corpus Scriptorum Latinorum Paravianum. Aug. Taurinorum / Mediolani / Patavii / Bononiae / Florentiae / Aterni / Romae / Neapoli / Barii / Panormi, 1979 [*ORF⁴*: index].

Additional material by Malcovati:

Malcovati, E. notice of Malcovati 1955. *Athenaeum* 33 (1955): 377.

―――. "Per una nuova edizione degli *Oratorum Romanorum Fragmenta*." *Athenaeum* 43 (1965): 209–16.

―――. notice of Malcovati 1967. *Athenaeum* 45 (1967): 455–56.

―――. "† Helmut Gugel." *Athenaeum* 51 (1973): 484–85.

―――. notice of Malcovati 1976. *Athenaeum* 55 (1977): 228–29.

Reviews of first edition:

Bione, C. *CM* (1931): 1186.

Craig, J. D. *CR* 45 (1931): 182–83.

Faider, P. *RBPh* 10 (1931): 187–88.

Frank, T. *AJPh* 52 (1931): 290–91.

Klotz, A. *PhW* 51.39 (1931): 1175–78.

Marouzeau, J. *REL* 9 (1931): 132.
Valgimigli, M. *Leonardo* (1931): 248
Ernout, A. *RPh* s. 3, 6 (1932): 81–82.
Lenchantin, M. *BFC* 38 (1932): 166–69.
Tescari, O. *RFIC* n.s. 10 (1932): 260–62.
Muller, *MPh* 40 (1933): 230.

Reviews of second edition:
d'Agostino, V. *RSC* 3 (1955): 221–23.
Marouzeau, J. *REL* 33 (1955): 447.
Badian, E. *JRS* 46 (1956): 218–21 [repr. in E. Badian, *Studies in Greek and Roman History*, 243–49. Oxford, 1964 (repr. 1968)].
Bardon, M. *Latomus* 15 (1956): 88.
Browning, R. *CR* 6 (1956): 244–45.
Cataudella, Q. *Iura* 7 (1956): 191–92.
Delande, J. *LEC* 24 (1956): 188.
Rambaud, M. *REA* 58 (1956): 402–4.
van de Woestijne, P. *AC* 25 (1956): 190.
Frassinetti, P. *A&R* 3 (1958): 50–53.
Enk, P. J. *Mnemosyne* 12 (1959): 167–68.
Till, R. *Gnomon* 32 (1960): 672–73.

Reviews of third edition:
Badian, E. *JRS* 58 (1968): 256.
Garzetti, A. *Aevum* 42 (1968): 195.

Reviews of fourth edition:
Frassinetti, P. *A&R* 25 (1980): 193–94 [index].
Mazzoli, G. *Athenaeum* 58 (1980): 247–49 [index].

BIBLIOGRAPHY

3. SECONDARY LITERATURE

von Albrecht, Michael. *Masters of Roman Prose from Cato to Apuleius. Interpretative Studies*. ARCA 23. Translated by Neil Adkin. Leeds, 1989 [German orig. 1971].

Alexander, Michael C.: see *TLRR*.

———. *The Case for the Prosecution in the Ciceronian Era*. Ann Arbor, 2002.

Astin, A. E. *Scipio Aemilianus*. Oxford, 1967.

Aubert-Baillot, Sophie. "La rhétorique du Stoïcien Rutilius Rufus dans le *Brutus*." In Aubert-Baillot and Guérin 2014, 123–40.

Aubert-Baillot, Sophie, and Charles Guérin, eds. *Le Brutus de Cicéron. Rhétorique, politique et histoire culturelle*. Mnemosyne Suppl. 371. Leiden / Boston, 2014.

Badian, E. "L. Papirius Fregellanus." *CR* 5 (1955): 22–23.

———. "The *Lex Thoria*: A Reconsideration." In *Studi in onore di Biondo Biondi*, 187–96. Milano, 1965; repr. in E. Badian, *Studies in Greek and Roman History*, 235–42. Oxford, 1964 (repr. 1968).

———. "Which Metellus? A Footnote to Professor Barchiesi's Article." *AJAH* 13 (1988 [1996–97]): 106–12.

Balbo, Andrea. "Marcus Junius Brutus the Orator: Between Philosophy and Rhetoric." In Steel and van der Blom 2013, 315–28.

Bardon, Henry. *La littérature latine inconnue. Tome I: L'époque républicaine*. Paris, 1952; *Tome II: L'époque impériale*. Paris, 1956.

Bates, Richard L. "*Rex in Senatu*: A Political Biography of M. Aemilius Scaurus." *Proceedings of the American Philosophical Society* 130 (1986): 251–88.

Bätz, Alexander. *Sacrae Virgines. Studien zum religiösen und gesellschaftlichen Status der Vestalinnen.* Paderborn / München / Wien / Zürich, 2012.

Bauman, Richard A. *The Crimen Maiestatis in the Roman Republic and Augustan Principate.* Johannesburg, 1967.

———. *Crime and Punishment in Ancient Rome.* London / New York, 1996.

Benner, Herbert. *Die Politik des P. Clodius Pulcher. Untersuchungen zur Denaturierung des Clientelwesens in der ausgehenden römischen Republik.* Historia Einzelschriften 50. Stuttgart, 1987.

Bländsdorf, Jürgen: see *FPL*[4].

van der Blom, Henriette. "Fragmentary Speeches: The Oratory and Political Career of Piso Caesoninus." In Steel and van der Blom 2013, 299–314.

———. *Oratory and Political Career in the Late Roman Republic.* Cambridge, 2016.

———. "Caesar's Orations." In *The Cambridge Companion to the Writings of Julius Caesar*, edited by Luca Grillo and Christopher B. Krebs, 193–205. Cambridge, 2017.

Bonnefond-Coudry, Marianne. *Le Sénat de la République romaine de la guerre d'Hannibal à Auguste: pratiques délibératives et prise de decision.* BEFAR 273. Paris / Roma, 1989.

Brennan, T. Corey. *The Praetorship in the Roman Republic.* 2 vols. Oxford, 2000.

Broughton, T. R. S.: see *MRR*.

Burden-Strevens, Christopher. "Fictitious Speeches, Envy, and the Habituation to Authority: Writing the Collapse of the Roman Republic." In *Cassius Dio. Greek Intellectual and Roman Politician*, edited by Carsten Hjort

Lange and Jesper Majbom Madsen, 191–216. Historiography of Rome and Its Empire 1. Leiden / Boston, 2016.

———. "Reconstructing Republican Oratory in Cassius Dio's Roman History." In Gray, Balbo, Marshall, and Steel 2018, 111–134.

Calboli, Gualtiero. "The Asiatic Style of Antony: Some considerations." In *Vir bonus dicendi peritus. Festschrift für Alfons Weische zum 65. Geburtstag*, edited by Beate Czapla, Tomas Lehmann, and Susanne Liell, 13–26. Wiesbaden, 1997.

Cavarzere, Alberto. *Oratoria a Roma. Storia di un genere pragmatico*. Roma, 2000.

———. "Gaius Titius, *Orator* and *Poeta*. (Cic. *Brut.* 167 and Macrob. *Sat.* 3.16.4–16)." In Gray, Balbo, Marshall, and Steel 2018, 153–70.

CCMR: Pina Polo, Francisco. *Las contiones civiles y militares en Roma*. Zaragoza, 1989.

Clarke, M. L. *Rhetoric at Rome. A Historical Survey*. London, 1953; 3rd ed., rev. and with a new introduction by D. H. Berry. London / New York, 1996.

Coleman, Robert. *Vergil. Eclogues*. Cambridge Greek and Latin Classics. Cambridge, 1977.

Corbeill, Anthony. "Clodius' *Contio de haruspicum responsis*." In Gray, Balbo, Marshall, and Steel 2018, 171–190.

Cornell, T. J.: see *FRHist*.

Courtney, Edward. *Archaic Latin Prose*. American Philological Association, American Classical Studies 42. Atlanta, 1999.

Crawford, Jane W. *M. Tullius Cicero. The Lost and Unpublished Orations*. Hypomnemata 80. Göttingen, 1984.

————. *M. Tullius Cicero. The Fragmentary Speeches. An Edition with Commentary.* 2nd ed. American Classical Studies 37. Atlanta, 1994.

D'Arms, J. H. "Senators' Involvement in Commerce in the Late Republic: Some Ciceronian Evidence." *MAAR* 36 (1980): 77–89.

David, Jean-Michel. "*Eloquentia popularis et urbanitas.* Les orateurs originaires des villes italiennes à Rome à la fin de la république." *Actes de la recherche en sciences sociales* 60 (1985): 68–71.

Dobesch, Gerhard. "Zu einigen lateinischen Rednerfragmenten." *WS* 88, NF 9 (1975): 109–17.

Dominik, William, and Jon Hall, eds. *A Companion to Roman Rhetoric.* Blackwell Companions to the Ancient World. Malden, MA / Oxford, 2007.

Dugan, John. "*Scriptum* and *voluntas* in Cicero's *Brutus.*" In *Letteratura e Civitas. Transizioni dalla Repubblica all'Impero. In ricordo di Emanuele Narducci*, edited by Mario Citroni, 117–28. Testi e studi di cultura classica 53. Pisa, 2012.

————. "Netting the Wolf-Fish: Gaius Titius in Macrobius and Cicero." In Gray, Balbo, Marshall, and Steel 2018, 135–51.

Elster, M. *Die Gesetze der mittleren römischen Republik. Text und Kommentar.* Darmstadt, 2003.

Ferrary, Jean-Louis, Aldo Schiavone, and Emanuele Stolfi, eds. *Quintus Mucius Scaevola. Opera.* Scriptores Iuris Romani I. Roma, 2018.

Flach, Dieter. "Antike Grabreden als Geschichtsquelle." In *Leichenpredigten als Quelle historischer Wissenschaften*, edited by Rudolf Lenz, 1:1–35. Erstes

Marburger Personalschriftensymposion, Forschungsschwerpunkt Leichenpredigten. Köln / Wien, 1975.

Flaig, Egon. *Ritualisierte Politik. Zeichen, Gesten und Herrschaft, 2. Auflage*. Historische Semantik 1. Göttingen, 2004.

Fomin, Andriy. "Speeches in Dio Cassius." In *Cassius Dio. Greek Intellectual and Roman Politician*, edited by Carsten Hjort Lange and Jesper Majbom Madsen, 217–237. Historiography of Rome and Its Empire 1. Leiden / Boston, 2016.

FPL[4]: Blänsdorf, Jürgen, ed. *Fragmenta poetarum Latinorum epicorum et lyricorum praeter Enni Annales et Ciceronis Germanicique Aratea, post W. Morel et K. Büchner editionem quartam auctam curavit*. Berlin / New York, 2011.

FRHist: Cornell, T. J., et al., eds. *The Fragments of the Roman Historians*. 3 vols. Oxford, 2013.

Frier, Bruce W. *The Rise of the Roman Jurists. Studies in Cicero's pro Caecina*. Princeton, 1985.

Funaioli, Hyginus: see *GRF*.

Garcea, Alessandro, and Valeria Lomanto. "Hortensius dans le *Brutus*: une polémique rhétorique sous forme d'éloge funèbre." In Aubert-Baillot and Guérin 2014, 141–60.

Gelzer, Matthias. *Caesar. Der Politiker und Staatsmann*. Neudruck der Ausgabe von 1983 mit einer Einführung und einer Auswahlbibliographie von Ernst Baltrusch. Stuttgart, 2008.

———. *Pompeius. Lebensbild eines Römers. Neudruck der Ausgabe von 1984 mit einem Forschungsüberblick und einer Ergänzungsbibliographie von Elisabeth Herrmann-Otto*. Stuttgart, 2005.

Giomini, Remo. "Su alcuni frammenti di orazioni traman-
dati da G. Vittore e dal grammatico Pompeo." *RCCM*
20 (1978): 947–52.

Gowing, Alain. "Memory and Silence in Cicero's *Brutus*."
Eranos 98 (2000): 39–64.

Gray, Christa, Andrea Balbo, Richard M. A. Marshall, and
Catherine E. W. Steel, eds. *Reading Republican Oratory. Reconstructions, Contexts, Receptions*. Oxford,
2018.

Greenidge, A. H. J. *The Legal Procedure of Cicero's Time*.
London, 1901 (repr. New York / South Hackensack, NJ,
1971).

GRF: Funaioli, Hyginus, ed. *Grammaticae Romanae
Fragmenta. Collegit recensuit. Editio stereotypa editionis anni MCMVII*. Stuttgart, 1969.

Gruen, Erich S. "The *Lex Varia*." *JRS* 55 (1965): 59–73.

———. "Cicero and Licinius Calvus." *HSCP* 71 (1967):
215–33.

———. *Roman Politics and the Criminal Courts, 149–78
B.C.* Cambridge, MA, 1968a.

———. "M. Antonius and the Trial of the Vestal Virgins."
RhM 111 (1968b): 59–63.

———. "Some Criminal Trials of the Late Republic: Political and Prosopographical Problems." *Athenaeum* 49
(1971): 54–69.

———. *The Last Generation of the Roman Republic*.
Berkeley / Los Angeles / London, 1974.

Gwyn Morgan, M. "Glaucia and Metellus. A Note on Cicero, *De oratore* II 263 and III 164." *Athenaeum* 52
(1974): 314–19.

Hall, Jon. "Cicero's *Brutus* and the Criticism of Oratorical
Performance." *CJ* 110 (2014): 43–59.

Häpke, Natalie. *C. Semproni Gracchi oratoris Romani*

fragmenta collecta et illustrata. PhD diss. München, 1915.

Hill, H. "The so-called *Lex Aufeia* (Gellius xi. 10)." *CR* 62 (1948): 112–13.

Holford-Strevens, L. A. "1. Two Notes on Minor Greek Poets, 2. Five Notes on Aulus Gellius." *LCM* 8.9 (1983): 143–44.

HRR: Historicorum Romanorum Reliquiae. Iteratis curis disposuit recensuit praefatus est Hermannus Peter. Volumen prius. Leipzig, 1914 / *Historicorum Romanorum Reliquiae. Collegit disposuit recensuit praefatus est* Hermannus Peter. Volumen alterum. Leipzig, 1906.

Huzar, Eleanor. "The Literary Efforts of Mark Antony." *ANRW* II.30.1 (1982): 639–57.

Jones, A. H. M. *The Criminal Courts of the Roman Republic and Principate.* With a preface by John Crook. Oxford, 1972.

Kaser, Max, and Karl Hackl. *Das römische Zivilprozessrecht von Max Kaser. Zweite Auflage, neu bearbeitet von Karl Hackl.* HbdA IX.3.4. München, 1996.

Kemezis, Adam. "Dio, Caesar and the Vesontio Mutineers (38.34–47): A Rhetoric of Lies." In *Cassius Dio. Greek Intellectual and Roman Politician,* edited by Carsten Hjort Lange and Jesper Majbom Madsen, 238–257. Historiography of Rome and Its Empire 1. Leiden / Boston, 2016.

Kennedy, G. *The Art of Rhetoric in the Roman World 300 B.C.–A.D. 300.* Princeton, 1972.

Kierdorf, Wilhelm. *Laudatio Funebris. Interpretationen und Untersuchungen zur Entwicklung der römischen Leichenrede.* Beiträge zur Klassischen Philologie 106. Meisenheim am Glan, 1980.

Kunkel, Wolfgang. *An Introduction to Roman Legal and*

Constitutional History. Second Edition Based on the Sixth German Edition of Römische Rechtsgeschichte. Translated by J.M. Kelly. Oxford, 1973.

Kytzler, Bernhard, ed. and trans. *Marcus Tullius Cicero. Brutus. Lateinisch–Deutsch.* Sammlung Tusculum. München, 1970.

Lausberg, H. *Handbook of Literary Rhetoric. A Foundation of Literary Study. Foreword by G. A. Kennedy. Translated by M. T. Bliss, A. Jansen, D. E. Orton. Edited by D. E. Orton & D. Anderson.* Leiden / Boston / Köln, 1998 [translated from original German edition, first published in 1960].

Leeman, Anton D., Harm Pinkster, and Hein L. W. Nelson. *M. Tullius Cicero. De oratore libri III. Kommentar. 1. Band: Buch I, 1–165.* Wissenschaftliche Kommentare zu griechischen und lateinischen Schriftstellern. Heidelberg, 1981.

———. *M. Tullius Cicero. De oratore libri III. Kommentar. 2. Band: Buch I, 166–265, Buch II, 1–98.* Wissenschaftliche Kommentare zu griechischen und lateinischen Schriftstellern. Heidelberg, 1985.

Leeman, Anton D., Harm Pinkster, and Edwin Rabbie. *M. Tullius Cicero, De oratore libri III. Kommentar. 3. Band: Buch II, 99–290.* Wissenschaftliche Kommentare zu griechischen und lateinischen Schriftstellern. Heidelberg, 1989.

Leeman, Anton D., Harm Pinkster, and Jakob Wisse. *M. Tullius Cicero. De oratore libri III. Kommentar. 4. Band: Buch II, 291–367, Buch III, 1–95.* Wissenschaftliche Kommentare zu griechischen und lateinischen Schriftstellern. Heidelberg, 1996. [cf. s.n. Wisse]

Levick, Barbara. *Catiline.* Ancients in Action. London / New Delhi / New York / Sydney, 2015.

Linderski, Jerzy. "Two Speeches of Q. Hortensius. A Contribution to the *corpus oratorum* of the Roman Republic." *PP* 16 (1961): 304–11.

———. "Three Trials in 54 B.C.: Sufenas, Cato, Procilius and Cicero, 'Ad Atticum,' 4.15.4." In *Studi in onore di Edoardo Volterra*, 2:281–302. Milano, 1969.

———. "A Witticism of Appuleius Saturninus." *RFIC* 111 (1983): 452–59.

Lintott, Andrew. *Violence in Republican Rome*. 2nd ed. Oxford, 1999a.

———. *The Constitution of the Roman Republic*. Oxford, 1999b.

Lowrie, Michèle. "Cicero in Caesar or Exemplum and Inability in the *Brutus*." In *Vom Selbstverständnis in Antike und Neuzeit / Notions of the Self in Antiquity and Beyond*, edited by Alexander Arweiler und Melanie Möller, 131–154. Transformationen der Antike 8. Berlin / New York, 2008.

LPPR: Rotondi, Giovanni. *Leges publicae populi Romani. Elenco cronologico con una introduzione sull'attività legislativa dei comizi romani. Estratto dalla Enciclopedia Giuridica Italiana*. Milano, 1912 (repr. Hildesheim, 1966: with supplement from: Giovanni Rotondi, *Scritti Giuridici I*. Milano, 1922).

Mahy, Trehor. "Antonius, Triumvir and Orator: Career, Style, and Effectiveness." In Steel and van der Blom 2013, 329–44.

Malcovati, E. "L. Papirius Fregellanus." *Athenaeum* 33 (1955): 137–40.

———. "Una *laudatio funebris* recuperata (Addendum a ORF[4] n. 41)." *Athenaeum* 59 (1981): 185–87.

Marchese, Rosa Rita. *Cicerone, Bruto. Introduzione, traduzione e commento*. Classici 15. Roma, 2011.

Marshall, B. A. *Crassus. A Political Biography*. Amsterdam, 1976.

———. *A Historical Commentary on Asconius*. Columbia, 1985.

Mau, August. "Bart." *RE* III 1 (1897): 30–34.

Meier, Christian. *Caesar*. Translated from the German by David McLintock. London / New York / Sydney / Toronto, 1995.

Millar, F. *The Crowd in Rome in the Late Republic*. Ann Arbor, 1998.

Miller, N. P. "Dramatic Speech in the Roman Historians." *G&R* 22 (1975): 45–57.

Morstein-Marx, R. *Mass Oratory and Political Power in the Late Roman Republic*. Cambridge, 2004.

Mouritsen, Henrik. *Plebs and Politics in the Late Roman Republic*. Cambridge, 2001.

———. "From Meeting to Text: The *Contio* in the Late Republic." In Steel and van der Blom 2013, 63–82.

MRR I: Broughton, T. R. S. *The Magistrates of the Roman Republic. Vol. I. 509 B.C.–100 B.C.* Philological Monographs XV, Vol. I. New York, 1951.

MRR II: Broughton, T. R. S. *The Magistrates of the Roman Republic. Vol. II. 99 B.C.–31 B.C.* Philological Monographs XV, Vol. II. New York, 1952.

MRR III: Broughton, T. R. S. *The Magistrates of the Roman Republic. Vol. III. Supplement*. Philological Monographs XV, Vol. III. Atlanta, GA, 1986.

van Ooteghem, J. *Lucius Licinius Lucullus*. Académie Royale de Belgique, Classe des Lettres, Mémoirs, Deuxième série, Tome LIII, fasc. 4. Bruxelles, 1959.

Pina Polo, Francisco: see *CCMR*.

————. *Contra arma verbis. Der Redner vor dem Volk in der späten römischen Republik*. Aus dem Spanischen von Edda Liess. Stuttgart, 1996.

Piras, Giorgio. "Tradizione indiretta e testi frammentari: Ennio, *Ann.* 303–308 V.^{2} (304–308 Sk.), Cicerone e Gellio." In *Le strade della filologia. Per Scevola Mariotti*, edited by Leopoldo Gamberale, Mario De Nonno, Carlo Di Giovine, and Marina Passalacqua, 41–69. Storia e letteratura 277. Roma, 2012.

du Plessis, Paul J., Clifford Ando, and Kaius Tuori, eds. *The Oxford Handbook of Roman Law and Society*. Oxford, 2016.

Porter, S. E., ed. *Handbook of Classical Rhetoric in the Hellenistic Period 330 B.C.–A.D. 400*. Leiden / New York / Köln, 1997.

Rosillo López, C. "The Common (*Mediocris*) Orator of the Late Republic: The Scribonii Curiones." In Steel and van der Blom 2013, 287–98.

Rotondi, Giovanni: see *LPPR*.

Ryan, F. X. "The Praetorship of Favonius." *AJPh* 115 (1994): 587–601.

Schütz, Günter. *L. Licinius Lucullus. Studien zu den frühen Jahren eines Nobilis (117–75 v. Chr.)*. PhD diss. Regensburg, 1994.

Sciarrino, Enrica. "Roman Oratory Before Cicero: The Elder Cato and Gaius Gracchus." In Dominik and Hall 2007, 54–66.

Scullard, H. H. *Scipio Africanus: Soldier and Politician*. London, 1970.

Seager, Robin. *Pompey the Great. A Political Biography. Second Edition*. Oxford, 2002.

Shackleton Bailey, D. R. *Two Studies in Roman Nomenclature*. 2nd ed. American Philological Association, American Classical Studies 03. Atlanta, GA, 1991.

Steel, C. E. W. "Cicero's *Brutus*: The End of Oratory and the Beginning of History?" *BICS* 46 (2003): 195–211.

———. *Roman Oratory*. Greece & Rome, New Surveys in the Classics No. 36. Cambridge, 2006.

———. "Lost Orators of Rome." In Dominik and Hall 2007, 237–49.

———. "Pompeius, Helvius Mancia, and the Politics of Public Debate." In Steel and van der Blom 2013, 151–59.

Steel, Catherine, and Henriette van der Blom, eds. *Community and Communication. Oratory and Politics in Republican Rome*. Oxford, 2013.

Stevenson, Tom. *Julius Caesar and the Transformation of the Roman Republic*. London / New York, 2015.

Stockton, David. *The Gracchi*. Oxford, 1979.

Sumner, G. V. "Manius or Mamercus?" *JRS* 54 (1964): 41–48.

———. "Asconius and the Acta." *Hermes* 93 (1965): 134–36.

———. *The Orators in Cicero's Brutus: Prosopography and Chronology*. Phoenix Suppl. XI. Toronto, 1973.

Tatum, W. J. *The Patrician Tribune. Publius Clodius Pulcher*. Studies in the History of Greece and Rome. Chapel Hill / London, 1999.

Tempest, Kathryn. *Brutus. The Noble Conspirator*. New Haven / London, 2017.

TLRR: Alexander, Michael C. *Trials in the Late Roman Republic, 149 BC to 50 BC*. Phoenix Suppl. XXVI. Toronto / Buffalo / London, 1990.

Vogt-Spira, Gregor. "Rednergeschichte als Literaturge-schichte. Ciceros *Brutus* und die Tradition der Rede in Rom." In *Rede und Redner. Bewertung und Darstellung in den antiken Kulturen. Kolloquium Frankfurt a.M., 14.–16. Oktober 1998,* edited by Christoff Neumeister and Wulf Raeck, 207–25. Frankfurter Archäologische Schriften 1. Möhnesee, 2000.

Walt, S. *Der Historiker C. Licinius Macer. Einleitung, Fragmente, Kommentar.* BzA 103. Stuttgart / Leipzig, 1997.

Weinstock, Stefan. *Divus Julius.* Oxford, 1971.

Williamson, Callie. *The Laws of the Roman People. Public Law in the Expansion and Decline of the Roman Republic.* Ann Arbor, 2005.

Wiseman, T. P. *New Men in the Roman Senate 139 BC–14 AD.* Oxford, 1971.

Wisse, Jakob, Michael Winterbottom, and Elaine Fantham. *M. Tullius Cicero. De oratore libri III. A Commentary on Book III, 96–230. Volume 5 of the commentary initiated by Anton D. Leeman and Harm Pinkster.* Wissenschaftliche Kommentare zu griechischen und lateinischen Schriftstellern. Heidelberg, 2008.

ORATORY
PART 1

1 AP. CLAUDIUS CAECUS

Ap. Claudius Caecus (censor 312, cos. 307, 296 BC; RE Claudius 91) initiated a number of political reforms and building projects over the course of his career. Appius also composed poetry (FPL⁴, pp. 11–13) and seems to have discussed issues of spelling (GRF, p. 1).

Cicero implies that Appius was one of the earliest Roman speakers who deserve notice (F 6) and that a speech

T 1 Sen. *Ep.* 114.13

multi ex alieno saeculo petunt verba, duodecim tabulas loquuntur; Gracchus illis et Crassus et Curio nimis culti et recentes sunt, ad Appium usque et Coruncanium redeunt.

T 2 Tac. *Dial.* 18.4

[Aper:] num dubitamus inventos qui pro Catone Appium Caecum magis mirarentur?

T 3 Tac. *Dial.* 21.7

[Aper:] Asinius quoque, quamquam propioribus temporibus natus sit, videtur mihi inter Menenios et Appios stu-

1 AP. CLAUDIUS CAECUS

of his was extant in his time, in addition to Ennius' recre-
ating utterances of Appius in poetic form (F 4). In the later
tradition, Appius is described as eloquent (Liv. 10.19.6;
F 8), while some regarded him as a representative of an
antiquated style (T 1–3); Isidore (F 9) identifies Appius as
the first Roman to use prose.

T 1 Seneca, *Epistles*

Many [orators] seek out words from another epoch; they
speak in the language of the Twelve Tables. Gracchus [C.
Sempronius Gracchus (**48**)] and Crassus [L. Licinius
Crassus (**66**)], and Curio [C. Scribonius Curio (**47**)] are
too refined and modern for them; they go back right up to
Appius and Coruncanius [Ti. Coruncanius, cos. 280 BC].

T 2 Tacitus, *Dialogue on Oratory*

[APER:] We do not doubt, do we, that some could be found
who admire Appius Caecus more than Cato [M. Porcius
Cato (**8**)]?

T 3 Tacitus, *Dialogue on Oratory*

[APER:] Asinius [C. Asinius Pollio (**174**)] too, though he
was born in times nearer [to us], seems to me to have
pursued his studies among people like Menenius [Agrippa

duisse. Pacuvium certe et Accium non solum tragoediis
sed etiam orationibus suis expressit; adeo durus et siccus
est.

On King Pyrrhus in the Senate (F 4–11)

*In 280 BC, when, after the Battle of Heraclea, the Senate
debated whether to make peace with King Pyrrhus of
Epirus, Appius, already old and blind, made an effective*

F 4 Cic. *Sen.* 16

[CATO:] ad Appi Claudi senectutem accedebat etiam ut
caecus esset; tamen is cum sententia senatus inclinaret ad
pacem cum Pyrrho foedusque faciendum, non dubitavit
dicere illa quae versibus persecutus est Ennius [Enn. *Ann.*
199–200 Sk. = 6 *Ann.* F 15 *FRL*]: "quo vobis mentes,
rectae quae stare solebant / antehac, dementes sese flex-
ere † via[1]?" ceteraque gravissime; notum enim vobis car-
men est, et tamen ipsius Appi exstat oratio.

    [1] † via *Skutsch*: via *codd.*: ruina *codd. rec. aliquot*: viai *Lam-
binus*: vietae *Scaliger*

F 5 Cic. *Brut.* 55

[CICERO:] possumus Appium Claudium suspicari disertum, quia senatum iamiam inclinatum a Pyrrhi pace revo-
caverit . . .

F 6 Cic. *Brut.* 61

[CICERO:] nec vero habeo quemquam antiquiorem, cuius
quidem scripta proferenda putem, nisi quem Appi Caeci

Menenius Lanatus, cos. 503 BC] and Appius. At any rate he modeled his expression upon Pacuvius and Accius not only in his tragedies, but also in his speeches: so stiff and dry is he.

On King Pyrrhus in the Senate (F 4–11)

speech and prevented a peace deal (e.g., Val. Max. 8.13.5; Suet. Tib. 2.1; Cic. Phil. 1.11; Ov. Fast. 6.203–4; Flor. 1.13.20; Vir. ill. 34.9; Pompon. Dig. 1.2.2.36).

F 4 Cicero, *On Old Age*

[CATO:] There was also added to the old age of Appius Claudius the fact that he was blind. Nevertheless, when opinion in the Senate was inclining toward peace with Pyrrhus and making a treaty, he did not hesitate to say what Ennius has captured in verse [Enn. *Ann.* 199–200 Sk. = 6 *Ann.* F 15 *FRL*]: "where have your senses, which before used to stand upright, wandered off senseless and bent down [?]?", and the rest, most impressively. For the poem is known to you, and, after all, the speech of Appius himself is extant.

F 5 Cicero, *Brutus*

[CICERO:] We may assume that Appius Claudius was a skilled speaker, since he recalled the Senate, already inclining toward it, from peace with Pyrrhus . . .

F 6 Cicero, *Brutus*

[CICERO:] Still, I do not have anyone earlier whose writings I believe should be brought up [than M. Porcius Cato

oratio haec ipsa de Pyrrho et non nullae mortuorum lau-
dationes forte delectant.

F 7 Liv. *Epit.* 13.5–6

Cineas legatus a Pyrrho ad senatum missus petiit, ut con-
ponendae pacis causa rex in urbem reciperetur. [6] de qua
re cum ad frequentiorem senatum referri placuisset, Appius Claudius, qui propter valetudinem oculorum iam diu
consiliis publicis se abstinuerat, venit in curiam et sententia sua tenuit, ut id Pyrrho negaretur.

F 8 Quint. *Inst.* 2.16.7

num igitur negabitur deformem Pyrrhi pacem Caecus ille
Appius dicendi viribus diremisse?

F 9 Isid. *Orig.* 1.38.2

praeterea tam apud Graecos quam apud Latinos longe
antiquiorem curam fuisse carminum quam prosae. omnia
enim prius versibus condebantur; prosae autem studium
sero viguit. primus apud Graecos Pherecydes Syrus soluta
oratione scripsit; apud Romanos autem Appius Caecus
adversus Pyrrhum solutam orationem primus exercuit.

(**8**)], unless by chance this very speech of Appius Caecus concerning Pyrrhus and some eulogies of the dead delight anyone.

F 7 Livy, *Epitome*

Cineas, having been sent by Pyrrhus as an envoy to the Senate, asked that the king might be received into the city to arrange the terms of the peace. [6] When it had been decided to refer this matter to a fuller meeting of the Senate, Appius Claudius, who, because of the weakness of his eyes, had kept himself away from public deliberations already for a long time, entered the Senate house and by his statement achieved that this was denied to Pyrrhus.

F 8 Quintilian, *The Orator's Education*

Will it then be possible to deny that the well-known Appius Caecus pulled apart the shameful peace with Pyrrhus by the force of his speaking?

F 9 Isidore, *Origins*

Moreover, among the Greeks as among the Latins attention to poetry was far older than to prose. For initially everything was expressed in verse; but the application to prose flourished late. Among the Greeks Pherecydes of Syros[1] was the first to write in prose; and among the Romans Appius Caecus, against Pyrrhus, was the first to use prose.

[1] Pherecydes of Syros (D.-K. 7) was a mythographer and cosmologist in the sixth century BC; he probably wrote in prose.

F 10 Plut. *Pyrr.* 19.1–5

ὁ δ᾽ αὐτόθεν καταστὰς "πρότερον μέν" ἔφη "τὴν περὶ
τὰ ὄμματα τύχην ἀνιαρῶς ἔφερον, ὦ Ῥωμαῖοι, νῦν δ᾽
ἄχθομαι πρὸς τῷ τυφλὸς εἶναι μὴ καὶ κωφὸς ὤν, ἀλλ᾽
ἀκούων αἰσχρὰ βουλεύματα καὶ δόγμαθ᾽ ὑμῶν, ἀνα-
τρέποντα τῆς Ῥώμης τὸ κλέος. [2] ποῦ γὰρ ὑμῶν ὁ
πρὸς ἅπαντας ἀνθρώπους θρυλούμενος ἀεὶ λόγος, ὡς
εἰ παρῆν ἐκεῖνος εἰς Ἰταλίαν ὁ μέγας Ἀλέξανδρος καὶ
συνηνέχθη νέοις ἡμῖν καὶ τοῖς πατράσιν ἡμῶν ἀκμά-
ζουσιν, οὐκ ἂν ὑμνεῖτο νῦν ἀνίκητος, ἀλλ᾽ ἢ φυγὼν
ἂν ἢ που πεσὼν ἐνταῦθα τὴν Ῥώμην ἐνδοξοτέραν
ἀπέλιπε; [3] ταῦτα μέντοι κενὴν ἀλαζονείαν καὶ κόμ-
πον ἀποδείκνυτε, Χάονας καὶ Μολοσσοὺς τὴν ἀεὶ
Μακεδόνων λείαν δεδιότες, καὶ τρέμοντες Πύρρον, ὃς
τῶν Ἀλεξάνδρου δορυφόρων ἕνα γοῦν ἀεὶ περιέπων
καὶ θεραπεύων διατετέλεκε, καὶ νῦν οὐ βοηθῶν τοῖς
ἐνταῦθα μᾶλλον Ἕλλησιν ἢ φεύγων τοὺς ἐκεῖ πολε-
μίους πλανᾶται περὶ τὴν Ἰταλίαν, ἐπαγγελλόμενος
ἡμῖν τὴν ἡγεμονίαν ἀπὸ ταύτης τῆς δυνάμεως, ἢ μέ-
ρος μικρὸν αὐτῷ Μακεδονίας οὐκ ἤρκεσε διαφυλάξαι.
[4] μὴ τοῦτον οὖν ἀπαλλάξειν νομίζετε ποιησάμενοι
φίλον, ἀλλ᾽ ἐκείνους ἐπάξεσθαι καταφρονήσαντας
ὑμῶν ὡς πᾶσιν εὐκατεργάστων, εἰ Πύρρος ἄπεισι μὴ
δοὺς δίκην ὧν ὕβρισεν, ἀλλὰ καὶ προσλαβὼν μισθὸν
τὸ ἐπεγγελάσαι Ῥωμαίοις Ταραντίνους καὶ Σαυνί-
τας." [5] τοιαῦτα τοῦ Ἀππίου διαλεχθέντος, ὁρμὴ
παρέστη πρὸς τὸν πόλεμον αὐτοῖς, καὶ τὸν Κινέαν

F 10 Plutarch, *Life of Pyrrhus*

Then he [Appius] raised himself up from that very place and said: "Previously I have borne the misfortune affecting my eyes as an affliction, Romans, but now I am grieved that, in addition to being blind, I am not deaf, but instead hear your shameful resolutions and decrees, overturning the glory of Rome. [2] For what becomes of your words continuously spread about to all men, namely that, if the famous Alexander the Great had come to Italy and had come into conflict with us, when we were young men, and with our fathers, when they were in their prime, he would not now be celebrated as invincible, but would either have fled, or, perhaps, have fallen there, and so have left Rome more glorious still? [3] Surely you are proving that this was empty boasting and noise, since you are afraid of Chaonians and Molossians [tribes in Epirus], ever the prey of the Macedonians, and you tremble before Pyrrhus, who has always been an attendant and servant of at least one of Alexander's bodyguards, and now wanders over Italy, not so much to help the Greeks here as to escape his enemies there, promising to win for us the supremacy with that force that was not able to preserve for him a small portion of Macedonia. [4] Do not suppose that you will rid yourselves of that man by making him your friend; instead, you will bring against you those who will despise you as men easily subdued by anybody, if Pyrrhus goes away without having been punished for his insults, but actually having received as a reward that Tarantines and Samnites mock at the Romans." [5] After Appius had said such things, eagerness to prosecute the war arose among them,

ἀποπέμπουσιν ἀποκρινάμενοι Πύρρον ἐξελθόντα τῆς
Ἰταλίας, οὕτως εἰ δέοιτο περὶ φιλίας καὶ συμμαχίας
διαλέγεσθαι . . .

F 11 App. *Samn.* F 10.4–6

οἱ δ' ἐνεδοίαζον ἐπὶ πλεῖστον, τῇ τε δόξῃ τοῦ Πύρρου
καὶ τῷ συμβεβηκότι πάθει καταπλαγέντες, ἕως Ἄππιος Κλαύδιος ὁ Καῖκος ἐπίκλησιν, ἤδη τετυφλωμέ-
νος, ἐς τὸ βουλευτήριον τοῖς παισὶν αὐτὸν ἀγαγεῖν
κελεύσας [5] "ἠχθόμην," εἶπεν, "ὅτι μὴ βλέπω, νῦν δ',
ὅτι ἀκούω. τὰ γὰρ τοιαῦτα ὑμῶν βουλεύματα ἠξίουν
μήθ' ὁρᾶν μήτ' ἀκούειν, οἳ δι' ἓν ἀτύχημα ἀθρόως
οὕτως ἑαυτῶν ἐκλέλησθε καὶ τὸν τοῦτο δράσαντα
αὐτόν τε καὶ τοὺς ἐπαγαγομένους αὐτὸν βουλεύεσθε
φίλους ἀντὶ πολεμίων θέσθαι καὶ τὰ τῶν προγόνων
κτήματα Λευκανοῖς καὶ Βρεττίοις δοῦναι. τί τοῦτ'
ἐστὶν ἢ Ῥωμαίους ἐπὶ Μακεδόσι γενέσθαι; καὶ ταῦτά
τινες εἰρήνην ἀντὶ δουλείας τολμῶσιν ὀνομάζειν." [6]
ἄλλα τε πολλὰ ὅμοια τούτοις ὁ Ἄππιος εἰπὼν καὶ
ἐρεθίσας εἰσηγήσατο Πύρρον, εἰ δέοιτο τῆς Ῥωμαίων
φιλίας καὶ συμμαχίας, ἐξ Ἰταλίας ἀπελθόντα πρε-
σβεύειν, παρόντα δὲ μήτε φίλον ἡγεῖσθαι μήτε σύμ-
μαχον μήτε Ῥωμαίοις δικαστὴν ἢ διαιτητήν. καὶ ἡ
βουλὴ ταῦθ', ἅπερ καὶ Ἄππιος εἶπεν, ἀπεκρίνατο Κι-
νέᾳ.

and they sent back Cineas [Pyrrhus' envoy], with the reply
that Pyrrhus must leave Italy, and then, if he wished, one
could talk about friendship and alliance . . .

F 11 Appian, *Samnite History*

They [the Romans] were uncertain for a long time, in-
timidated by the prestige of Pyrrhus and by the calamity
that had befallen them, until Appius Claudius, with the
nickname Caecus, who had already gone blind by that
time, ordered his sons to lead him into the Senate house
and said: [5] "I was grieved that I cannot see, now that I
can hear. For never did I expect to see or hear deliberations of this kind from you, who, as a result of a single
misfortune, immediately have so forgotten yourselves that
you wish to take the man who brought it upon you and
those who called him hither for friends instead of enemies,
and to give the possessions of your ancestors to Lucanians
and Bruttians [tribes in southern Italy]. What is this other
than Romans becoming servants of Macedonians? And
some dare to call this peace instead of servitude." [6] Voic-
ing many other points similar to these and rousing their
spirit, Appius proposed that, if Pyrrhus wanted the friendship of the Romans and alliance, he should withdraw from
Italy and send an embassy; as long as he remained, he
should be considered neither friend nor ally, neither judge
nor arbitrator of the Romans. And the Senate replied to
Cineas [Pyrrhus' envoy] what Appius had said.

2 C. MARCIUS RUTILUS CENSORINUS

On Censorial Power to the People (F 1)

When elected censor for the second time, Censorinus delivered a speech criticizing the People for that decision (CCMR, App. A: 108) and supported a law forbidding

F 1 Val. Max. 4.1.3

par Furio moderatione Marcius Rutil{i}us[1] Censorinus: iterum enim censor creatus ad contionem populum vocatum quam potuit gravissima oratione corripuit, quod eam potestatem bis sibi detulisset, cuius maiores, quia nimis magna videretur, tempus coartandum iudicassent. uterque recte, et Censorinus et populus: alter enim ut moderate honores crederent praecepit, alter se moderato credidit.

[1] Rutil{i}us *Kempf*: Rutilius *codd.*

2 C. MARCIUS RUTILUS CENSORINUS

C. Marcius Rutilus Censorinus (tr. pl. 311, cos. 310, pontifex et augur 300, censor 294, 265 BC; RE Marcius 98) was censor twice and therefore was the first in his family to bear the cognomen *Censorinus (cf. also Plut. Cor. 1.1).*

On Censorial Power to the People (F 1)

reelection to the censorship (Plut. Cor. 1.1; Lex de censura non iteranda: LPPR, *p. 244).*

F 1 Valerius Maximus, *Memorable Doings and Sayings*

Equal to Furius [M. Furius Camillus] in moderation was Marcius Rutilus Censorinus: for, when elected censor for the second time, he summoned the People to a public meeting and rebuked them in as stern a speech as he possibly could since they had conferred upon him twice that power whose duration their ancestors had thought proper to be curtailed because it seemed too great. Each was in the right, both Censorinus and the People: for the former advised them to entrust offices moderately, the latter entrusted itself to a man of moderation.

3 Q. FABIUS MAXIMUS VERRUCOSUS CUNCTATOR

Q. Fabius Maximus Verrucosus Cunctator (RE Fabius 116) was consul five times (233, 228, 215, 214, 209 BC), censor (230 BC), dictator twice (221, 217 BC), pontifex from 216 BC, and augur (on his life, see Plut. Fab. Max.). He received the cognomen *Cunctator since he famously defeated the Carthaginians in the Second Punic War by*

T 1 Cic. *Brut.* 57

[CICERO:] Q. etiam Maximus Verrucosus orator habitus est temporibus illis . . .

Funeral Oration for His Son Quintus (F 2–5)

F 2 Cic. *Sen.* 12

[CATO:] multa in eo viro praeclara cognovi, sed nihil admirabilius quam quomodo ille mortem fili tulit, clari viri et consularis; est in manibus laudatio, quam cum legimus, quem philosophum non contemnimus?

3 Q. FABIUS MAXIMUS VERRUCOSUS CUNCTATOR

"hesitating" to start an open battle (Enn. 363–65 Sk. = 12 Ann. F 1 FRL).

In Cicero it is noted that Fabius Maximus was regarded as an orator in an early period (T 1). His speech was said to be unadorned but made weighty by its content (Plut. Fab. Max. 1.7–8).

T 1 Cicero, *Brutus*

[CICERO:] Q. Maximus Verrucosus, too, was accounted an orator in those times . . . [**6 T 1**]

Funeral Oration for His Son Quintus (F 2–5)

Fabius Maximus' funeral oration for his son Quintus (cos. 213 BC) was delivered after the son's death in 207 BC and apparently published afterward (CCMR, App. A: 132; see Kierdorf 1980, 83–85).

F 2 Cicero, *On Old Age*

[CATO:] Many are the remarkable things I have observed in that great man [Fabius Maximus], but nothing more admirable than the manner in which he bore the death of his son, a noble man and a former consul. The funeral eulogy is generally available, and, when we read it, what philosopher do we not look down upon?

F 3 Plut. *Fab. Max.* 1.7–9

ὁρῶν δὲ καὶ τῆς πολιτείας τὸ μέγεθος καὶ τῶν πολέ-
μων τὸ πλῆθος, ἤσκει τὸ μὲν σῶμα πρὸς τοὺς πολέμους ὥσπερ ὅπλον σύμφυτον, τὸν δὲ λόγον ὄργανον
πειθοῦς πρὸς τὸν δῆμον, εὖ μάλα τῷ βίῳ πρεπόντως
κατακεκοσμημένον. [8] οὐ γὰρ ἐπῆν ὡραϊσμὸς οὐδὲ
κενὴ καὶ ἀγοραῖος χάρις, ἀλλὰ νοῦς ἴδιον καὶ περιτ-
τὸν ἐν γνωμολογίαις σχῆμα καὶ βάθος ἔχων, ἃς μάλιστα ταῖς Θουκυδίδου προσεοικέναι λέγουσι. [9] δια-
σῴζεται γὰρ αὐτοῦ λόγος ὃν εἶπεν ἐν τῷ δήμῳ, τοῦ
παιδὸς αὐτοῦ μεθ᾽ ὑπατείαν ἀποθανόντος ἐγκώμιον.

F 4 Plut. *Fab. Max.* 24.6

τοῦ δὲ Φαβίου τὸν υἱὸν ἀποθανεῖν συνέβη, καὶ τὴν
μὲν συμφορὰν ὡς ἀνήρ τε φρόνιμος καὶ πατὴρ χρη-
στὸς ἤνεγκε μετριώτατα, τὸ δ᾽ ἐγκώμιον ὃ ταῖς ἐκκο-
μιδαῖς τῶν ἐπιφανῶν οἱ προσήκοντες ἐπιτελοῦσιν,
αὐτὸς εἶπε καταστὰς ἐν ἀγορᾷ καὶ γράψας τὸν λόγον
ἐξέδωκεν.

F 5 Prisc., *GL* II, p. 380.9–10

Fabius Maximus: "amitti quam apisci." passive omnia sunt
prolata.

F 3 Plutarch, *Life of Fabius Maximus*

Seeing both the greatness of the task of running the Republic and the large number of wars, he [Fabius Maximus] trained his body for the wars like natural armor and his speech as an instrument of persuasion with the People, thus shaped in a way right well befitting his manner of life. [8] For there was no affectation nor any empty and forensic grace, but a mind having a peculiar form and weight in an abundance of maxims, which, they say, most resembled those of Thucydides. [9] And a speech of his is preserved, which he delivered before the People, as a eulogy of his son, who had died after his consulship.

F 4 Plutarch, *Life of Fabius Maximus*

And the son of Fabius happened to die, and this affliction he bore with the greatest equanimity, like a wise man and a good father. The funeral eulogy, which the kinsmen offer at the obsequies of illustrious men, he delivered himself, standing in the Forum, and then he wrote out the speech and published it.

F 5 Priscian

Fabius Maximus: "to be lost rather than to be obtained." All these [words: this and preceding examples] have been uttered in the passive voice [for verbs normally deponent].[1]

---

[1] The attribution of this fragment to this Fabius Maximus and to this speech is conjectural, based on the fact that Q. Fabius Maximus Cunctator was the most famous bearer of that name.

17

On Lex Cincia *(F 6)*

Fabius Maximus' speech in support of the Lex Cincia *dates to 204 BC: this bill, proposed by the Tribune of the People M. Cincius Alimentus, was to prohibit donations to law-*

F 6 Cic. *Sen.* 10

[CATO:] quaestor deinde quadriennio post factus sum, quem[1] magistratum gessi consulibus Tuditano et Cethego, cum quidem ille admodum senex suasor legis Cinciae de donis et muneribus fuit.

---

[1] quaestor . . . quem *Pighius*: quaestor. deinde aedilis. quadriennio post factus sum praetor. quem *vel* quaestor. quem *vel* quaestor. quō *vel* quaestor. *codd.*

4 P. CORNELIUS SCIPIO AFRICANUS MAIOR

P. Cornelius Scipio Africanus maior (ca. 235–183 BC; cos. 205, 194, censor 199 BC; RE Cornelius 336) became proconsul in Hispania after the deaths of his father and uncle during the Second Punic War. He eventually defeated the Carthaginians in the battle at Zama in 202 BC. Thereupon, Scipio celebrated a triumph and was honored with the cognomen *Africanus (Polyb. 16.23.5–7; Liv. 30.45).*

T 1 Cic. *Brut.* 77

[CICERO:] cum hoc Catone grandiores natu fuerunt C. Flaminius C. Varro Q. Maximus Q. Metellus P. Lentulus

On Lex Cincia *(F 6)*

*yers and the offering of extensive gifts (*Lex Cincia de donis et muneribus: LPPR, *pp. 261–62).*

F 6 Cicero, *On Old Age*

[CATO:] Then, after four years, I was made quaestor, which office I held in the consulship of Tuditanus and Cethegus [204 BC], when that man [Fabius Maximus], far advanced in age, was a supporter of the Cincian Law on gifts and donations.

4 P. CORNELIUS SCIPIO AFRICANUS MAIOR

His successes and unusual career later led to resentment among the Roman nobility: Scipio Africanus left Rome toward the end of his life and died near Liternum (Liv. 38.50.4–56.13; on his life see, e.g., Scullard 1970).

In Cicero, Scipio Africanus is described as a decent orator (T 1); it is also mentioned that he left nothing in writing (T 2; see F 3–5).

T 1 Cicero, *Brutus*

[CICERO:] Older contemporaries of this Cato [M. Porcius Cato (**8**)] were C. Flaminius [C. Flaminius Nepos, cos. 223, 217 BC], C. Varro [C. Terentius Varro, cos. 216 BC],

P. Crassus, qui cum superiore Africano consul fuit. ipsum Scipionem accepimus non infantem fuisse.

T 2 Cic. *Off.* 3.4

quamquam Africanus maiorem laudem meo iudicio adsequebatur. nulla enim eius ingenii monumenta mandata litteris, nullum opus otii, nullum solitudinis munus exstat . . .

Defense Speech Against Tribunes of the People
(F 3–5)

Although the remark that Africanus left nothing in writing (T 2) is part of a specific argument, it may suggest that extracts from a defense speech by Scipio Africanus against the Tribunes of the People M. Naevius (tr. pl. 184 BC) or the two Q. Petillii (tr. pl. 187 BC), as reported in later authors (F 3–5, 3A; App. Syr. *40.206–11; CCMR, App. A:*

F 3 Gell. *NA* 4.18.3–6

cum M. Naevius tribunus plebis accusaret eum ad populum diceretque accepisse a rege Antiocho pecuniam, ut condicionibus gratiosis et mollibus pax cum eo populi

Q. Maximus [Q. Fabius Maximus Cunctator (3)], Q. Metellus [Q. Caecilius Metellus (6)], P. Lentulus [P. Cornelius Lentulus Caudinus, prob. praet. 203 BC], P. Crassus [P. Licinius Crassus Dives, cos. 205 BC], who was consul with the elder Africanus. Scipio himself, we learn, was not at all without the ability to speak.

T 2 Cicero, *On Duties*

And yet, in my judgment, Africanus earned the higher praise. For no monuments of his genius have been committed to writing, no work of leisure, no product of his solitude exists[1] . . .

[1] Since Africanus was still thinking about political affairs in his solitude and leisure, rather than writing treatises, as Cicero does.

Defense Speech Against Tribunes of the People
(F 3–5)

150), might not be "authentic"; there was already doubt in antiquity (F 3–4). The incident must have taken place (F 3) after the Treaty of Apamea (188 BC) with Antiochus, king of the Seleucids, which imposed harsh terms and required huge payments.

F 3 Gellius, *Attic Nights*

When M. Naevius, a Tribune of the People, accused him [Scipio] before the People and said that he had accepted money from king Antiochus [king of the Seleucids], so that peace was arranged with him in the name of the Roman

Romani nomine fieret, et quaedam item alia crimini daret indigna tali viro, tum Scipio pauca praefatus, quae dignitas vitae suae atque gloria postulabat: "memoria," inquit, "Quirites, repeto, diem esse hodiernum, quo Hannibalem Poenum imperio vestro inimicissimum magno proelio vici in terra Africa pacemque et victoriam vobis peperi inspectabilem. non igitur simus adversum deos ingrati et, censeo, relinquamus nebulonem hunc, eamus hinc protinus Iovi optimo maximo gratulatum." [4] id cum dixisset, avertit et ire ad Capitolium coepit. [5] tum contio universa, quae ad sententiam de Scipione ferendam convenerat, relicto tribuno Scipionem in Capitolium comitata atque inde ad aedes eius cum laetitia et gratulatione sollemni prosecuta est. [6] fertur etiam oratio, quae videtur habita eo die a Scipione, et qui dicunt eam non veram, non eunt infitias, quin haec quidem verba fuerint, quae dixi, Scipionis.

F 3A Liv. 38.50.10–51.12

nec alius antea quisquam nec ille ipse Scipio consul censorve maiore omnis generis hominum frequentia quam reus illo die in forum est deductus. [11] iussus dicere causam, sine ulla criminum mentione orationem adeo magnificam de rebus ab se gestis est exorsus ut satis constaret neminem umquam neque melius neque verius laudatum esse. [12] dicebantur enim ab ⟨eo⟩ eodem animo

People under favorable and gentle conditions, and equally put forward as reproaches some other things unworthy of such a man, then Scipio, after he had mentioned initially a few things that the dignity and glory of his life demanded, said: "I recall in my mind, Romans, that today is the day on which I defeated the Carthaginian Hannibal, a stern enemy of your empire, in a great battle in Africa and achieved peace and a glorious victory for you. Therefore, let us not be ungrateful toward the gods and, I believe, let us leave this sorry wretch behind; let us go from here immediately to render thanks to Iuppiter Optimus Maximus." [4] When he had said this, he turned and started to walk to the Capitol. [5] Then the entire assembly, who had come together to cast their vote on Scipio, left the Tribune behind, accompanied Scipio to the Capitol and from there followed him to his house with joy and solemn congratulation. [6] There is in circulation even an oration that is believed to have been delivered on that day by Scipio, and those who say that it is not the true one do not deny that at least those words that I quoted are those of Scipio.

F 3A Livy, *History of Rome*

And no other man previously, not even this Scipio himself, when consul or censor, was ever escorted to the Forum by a greater crowd of men of every rank than he on that day as the defendant. [11] Asked to plead his cause, he began so magnificent a speech about his achievements, without any mention of the accusations, that it was sufficiently clear that no man had ever been eulogized better or more truthfully. [12] For his deeds were mentioned by ⟨him⟩ in

ingenioque {a} quo[1] gesta erant, et aurium fastidium aberat, quia pro periculo, non in gloriam referebantur. [51.1] . . . [5] orationibus in noctem perductis prodicta dies est. ubi ea venit, tribuni in rostris prima luce consederunt; [6] citatus reus magno agmine amicorum clientiumque per mediam contionem ad rostra subiit, [7] silentioque facto "hoc" inquit "die, tribuni plebis vosque, Quirites, cum Hannibale et Carthaginiensibus signis conlatis in Africa bene ac feliciter pugnavi. [8] itaque, cum hodie litibus et iurgiis supersederi aequum sit, ego hinc extemplo in Capitolium ad Iovem optimum maximum Iunonemque et Minervam, ceterosque deos qui Capitolio atque arci praesident, salutandos ibo, [9] iisque gratias agam quod mihi et hoc ipso die et saepe alias egregie gerendae rei publicae mentem facultatemque dederunt. [10] vestrum quoque quibus commodum est, Quirites, [11] ite mecum, et orate deos ut mei similes principes habeatis, ita, si ab annis septemdecim ad senectutem semper vos aetatem meam honoribus vestris anteistis, ego vestros honores rebus gerendis praecessi." [12] ab rostris in Capitolium escendit. simul se universa contio avertit et secuta Scipionem est, adeo ut postremo scribae viatoresque tribunos relinquerent, nec cum iis praeter servilem comitatum et praeconem, qui reum ex rostris citabat, quisquam esset.

[1] ab e<o> eodem . . . {a} quo *Burman*: ab eodem . . . a quo *codd.*: eodem . . . quo *Ruhnken*

the same temper and spirit in which they had been performed, and there was no resentment among the hearers, since they were recalled in view of the peril, not for boasting. [51.1] . . . [5] When the speeches had continued until nightfall, the matter was adjourned. When that date came, the Tribunes [Q. Petillii] took their seats on the Rostra at dawn; [6] the defendant, when summoned, approached the Rostra with a great throng of friends and clients through the midst of the public meeting, [7] and, when silence ensued, he said: "On this day, Tribunes of the People and you, Romans, I fought well and successfully in pitched battle with Hannibal and the Carthaginians in Africa. [8] Therefore, since it is appropriate to refrain today from trials and quarrels, I shall proceed at once from here to the Capitol to pay my respects to Iuppiter Optimus Maximus and Juno and Minerva and other gods who preside over the Capitoline and the citadel, [9] and I shall give thanks to them because both on this very day and often on other occasions they have given me the mind and the capacity to render conspicuous service to the Republic. [10] Those of you too, Romans, for whom it is convenient, [11] come with me and pray to the gods that you may have leaders like me, on this condition, that, if from the age of seventeen to my old age you have always gone ahead of my years in bestowing honors upon me, I have come before your honors with my deeds." [12] From the Rostra he went up to the Capitol. At the same time the whole public meeting turned and followed Scipio, so that finally even the clerks and messengers left the Tribunes, nor did anyone remain with them except their retinue of slaves and the herald, who was summoning the defendant from the Rostra.

25

F 4 Liv. 38.56.1–6

multa alia in Scipionis exitu maxime vitae dieque dicta,
morte, funere, sepulcro in diversum trahunt, ut cui famae,
quibus scriptis adsentiar non habeam. [2] non de accusa-
tore convenit (alii M. Naevium, alii Petillios diem dixisse
scribunt), non de tempore quo dicta dies sit, non de anno
quo mortuus sit, non ubi mortuus aut elatus sit; . . . [5] nec
inter scriptores rerum discrepat solum, sed orationes quoque, si modo ipsorum sunt quae feruntur, P. Scipionis et
Ti. Gracchi abhorrent inter se. [6] index orationis P. Scipionis nomen M. Naevi tribuni plebis habet, ipsa oratio
sine nomine est accusatoris; modo nebolunem, modo nugatorem appellat.

F 5 Liv. 39.52.3

Antiatem auctorem refellit tribunus plebis M. Naevius,
adversus quem oratio inscripta P. Africani est.

F 4 Livy, *History of Rome*

Many other things concerning particularly the end of
Scipio's life and his trial, death, funeral and tomb go in
opposite directions, so that I do not know which tradition,
which writings I should subscribe to. [2] There is no agreement as regards the accuser (some write that M. Naevius,
some that the Petillii called him to court), neither about
the time for which the appearance in court was set, nor
about the year in which he died, nor where he died or was
buried. . . . [5] And there is a discrepancy not only among
historiographers, but also the speeches (provided that
those that are in circulation are works of these men themselves) of P. Scipio and Ti. Gracchus [Ti. Sempronius
Gracchus (**10**), F 1A] are inconsistent with one another.
[6] The title of the speech by P. Scipio contains the name
of M. Naevius, Tribune of the People; the speech itself is
without the name of the accuser; it calls him now a scoundrel, now a trifler.

F 5 Livy, *History of Rome*

The author [Valerius] Antias [Roman historian of 1st cent.
BC; *FRHist* 25] is refuted [as regards his view on the date
of Scipio's death] by the Tribune of the People M. Naevius, against whom an oration by P. Africanus exists enti-
tled after him.

5 M. CLAUDIUS MARCELLUS

*Funeral Oration for His Father
M. Claudius Marcellus (F 1)*

*Marcellus delivered the funeral oration for his father
(CCMR, App. A: 127; Kierdorf 1980, 108), when the latter
fell in an ambush near Venusia (modern Venosa) in 208 BC*

F 1 Liv. 27.27.12–14

multos circa unam rem ambitus fecerim si quae de Marcelli morte variant auctores omnia exsequi velim. [13] ut
omittam alios, Coelius triplicem gestae rei ‹mem›oriam[1]
edit, unam traditam fama, alteram scriptam laudationem[2]
filii qui rei gestae interfuerit, tertiam quam ipse pro inqui-
sita ac sibi comperta adfert. [14] ceterum ita fama variat
ut tamen plerique loci speculandi causa castris egressum,
omnes insidiis circumventum tradant.

[1] ‹mem›oriam *Luchs*: ordinem *codd.*: ordine ‹memoria›m
Castiglioni: seriem *Perizonius*: rationem *Weissenborn*: recorda-
tionem *Madvig dubitanter*: *alii alia*   [2] scriptam laudationem *vel* scripta laudatione *vel* scriptam in laudatione *codd.*

5 M. CLAUDIUS MARCELLUS

M. Claudius Marcellus (cos. 196, censor 189 BC; RE Claudius 222) was the son of the M. Claudius Marcellus who was consul five times and conquered Syracuse in 212 BC.

Funeral Oration for His Father
M. Claudius Marcellus (F 1)

during his last consulship (Polyb. 10.32; Plut. Marc. 29–30; Liv. 27.26–27). In 205 BC the son dedicated the Temple of Virtus vowed and begun by his father (Liv. 29.11.13).

F 1 Livy, *History of Rome*

I would be making many twists and turns around a single matter, if I wished to go through everything in which writers differ concerning the death of Marcellus. [13] Not to mention others, Coelius [L. Coelius Antipater, Roman historian at end of 2nd cent. BC; *FRHist* 15] provides a threefold record of the event: one as transmitted by tradition, a second the eulogy, written down, by the son, who was present at the event, a third that he himself adds as investigated and discovered by him. [14] In any case, the reports vary in such a way that, still, most writers relate that he [Marcellus] left the camp to explore the locality and all that he was overwhelmed by an ambush.

6 Q. CAECILIUS METELLUS

T 1 Cic. *Brut.* 57

[CICERO:] Q. etiam Maximus Verrucosus orator habitus est temporibus illis et Q. Metellus, is qui bello Punico secundo cum L. Veturio Philone consul fuit.

Funeral Oration for His Father
L. Caecilius Metellus (F 2)

F 2 Plin. *HN* 7.139–40

Q. Metellus in ea oratione, quam habuit supremis laudibus patris sui L. Metelli pontificis, bis consulis, dictatoris, magistri equitum, XVviri agris dandis, qui p⟨lu⟩rimos[1] elephantos ex primo Punico bello duxit in triumpho, scriptum reliquit decem maximas res optimasque, in quibus quaerendis sapientes aetatem exigerent, consummasse eum: [140] voluisse enim primarium bellatorem esse,

---

[1] p⟨lu⟩rimos *Pintianus*: primus *codd., edd. vet.*

30

6 Q. CAECILIUS METELLUS

Q. Caecilius Metellus (cos. 206, dictator 205 BC; RE Cae-
cilius 81) was active during the Second Punic War and is
recognized as an early orator in Cicero (T 1).

T 1 Cicero, *Brutus*

[CICERO:] Q. Maximus Verrucosus [Q. Fabius Maximus
Verrucosus Cunctator (**3**), T 1], too, was accounted an
orator in those times, and Q. Metellus, who was consul
during the Second Punic War with L. Veturius Philo [206
BC].

Funeral Oration for His Father
L. Caecilius Metellus (F 2)

In 221 BC Caecilius delivered the funeral oration for his
father L. Caecilius Metellus (cos. 251, 247, dictator 224
BC), which he seems to have written up (CCMR, App. A:
110; see Kierdorf 1980, 10–21).

F 2 Pliny the Elder, *Natural History*

Q. Metellus, in that oration that he delivered for the final
eulogy of his father L. Metellus—*pontifex*, twice consul,
dictator, master of the horse, and *quindecimvir* for the
assignation of land, who led a great number of elephants
in a triumph on account of the First Punic War [in 250
BC]—has left it in writing that he [his father] had achieved
the ten greatest and highest objects in the pursuit of which
wise men pass their lives: [140] for he had wished to be a

optimum oratorem, fortissimum imperatorem, auspicio suo maximas res geri, maximo honore uti, summa sapientia esse, summum senatorem haberi, pecuniam magnam bono modo invenire, multos liberos relinquere et clarissimum in civitate esse; haec contigisse ei nec ulli alii post Romam conditam.

On Carthage in the Senate (F 3)

F 3 Val. Max. 7.2.3

Q. quoque Metelli cum gravis tum etiam alta in senatu sententia, qui devicta Carthagine nescire[1] se illa victoria bonine plus an mali rei publicae attulisset adseveravit, quoniam ut pacem restituendo profuisset, ita Hannibalem submovendo nonnihil nocuisset: eius enim transitu in Italiam dormientem iam populi Romani virtutem excitatam, metuique debere ne acri aemulo liberata in eundem somnum revolveretur. in aequo igitur malorum posuit uri tecta, vastari agros, exhauriri aerarium, et prisci roboris nervos hebetari.

[1] nescire *vel* scire *codd.*

first-class warrior, a supreme orator, a very brave general, matters of the highest importance to be directed by his military leadership, to enjoy the greatest honor, to be of outstanding wisdom, to be deemed a most eminent senator, to obtain great wealth in an honorable way, to leave many children, and to be most distinguished in the community; that these things had fallen to his lot and not to that of anyone else since Rome's foundation.

On Carthage in the Senate (F 3)

Metellus' comment about the impact of the conquest of Carthage (201 BC) on Rome comes from a later utterance in the Senate.

F 3 Valerius Maximus, *Memorable Doings and Sayings*

There is also a statement by Q. Metellus in the Senate, both impressive and particularly profound, as he asserted, after the conquest of Carthage, that he did not know whether that victory had brought more good or harm to the Republic; for, while by restoring peace it had been beneficial, equally, by removing Hannibal, it had done not a little harm. For by his passage into Italy the already dormant prowess of the Roman People had been aroused, and it was to be feared that, freed of its fierce competitor, it would sink again into the same slumber. Thus, he placed the burning of houses, the laying waste of fields, the exhaustion of the treasury, and the slackening of the sinews of former strength on an equal plane of evils.

7 M. CORNELIUS CETHEGUS

M. Cornelius Cethegus (censor 209, cos. 204 BC; RE Cornelius 92), according to Cicero (T 1), was the first Roman for whom there is evidence that he was eloquent and regarded as such: as proof Cicero refers to lines from Ennius'

T 1 Cic. *Brut.* 57–60

[CICERO:] quem vero exstet et de quo sit memoriae proditum eloquentem fuisse et ita esse habitum, primus est M. Cornelius Cethegus, cuius eloquentiae est auctor et idoneus quidem mea sententia Q. Ennius, praesertim cum et ipse eum audiverit et scribat de mortuo: ex quo nulla suspicio est amicitiae causa esse mentitum. [58] est igitur sic apud illum in nono ut opinor annali [Enn. *Ann.* 304–8 Sk. = 9 *Ann.* F 6 *FRL*]: "additur orator Cornelius suaviloquenti / ore Cethegus Marcus Tuditano conlega / Marci filius," et oratorem appellat et suaviloquentiam tribuit, quae nunc quidem non tam est in plerisque (latrant enim iam quidam oratores, non loquuntur), sed est ea laus eloquentiae certe maxima "is dictust ollis popularibus olim, / qui tum vivebant homines atque aevum agitabant,[1] / flos delibatus populi," probe vero; [59] ut enim hominis decus ingenium, sic ingeni ipsius lumen est eloquentia, qua virum excellentem praeclare tum illi homines florem populi esse dixerunt "Suadaeque medulla." Πειθώ quam vocant Graeci, cuius effector est orator, hanc Sua-

---

[1] agitabant *Gell. NA* 12.2.3: agebant *codd. Cic.*

7 M. CORNELIUS CETHEGUS

Annales *(Enn. Ann. 304–8* Sk. = 9 Ann. F 6 FRL; *see Piras 2012), praising Cethegus' sweet-speaking tongue and his faculties of persuasion (see also Cic. Sen. 50; Quint. Inst. 2.15.4–5, 11.3.31; Gell. NA 12.2.3).*

T 1 Cicero, *Brutus*

[CICERO:] The first, however, who is on record and known to have been eloquent and recognized as such, is M. Cornelius Cethegus, of whose eloquence Q. Ennius is a witness, and indeed a suitable one in my view, especially since he heard him himself and writes about him after his death; hence there is no suspicion that he lied for the sake of friendship. [58] There is thus the following in him [Ennius] in, I believe, the ninth book of the *Annals* [Enn. *Ann.* 304–8 Sk. = 9 *Ann.* F 6 *FRL*]: "there is added the orator Cornelius, of sweet-speaking tongue, Cethegus Marcus, Marcus' son, to Tuditanus [P. Sempronius Tuditanus, cos. 204 BC] as his colleague." He both calls him an orator and attributes to him sweetness of speech, which nowadays at least is not so much found in most of them (for some orators now bark, they do not speak); but this is surely the greatest praise of eloquence: "he was called by those countrymen in the past, who were then alive and living out their years, the choice flower of the People," truly well said; [59] for just as a man's distinction is his talent, so the highlight of talent itself is eloquence; and someone excelling in that was well called by the men of that time the flower of the People "and the marrow of Persuasion." What the Greeks call Πειθώ [*Peitho*, "Persuasion"], of

dam appellavit Ennius, eius autem Cethegum medullam fuisse vult, ut, quam deam in Pericli labris scripsit Eupolis sessitavisse [Eupolis, F 102 K.-A.], huius hic medullam nostrum oratorem fuisse dixerit. [60] at hic Cethegus consul cum P. Tuditano fuit bello Punico secundo quaestorque his consulibus M. Cato modo plane annis CXL ante me consulem; et id ipsum nisi unius esset Enni testimonio cognitum, hunc vetustas, ut alios fortasse multos, oblivione obruisset. illius autem aetatis qui sermo fuerit ex Naevianis scriptis intellegi potest.

9 M. SERGIUS SILUS

On His Achievements When Debarred from Sacrifices (F 1)

F 1 Plin. *HN* 7.104–5

verum in his sunt quidem virtutis opera magna, sed maiora fortunae. M. Sergio, ut equidem arbitror, nemo quem-

which the orator is the creator, Ennius named *Suada*, and he wishes Cethegus to have been the marrow of that, so that of that goddess [Peitho], of whom Eupolis wrote that she had dwelt on the lips of Pericles [Eupolis, F 102 K.-A.], our orator was, he said, the marrow. [60] Now this Cethegus was consul with P. Tuditanus in the Second Punic War, and M. Cato [M. Porcius Cato (**8**)] was quaestor under these consuls [204 BC], only one hundred and forty years exactly before my consulship; and were that very fact not known to us by the testimony of Ennius alone, antiquity would have buried him in oblivion, as it has perhaps many others. And what the language of that period was like can be learned from the writings of Naevius.

9 M. SERGIUS SILUS

*M. Sergius Silus (praet. 197 BC; RE Sergius 40) was a fearless general and fighter and also the great-grandfather of the conspirator L. Sergius Catilina (**112**).*

On His Achievements When Debarred from Sacrifices (F 1)

As praetor in 197 BC, Sergius delivered a speech about his achievements, when he was debarred from sacrifices by his colleagues on account of life-changing wounds incurred during his military career.

F 1 Pliny the Elder, *Natural History*

But, although in these instances [the examples just mentioned] there are certainly great deeds of valor, yet there

37

quam hominum iure praetulerit, licet pronepos Catilina
gratiam nomini deroget. secundo stipendio dextram manum perdidit; stipendiis duobus ter et viciens vulneratus
est, ob id neutra manu, neutro pede satis utilis, animo[1]
tantum salvus,[2] plurimis postea stipendiis debilis miles. bis
ab Hannibale captus—neque enim cum quolibet hoste res
fuit—bis vinculorum eius profugus, in viginti mensibus
nullo non die in catenis aut compedibus custoditus. [105]
sinistra manu sola quater pugnavit, duobus equis insidente
eo suffossis. dextram sibi ferream fecit eaque religata
proeliatus Cremonam obsidione exemit, Placentiam tutatus est, duodena castra hostium in Gallia cepit, quae omnia ex oratione eius adparent habita cum in praetura sacris
arceretur a collegis ut debilis . . .

[1] animo *Detlefsen*: uno (*sc.* stipendio) *codd., edd. vet.*: (utili)
sumpto *Müller*: trunco *Rossbach*   [2] salvus *Welzhofer*: seruū
unus cod.: seruo *codd. rel., edd. vet.*: salvo *Detlefsen*: seruato
Rossbach

Cf. Solin. 1.104–5.

10 TI. SEMPRONIUS GRACCHUS PATER

*Ti. Sempronius Gracchus pater (tr. pl. 184 BC, cos. 177,
163, censor 169 BC; RE Sempronius 53), the father of the
brothers Gracchi (34 + 48), had a distinguished political
and military career. He is described as eloquent in Cicero's*

are greater ones of fortune. Nobody, in my judgment at any rate, could rightly rank any human being above M. Sergius, albeit his great-grandson Catilina [L. Sergius Catilina (**112**)] diminishes the credit of his name. In his second campaign he [Sergius] lost his right hand; in two campaigns he was wounded twenty-three times; for that reason not being able to use either hand or either foot fully, being unharmed only in spirit, he, although disabled, served in numerous campaigns afterward as a soldier. Twice he was taken prisoner by Hannibal—for he was not engaged with an ordinary foe—twice he escaped from his [Hannibal's] fetters, although kept in chains or shackles every single day for twenty months. [105] He fought four times with only his left hand, having two horses he was riding stabbed under him. He had a right hand of iron made for him and, having it tied to his arm, went into battle, raised the siege of Cremona, saved Placentia [modern Piacenza], captured twelve enemy camps in Gaul: all of these exploits become apparent from his speech delivered when, during his praetorship, he was debarred from the sacrifices, as infirm, by his colleagues . . .

10 TI. SEMPRONIUS GRACCHUS PATER

*history of Roman orators (F 1); elsewhere, Cicero has an interlocutor state that the father, in comparison with his sons, was not really an orator, but rather a man of action (Cic. De or. 1.38; **34** T 5).*

In Support of L. Cornelius Scipio Asiaticus
(F 1A–B)

*As Tribune of the People in 184 BC, Gracchus is said to
have supported L. Cornelius Scipio Asiaticus, the brother
of P. Cornelius Scipio Africanus maior (4), when Lucius*

F 1A Liv. 38.56.5–57.1

nec inter scriptores rerum discrepat solum, sed orationes
quoque, si modo ipsorum sunt quae feruntur, P. Scipionis
et Ti. Gracchi abhorrent inter se. [6] index orationis P.
Scipionis nomen M. Naevii tribuni plebis habet, ipsa oratio sine nomine est accusatoris; modo nebulonem, modo
nugatorem appellat. [7] ne Gracchi quidem oratio aut
Petilliorum accusatorum Africani aut diei dictae Africano
ullam mentionem habet. [8] alia tota serenda fabula est
Gracchi orationi conveniens, et illi auctores sequendi sunt
qui cum L. Scipio et accusatus et damnatus sit pecuniae
captae ab rege legatum in Etruria fuisse Africanum tradunt; [9] † quo †[1] post famam de casu fratris allatam relicta
legatione cucurrisse eum Romam, et cum a porta recta ad
forum se contulisset, quod in vincula duci fratrem dictum
erat, reppulisse a corpore eius viatorem, et tribunis reti-

---

[1] quo *vel* quod *codd.*: ‹a›tque *vel* inde *Weissenborn*: ‹addun›t-
que *Madvig*: qua *Harant*: ‹adiciun›tque *M. Müller*

In Support of L. Cornelius Scipio Asiaticus
(F 1A–B)

was prosecuted by other Tribunes for the brothers' deal-
ings with King Antiochus (see **4**).

F 1A Livy, *History of Rome*

And there is a discrepancy not only among historiographers, but also the speeches (provided that those that are
in circulation are works of these men themselves) of P.
Scipio [P. Cornelius Scipio Africanus maior (**4**), F 4] and
Ti. Gracchus are inconsistent with one another. [6] The
title of the speech by P. Scipio contains the name of M.
Naevius, Tribune of the People [184 BC]; the speech itself
is without the name of the accuser; it calls him now a
scoundrel, now a trifler. [7] Not even Gracchus' speech
makes any mention at all either of the Petillii [tr. pl. 187
BC] as accusers of Africanus or of the prosecution of Africanus. [8] An entirely different story must be put together, consistent with Gracchus' speech, and those writers must be followed who say that, when L. Scipio was
both accused and convicted of taking money from the
king, Africanus was an envoy in Etruria [184 BC; cf. *MRR*
I 377 and n. 7]; [9] that, after a report about his brother's
downfall had been brought to him, he abandoned the embassy and hastened to Rome, and that, when he had gone
from the gate straight to the Forum, because it was said
that his brother was being led to prison, he pushed back
the official from his body, and that, when the Tribunes
tried to hold him back, he attacked them, with more fa-

nentibus magis pie quam civiliter vim fecisse. [10] haec
enim ipsa Ti. Gracchus queritur, dissolutam esse a privato
tribuniciam potestatem, et ad postremum, cum auxilium
L. Scipioni pollicetur, adicit tolerabilioris exempli esse a
tribuno plebei potius quam a privato victam videri et tribuniciam potestatem et rem publicam esse. [11] sed ita
hanc unam impotentem eius iniuriam invidia onerat ut
increpando, quod degenerarit² tantum a se ipse, cumulatas ei³ veteres laudes moderationis et temperantiae pro
reprehensione praesenti reddat: [12] castigatum enim
quondam ab eo populum ait quod eum perpetuum consulem et dictatorem vellet facere; prohibuisse statuas sibi
in comitio, in rostris, in curia, in Capitolio, in cella Iovis
poni; [13] prohibuisse ne decerneretur ut imago sua
triumphali ornatu e templo Iovis optimi maximi exiret.
[57.1] haec vel in laudatione posita ingentem magnitudinem animi moderantis ad civilem habitum honoribus sig-
nificarent, quae exprobrando inimicus fatetur.

² degenerarit *ed. Frobeniana 1535*: generaverit *vel* generavit
vel graviter *vel* degeneraverit *codd.*   ³ cumulatas ei *ed. Frobeniana 1535*: cumulata sed *vel* cumulatas et *codd.*

F 1B Gell. *NA* 6.19.1–7

pulcrum atque liberale atque magnanimum factum Tibe-
rii Sempronii Gracchi in exemplis repositum est. [2] id
exemplum huiuscemodi est: L. Scipioni Asiatico, P. Sci-

milial affection than in line with a citizen's behavior. [10] For this is what Ti. Gracchus complains of, that the tribunician power has been infringed by a private citizen, and at the end, when he promises his official assistance to L. Scipio, he adds that it is a more acceptable precedent that a Tribune of the People, rather than a private citizen, is seen to have prevailed against both the tribunician power and the Republic. [11] But this single act of intemperate violence on the other's part he loads with reproaches in such a way that, by taunting him on the grounds that he had fallen so far below his own standards, he pays him accumulated and long-standing praises for his integrity and self-command as compensation for his present criticism: [12] for he says that the People have once been rebuked by him because they wished to make him perpetual consul and dictator; that he forbade statues to himself to be erected in the *comitium*, on the Rostra, in the Senate house, on the Capitol, in the temple chamber of Jupiter; [13] that he prevented a decree that his image in triumphal dress should be coming out of the temple of Iuppiter Optimus Maximus. [57.1] Such statements, even if included in a eulogy, would indicate the remarkable greatness of a soul limiting distinctions in accordance with the circumstances of a citizen, and they were made by an enemy in censure.

F 1B Gellius, *Attic Nights*

A fine, noble and generous action of Tiberius Sempronius Gracchus is recorded in the *Examples* [by Cornelius Nepos; see Gell. *NA* 6.18.11] [2] This example runs as follows: C. Minucius Augurinus, Tribune of the People [in

pionis Africani superioris fratri, C. Minucius Augurinus tribunus plebi multam irrogavit eumque ob eam causam praedes poscebat. [3] Scipio Africanus fratris nomine ad collegium tribunorum provocabat petebatque, ut virum consularem triumphalemque a collegae vi defenderent. [4] . . . [6] post hoc decretum cum Augurinus tribunus L. Scipionem praedes non dantem prendi et in carcerem duci iussisset, tunc Tiberius Sempronius Gracchus tr. pl., pater Tiberi atque C. Gracchorum, cum P. Scipioni Africano inimicus gravis ob plerasque in republica dissensiones esset, iuravit palam in amicitiam inque gratiam se cum P. Africano non redisse, atque ita decretum ex tabula recitavit. [7] eius decreti verba haec sunt: "cum L. Cornelius Scipio Asiaticus triumphans hostium duces in carcerem coniectarit, alienum videtur esse dignitate reipublicae in eum locum imperatorem populi Romani duci, in quem locum ab eo coniecti sunt duces hostium; itaque L. Cornelium Scipionem Asiaticum a collegae vi prohibeo."

187 BC], imposed a fine on L. Scipio Asiaticus, brother of
P. Scipio Africanus the Elder [P. Cornelius Scipio Africanus maior (**4**)], and demanded guarantors from him for
that matter. [3] Scipio Africanus appealed to the college
of Tribunes in the name of his brother and asked them to
defend a man who had been consul and triumphator
against the violence of their colleague. [4] . . . [6] When,
after this decree [of the Tribunes], L. Scipio did not give
guarantors, and Augurinus, the Tribune, had ordered him
to be arrested and taken to prison, then Tiberius Sempronius Gracchus, Tribune of the People [184 BC], the father
of Tiberius and C. Gracchus [**34 + 48**], although he was a
bitter personal enemy of P. Scipio Africanus because of
numerous disagreements on political questions, publicly
swore an oath that he had not won again the friendship
and favor of P. Africanus, and thus read a decree from a
tablet. [7] The words of that decree are as follows:
"Whereas L. Cornelius Scipio Asiaticus, celebrating a triumph, cast the leaders of the enemy into prison, it seems
contrary to the dignity of the Republic that the Roman
People's commander should be consigned to the same
place into which the leaders of the enemy had been thrown
by him; therefore I protect L. Cornelius Scipio Asiaticus
from the violence of my colleague."

Greek Speech Delivered at Rhodes (F 1)

F 1 Cic. *Brut.* 79

[CICERO:] erat isdem temporibus Ti. Gracchus P. f., qui bis consul et censor fuit, cuius est oratio Graeca apud Rhodios; quem civem cum gravem tum etiam eloquentem constat fuisse.

11 L. PAPIRIUS FREGELLANUS

*On Behalf of the People of Fregellae and
the Latin Colonists (F 1)*

*In 177 BC, when Ti. Sempronius Gracchus (**10**) and C. Claudius Pulcher were consuls, the Latin allies complained that large numbers of their citizens had moved to Rome and the Samnites and Paelignians were worried that people from their territory had moved to Fregellae; therefore,*

F 1 Cic. *Brut.* 170

[CICERO:] apud maiores autem nostros video disertissimum habitum ex Latio L. Papirium Fregellanum Ti.

Greek Speech Delivered at Rhodes (F 1)

This speech might date to ca. 165/4 or 161/0 BC, when Gracchus was a member of embassies to the East (Polyb. 30.27, 30.30.7, 30.31.19–20, 31.32–33, 32.1.1–3).

F 1 Cicero, *Brutus*

[CICERO:] In the same period there was Ti. Gracchus, Publius' son, who was consul twice and censor; of him there is an oration in Greek given before the people of Rhodes. It is well known that he was an influential citizen and also eloquent.

11 L. PAPIRIUS FREGELLANUS

L. Papirius Fregellanus / of Fregellae (RE Papirius 19) is known only from Cicero, where he appears among the noteworthy speakers from outside Rome (F 1).

On Behalf of the People of Fregellae and the Latin Colonists (F 1)

they asked the Roman Senate to take action (Liv. 41.8.6–12). In this context Papirius might have spoken on behalf of the inhabitants of Fregellae and the Latin colonists in the Roman Senate (for contrasting interpretations see Badian 1955; Malcovati 1955).

F 1 Cicero, *Brutus*

[CICERO:] And among our ancestors I see that L. Papirius of Fregellae was considered the most eloquent speaker

Gracchi P. f. fere aetate; eius etiam oratio est pro Fregellanis colonisque Latinis habita in senatu.

12 L. AEMILIUS PAULLUS

L. Aemilius Paullus (cos. 182, 168 BC; RE Aemilius 114), the biological father of P. Cornelius Scipio Aemilianus Africanus (21), celebrated triumphs during both his consulships, first over the Ligures Ingauni (in northwestern Italy) and then over the Macedonian king Perseus; the

T 1 Cic. *Brut.* 80

[CICERO:] . . . atque etiam L. Paullus Africani pater personam principis civis facile dicendo tuebatur.

On His Consulship and the War in Macedonia
(F 2A–D)

F 2A Plut. *Paul.* 11.1–4

Paullus is said to have stated in a speech to the People upon obtaining his second consulship that he stood for his first consulship because he wanted office and for his second because the People wanted a general. Therefore, he would

48

from Latium, in about the time of Ti. Gracchus, Publius'
son [Ti. Sempronius Gracchus (**10**)]. From him there exists even a speech, on behalf of the people of Fregellae
and the Latin colonists, delivered in the Senate.

12 L. AEMILIUS PAULLUS

*latter victory brought an enormous amount of money to
the Roman treasury (Liv. 45.40–41; on his life see CIL I,
p. 289; Plut. Aem.).*

*In Cicero it is noted that Paullus' eloquence was condu-
cive to his prominent public position (T 1).*

T 1 Cicero, *Brutus*

[CICERO:] . . . and also L. Paullus, Africanus' father, easily
maintained the role of first citizen by his eloquence.

*On His Consulship and the War in Macedonia
(F 2A–D)*

*Several speeches connected with Paullus' election to his
second consulship in 168 BC and his subsequent waging
of war in Macedonia have been put into his mouth by
ancient historians (CCMR, App. A: 168).*

F 2A Plutarch, *Life of Aemilius Paulus*

*be happy to step back if someone better was found; if,
however, they supported him, they would have to follow
his command. Thereupon, the People felt happy with their
choice.*

F 2B Liv. 44.22.1–16

*Just before Paullus is about to set off for Macedonia, Livy
puts a speech to the People in Paullus' mouth: in it he notices that he received greater congratulations when he was
allotted Macedonia as his province than when he was
elected consul or entered office. He explains this discrepancy by the fact that the People believed that he was the
right person to bring the drawn-out war in Macedonia to*

F 2C Liv. 44.34.1–6

*In an assembly of the soldiers Paullus is said to have ex-
plained that a single general in an army should foresee and
plan the procedure; soldiers should look after their bodies,
weapons, and food supply, and otherwise trust the general;*

F 2D Liv. 44.37.13–40.1

On King Perseus (F 2E–F)

F 2E Liv. 45.8.1–7

*Livy reports that Paullus asked king Perseus in Greek why
he was prompted to make war on the Roman People, although he had experienced their power in war and their
good faith in peace. When the king did not reply, Paullus
offered him mercy. Paullus is said to have gone on to point*

F 2B Livy, *History of Rome*

an end. He promises to do all he can to meet these expectations. At the same time Paullus warns the People not to believe rumors and not to give advice on the best military strategy at dinner parties in the city of Rome: they should either turn their attention elsewhere or, if they could be true military experts, accompany the general.

F 2C Livy, *History of Rome*

he would offer them opportunities for successful action. After that speech even the veterans commented that on that day they had for the first time learned how military matters should be handled.

F 2D Livy, *History of Rome*

A long speech, given in council, is put into Paullus' mouth: in it he responds to criticism and explains with a number of reasons why he postponed the battle and decided not to fight on the preceding day.

On King Perseus (F 2E–F)

F 2E Livy, *History of Rome*

out in Latin to his men this notable example of the changefulness of human affairs. Therefore, he advises his men not to offer insult or violence to anyone, while one is in favorable circumstances, since conditions might change quickly.

F 2F Polyb. 29.20.1–4

Polybius reports that Paullus pointed out the fate of king
Perseus to his men and told them in Latin never to boast
unduly of achievements and never to plan anything over-

On the Mutability of Fortune (F 2, 2G–H)

When two of his sons died around the time of his triumph
in 167 BC, Paullus commented on this situation in a speech
before the People, versions of which have been provided

F 2 Val. Max. 5.10.2

Aemilius Paulus, nunc felicissimi nunc miserrimi patris
clarissima repraesentatio, ex quattuor filiis formae insignis
egregiae indolis duos iure adoptionis in Corneliam Fa-
biamque gentem translatos sibi ipse denegavit: duos ei
fortuna abstulit. quorum alter triumphum patris funere
suo quartum ante diem praecessit, alter in triumphali
curru conspectus post diem tertium exspiravit. itaque qui
ad donandos usque liberos abundaverat, in orbitate subito
destitutus est. quem casum quo robore animi sustinuerit
oratione, quam de rebus a se gestis apud populum habuit,
hanc adiciendo clausulam nulli ambiguum reliquit: "cum
in maximo proventu felicitatis nostrae, Quirites, timerem
ne quid mali fortuna moliretur, Iovem Optimum Maximum Iunonemque Reginam et Minervam precatus sum
ut si quid adversi populo Romano inmineret, totum in
meam domum converteretur. quapropter bene habet:

F 2F Polybius, *Histories*

bearing or merciless to anyone; they should be aware of the opposite extreme of fortune when successful.

On the Mutability of Fortune (F 2, 2G–H)

by ancient authors (CCMR, App. A: 172; see also Diod. Sic. 31.11; Vell. Pat. 1.10.3–5; Cic. Fam. 4.6.1; Sen. Dial. 6.13.3; Plut. Aem. 35–36; Ampel. Lib. mem. 18.13).

F 2 Valerius Maximus, *Memorable Doings and Sayings*

Aemilius Paulus is the most famous model of a father at one point very happy, at another very wretched: of his four sons, with remarkable handsomeness and outstanding natural gifts, he transferred two to the Cornelian and Fabian families by right of adoption and thus denied them to himself; Fortune took two away from him. One of these preceded his father's triumph [167 BC] with his own death by three days, the other was seen in the triumphal car, but died three days later. Thus he, who had had so many children that he could give some away, was suddenly left forlorn in childlessness. With what strength of mind he bore this calamity he did not leave unclear to anyone in the speech that he delivered to the People concerning his achievements, by adding these final words: "Since I feared lest in the great harvest of our felicity, Romans, Fortune might set in motion something bad, I prayed to Iuppiter Optimus Maximus and queen Juno and Minerva that, if any adversity threatened the Roman People, it might all be turned against my house. Therefore, all is well: for by

adnuendo enim votis meis id egerunt ut vos potius meo casu doleatis quam ego vestro ingemescerem."

F 2G Liv. 45.40.6–42.1

Livy describes Paullus' situation and then reports a speech he delivered as the victorious general (in direct discourse): Paullus sketches his journey to victory. Therefore, he says, he felt that this good fortune seemed excessive and thus suspicious, but he hoped that his personal fortune would

F 2H App. *Mac.* 19.1–3

13 P. CORNELIUS SCIPIO AFRICANI MAIORIS FILIUS

P. Cornelius Scipio Africani maioris filius (RE Cornelius 331) was augur from 180 BC (Liv. 40.42.13); he was the son of P. Cornelius Scipio Africanus maior (4) and adopted the later P. Cornelius Scipio Aemilianus Africanus minor (21) (on his life see FRHist 1:184).

T 1 Cic. *Brut.* 77

[CICERO:] ipsum Scipionem accepimus non infantem fuisse. filius quidem eius, is qui hunc minorem Scipionem a Paullo adoptavit, si corpore valuisset, in primis habitus

granting my prayers they saw to it that you rather grieve for my misfortune than that I groan over yours."

F 2G Livy, *History of Rome*

suffer a blow rather than the Republic. Although, he adds, he is now almost more unfortunate than the captured king Perseus, he is consoled by the happiness of the Roman People and the public good fortune.

F 2H Appian, *Macedonian History*

Appian gives a report of Paullus' speech similar to that in Livy; his description is shorter and partly in direct and partly in indirect speech (in Greek).

13 P. CORNELIUS SCIPIO AFRICANI MAIORIS FILIUS

According to Cicero, this Scipio's oratorical abilities were constrained by his ill health (T 1; Cic. Sen. 35; Off. 1.121; cf. also Vell. Pat. 1.10.3). Still, in Cicero's time some speeches of Scipio were available (T 1).

T 1 Cicero, *Brutus*

[CICERO:] Scipio [P. Cornelius Scipio Africanus maior (**4**)] himself, we learn, was not at all without the ability to speak. His son, who adopted the younger Scipio [P. Cornelius Scipio Aemilianus Africanus minor (**21**)] from Paullus [L. Aemilius Paullus (**12**)], would certainly have been

esset disertus; indicant cum oratiunculae tum historia quaedam Graeca scripta dulcissime [*FRHist* 3 T 1].

14 C. SULPICIUS GALUS

C. Sulpicius Galus (cos. 166 BC; RE Sulpicius 66) had a military career and was a learned and cultured man. In Cicero it is attested that he was regarded as an orator

T 1 Cic. *Brut.* 78

[Cicero:] de minoribus autem C. Sulpicius Galus, qui maxime omnium nobilium Graecis litteris studuit; isque et oratorum in numero est habitus et fuit reliquis rebus ornatus atque elegans. iam enim erat unctior quaedam splendidiorque consuetudo loquendi.

On an Eclipse of the Moon (F 2)

*Since Galus was an expert in astronomy (Cic. Sen. 49), he is said to have predicted an eclipse of the moon to the soldiers when he was fighting as a military tribune with L. Aemilius Paullus (**12**) in Macedonia in 168 BC (CCMR,*

F 2 Liv. 44.37.5–9

castris permunitis, C. Sulpicius Gal{l}us,[1] tribunus militum secundae legionis, qui praetor superiore anno fuerat,

---

[1] Gal{l}us *Heraeus*: Gallus *cod.*

accounted eloquent among the first had he possessed
bodily strength; some little orations show it, and especially
a piece of historical narrative in Greek written with great
charm [*FRHist* 3 T 1].

14 C. SULPICIUS GALUS

(*T 1*). *Galus acted as an advocate supporting the inhabitants of Hispania ulterior in a trial for the recovery of extorted money (Liv. 43.2.3–10).*

T 1 Cicero, *Brutus*

[CICERO:] Now, out of the younger contemporaries [of M.
Porcius Cato (**8**)] there was C. Sulpicius Galus, who of all
the noblemen studied Greek literature most. And he was
counted among the group of orators, and in other matters
too he was cultured and refined. For by that time there
was already a more elaborate and more brilliant habit of
speaking.

On an Eclipse of the Moon (F 2)

*App. B: 74; cf. Cic. Rep. 1.23; Val. Max. 8.11.1; Quint. Inst.
1.10.47; Frontin. Str. 1.12.8; Zonar. 9.23). According to
Pliny, Galus published on the eclipse soon afterward,
though probably not the text of the speech (Plin. HN 2.53).*

F 2 Livy, *History of Rome*

After the fortification of the camp was complete, C. Sulpicius Galus, a military tribune with the second legion,
who had been praetor in the previous year [169 BC], sum-

consulis permissu ad contionem militibus vocatis, pronun-
tiavit [6] nocte proxima, ne quis id pro portento acciperet,
ab hora secunda usque ad quartam horam noctis lunam
defecturam esse. id quia naturali ordine statis temporibus
fiat, et sciri ante et praedici posse. [7] itaque quem ad
modum, quia certi solis lunaeque et ortus et occasus sint,
nunc pleno orbe nunc senescente<m>[2] exiguo cornu
fu<l>gere[3] lunam non mirarentur, ita ne obscurari quidem, cum condatur umbra terrae, trahere in prodigium
debere. [8] nocte quam pridie nonas Septembres insecuta
est dies edita luna hora cum defecisset, Romanis militibus
Gal{l}i sapientia prope divina videri; [9] Macedonas ut
triste prodigium, occasum regni perniciemque gentis por-
tendens, movit, nec aliter vates. clamor ululatusque in castris Macedonum fuit, donec luna in suam lucem emersit.

[2] senescente<m> *Florebellus*: senescente *cod.*   [3] fu<l>gere
ed. Frobeniana 1531: fugere *cod.*

15 P. CORNELIUS LENTULUS

*P. Cornelius Lentulus (cos. suff. 162 BC; RE Cornelius
202) had a successful public career and was* princeps senatus *from 125 BC (T 1); he was wounded in the conflict*

moned the soldiers to an assembly, by permission of the consul [L. Aemilius Paullus (**12**)], and announced: [6] that no one should regard this as a bad omen when in the following night an eclipse of the moon would take place from the second to the fourth hour of the night. Since this occurred in the regular order of nature at fixed times, it could both be known in advance and be foretold. [7] Therefore, just as they were not surprised when they saw the moon shining now with its full circle, now during its wane with a narrow arc, since both the risings and the settings of the sun and the moon were certain, so they should not regard as a prodigy even that it was darkened when it was hidden by the shadow of the earth. [8] In the night that was followed by the day preceding the Nones of September [September 4], when the moon had been eclipsed at the predicted hour, the wisdom of Galus seemed almost divine to the Roman soldiers; [9] [the incident] moved the Macedonians like a dire portent, indicating the downfall of the kingdom and the ruin of the nation, and the soothsayers likewise. There was uproar and wailing in the camp of the Macedonians until the moon emerged back to its usual light.

15 P. CORNELIUS LENTULUS

*with C. Sempronius Gracchus (**48**) in 121 BC, but was able to escape (Val. Max. 5.3.2f; Cic. Cat. 4.13; Phil. 8.14).*

In Cicero Lentulus is said to have been adequately eloquent for political affairs (T 1).

T 1 Cic. *Brut.* 108

[CICERO:] tum etiam P. Lentulus ille princeps ad rem publicam dumtaxat quod opus esset satis habuisse eloquentiae dicitur . . .

Against M'. Aquillius (F 2)

F 2 Cic. *Div. Caec.* 69

cuius consuetudinis atque instituti patres maioresque nostros non paenitebat tum cum P. Lentulus, is qui princeps senatus fuit, accusabat M'. Aquillium subscriptore C. Rutilio Rufo . . .

16 L. CORNELIUS LENTULUS LUPUS

L. Cornelius Lentulus Lupus (cos. 156, censor 147, princeps senatus *from 131 BC;* RE Cornelius 224) *was sufficiently notorious to be mocked by the satirist Lucilius (Lucil. 784–90 Marx). After his consulship Lentulus was*

T 1 Cic. *Brut.* 79

[CICERO:] . . . habitum eloquentem aiunt . . . dicunt etiam L. Lentulum, qui cum C. Figulo consul fuit.

T 1 Cicero, *Brutus*

[CICERO:] Then too, P. Lentulus, that leader [of the Senate], is reported to have possessed an eloquence adequate at least for what was required for political affairs . . .

Against M'. Aquillius (F 2)

The prosecution of M'. Aquillius (cos. 129 BC) took place in 125 or 124 BC; the defendant was acquitted (Cic. Font. 38; App. B Civ. 1.22.92; Mith. 57.231) (TLRR 23).

F 2 Cicero, *Against Caecilius*

This custom and practice [of having honorable judges] did not dissatisfy our fathers and ancestors, at that time when P. Lentulus, he who was leader of the Senate, prosecuted M'. Aquillius, and C. Rutilius Rufus supported him . . .

16 L. CORNELIUS LENTULUS LUPUS

charged with extortion and found guilty (Val. Max. 6.9.10); nevertheless, he was able to proceed to the censorship.
    Lentulus is reported in Cicero to have been regarded as eloquent (T 1).

T 1 Cicero, *Brutus*

[CICERO:] . . . was, they say, regarded as eloquent . . . they say the same of L. Lentulus, who was consul with C. Figulus [C. Marcius Figulus, cos. 162, 156 BC].

On the Senate Decree Concerning the People of Tibur (F 2A)

As praetor (in around 160 BC) Lentulus enabled envoys from Tibur to defend themselves in the Senate and initiated a Senate decree on their behalf. The Senate speech that he must have given on that occasion does not survive;

F 2A *CIL* I² 586 = XIV 3584 = *ILS* 19 = *ILLRP* 512

L. Cornelius Cn. f. pr(aetor) sen(atum) cons(uluit) a. d. III nonas Maias sub aede Kastorus. scr(ibendo) adf(uerunt) A. Manlius A. f., Sex. Iulius . . . L. Postumius S(p.) f. quod Teiburtes v(erba) f(ecistis) quibusque de rebus vos purgavistis ea senatus animum advortit ita utei aequom fuit. nosque ea ita audiveramus, ut vos deixsistis vobeis nontiata esse. ea nos animum nostrum non indoucebamus ita facta esse propter ea quod scibamus ea vos merito nostro facere non potuisse, neque vos dignos esse quei ea faceretis neque id vobeis neque rei poplicae vostrae oitile esse facere. et postquam vostra verba senatus audivit, tanto magis animum nostrum indoucimus, ita utei ante arbitrabamur, de eieis rebus af vobeis peccatum non esse. quonque de eieis rebus senatuei purgati estis, credimus vosque animum vostrum indoucere oportet, item vos populo Romano purgatos fore.

*On the Senate Decree Concerning the
People of Tibur (F 2A)*

*the report of the Senate decree to the People of Tibur, re-
corded on a bronze tablet now lost, gives a flavor of the
content.*

F 2A An inscription

L. Cornelius, Gnaeus' son, the praetor, consulted the Senate on the third day before the Nones of May [May 5] in
the Temple of Castor. To write up [the decree] there were
A. Manlius, Aulus' son, Sex. Iulius . . . L. Postumius, Spurius' son. As regards the fact that you, people of Tibur,
gave a speech and the matters concerning which you ex-
onerated yourselves, the Senate gave heed to it in such
way as was appropriate. And we had heard those things in
such a way as you said they had been reported to you. We
were not of the view that it had been done thus, for the
reason that we knew that you had not been able to do it in
line with what we deserve, nor that it would be appropriate for you to do this, nor that this was useful to do for you
or your state. And after the Senate has heard your speech,
all the more we are of the opinion, just as we thought
previously, that with regard to these matters no fault was
committed by you. And since you have been cleared of
these matters in the eyes of the Senate, we believe that
you must be of the opinion that you will have been equally
cleared in the eyes of the Roman People.

17 T. ANNIUS LUSCUS

T. Annius Luscus (cos. 153 BC; RE Annius 64) was a fierce opponent of the Tribune of the People Ti. Sempronius Gracchus (34) in 133 BC. This is obvious from speeches against Gracchus in the Senate and before the People (F 3–5; CCMR, App. A: 183).

T 1 Cic. *Brut.* 79

[CICERO:] . . . et T. Annium Luscum huius Q. Fulvi collegam non indisertum dicunt fuisse . . .

T 2 Plut. *Ti. Gracch.* 14.5

= F 4.

Speeches Against Ti. Sempronius Gracchus
(F 3–5)

F 3 Liv. *Epit.* 58.1–6

Tib. Sempronius Gracchus trib. pleb. cum legem agrariam ferret adversus voluntatem senatus et equestris ordinis: nequis ex publico agro plus quam ∞[1] iugera possideret, in eum furorem exarsit, ut M. Octavio collegae causam diversae partis defendenti potestatem lege lata abrogaret,

---

[1] ∞ *vel* c *vel* cc *vel* decem *codd.*

17 T. ANNIUS LUSCUS

In Cicero it is said that Luscus was regarded as a decent orator (T 1), and in Plutarch that he was good at discussions carried out by question and answer (T 2).

T 1 Cicero, *Brutus*

[CICERO:] . . . and they say that T. Annius Luscus, the colleague of this Q. Fulvius [Q. Fulvius Nobilior, cos. 153 BC], was not without command of oratory . . .

T 2 Plutarch, *Life of Tiberius Gracchus*

= F 4.

Speeches Against Ti. Sempronius Gracchus
(F 3–5)

F 3 Livy, *Epitome*

When Tib. Sempronius Gracchus [**34**], Tribune of the People [in 133 BC], put forward a land law against the wishes of the Senate and the equestrian order, to the effect that no one should occupy more than a thousand[1] acres of public land, he went to such a point of madness as to remove from office his colleague M. Octavius, who was supporting the case of the other side, by putting forward a law,

---

[1] The transmission of the figure is uncertain; it is inferred from a combination of other sources (*Vir. ill.* 64.3; App. *B Civ.* 1.9.37) on this law (*Lex Sempronia agraria*: *LPPR*, pp. 298–99).

seque et ⟨C.⟩[2] Gracchum fratrem et Appium Claudium socerum triumviros ad dividendum agrum crearet. [2] promulgavit et aliam legem agrariam, qua sibi latius agrum patefaceret, ut idem triumviri iudicarent, qua publicus ager, qua privatus esset. [3] deinde cum minus agri esset quam quod dividi posset sine offensa etiam plebis, qu⟨oni⟩am[3] eos ad cupiditatem amplum modum sperandi incitaverat, legem se promulgaturum ostendit, ut his qui Sempronia lege agrum accipere deberent pecunia, quae regis Attali fuisset, divideretur. [4] heredem autem populum Romanum reliquerat Attalus, rex Pergami, Eumenis filius. [5] tot indignitatibus commotus graviter senatus, ante omnis T. Annius consul⟨aris⟩.[4] [6] qui cum[5] in senatu in Gracchum perorasset, raptus ab eo ad populum delatusque plebi, rursus in eum pro rostris contionatus est.

2 C. *om. codd., ed. princ.*: fratrem Caium *codd. Sigonii*

3 qu⟨oni⟩am *ed. princ.*: qua in *vel* qua *vel* quam *vel* quod *codd.*

4 t. *vel* c. *vel. om. codd.*   annius *vel* antonius *codd.*   consul⟨aris⟩ *Drakenborchius*: proconsul *vel* cos. *codd.*

5 cum *vel om. codd.*

F 4 Plut. *Ti. Gracch.* 14.5–9

Τίτος δ᾽ Ἄννιος, οὐκ ἐπιεικὴς μὲν ὢν οὐδὲ σώφρων ἄνθρωπος, ἐν δὲ λόγοις περὶ τὰς ἐρωτήσεις καὶ τὰς ἀποκρίσεις ἄμαχος εἶναι δοκῶν, εἰς ὁρισμόν τινα προὐκαλεῖτο τὸν Τιβέριον, ἦ μὴν ἱερὸν ὄντα καὶ ἄσυλον ἐκ τῶν νόμων ἠτιμωκέναι τὸν συνάρχοντα. [6] θορυβούντων δὲ πολλῶν, ἐκπηδήσας ὁ Τιβέριος τόν

and to have himself, his brother <C.> Gracchus [C. Sempronius Gracchus (**48**)] and his father-in-law Appius Claudius [Ap. Claudius Pulcher (**24A**)] elected as the board of three in charge of distributing the land. [2] He also proposed a second land law, in order to put more land at his disposal, that the same board of three should judge where land was public and where private. [3] Then, when there was less land than could be divided up without offending even the commons, because he had stirred them up to be greedy enough to hope for a large amount, he declared that he would propose a law to the effect that the fortune which had belonged to king Attalus should be divided among those who ought to receive land under the Sempronian Law. [4] Now Attalus, king of Pergamum, son of Eumenes, had made the Roman People his heir [when he died in 133 BC]. [5] By so many acts of insulting treatment the Senate was deeply moved, above all the ex-consul T. Annius. [6] After he had finished a speech in the Senate against Gracchus, he was dragged by him before the People and accused before the commons; in return, he delivered a speech against him [Gracchus] from the front of the Rostra before the People.

F 4 Plutarch, *Life of Tiberius Gracchus*

Titus Annius, too, a man of no high character nor sound mind, but thought to be invincible in arguments carried on by questions and answers, challenged Tiberius to some judicial wager, solemnly asserting that he [Gracchus] had branded with infamy his colleague [M. Octavius, tr. pl. 133 BC], who was sacred and inviolable by law. [6] As many applauded this speech, Tiberius leaped out [of the Senate

τε δῆμον συνεκάλει, καὶ τὸν Ἄννιον ἀχθῆναι κελεύσας ἐβούλετο κατηγορεῖν. [7] ὁ δὲ καὶ τῷ λόγῳ καὶ τῇ δόξῃ πολὺ λειπόμενος, εἰς τὴν ἑαυτοῦ δεινότητα κατεδύετο, καὶ παρεκάλει μικρὰ πρὸ τῶν λόγων ἀποκρίνασθαι τὸν Τιβέριον. [8] συγχωροῦντος δὲ ἐρωτᾶν ἐκείνου καὶ σιωπῆς γενομένης εἶπεν ὁ Ἄννιος· "ἂν σὺ μὲν ἀτιμοῦν με βούλῃ καὶ προπηλακίζειν, ἐγὼ δέ τινα τῶν σῶν ἐπικαλέσωμαι συναρχόντων, ὁ δ' ἀναβῇ βοηθήσων, σὺ δὲ ὀργισθῇς, ἆρά γ' αὐτοῦ τὴν ἀρχὴν ἀφαιρήσῃ;" [9] πρὸς ταύτην λέγεται τὴν ἐρώτησιν οὕτως διαπορηθῆναι τὸν Τιβέριον ὥστε πάντων ὄντα καὶ τὸ λέγειν ἑτοιμότατον καὶ τῷ θαρρεῖν ἰταμώτατον ἀποσιωπῆσαι.

F 5 Fest., p. 416.13–21 L.

SATURA, et cibi genus ex | variis rebus conditum est, et lex | <mul>tis[1] alis legibus conferta. . . . T. Annius Luscus in ea, {quam}[2] | quam dixit adversus Ti. Gracchum: | "imperium quod plebes per saturam | dederat, id abrogatum est."

[1] *suppl. ex Epit.*   [2] *del. edd.*

house], called the People together, and, ordering Annius to be brought before them, intended to denounce him. [7] But he, who was far inferior both in eloquence and in reputation, had recourse to his own particular strength and called upon Tiberius to give a few answers before the speeches. [8] When the latter assented to the questioning and silence was made, Annius said: "If you wish to dishonor me and heap insult upon me, and I invoke the aid of one of your colleagues, and he mounts the Rostra to support me and you get angry, will you take the office away from him?" [9] At this question, it is said, Tiberius was so disconcerted that, although of all men he was most ready in speech and most vehement in boldness, he fell silent.[1]

[1] A variation of the practice of *sponsio*, when a catch question is employed to place the opponent in a politically difficult position (on this instance see Flaig 2004, 203–5).

F 5 Festus

satura ["medley"] is both a kind of dish put together from various things and a law made up of many other laws. . . . T. Annius Luscus in that [speech] that he delivered against Ti. Gracchus: "That power that the people had given en bloc [*per saturam*][1] has been annulled."

[1] In political contexts *per saturam* means that various matters are combined into a single item to be voted on.

18 Q. CAECILIUS METELLUS MACEDONICUS

Q. Caecilius Metellus Macedonicus (cos. 143, censor 131 BC; RE Caecilius 94), presumably a son of Q. Caecilius Metellus (6), was a successful general and politician; he triumphed over Macedonia and its king Andriscus and therefore adopted the cognomen Macedonicus (Plut. Mar. 1.1).

On Behalf of L. Aurelius Cotta Against Scipio Aemilianus (F 1)

When P. Cornelius Scipio Aemilianus Africanus minor (21 F 23–26) prosecuted L. Aurelius Cotta (cos. 144 BC), presumably on a charge of extortion, in 138 BC or between 132 and 129 BC (Cic. Mur. 58 [though Cicero may be

F 1 Cic. *Brut.* 81

[Cicero:] nam Q. Metellus, is cuius quattuor filii consulares fuerunt, in primis est habitus eloquens, qui pro L. Cotta dixit accusante Africano . . .

On Ti. Sempronius Gracchus (F 2–3)

The speech criticizing Ti. Sempronius Gracchus (34) was given when the latter was Tribune of the People (133 BC), apparently after he had proposed a bill concerning the bequest from King Attalus (Plut. Ti. Gracch. 14.1–2; see

18 Q. CAECILIUS METELLUS MACEDONICUS

Metellus was a cultured man; in Cicero he is mentioned as an eloquent speaker (F 1; Cic. De or. 1.215).

In about 138 BC Macedonicus appeared as a witness at a trial of Q. Pompeius (30 F 4A–B; TLRR 8).

On Behalf of L. Aurelius Cotta Against Scipio Aemilianus (F 1)

inaccurate]), Metellus defended the accused, who was acquitted (Cic. Div. Caec. 69; Font. 38; Ps.-Asc. in Cic. Div. Caec. 69 [p. 204.3–4 St.]; Tac. Ann. 3.66.1–2; Val. Max. 8.1.abs.11; Liv. Epit. Ox. 55; App. B Civ. 1.3.22; TLRR 9).

F 1 Cicero, *Brutus*

[CICERO:] For Q. Metellus, whose four sons were former consuls, was regarded as particularly eloquent; he spoke on behalf of L. Cotta, when Africanus [P. Cornelius Scipio Aemilianus Africanus minor (**21**), F 23–26] was the prosecutor . . . [continued by F 2]

On Ti. Sempronius Gracchus (F 2–3)

17 F 3). Cicero knew a version of the speech included in the Annals *of C. Fannius (FRHist 12 T 2), not necessarily "authentic" (F 2).*

F 2 Cic. *Brut.* 81

[CICERO:] . . . cuius et aliae sunt orationes et contra Ti. Gracchum exposita est in C. Fanni annalibus.

F 3 Plut. *Ti. Gracch.* 14.3–4

. . . καὶ Πομπήιος μὲν ἀναστὰς ἔφη γειτνιᾶν τῷ Τι-βερίῳ, καὶ διὰ τοῦτο γινώσκειν Εὔδημον αὐτῷ τὸν Περγαμηνὸν τῶν βασιλικῶν διάδημα δεδωκότα καὶ πορφύραν, ὡς μέλλοντι βασιλεύειν ἐν Ῥώμῃ· [4] Κόιντος δὲ Μέτελλος ὠνείδισε τὸν Τιβέριον ὅτι τοῦ μὲν πατρὸς αὐτοῦ τιμητεύοντος, ὁσάκις ἀναλύοι⟨εν⟩[1] μετὰ δεῖπνον οἴκαδε, τὰ φῶτα κατεσβέννυσαν οἱ πο-λῖται, φοβούμενοι μὴ πορρωτέρω τοῦ μετρίου δόξω-σιν ἐν συνουσίαις εἶναι καὶ πότοις, τούτῳ δὲ παρα-φαίνουσι νυκτὸς οἱ θρασύτατοι καὶ ἀπορώτατοι τῶν δημοτῶν . . .

[1] *add. Kurtz*

On Marriage and Childbearing (F 4–7)

F 4 Liv. *Epit.* 59.6–9

Q. Pompeius Q. Metellus, tunc primum uterque ex plebe facti censores, lustrum condiderunt. [7] . . . [8] Q. Metel-

F 2 Cicero, *Brutus*

[CICERO:] . . . [continued from F 1]; from him [Metellus] there exist other orations, and the one against Ti. Gracchus is set forth in the *Annals* of C. Fannius.

F 3 Plutarch, *Life of Tiberius Gracchus*

. . . and Pompeius [Q. Pompeius (**30**), F 5–7], having risen to speak, said that he was a neighbor of Tiberius and therefore knew that Eudemus of Pergamum [envoy of the king] had presented him [Tiberius] with things pertaining to a king, a diadem and a purple robe, as if he was going to be king in Rome. [4] Moreover, Quintus Metellus upbraided Tiberius, saying that, whenever his father [Ti. Sempronius Gracchus (**10**)], during his censorship [169 BC], was returning home after a supper, the citizens put out their lights, fearing they might be thought to be indulging too immoderately in entertainments and drinking bouts, whereas for him [Tiberius] the most reckless and neediest of the citizens put on lights at night . . .

On Marriage and Childbearing (F 4–7)

The laws on marriage and childbearing that Metellus proposed as censor were ridiculed by the satirist Lucilius (Book 26). The speech presenting these laws was still available in the time of the emperor Augustus (F 4–5).

F 4 Livy, *Epitome*

Q. Pompeius [**30**] and Q. Metellus, then for the first time both from plebeian rank made censors, formally concluded the census. [7] . . . [8] Q. Metellus, the censor,

lus censor censuit ut cogerentur omnes ducere uxores li-
berorum creandorum causa. [9] extat oratio eius, quam
Augustus Caesar, cum[1] de maritandis ordinibus[2] ageret,
velut in haec tempora scriptam in senatu recitavit.

1 cum *vel om. codd.*   2 ordinibus *vel* omnibus *codd.*

F 5 Suet. *Aug.* 89.2

etiam libros totos et senatui recitavit et populo notos per
edictum saepe fecit, ut orationes Q. Metelli de prole
augenda et Rutili de modo aedificiorum, quo magis per-
suaderet utramque rem non a se primo animadversam,
sed antiquis iam tunc curae fuisse.

F 6 Gell. *NA* 1.6.1–2

multis et eruditis viris audientibus legebatur oratio Metelli Numidici, gravis ac diserti viri, quam in censura dixit
ad populum de ducendis uxoribus, cum eum ad matrimo-
nia capessenda hortaretur. [2] in ea oratione ita scriptum
fuit: "si sine uxore possemus,[1] Quirites, omnes ea molestia
careremus; set quoniam ita natura tradidit, ut nec cum
illis satis commode, nec sine illis ullo modo vivi possit,
saluti perpetuae potius quam brevi voluptati consulendum
est."

1 possemus *codd.*: <vivere> possemus *Hertz*

---

1 Gellius assigns this passage and the following excerpt (F 7)
to a speech by Q. Caecilius Metellus Numidicus (**58**). Gellius
may have confused the *cognomina Macedonicus* and *Numidicus*.
Moreover, he has the speech addressed to the People (rather than
the Senate); thus, either there must be even more confusion in

proposed that all should be forced to take wives in order to produce children. [9] His speech is extant; Augustus Caesar read it out in the Senate as though written for that time, when he was leading discussions about marriage within classes.

F 5 Suetonius, *Life of Augustus*

He [Augustus] even both read out entire volumes to the Senate and frequently made them known to the People by an edict, like the speeches of Q. Metellus on increasing [the number of] offspring and of Rutilius on the size of buildings [P. Rutilius Rufus (**44**), F 2], so as to convince them all the more that neither matter was picked up by him as the first person to do so, but that they had already at that time been a concern for the men of the past.

F 6 Gellius, *Attic Nights*

While many learned men were listening, there was a reading of a speech by Metellus Numidicus,[1] an earnest and eloquent man, a speech that he delivered to the People during his censorship, on taking wives, whereby he urged them to enter marriages. [2] In that speech the following was written: "If we could [produce offspring] without a wife, Romans, all of us would avoid that annoyance; but since nature has ordained it in such a way that one can neither live sufficiently comfortably with them nor in any way without them, we must take thought for our lasting preservation rather than for short-lived pleasure."

the sources, or there were two similar speeches by two Metelli (thus Badian 1988 [1996–97]).

F 7 Gell. *NA* 1.6.7–8

hoc quoque aliud ex eadem oratione Q. Metelli dignum
esse existimavimus adsidua lectione non hercle minus,
quam quae a gravissimis philosophis scripta sunt. [8] verba
Metelli haec sunt: "di immortales plurimum possunt; sed
non plus velle nobis debent quam parentes. at parentes, si
pergunt liberi errare, bonis exheredant. quid ergo nos ab
immortalibus dissimilius[1] expectemus, nisi malis rationibus finem facimus? is demum deos propitios esse aequum
est, qui sibi adversarii non sunt. dii immortales virtutem
adprobare, non adhibere debent."

[1] dissimilius *Hosius*: DISSIMILIVSDIVITIVS *vel* diutius
codd.: divinitus *e codd. suis Carrio*

19 SER. SULPICIUS GALBA

*Ser. Sulpicius Galba (cos. 144 BC; RE Sulpicius 58) was
a clever general and an independent-minded politician
(father of C. Sulpicius Galba [53]).*

*In Cicero it is acknowledged that Galba was well edu-
cated and an excellent speaker, well versed in the tech-
niques of oratory (some of which he was the first to use in
Rome), even though his extant speeches did not appear too
impressive, since his orations were based on talent, expressive delivery, and the emotions of the moment (T 1–6; Cic.*

T 1 Cic. *Brut.* 82

[CICERO:] sed inter hos aetate paulum his antecedens sine
controversia Ser. Galba eloquentia praestitit; et nimirum

F 7 Gellius, *Attic Nights*

This other passage also from the same speech of Q. Metellus we regard as deserving of constant reading, no less, by Hercules, than what has been written by the most serious philosophers. [8] The words of Metellus are these: "The immortal gods have the greatest power, but they are not expected to be more indulgent to us than parents. Yet parents, if their children persist in wrongdoing, disinherit them from their fortune. What then are we to expect differently from the immortal gods, unless we put an end to our evil ways? It is fair that the gods are favorable only toward those who are not enemies to themselves. The immortal gods ought to approve, not supply, virtue."

19 SER. SULPICIUS GALBA

Brut. 98; De or. 1.58, 1.255; Rep. 3.9, 3.42; Tusc. 1.5; cf. Val. Max. 8.7.1). In the Rhetorica ad Herennium Galba is listed as one of the writers from whom examples for students could be drawn (Rhet. Her. 4.7: **25** T 5), while in Tacitus' time some regarded Galba as belonging to the "ancient" orators of unpolished style (T 9–10). Written versions of his speeches were available in antiquity (T 1–3; Liv. Epit. 49).

T 1 Cicero, *Brutus*

[CICERO:] But among these, preceding these [generation of C. Laelius Sapiens (**20**) and P. Cornelius Scipio Aemilianus Africanus minor (**21**)] a little in time, Ser. Galba,

is princeps ex Latinis illa oratorum propria et quasi legi-
tima opera tractavit, ut egrederetur a proposito ornandi
causa, ut delectaret animos, ut permoveret, ut augeret
rem, ut miserationibus, ut communibus locis uteretur. sed
nescio quo modo huius, quem constat eloquentia praesti-
tisse, exiliores orationes sunt et redolentes magis antiquitatem quam aut Laeli ‹aut›[1] Scipionis aut etiam ipsius
Catonis, itaque exaruerunt vix iam ut appareant.

[1] *add. edd.*: *om. codd.*

T 2 Cic. *Brut.* 91–94

"quid igitur," inquit, "est causae," BRUTUS, "si tanta virtus
in oratore Galba fuit, cur ea nulla in orationibus eius appa-
reat? quod mirari non possum in eis qui nihil omnino
scripti reliquerunt." [CICERO:] ". . . [92] . . . alios, quod
melius putent dicere se posse quam scribere, quod perin-
geniosis hominibus neque satis doctis plerumque contin-
git, ut ipsi Galbae. [93] quem fortasse vis non ingeni solum
sed etiam animi et naturalis quidam dolor dicentem incen-
debat efficiebatque ut et incitata et gravis et vehemens
esset oratio; dein cum otiosus stilum prenderat motusque
omnis animi tamquam ventus hominem defecerat, flacces-
cebat oratio. quod eis qui limatius dicendi consectantur
genus accidere non solet, propterea quod prudentia numquam deficit oratorem, qua ille utens eodem modo possit

beyond question, was preeminent in eloquence. And, without doubt, of the Latins, he was the first to employ the specific and almost legally prescribed resources of orators, namely to digress from the point for embellishment, to delight the minds, to move them, to amplify the subject matter, to employ expressions of grief and commonplaces. But for some reason, the orations of this man, who is well attested to have been preeminent in eloquence, are more meager and savor more of antiquity than those of either Laelius [C. Laelius Sapiens (**20**)] <or> Scipio [P. Cornelius Scipio Aemilianus Africanus minor (**21**)] or even of Cato [M. Porcius Cato (**8**)] himself; and they have dried up so much that they are scarcely still visible.

T 2 Cicero, *Brutus*

"What is the reason then," BRUTUS said, "if there was such skill in Galba as an orator, why nothing of it appears in his orations? I cannot wonder at that in relation to those who have left nothing written at all." [CICERO:] ". . . [92] . . . still others [do not write] because they believe that they can speak better than write, which frequently happens with men of outstanding talent and insufficient training, like this very Galba. [93] He was perhaps fired, when he spoke, not only by the force of his intellect, but also of passion and by a kind of natural ability to rouse sad emotions, and the result was that his speech was fast-moving, impressive, and powerful; then, when he had taken up his pen at leisure and all that passion of the mind, like a storm, had left the man, his language flagged. That does not tend to happen to those who seek a more careful style of speaking, because reason never leaves the orator, and, relying

et dicere et scribere; ardor animi non semper adest, isque cum consedit, omnis illa vis et quasi flamma oratoris exstinguitur. [94] hanc igitur ob causam videtur Laeli mens spirare etiam in scriptis, Galbae autem vis occidisse. . . ."

T 3 Cic. *Brut.* 295

[Atticus:] Galbam laudas. si ut illius aetatis principem, adsentior—sic enim accepimus—; sin ut oratorem, cedo quaeso orationes—sunt enim—et dic hunc, quem tu plus quam te amas, Brutum velle te illo modo dicere.

T 4 Cic. *Brut.* 333

[Cicero:] nonne cernimus vix singulis aetatibus binos oratores laudabilis constitisse? Galba fuit inter tot aequalis unus excellens, cui, quem ad modum accepimus, et Cato cedebat senior et qui temporibus illis aetate inferiores fuerunt, Lepidus postea, deinde Carbo . . .

T 5 Cic. *De or.* 1.40

[Scaevola:] equidem et Ser. Galbam memoria teneo divinum hominem in dicendo et M. Aemilium Porcinam et C. ipsum Carbonem, quem tu adolescentulus perculisti,

upon that, he would be able both to write and to speak in the same manner; agitation of the mind is not always present, and when that has subsided, all that force, and almost the fire, of the orator is extinguished. [94] For this reason, then, the mind of Laelius [C. Laelius Sapiens (**20**)] seems to breathe even in his writings, but the force of Galba seems to have vanished. . . ."

T 3 Cicero, *Brutus*

[ATTICUS:] You praise Galba; if as the foremost man of that period, I agree—for thus we are told—; but if as an orator, please produce his orations—for they are extant—and say that you would like Brutus here, whom you love more than yourself, to speak in that fashion.

T 4 Cicero, *Brutus*

[CICERO:] Do we not see that in every single period scarcely two orators each have established themselves as praiseworthy? Galba, among so many contemporaries, was the only one preeminent, to whom, as we are told, both Cato [M. Porcius Cato (**8**)], of the older generation, gave way and those who were his juniors in age in that period, afterward Lepidus [M. Aemilius Lepidus Porcina (**25**)], then Carbo [C. Papirius Carbo (**35**)] . . .

T 5 Cicero, *On the Orator*

[SCAEVOLA:] Indeed I remember that Ser. Galba, a divine man with regard to speaking, and M. Aemilius Porcina [M. Aemilius Lepidus Porcina (**25**)] and C. Carbo [C. Papirius Carbo (**35**)] himself, whom you, as a very young man [L. Licinius Crassus (**66**), F 13–14], crushed, were ignorant

ignarum legum, haesitantem in maiorum institutis, rudem
in iure civili . . .

T 6 Cic. *De or.* 3.28

[CRASSUS:] gravitatem Africanus, lenitatem Laelius, aspe-
ritatem Galba, profluens quiddam habuit Carbo et canorum. quis horum non princeps temporibus illis fuit? et suo
tamen quisque in genere princeps.

T 7 Lactant. *Div. inst.* 5.14.3 [Cic. *Rep.* 3.9]

Carneades Academicae sectae philosophus, cuius in disserendo quae vis fuerit, quae eloquentia, quod acumen, qui
nescit ipsum, ex praedicatione Ciceronis intelleget . . . is
cum legatus ab Atheniensibus Romam missus esset, dis-
putavit de iustitia copiose audiente Galba et Catone Cen-
sorio maximis tunc oratoribus.

T 8 Liv. 45.39.16

ille nihil praeterquam loqui, et ⟨id⟩ ipsum[1] maledice et
maligne, didicit . . .

[1] ⟨id⟩ ipsum *ed. Aldina*: ipsud *cod.*: ipsum *Vascosanus*: ipsum
⟨id⟩ *Gronovius*: ⟨hoc⟩ ipsum *anon. ap. Drakenborch*

of the statutes, uncertain about the institutions of the ancestors, uninstructed in civil law . . .

T 6 Cicero, *On the Orator*

[CRASSUS:] Africanus [P. Cornelius Scipio Aemilianus Africanus minor (**21**)] had weight, Laelius [C. Laelius Sapiens (**20**)] smoothness, Galba harshness, Carbo [C. Papirius Carbo (**35**)] a kind of flow and melody. Which of these was not eminent in that period? And yet each [was] eminent in their own style.

T 7 Lactantius, *Divine Institutions* [Cicero, *On the Republic*]

As regards Carneades, a philosopher of the Academic school, what force there was in his arguing, what eloquence, what shrewdness, whoever does not know him personally will see it from Cicero's commendation . . . when he was sent as an envoy by the Athenians to Rome [in 155 BC], he argued about justice copiously while Galba and Cato Censorius [M. Porcius Cato (**8**)], the greatest orators at the time, were listening.

T 8 Livy, *History of Rome*

He [Galba] has learned nothing except speaking, and ⟨that⟩ in a slanderous and malicious way . . .

T 9 Tac. *Dial.* 18.1

[APER:] haec ideo praedixi, ut si qua ex horum oratorum fama gloriaque laus temporibus adquiritur, ea{nde}m[1] docerem in medio sitam et propiorem nobis quam Servio Galbae aut C. Carboni quosque alios merito antiquos vocaverimus; sunt enim horridi et impoliti et rudes et informes et quos utinam nulla parte imitatus esset Calvus vester aut Caelius aut ipse Cicero.

[1] ea{nde}m *Halm*: eandem *codd.*

T 10 Tac. *Dial.* 25.7

[MESSALLA:] quod ad Servium Galbam et C. Laelium attinet et si quos alios antiqu⟨i⟩orum[1] agitare non destitit, non exigit defensorem, cum fatear quaedam eloquentiae eorum ut nascenti adhuc nec satis adultae defuisse.

[1] antiqu⟨i⟩orum *P. Voss*: antiquorum *codd.*   Aper *post* antiqu⟨i⟩orum *add. Voss*

Against a Triumph of L. Aemilius Paullus (F 11)

F 11 Liv. 45.35.8–36.6

sed eos Ser. Sulpicius Galba, qui tribunus militum secundae legionis in Macedonia fuerat, privatim imperatori ini-

T 9 Tacitus, *Dialogue on Oratory*

[APER:] I have mentioned this in advance for this reason, so that I could show that, if from the fame and glory of these orators [of the late Republican / early Augustan period] any kudos is obtained for their times, that is within reach and nearer to us than to Servius Galba or C. Carbo [C. Papirius Carbo (**35**)] and others whom we may justly call ancients; for they are rough, uncultivated, crude, without any proper shape and of such a kind that one would hope that neither your Calvus [C. Licinius Macer Calvus (**165**)], nor Caelius [M. Caelius Rufus (**162**)], nor Cicero himself had imitated them in anything.

T 10 Tacitus, *Dialogue on Oratory*

[MESSALLA:] As for Servius Galba and C. Laelius [C. Laelius Sapiens (**20**)] and if there are others of the more ancient [speakers] whom he [Aper] has not ceased to disparage, their case does not demand a defender since I admit that some things were wanting in their eloquence, as it was still in its infancy and not yet fully grown up.

Against a Triumph of L. Aemilius Paullus (F 11)

*In 167 BC Galba spoke against the approval of a triumph for L. Aemilius Paullus (**12**), who had defeated Perseus (Plut. Aem. 30.4–8) and thus ended the Third Macedonian War.*

F 11 Livy, *History of Rome*

But Ser. Sulpicius Galba, who had been a military tribune of the second legion in Macedonia, personally an enemy

micus, prensando ipse et per suae legionis milites sollici-
tando stimulaverat ut frequentes ad suffragium adessent.
[9] imperiosum ducem et malignum antiquando rogationem quae de triumpho eius ferretur ulciscerentur. plebem urbanam secuturam esse militum iudicia. pecuniam
illum dare non potuisse: militem honorem dare posse. ne
speraret ibi fructum gratiae ubi non meruisset. [36.1] i<i>s
incitatis cum in Capitolio rogationem eam T<i>.[1] Sempronius tribunus plebis ferret et privatis <de>[2] lege dicendi
locus esset, ad suadendum, ut in re minime dubia, haud
quisquam procederet, [2] Ser. Galba repente processit et
a tribunis postulavit ut quoniam hora iam octava diei esset,
nec satis temporis ad demonstrandum haberet cur L.
Aemilium non iuberent triumphare, in posterum diem
differrent et mane eam rem agerent: integro sibi die ad
causam eam orandam opus esse. [3] cum tribuni dicere
eo die, si quid vellet, iuberent, in noctem rem dicendo
extraxit referendo admonendoque exacta acerbe munia
militiae; plus laboris plus periculi quam desiderasset res
iniunctum; contra in praemiis in honoribus omnia artata;
[4] militiamque, si talibus succedat ducibus, horridiorem
asperioremque bellantibus, eandem victoribus inopem atque
inhonoratam futuram. Macedonas in meliore fortuna

---

[1] *add. Sigonius*   [2] *add. Gronovius*

of the general, by buttonholing himself and by pestering through the soldiers of his own legion, had incited them [the soldiers of L. Aemilius Paullus' army] to turn up in great numbers at the voting. [9] They should take revenge on a domineering and mean leader by rejecting the proposal that was being brought forward about that man's triumph. The urban populace would follow the judgment of the soldiers. That man had not been able to give them money: the soldiers were able to give an honor. He should not hope for the fruit of gratitude there where he had not earned it. [36.1] Thus they [the soldiers] had been roused; then, when, on the Capitol, Ti. Sempronius, a Tribune of the People [167 BC], brought forward that proposal and there was an opportunity for private individuals to speak <about> the law, and hardly anyone came forward to argue for its passing, like in a matter in no way doubtful, [2] Ser. Galba suddenly came forward and demanded from the Tribunes that, since it was already the eighth hour of the day and he did not have sufficient time to demonstrate why they should not order L. Aemilius to triumph, they should adjourn until the following day and bring this matter up early: a full day was necessary for him to plead the case. [3] When the Tribunes ordered him to speak on that day, if he wished [to say] anything, he prolonged the matter until the night by speaking, reminding them and recalling the harshly enforced duties of military service; more toil and more risk than the situation had demanded had been imposed; by contrast, everything concerning rewards and honors had been reduced; [4] and military service, if it prospers for such generals, would become more dreadful and harsher for the fighters, and equally would be without funds and without honors for the victors. The

quam milites Romanos esse. [5] si frequentes postero die
ad legem antiquandam adessent, intellecturos potentes
viros non omnia in ducis, aliquid et in militum manu esse.
[6] his vocibus incitati, postero die milites tanta frequentia
Capitolium compleverunt ut aditus nulli praeterea ad suffragium ferendum esset.

In 149 BC Galba delivered two speeches against the Tri-
*bune of the People L. Scribonius Libo (**29** F 2–4; cf. Cic.*
De or. 2.263) and one against L. Cornelius Cethegus in his
own defense (CCMR, App. A: 173), when his behavior

In His Defense Against L. Scribonius Libo
(F 12–14)

F 12   Liv. *Epit.* 49.17–20

cum L. Scribonius tr. pl. rogationem promulgasset, ut
Lusitani, qui in fidem populo R. dediti ab Servio Galba in
Galliam venissent, in libertatem restituerentur, M. Cato
acerrime suasit. [18] extat oratio in annalibus ipsius in-
clusa. [19] Q. Fulvius Nobilior ei,[1] saepe ab eo in senatu
laceratus, respondit pro Galba; ipse quoque Galba cum se
damnari videret, complexus duos filios praetextatos et Sul-

---

[1] ei *Iahn*: et *codd.*

Macedonians were in a better position than the Roman soldiers. [5] If they came in large numbers on the following day to reject the law, the powerful men would understand that not everything is in the hand of the leader and that something is also in that of the soldiers. [6] Incited by these words, on the following day the soldiers filled the Capitol in such large numbers that, besides [them], there was access for nobody to cast a vote.

toward the Lusitanians (in Hispania) was criticized (Cic. De or. 1.227; Att. 12.5b; Mur. 59; Val. Max. 8.7.1; Liv. 39.40.12; Epit. Ox. 49; Quint. Inst. 2.15.8; cf. Brennan 2000, 175) (TLRR 1).

In His Defense Against L. Scribonius Libo
(F 12–14)

F 12 Livy, *Epitome*

When L. Scribonius [L. Scribonius Libo (**29**), F 3], a Tribune of the People [149 BC], had promulgated a bill that the Lusitanians, who had surrendered themselves to the protection of the Roman People and had been sold by Servius Galba into Gaul, should be restored to freedom, M. Cato [M. Porcius Cato (**8**)] most vigorously spoke in favor. [18] The speech is extant, included in his own annals [*Origines*; **8** *ORF*⁴ F 196–99]. [19] Q. Fulvius Nobilior [**19A** F 2], often railed at by him [Cato] in the Senate [i.e., because of losses incurred when fighting in Hispania], answered him on behalf of Galba; Galba himself, too, when he saw that he was being condemned, clasping his two young sons and the son of Sulpicius Galus [C. Sulpicius

pici Gali[2] filium, cuius tutor erat, ita miserabiliter pro se locutus est ut rogatio antiquaretur. [20] exstant tres orationes eius, duae adversus Libonem tr. pl. rogationemque eius habitae de Lusitanis, una contra L. Cornelium Cethegum, in qua Lusitanos prope se castra habentis caesos fatetur, quod compertum habuerit, equo atque homine suo ritu immolatis per speciem pacis adoriri exercitum suum in animo habuisse.

2 sulpicii galli *vel* g. s. *vel* sulpicii *vel* sulpicali (*vel similia*) *codd.*

F 13 Cic. *Brut.* 89–90

[CICERO:] ex hac Rutili narratione suspicari licet, cum duae summae sint in oratore laudes, una subtiliter disputandi ad docendum, altera graviter agendi ad animos audientium permovendos, multoque plus proficiat is qui inflammet iudicem quam ille qui doceat, elegantiam in Laelio, vim in Galba fuisse. quae quidem vis tum[1] maxime cognita est, cum Lusitanis a Ser. Galba praetore contra interpositam, ut existimabatur, fidem interfectis L.[2] Libone tribuno plebis populum incitante et rogationem in Galbam privilegi similem ferente, summa senectute, ut ante dixi, M. Cato legem suadens in Galbam multa dixit; quam orationem in Origines suas rettulit, paucis ante quam mortuus est {an}[3] diebus an mensibus. [90] tum igitur ‹nihil›[4] recusans Galba pro sese et populi Romani

1 vis tum *edd.*: is est istum *codd.*   2 L. *Corradus:* T. *codd.*   3 *del. Pareus*   4 *add. Corradus*

Galus (**14**)], whose guardian he was, spoke so pitiably in his defense that the proposal was rejected. [20] Three speeches by him are extant, two delivered against Libo, the Tribune of the People, and his proposal concerning the Lusitanians, one against L. Cornelius Cethegus [cf. F 15], in which he admits that the Lusitanians who had their camp near him were killed, since he had discovered that, after having sacrificed a horse and a man according to their rites, they had in mind to attack his army under the cover of peace.

F 13 Cicero, *Brutus*

[CICERO:] From this story [F 16] of Rutilius [P. Rutilius Rufus (**44**)] it can be inferred that, as there are two very praiseworthy qualities of an orator, one of arguing subtly to instruct, the other of acting forcefully to move the minds of the listeners, and that he achieves far more who inflames the judge than he who instructs, there was skill of presentation in Laelius [C. Laelius Sapiens (**20**)] and force in Galba. This force was then particularly noticed when, after the Lusitanians had been killed by Ser. Galba, when praetor, against pledged faith, as was believed, and when L. Libo [L. Scribonius Libo (**29**), F 2], a Tribune of the People, incited the People and put forward a bill against Galba, like a measure directed against him in person, M. Cato [M. Porcius Cato (**8**) *ORF*[4] F 196–99], in extreme old age, as I have mentioned, arguing for the law, said a lot against Galba; he recorded this speech in his *Origines*, a few days or months before he died. [90] Then Galba, <not> putting in <any> objections on his own behalf and appealing to the good faith of the Roman People, in

fidem implorans cum suos pueros tum C. Gal{l}i etiam filium flens commendabat, cuius orbitas et fletus mire miserabilis fuit propter recentem memoriam clarissimi patris; isque se tum eripuit flamma, propter pueros misericordia populi commota, sicut idem scriptum reliquit Cato.

F 14 Val. Max. 8.1.abs.2

cum a Libone tribuno pl. Ser. Galba pro rostris vehementer increparetur, quod Lusitanorum magnam manum interposita fide praetor in Hispania interemisset, actionique tribuniciae M. Cato ultimae senectutis oratione sua, quam in Origines retulit, suscriberet, reus pro se iam nihil recusans parvulos liberos suos et Gal{l}i[1] sanguine sibi coniunctum filium flens commendare coepit eoque facto mitigata contione qui omnium consensu periturus erat paene nullum triste suffragium habuit.

[1] Gal{l}i *Briscoe*: Galli *codd.*: C. Galli *Halm*

In His Defense Against L. Cornelius Cethegus
(F 15)

F 15 Liv. *Epit.* 49.17–20
= F 12.

tears, began to commend to them his sons and particularly the son of C. Galus [C. Sulpicius Galus (**14**)], whose orphaned state and tears were remarkably pitiable because of the recent memory of his great father. And, at that time, he rescued himself from the flame, when the sympathy of the People had been moved because of the boys, as Cato has also transmitted in writing.

F 14 Valerius Maximus, *Memorable Doings and Sayings*

When Ser. Galba was vehemently criticized by Libo [L. Scribonius Libo (**29**), F 4], a Tribune of the People, from the front of the Rostra, because after faith had been pledged he had killed a large number of Lusitanians as praetor in Hispania and M. Cato [M. Porcius Cato (**8**) *ORF*⁴ F 196–99], in extreme old age, supported the tribunician action by his speech that he has transferred into the *Origines*, the accused, no longer putting in any objections on his own behalf, in tears, began to commend his young sons and the son of Galus [C. Sulpicius Galus (**14**)], a blood relation of his, and once the meeting was softened by that deed, he, who was on the point of perishing by the consensus of all, suffered hardly any negative vote.

In His Defense Against L. Cornelius Cethegus
(F 15)

F 15 Livy, *Epitome*
= F 12.

On Behalf of the Tax Collectors (F 16)

F 16 Cic. *Brut.* 85–88

[CICERO:] memoria teneo Smyrnae me ex P. Rutilio Rufo audivisse, cum diceret adulescentulo se accidisse, ut ex senatus consulto P. Scipio et D. Brutus, ut opinor, consules de re atroci magnaque quaererent. nam cum in silva Sila[1] facta caedes esset notique homines interfecti insimulareturque familia, partim etiam liberi societatis eius, quae picarias de P. Cornelio L. Mummio censoribus redemisset, decrevisse senatum, ut de ea re cognoscerent et statuerent consules. [86] causam pro publicanis accurate, ut semper solitus esset, eleganterque dixisse Laelium. cum consules re audita "amplius" de consili sententia pronuntiavissent, paucis interpositis diebus iterum Laelium multo diligentius meliusque dixisse iterumque eodem modo a consulibus rem esse prolatam. tum Laelium, cum eum socii domum reduxissent egissentque gratias et ne defatigaretur oravissent, locutum esse ita: se, quae fecisset, honoris eorum causa studiose accurateque fecisse, sed

---

[1] in silva Sila *Turnebus*: in siuas ita *vel* istiuas ita *vel* Stiuas ita *codd.*

On Behalf of the Tax Collectors (F 16)

*In 138 BC, taking over from C. Laelius Sapiens (**20** F 20), Galba secured the acquittal of a group of tax collectors by a speech described as impressive in Cicero (TLRR 10).*

F 16 Cicero, *Brutus*

[CICERO:] I remember that I heard from P. Rutilius Rufus [**44**] in Smyrna, when he said that it had happened when he was a very young man that, on the basis of a Senate decree, the consuls, P. Scipio and D. Brutus, as I believe [138 BC], inquired into a shocking and serious matter. For when a murder had been committed in the Silan forest [in Bruttium / Calabria], well-known people had been killed, and the household slaves were blamed, as well as some free men from that corporation that had leased pitch huts from the censors P. Cornelius and L. Mummius [142 BC], the Senate had decreed that the consuls investigate this matter and pass judgment. [86] The case on behalf of the tax collectors had been presented with precision, as he was always accustomed to do, and with skillful use of words by Laelius [C. Laelius Sapiens (**20**), F 20]. When the consuls, after listening to the matter, had announced "a further hearing" on the advice of their counsel, after an interval of a few days Laelius had spoken again, far more carefully and better, and again in the same way the matter had been adjourned by the consuls. Then, when the members of the corporation had escorted him to his house, had thanked him, and had begged that he should not relax, Laelius had spoken thus: what he had done, he had done assiduously and meticulously out of regard for their honor, but he

se arbitrari causam illam a Ser. Galba, quod is in dicendo atrocior[2] acriorque esset, gravius et vehementius posse defendi. itaque auctoritate C. Laeli publicanos causam detulisse ad Galbam; [87] illum autem, quod ei viro succedendum esset, verecunde et dubitanter recepisse. unum quasi comperendinatus medium diem fuisse, quem totum Galbam in consideranda causa componendaque posuisse; et cum cognitionis dies esset et ipse Rutilius rogatu sociorum domum ad Galbam mane venisset, ut eum admoneret et ad dicendi tempus adduceret, usque illum, quoad ei nuntiatum esset consules descendisse, omnibus exclusis commentatum in quadam testudine cum servis litteratis fuisse, quorum ‹alii›[3] aliud dictare eodem {a}[4] tempore solitus esset. interim cum esset ei nuntiatum tempus esse, exisse in aedis eo colore et iis oculis, ut egisse causam, non commentatum putares. [88] addebat etiam idque ad rem pertinere putabat, scriptores illos male mulcatos exisse cum Galba; ex quo significabat illum non in agendo solum, sed etiam in meditando vehementem atque incensum fuisse. quid multa? magna exspectatione, plurimis audientibus, coram ipso Laelio sic illam causam tanta vi tantaque gravitate dixisse Galbam ut nulla fere pars orationis silen-

---

[2] atrocior *Friller*: adhortor *codd.*: asperior *Martha*: ardentior *Corradus*: *alii alia*   [3] *add. hic Manutius*: *post* dictare *Fuchs*: *post* eodem *Reis, Barwick*   [4] *del. edd.*

believed that this case could be defended more strongly
and forcefully by Ser. Galba, since he was fiercer and
sharper in speaking. Thus, on the authority of C. Laelius,
the tax collectors had transferred their case to Galba. [87]
He, however, since it was a matter of succeeding such a
man, had accepted with scruples and hesitation. There
had been available practically a single day of the trial's
adjournment to the third day, the middle one, which
Galba had spent entirely on considering and shaping the
case. And when it was the day of the hearing and Rutilius
himself, upon the request of the members of the corporation, had come early to the house of Galba, to remind him
and bring him over for the time of his appearance as
speaker, he, until it had been announced to him that the
consuls had come down, continued to prepare in a kind of
a shell, with everyone excluded, surrounded by his literate
slaves, of whom he had the habit of dictating one thing <to
one of them> and another thing <to another> at the same
time.[1] Meanwhile, when it had been announced to him
that the time had arrived, he had come out into the hall
with such a color and such eyes that you would think he
had presented a case, not prepared it. [88] He [Rutilius]
also added, and he believed that this was relevant to the
matter, that those scribes had come out along with Galba
having been badly treated; thereby he showed that he
[Galba] was not only in pleading, but also in preparing,
vehement and fiery. What else? Amid great expectation,
with a very large number of listeners, in front of Laelius
himself, Galba had pleaded that case with such great force

---

[1] For a similar practice attributed to Caesar, see Plut. *Caes.*
17.7; Plin. *HN* 7.91.

tio praeteriretur. itaque multis querelis multaque misera-
tione adhibita socios omnibus approbantibus illa die
quaestione liberatos esse.

19A Q. FULVIUS NOBILIOR

*Q. Fulvius Nobilior (cos. 153, censor 136 BC; RE Fulvius
95) is known for having obtained Roman citizenship for
the poet Q. Ennius, who had accompanied his father on*

T 1 Cic. *Brut.* 79

Q. Nobiliorem M. f. iam patrio[1] instituto deditum studio
litterarum . . . non indisertum dicunt fuisse . . .

[1] patrio *edd.*: patre *codd.*

In Support of Ser. Sulpicius Galba (F 2)

*When the Tribune of the People L. Scribonius Libo (29
F 2–4) promulgated a bill reverting the actions of Ser.
Sulpicius Galba (19) in Gaul, which was supported by M.*

F 2 Liv. *Epit.* 49.19

= **19** F 12.

and such great gravity that hardly any part of the oration was passed by in silence. Thus, as a result of many pitiful utterances and much compassion adduced, with the approval of all, the members of the corporation had been freed from the charge on that day. [continued by F 13]

19A Q. FULVIUS NOBILIOR

his campaign to Aetolia (Cic. Brut. 79). In Cicero Fulvius is described as a decent speaker (T 1); one particular instance of an oratorical intervention of his is attested (F 2).

T 1 Cicero, *Brutus*

About Q. Nobilior, Marcus' son [M. Fulvius Nobilior, cos. 189 BC], as a result already of his father's practice devoted to the study of letters, . . . they say that he was not without the ability to speak . . .

In Support of Ser. Sulpicius Galba (F 2)

Porcius Cato (8), Fulvius Nobilior responded on behalf of Galba (TLRR 1).

F 2 Livy, *Epitome*
= **19** F 12.

20 C. LAELIUS SAPIENS

*C. Laelius Sapiens (cos. 140 BC; RE Laelius 3) was a friend of P. Cornelius Scipio Aemilianus Africanus minor (**21**); he had philosophical and literary interests and was acquainted with the poets and philosophers Terence, Lucilius, Diogenes, and Panaetius (T 6); he appears as an interlocutor in several Ciceronian dialogues.*

In Cicero Laelius is described as an excellent orator, which could be perceived from the surviving written speeches (T 1, 3), as someone whose utterances are characterized by pure Latinity (T 4) and by a charming and natural diction (T 5, 7, 8, 10), and who was able to create

T 1 Cic. *Brut.* 82–83

[CICERO:] . . . sed C. Laelius et P. Africanus in primis eloquentes, quorum exstant orationes, ex quibus existimari de ingeniis oratorum potest. . . . [83] de ipsius Laeli et Scipionis ingenio quamquam ea est fama,[1] ut plurimum tribuatur ambobus, dicendi tamen laus est in Laelio inlustrior.

---

[1] fama *Baiter*: iam *codd.*

T 2 Cic. *Brut.* 89

= **19** F 13.

T 3 Cic. *Brut.* 93–94

= **19** T 2.

20 C. LAELIUS SAPIENS

different levels of style by slight variations rather than by exerting himself (Cic. De or. 1.255), even though Quintilian notes that the style may be regarded only as polished in relation to the early period in which Laelius was active (Quint. Inst. 12.10.10; for praise cf. also T 7, 11; Cic. De or. 1.58, 1.215; Vell. Pat. 2.9.1; Apul. Apol. 95.5). In the Rhetorica ad Herennium *Laelius is listed as one of the writers from whom examples for students could be drawn* (Rhet. Her. 4.7: **25** T 5).

Laelius is said to have delivered many speeches for the defense (T 9).

T 1 Cicero, *Brutus*

[Cicero:] ... but C. Laelius and P. Africanus [P. Cornelius Scipio Aemilianus Africanus minor (**21**)] [were regarded as] particularly eloquent; of them speeches are extant, from which one may judge their talent as orators. ... [**19** T 1] ... [83] Concerning the talent of Laelius himself and of Scipio, while their reputation is such that an enormous amount is attributed to both, still, in speaking, the reputation of Laelius is more illustrious. [continued by F 12]

T 2 Cicero, *Brutus*

= **19** F 13.

T 3 Cicero, *Brutus*

= **19** T 2.

T 4 Cic. *Brut.* 258

"solum quidem," inquit ille [ATTICUS], "et quasi funda-
mentum oratoris vides, locutionem emendatam et Lati-
nam, cuius penes quos laus adhuc fuit, non fuit rationis aut
scientiae, sed quasi bonae consuetudinis. mitto C. Laelium P.[1] Scipionem: aetatis illius ista fuit laus tamquam
innocentiae sic Latine loquendi—nec omnium tamen,
nam illorum aequalis Caecilium et Pacuvium male locutos
videmus—sed omnes tum fere, qui nec extra urbem hanc
vixerant neque eos aliqua barbaries domestica infuscave-
rat, recte loquebantur. . . ."

[1] P. *vel* Pilum *codd.*: P. illum *Stangl*

T 5 Cic. *Brut.* 295

[ATTICUS:] . . . quod item de Africano, de Laelio, cuius tu
oratione negas fieri quicquam posse dulcius, addis etiam
nescio quid augustius. nomine nos capis summi viri vitae-
que elegantissimae verissimis laudibus. remove haec: ne
ista dulcis oratio ita sit abiecta ut eam[1] aspicere nemo
velit.

[1] ut eam *edd.*: autem *codd.*

T 6 Cic. *De or.* 2.154

[CATULUS:] . . . et certe non tulit ullos haec civitas aut
gloria clariores aut auctoritate graviores aut humanitate

T 4 Cicero, *Brutus*

"The ground at any rate," he [ATTICUS] said, "and the foundation, as it were, of an orator is, you see, a faultless and pure Latin diction; those who have enjoyed this distinction so far have had it, not because of a system and expert knowledge, but because of good usage, as it were. I pass over C. Laelius and P. Scipio [P. Cornelius Scipio Aemilianus Africanus minor (**21**)]: the great distinction of that period was integrity of character as much as speaking pure Latin—though not of all men, for we see that their contemporaries Caecilius and Pacuvius spoke badly—still, at that time, almost all who had not lived outside this city or whom some crudeness at home had not corrupted spoke correctly. . . ."

T 5 Cicero, *Brutus*

[ATTICUS:] . . . the same [applies] to Africanus [P. Cornelius Scipio Aemilianus Africanus minor (**21**)] and to Laelius, compared with whose manner of speaking you [Cicero] say nothing could be more charming, you even add somehow more august. You take us in with the name of an outstanding man and the best-founded glory of the purest life. Take away these things: certainly, that sweet language would be so undistinguished that nobody would wish to take a glance at it.

T 6 Cicero, *On the Orator*

[CATULUS:] . . . and surely this community has produced no men more splendid in fame or weightier in influence or more refined in culture than P. Africanus [P. Cornelius

103

politiores P. Africano, C. Laelio, L. Furio, qui secum eruditissimos homines ex Graecia palam semper habuerunt.

T 7 Cic. *De or.* 3.28
= **19** T 6.

T 8 Cic. *De or.* 3.45

[CRASSUS:] equidem cum audio socrum meam Laeliam—facilius enim mulieres incorruptam antiquitatem conservant, quod multorum sermonis expertes ea tenent semper, quae prima didicerunt—sed eam sic audio, ut Plautum mihi aut Naevium videar audire; sono ipso vocis ita recto et simplici est, ut nihil ostentationis aut imitationis adferre videatur; ex quo sic locutum esse eius patrem iudico, sic maiores; non aspere, ut ille, quem dixi, non vaste, non rustice, non hiulce, sed presse et aequabiliter et leviter.[1]

[1] leviter *vel* leniter *codd.*

T 9 Cic. *Rep.* 3.42

"multas tu quidem," inquit [SCIPIO], "Laeli, saepe causas ita defendisti ut ego non modo tecum Servium Galbam, collegam nostrum, quem tu quoad vixit omnibus anteponebas, verum ne Atticorum quidem oratorum quemquam aut sua‹vitate . . .›"[1]

[1] *suppl. Mai*

Scipio Aemilianus Africanus minor (**21**)], C. Laelius, and
L. Furius [L. Furius Philus (**26**)], who had the most
learned men from Greece about themselves at all times
and in public.

T 7 Cicero, *On the Orator*

= **19** T 6.

T 8 Cicero, *On the Orator*

[CRASSUS:] For my own part, when I listen to my mother-
in-law Laelia—for women keep the old pronunciation
unspoiled more easily, as they do not take part in the conversations of the multitude and so always retain what they
learned initially—but I listen to her so that I believe I am
listening to Plautus or Naevius; she has such an unaffected
and natural sound of voice that she seems to introduce no
trace of display or affectation; hence I infer that her father
and her ancestors spoke like this: not harshly, like the
person I mentioned [Q. Valerius Soranus], nor in a coarse
manner, nor in a countrified way, nor with a jerky pronunciation, but neatly and evenly and smoothly.

T 9 Cicero, *On the Republic*

"You certainly have often defended, Laelius," he [SCIPIO]
said, "many cases in such a way that I [would not compare]
with you not only Servius Galba [Ser. Sulpicius Galba
(**19**)], our colleague [as augur], whom you put before everyone as long as he was alive, but not even any of the
Attic orators either in cha‹rm . . .›."

T 10 Quint. *Inst.* 1.1.6

. . . et Laelia C. filia[1] reddidisse in loquendo paternam elegantiam dicitur . . .

> [1] Laelia C. filia *H. Meyer*: lelia *vel* lelii filia *codd.*

T 11 Quint. *Inst.* 12.10.39

non Scipio, Laelius, Cato in loquendo[1] velut Attici Romanorum fuerunt?

> [1] eloquendo *ed. Ald.*: in loquendo *del. Winterbottom*

On the Priestly Colleges (F 12–16)

As praetor in 145 BC, Laelius successfully spoke against a bill of the Tribune of the People C. Licinius Crassus, proposing that the People should select the members of the

F 12 Cic. *Brut.* 83

[CICERO:] at oratio Laeli de collegiis non melior quam de multis quam voles Scipionis; non quo illa Laeli quicquam sit dulcius aut quo de religione dici possit augustius, sed multo tamen vetustior et horridior ille quam Scipio; et, cum sint in dicendo variae voluntates, delectari mihi magis antiquitate videtur et libenter verbis etiam uti paulo magis priscis Laelius.

T 10 Quintilian, *The Orator's Education*

... and Laelia, Gaius' daughter, is said to have echoed her father's elegance in her speech ...

T 11 Quintilian, *The Orator's Education*

Were not Scipio [P. Cornelius Scipio Aemilianus Africanus minor (**21**)], Laelius, and Cato [M. Porcius Cato (**8**)] like Attic orators of the Romans as regards their eloquence?

On the Priestly Colleges (F 12–16)

priestly colleges instead of co-option (Rogatio Licinia de sacerdotiis: LPPR, *p. 295*).

F 12 Cicero, *Brutus*

[CICERO:] [continued from T 1] But the speech of Laelius concerning the priestly colleges, however, is not better than any of the many speeches of Scipio [P. Cornelius Scipio Aemilianus Africanus minor (**21**)], not that anything could be more pleasing than that speech of Laelius, nor that anything more solemn could be said about religion, yet that man is much more archaic and harsher than Scipio. And, since in speaking there are varying preferences, Laelius seems to me to enjoy more what is ancient and also to use happily slightly more old-fashioned words.

F 13 Cic. *Amic.* 96

[LAELIUS:] atque ut ad me redeam, meministis, Q.
Maximo fratre Scipionis et L. Mancino consulibus, quam
popularis lex de sacerdotiis C. Licini Crassi videbatur;
cooptatio enim collegiorum ad populi beneficium trans-
ferebatur; atque is primus instituit in forum versus agere
cum populo; tamen illius vendibilem orationem religio
deorum immortalium, nobis defendentibus, facile vince-
bat. atque id actum est praetore me, quinquennio antequam consul sum factus; ita re magis quam summa auctoritate causa illa defensa est.

F 14 Cic. *Nat. D.* 3.5

[COTTA:] sed cum de religione agitur, Ti. Coruncanium P.
Scipionem P. Scaevolam pontifices maximos, non Ze-
nonem aut Cleanthen aut Chrysippum sequor, habeoque
C. Laelium augurem eundemque sapientem quem potius
audiam dicentem de religione in illa oratione nobili quam
quemquam principem Stoicorum.

F 15 Cic. *Nat. D.* 3.43

[COTTA:] quando enim me in hunc locum deduxit oratio,
docebo meliora me didicisse de colendis diis inmortalibus

F 13 Cicero, *On Friendship*

[LAELIUS:] And, to return to myself, you remember when Q. Maximus, Scipio's brother, and L. Mancinus were consuls [145 BC], how much in the interests of the People the law of C. Licinius Crassus [tr. pl. 145 BC] regarding the priestly offices seemed to be; for the right to co-opt into the colleges was being converted into a benefit from the People. And he was the first man to begin the practice of facing toward the Forum in addressing the People. Nevertheless, reverence for the immortal gods, with me as patron, easily prevailed over his oration appealing to the public taste. And this took place while I was praetor, five years before I was elected consul; thus, that cause was won more by its own merit than by great authority.

F 14 Cicero, *On the Nature of the Gods*

[COTTA:] But when a question of religion is being discussed, I follow Ti. Coruncanius [cos. 280; first plebeian pont. max. 254 BC], P. Scipio [P. Cornelius Scipio Nasica Corculum, cos. 162, 155; pont. max. 150 BC], and P. Scaevola [P. Mucius Scaevola, cos. 133; pont. max. 130 BC], *pontifices maximi*, not Zeno, or Cleanthes, or Chrysippus; and I have C. Laelius, an augur and also a wise man, to whom I would rather listen speaking about religion in that famous excellent oration than to any foremost man among the Stoics.

F 15 Cicero, *On the Nature of the Gods*

[COTTA:] For as my discourse has led me to this topic, I will show that I have learned more profitably about worshipping the immortal gods according to pontifical law and

iure pontificio et more maiorum capedunculis his, quas Numa nobis reliquit, de quibus in illa aureola oratiuncula dicit Laelius, quam rationibus Stoicorum.

F 16 Non., p. 398.28–31 M. = 640 L. (Cic. *Rep.* F inc. 9)

M. Tullius de Republica VI: "oratio Laeli,[1] quam omnes habemus in manibus, quam simpuia pontificum dis immortalibus grata sint Samiaeque, uti scribit, capudines."

[1] *Iunius*: M. Tullius de republ. lib. III et non pauper uti oratio et in libro sexto laeli (leli) *codd.*

On His Own Behalf Before the People (F 17–19)

F 17 Fest., p. 210.5–8 L.

OBSIDIUM tanquam praesi|dium, subsidium, recte dicitur. cuius etiam | auctor C. Laelius pro se apud populum: "ut in[1] | nobis terra marique simul obsidium facerent."

[1]ut in *cod.*: uti *Ant. Augustinus*

the customs of our ancestors from those little vessels[1] that Numa [Roman king] has bequeathed to us, which Laelius mentions in that little golden speech of his, than from the theories of the Stoics.

[1] The term *capeduncula* appears only here: it is a derivative of *capis/capedo* and denotes one-handled earthen vessels used in sacrifice (cf. F 16; Cic. *Parad.* 11).

F 16 Nonius (Cicero, *On the Republic*)

M. Tullius [Cicero in] *De re publica* 6 [?]: "the speech of Laelius, which we all have in our hands, [mentions] how pleasing to the immortal gods the pontiffs' ladles are, and, as he writes, the Samian vessels."

On His Own Behalf Before the People (F 17–19)

It is uncertain when Laelius delivered the speech on his own behalf (CCMR, App. A: 175) (TLRR 3).

F 17 Festus

obsidium ["blockade," "protection"] is rightly used like *praesidium* ["bulwark"] or *subsidium* ["support," "shelter"]. An authority for this is also C. Laelius [in the speech] on his own behalf before the People: "so that with us they created protection on land and on sea simultaneously."

F 18 Fest., pp. 196.36–98.7 L.

OREAE, freni quod ori inseruntur. | . . . C. Laelius[1] pro se
apud populum: "el|quusque mihi sub feminibus occisus
erat, oreas | detraho inspectante L. Stertinio."

[1] C. Laelius *Lion*: Coelius *codd.*

F 19 Fest., p. 416.13–25 L.

SATURA, et cibi genus ex | variis rebus conditum est, et lex
| <mul>tis[1] alis legibus conferta. . . . et C. Laellius in ea,
quam pro se dixit: <. . .> "dein | postero die, quasi per satu-
ram senten|tiis exquisitis in deditionem accipitur."

[1] *suppl. ex Epit.*

F 18 Festus

oreae ["mouthpiece of a bridle, bit"], bridle, because it is inserted into the mouth [*os, oris*]. . . . C. Laelius[1] [in the speech] on his own behalf before the People: "and my horse had been struck to death below the thighs; I remove the bit while L. Stertinius [perhaps the quaestor of 168 BC] watches."

[1] The attribution to C. Laelius Sapiens (and to this speech) depends on a (widely accepted) emendation of the transmitted name.

F 19 Festus

satura ["medley"] is both a kind of dish put together from various things and a law made up of many other laws. . . . And C. Laelius in that [speech] that he delivered on behalf of himself:[1] <. . .> "then, on the following day, after views have been sought out as if en bloc [*per saturam*],[2] he is accepted in surrender."

[1] Since the subsequent phrase is an extract from Sallust (Sall. *Iug.* 29.5), presumably a quotation from Laelius and the name of Sallust have been lost. From the context it can be inferred that Laelius' speech contained the term *satura*.   [2] The expression *per saturam* (see **17** F 5 n. 1) probably indicates that the discussion in the Senate covered several different issues.

On Behalf of the Tax Collectors (F 20)

F 20 Cic. *Brut.* 85–87
= **19** F 16.

Against Lex Papiria *(F 21)*

In 131 or 130 BC (MRR I 502 n. 1) Laelius argued against a proposal of the Tribune of the People C. Papirius Carbo (35 F 7) that Tribunes of the People should be eligible for

F 21 Cic. *Amic.* 96

[Laelius:] quibus blanditiis C. Papirius nuper influebat in aures contionis, cum ferret legem de tribunis plebis reficiendis! dissuasimus nos, sed nihil de me; de Scipione dicam libentius; quanta illa, di immortales, fuit gravitas, quanta in oratione maiestas, ut facile ducem populi Romani, non comitem diceres! sed adfuistis, et est in manibus oratio. itaque lex popularis suffragiis populi repudiata est.

On Behalf of the Tax Collectors (F 20)

In 138 BC Laelius defended a group of tax collectors at two hearings, before handing over the case to Ser. Sulpicius Galba (19 F 16) (TLRR 10).

F 20 Cicero, *Brutus*

= **19** F 16.

Against Lex Papiria *(F 21)*

reelection; P. Cornelius Scipio Aemilianus Africanus minor also spoke against it (21 F 28–29), while C. Sempronius Gracchus supported it (48 F 16–20).

F 21 Cicero, *On Friendship*

[LAELIUS:] With what flattering words C. Papirius [C. Papirius Carbo (**35**), F 7] not long ago tried to penetrate the ears of a meeting of the People, when he attempted to carry a law about making the Tribunes of the People eligible for reelection! We spoke against it, but nothing about myself; I will talk about Scipio [P. Cornelius Scipio Aemilianus Africanus minor (**21**), F 28–29] more happily. What great weight, by the immortal gods, what great majesty there was in his speech, so that one would easily say that he was the leader of the Roman People, not one of their group! But you [the interlocutors, C. Fannius (**32**) and Q. Mucius Scaevola (**50**)] both were present, and the speech is in everyone's hands. As a result, this "People's law" was rejected by the People's votes.

115

Funeral Eulogy of P. Cornelius Scipio Aemilianus
Africanus Minor (F 22–23)

*Upon the death (see **21**) of P. Cornelius Scipio Aemilianus*
*Africanus minor (**21**) in 129 BC, Laelius wrote the funeral*
eulogy (CCMR, App. A: 190; see Kierdorf 1980, 21–33),
to be delivered by the deceased's nephew Q. Fabius Maxi-

F 22 Schol. Bob. ad Cic. *Mil.* 16 (p. 118.11–17 Stangl)

super eius laudibus extat oratio C. Laeli Sapientis, qua
usus videtur Q. Fabius Maximus in laudatione mortui Scipionis, in cuius extrema parte haec verba sunt: "quiaprop-
ter neque tanta diis inmortalibus gratia haberi potest,
quanta habenda est, quod is cum illo animo atque ingenio
hac e civitate[1] potissimum natus est, neque moleste atque
aegre[2] ferri quam ferundum, cum isto modo mortem
obiit[3] et in eodem tempore[4] periit[5] cum et vobis et omnibus qui hanc rem p. salvam volunt maxime vivo opus est,
Quirites."

[1] hace civitate *Badian*   [2] aegre *Mai*: acre *codd.*
[3] *Stangl*: FERUN | SUMEUMESTCUMEO | MORBOR
UMTEMOUIT |, *at* CUME, *non solum* CUM, *del. lineola supra*
traducta: quod numero mortem obiit *Leo*: cum eum morbus tum
removit *Badian*: *alii alia*   [4] eo{dem} *Meyer*: eo dem‹um›
tempore *Badian*   [5] periit *edd.*: petuit *codd.*

F 23 Cic. *Mur.* 75

. . . quem cum supremo eius die Maximus laudaret, gratias
egit dis immortalibus quod ille vir in hac re publica potissimum natus esset; necesse enim fuisse ibi esse terrarum
imperium ubi ille esset.

Funeral Eulogy of P. Cornelius Scipio Aemilianus Africanus Minor (F 22–23)

mus Allobrogicus (**49** F 2–3), though Cicero elsewhere confuses the nephews and attributes the delivery to Q. Aelius Tubero (**45**) (Cic. De or. 2.341).

F 22 Scholia Bobiensia to Cicero, *Pro Milone*

With reference to his [Scipio's] eulogy there is extant the speech by C. Laelius Sapiens, which Q. Fabius Maximus [Q. Fabius Maximus Allobrogicus (**49**), F 2–3] seems to have used in the eulogy of the dead Scipio, in the final section of which the following words can be found: "Therefore, neither so much gratitude can be offered to the immortal gods as should be offered, because this man was born with that mind and intellect in this community out of all, nor can it be borne with grief and pain as it should be borne, because he died in that way and perished at the very same time when both for you and for all who wish this Republic safe there is very much the need for him to be alive, Romans."

F 23 Cicero, *Pro Murena*

. . . when on that man's last day Maximus [Q. Fabius Maximus Allobrogicus (**49**), F 2–3] eulogized him [Africanus], he gave thanks to the immortal gods because that man had been born in this Republic out of all; for it had been necessary for the world's government to be where he was.

Unplaced Fragment (F 24)

F 24 Cic. *De or.* 2.286

[CAESAR STRABO:] saepe etiam facete concedas adversario id ipsum, quod tibi ille detrahit: ut C. Laelius cum ei quidam malo genere natus diceret indignum esse suis maioribus: "at hercule" inquit "tu tuis dignus."

21 P. CORNELIUS SCIPIO AEMILIANUS AFRICANUS MINOR

P. Cornelius Scipio Aemilianus Africanus minor (185/84– 129 BC; cos. 147, 134, censor 142 BC; RE Cornelius 335) was the second son of L. Aemilius Paullus (12) and was adopted by P. Cornelius Scipio Africani maioris filius (13). Africanus conquered Carthage (146 BC) and Numantia (132 BC); he celebrated triumphs and, after the destruction of Carthage, was awarded the same cognomen *as his (adoptive) grandfather (Cic. Rep. 6.11; Val. Max. 2.7.1; Vell. Pat. 1.13.2; Eutr. 4.12.2). When Africanus was found dead in his home, there were suspicions that he might have been assassinated (Cic. Q Fr. 2.3.3; Mil. 16; Fat. 18; Fam. 9.21.3; Amic. 12; Oros. 5.10.9; Plut. C. Gracch. 31(10).5; on his life see Gell. NA 3.4.1; Astin 1967).*

Africanus was an educated man (T 5), a friend of C. Laelius Sapiens (20), and in close contact with the Greek philosopher Panaetius and the Greek historian Polybius (T 4, 8; Cic. Acad. 2.5; Polyb. 31.23–30) as well as the Roman poets Terence and Lucilius (T 10; Cic. Fin. 1.7 = Lucil. 594 Marx). After the battle of Pydna (168 BC), in which he participated as a young man, he received books

Unplaced Fragment (F 24)

F 24 Cicero, *On the Orator*

[CAESAR STRABO:] Also, you may often humorously yield to your opponent the very point that he is making against you: for instance, C. Laelius, when some lowborn person told him that he was not worthy of his ancestors, said: "But, by Hercules, you are worthy of yours."

21 P. CORNELIUS SCIPIO AEMILIANUS AFRICANUS MINOR

from the library of King Perseus from the spoils (Plut. Aem. 28.11). Africanus is a speaker in some of Cicero's dialogues; in particular, he is the main figure in De re publica *(for a collection of utterances attributed to Africanus, see Astin 1967, 248–69 [with the corresponding numbers indicated here]; for a selection of fragments with commentary, see Courtney 1999, 119–24).*

In Cicero, Africanus is described as an outstanding orator (T 1; Cic. De or. 1.215; cf. T 9; Vell. Pat. 2.9.1), as someone whose utterances are characterized by pure Latinity (T 2; cf. Gell. NA 2.20.5) and by gravitas (T 7), and as a representative of charming language in his day (T 3; cf. Quint. Inst. 12.10.10). In the Rhetorica ad Herennium *Africanus is listed as one of the writers from whom examples for students could be drawn (Rhet. Her. 4.7: **25** T 5). Fannius is said to have described Africanus as "ironic" in the Socratic way in his* Annals *(T 6; Cic. Brut. 299; Acad. 2.15; FRHist 12 F 6). Speeches by Africanus were available in Cicero's time (T 1).*

T 1 Cic. *Brut.* 82–83

= **20** T 1.

T 2 Cic. *Brut.* 258

= **20** T 4.

T 3 Cic. *Brut.* 295

= **20** T 5.

T 4 Cic. *Mur.* 66

huiusce modi Scipio ille fuit quem non paenitebat facere idem quod tu, habere eruditissimum hominem Panaetium domi; cuius oratione et praeceptis, quamquam erant eadem ista quae te delectant, tamen asperior non est factus sed, ut accepi a senibus, lenissimus.

T 5 Cic. *De or.* 2.154

= **20** T 6.

T 6 Cic. *De or.* 2.270

[CAESAR STRABO:] hoc in genere Fannius in annalibus suis Africanum hunc Aemilianum dicit fuisse et eum Graeco verbo appellat εἴρωνα[1] . . .

[1] verbo appellat εἴρωνα *vel* irona *codd. rec.*: verbo appellat ironiam *vel* verbo appellat ironia *vel* verbo (*sp. vac. 8 litt.*) -na *codd.*

T 1 Cicero, *Brutus*
= **20** T 1.

T 2 Cicero, *Brutus*
= **20** T 4.

T 3 Cicero, *Brutus*
= **20** T 5.

T 4 Cicero, *Pro Murena*

The famous Scipio was a man like that: he was not ashamed
to do what you [M. Porcius Cato (**126**), the prosecutor]
are doing, to entertain a very learned man, Panaetius, in
his house. By that man's speech and doctrines, although
they were the same as those that delight you, still, he
[Scipio] did not become harsher, but, as I have heard from
old men, extremely gentle.

T 5 Cicero, *On the Orator*
= **20** T 6.

T 6 Cicero, *On the Orator*

[CAESAR STRABO:] Fannius [*FRHist* 12 F 6] in his *Annals*
says that Africanus, the younger one called Aemilianus,
was well versed in this style [irony] and refers to him by
the Greek word *eirōn* ["dissembler"] . . .

T 7 Cic. *De or.* 3.28
= **19** T 6.

T 8 Vell. Pat. 1.13.3

diversi imperatoribus mores, diversa fuere studia; quippe Scipio tam elegans liberalium studiorum omnisque doctrinae et auctor et admirator fuit ut Polybium Panaetiumque, praecellentes ingenio viros, domi militiaeque secum habuerit. neque enim quisquam hoc Scipione elegantius intervalla negotiorum otio dispunxit semperque aut belli aut pacis serviit artibus: semper inter arma ac studia versatus aut corpus periculis aut animum disciplinis exercuit.

T 9 Quint. *Inst.* 12.10.39
= **20** T 11.

T 10 Porcius Licinus (F 3.2 *FPL*[4]), ap. Suet. / Donat. *Vita Ter.* 2

　　dum Africani vocem divinam[1] inhiat avidis auribus

　　[1] vocem divinam *Muretus*: voce divina *vel* vocē dum & *codd.*

T 11 Fronto, *Ad M. Caes.* 2.8.3 (p. 29.1–4 van den Hout)

[M. Aurelius ad Frontonem:] feci tamen mihi per hos dies excerpta ex libris sexaginta in quinque tomis, sed cum leges "sexaginta," inibi sunt et Novianae Atellaniolae et Scipionis oratiunculae, ne tu numerum nimis expavescas.

T 7 Cicero, *On the Orator*

= **19** T 6.

T 8 Velleius Paterculus, *Compendium of Roman History*

The commanders [Scipio and Mummius] had different characters, different interests. Indeed, Scipio was such a cultivated patron and admirer of liberal studies and every form of learning that he kept constantly with him, at home and in the field, Polybius and Panaetius, men outstanding by their intellect. For nobody punctuated the intervals between the duties of active life with leisure in a more refined way than this Scipio, and he always served the arts of either war or peace: always engaged in the pursuit of arms and studies, he was either training his body by dangers or his mind by studies.

T 9 Quintilian, *The Orator's Education*

= **20** T 11.

T 10 Porcius Licinus (F 3.2 *FPL*[4]), in Suetonius / Donatus, *Life of Terence*

> while he [Terence] was avid for Africanus' divine
>   voice with eager ears

T 11 Fronto, *Correspondence*

[MARCUS AURELIUS to Fronto:] Yet throughout these days I have made excerpts for myself from sixty books in five volumes; but when you read "sixty," there are included both brief Atellanae by Novius and little orations by Scipio, so that you should not become too frightened at the number.

Upon His Return from Africa (F 12)

F 12 Fest., p. 312.26–32 L.

QUATENUS signifi|cat, qua fine, ut hactenus, hac fine; at
quatinus, | quoniam. sed antiqui quatenoc dicebant, ut
Sci|pio Africanus in ea oratione, quam scribsit post quam
| ex Africa rediit: "uti negotium natum erat, quate|noc cas-
tra nostra ita munita erant, ut posses | partem exercitus
abducere."

On Morals as Censor (F 13–15)

*When he was censor in 142 BC, Africanus delivered a
speech with the aim of making the People observe the morals of the ancestors (Astin: F 15, 16, 56; CCMR, App. A:*

F 13 Gell. NA 4.20.1–10

inter censorum severitates tria haec exempla in litteris
sunt castigatissimae disciplinae. [2] unum est huiuscemodi: censor agebat de uxoribus sollemne iusiurandum;
[3] verba erant ita concepta: "ut tu ex animi tui sententia
uxorem habes?" qui iurabat, cavillator quidam et canicula
et nimis ridicularius fuit. [4] is locum esse sibi ioci dicundi
ratus, cum ita, uti mos erat, censor dixisset "ut tu ex animi
tui sententia uxorem habes?", [5] "habeo equidem" inquit

Upon His Return from Africa (F 12)

The speech composed after Africanus' return from Africa must date to 146 BC and deal with his achievements there (Astin: F 11).

F 12 Festus

quatenus means "to what point," like *hactenus* "to this point" (but *quatinus* [means] "because"). The ancients, however, said *quatenoc*, like Scipio Africanus in that speech that he wrote after he had returned from Africa: "when the question had arisen at what point our camp had been so fortified that you could lead away part of the army."

On Morals as Censor (F 13–15)

176; for other utterances during his censorship cf. Val. Max. 6.4.2a; Vir. ill. 58.9).

F 13 Gellius, *Attic Nights*

Among the severities of the censors these three examples of extremely strict discipline are recorded in literature. [2] The first is of this sort: The censor was administering the formal oath regarding wives; [3] the words were drawn up as follows: "Do you have, to the best of your knowledge, a wife?" The man who was to take the oath was a certain jester, a sarcastic dog, and too much of a buffoon. [4] Thinking that this was a chance for him to make a joke, when the censor had spoken as follows, as was customary: "Do you have, to the best of your knowledge, a wife?", [5]

"uxorem, sed non hercle ex animi mei sententia." [6] tum censor eum, quod intempestive lascivisset, in aerarios rettulit causamque hanc ioci scurrilis apud se dicti subscripsit. [7] altera severitas eiusdem sectae disciplinaeque est. [8] deliberatum est de nota eius, qui ad censores ab amico advocatus est et in iure stans clare nimis et sonore oscitavit atque inibi ut plecteretur fuit, tamquam illud indicium esset vagi animi et alucinantis et fluxae atque apertae securitatis. [9] sed cum ille deiurasset invitissimum sese ac repugnantem oscitatione victum tenerique eo vitio, quod "oscedo" appellatur, tum notae iam destinatae exemptus est. [10] Publius Scipio Africanus, Pauli filius, utramque historiam posuit in oratione, quam dixit in censura, cum ad maiorum mores populum hortaretur.

F 14 Gell. *NA* 5.19.15–16

animadvertimus in oratione P. Scipionis, quam censor habuit ad populum de moribus, inter ea, quae reprehen-

he said: "I indeed have a wife, but not, by Hercules, one according to my liking."[1] [6] Thereupon the censor reduced him to the class of *aerarii*,[2] because he had made a joke on an inappropriate occasion, and appended that the reason was a scurrilous joke made in front of him. [7] Here is another instance of the sternness of the same group and discipline [i.e., the censors]: [8] there was a deliberation about the punishment of a man who had been brought before the censors by a friend as his advocate and, standing in court, yawned very clearly and loudly. And he was on the point of being condemned, on the grounds that this was an indication of a fickle and wandering mind and of dissolute and undisguised carelessness. [9] But when that man had sworn that he had been overcome by the yawn very much against his will and in spite of his resistance, and that he was afflicted by that disorder that is called *oscedo* [morbid tendency to yawn], he was exempted from the penalty that had already been earmarked. [10] Publius Scipio Africanus, Paulus' son, included both these stories in a speech that he made during his censorship, when he urged the People to observe the customs of their ancestors.

[1] A play on the formula (cf. Cic. *Off.* 3.108) *ex animi sententia* (cf. Cic. *De or.* 2.260).—There seems to have been a special tax for unmarried men (Val. Max. 2.9.1).   [2] *aerarii* denotes a class of citizens who have to pay taxes to the *aerarium* but have been moved out of their *tribus* as a censorial punishment and thus have lost some of their citizen rights.

F 14 Gellius, *Attic Nights*

We have observed in a speech of P. Scipio, which he made to the People, on morals, when censor, that among the

debat, quod contra maiorum instituta fierent, id etiam eum culpavisse, quod filius adoptivos patri adoptatori inter praemia patrum prodesset. [16] verba ex ea oratione haec sunt: "in alia tribu patrem, in alia filium suffragium ferre, filium adoptivum tam procedere, quam si se natum habeat; absentis censeri iubere, ut ad censum nemini necessu‹s›[1] sit venire."

[1] necessu‹s› *Hertz*: necessu *codd.*: necessum *cod. corr.*

F 15 Paul. *Fest.*, p. 137.3–6 L.

MILLUS collare canum venaticorum, factum ex corio con|fixumque clavis ferreis eminentibus adversus impetum lu|porum. Scipio Aemilianus ad populum: "vobis," inquit, | "reique publicae praesidio erit is, quasi millus cani."

things that he criticized because they were done contrary to the conventions of the ancestors, he also found fault with this, that an adopted son was of profit to his adoptive father in gaining the rewards for paternity.[1] [16] This is the passage from that speech: "that a father votes in one tribe, the son in another, that an adopted son is of as much advantage as if one had a son of his own; that orders are given to take the census of absentees, so that it is not necessary for anyone to appear in person at the census."

[1] If the benefits of paternity offered by the government were enjoyed because of adopted children rather than one's own, the purpose of these measures, increasing the birthrate, would be thwarted (cf. Gell. *NA* 2.15.3–4).

F 15 Paul the Deacon, *Epitome of Festus*

millus, a collar for hunting dogs, made of leather and fastened together with projecting iron nails against the attack of wolves. Scipio Aemilianus [in the speech] to the People: "For you," he said, "and the Republic this man will serve as protection, just as a collar for a dog."[1]

[1] The attribution of the fragment to this speech is uncertain (see Astin 1967, 267).

In Front of the Temple of Castor (F 16)

F 16 Fest., p. 362.28–33 L.

REQUEAPSE | Scipio Africanus, Paulli filius, cum pro aede Calstoris dixit, hac conpositione usus est: "quibus | de hominibus ego saepe atque in multis locis | opera, factis, consiliis reque eapse {saepe}[1] bene | meritus siem,"[2] id est et re ipsa.

    [1] *del. Ant. Augustinus*   [2] siem *Scaliger*: spem *cod.*

On P. Sulpicius Galus (F 17)

F 17 Gell. *NA* 6.12.1–5

tunicis uti virum prolixis ultra brachia et usque in primores manus ac prope in digitos Romae atque in omni Latio indecorum fuit. [2] eas tunicas Graeco vocabulo nostri "chirodytas"[1] appellaverunt feminisque solis vestem

    [1] chirodyt- *Marx ad Lucil.*: chirodit- *vel* chyrodyt- *codd.*

---

    [1] According to *TLG*, this word for a type of garment is not attested in Greek texts, though χειριδωτός [χιτών], "sleeved [tunic]," exists. This word may have been substantivized in the feminine form in Latin (*chiridota*) and have undergone sporadic change because of the association with words of similar sound and

In Front of the Temple of Castor (F 16)

The speech in front of the Temple of Castor (Astin: F 18) presumably also dates to Africanus' censorship, since the censors typically set up the tribunal for the equestrian census in front of that temple.

F 16 Festus

requeapse, Scipio Africanus, Paulus' son, when he spoke in front of the Temple of Castor, used this combination: "for which men I have often and in many places done a service through labor, deeds, plans, and real action [*reque eapse*]," that is "and through real action" [*et re ipsa*].

On P. Sulpicius Galus (F 17)

The speech reproaching P. Sulpicius Galus (RE Sulpicius 68) with effeminate behavior might also be linked to Africanus' censorial office (Astin: F 20).

F 17 Gellius, *Attic Nights*

For a man to wear tunics stretching beyond the arms and as far as the wrists and almost to the fingers was considered unbecoming in Rome and in all Latium. [2] Such tunics our countrymen called by a Greek name *chirodytae*,[1] and they thought that a long and full-flowing garment

meaning. In different forms and spellings, the term was used as a loanword in early Latin (Nov. *Com.* 71 R.[2–3]: *chiridotam* [reading in ed. Aldina]; Lucil. 71 Marx: *chirodyti aurati*).

longe lateque diffusam {in}decere[2] existimaverunt ad ul-
nas cruraque adversus oculos protegenda. [3] viri autem
Romani primo quidem sine tunicis toga sola amicti fuerunt; postea substrictas et breves tunicas citra humerum
desinentis habebant, quod genus Graeci dicunt ἐξωμίδας.
[4] hac antiquitate indutus[3] P. Africanus, Pauli filius, vir
omnibus bonis artibus atque omni virtute praeditus, P.
Sulpicio Ga{u}lo,[4] homini delicato, inter pleraque alia,
quae obiectabat, id quoque probro dedit, quod tunicis
uteretur manus totas operientibus. [5] verba sunt haec
Scipionis: "nam qui cotidie unguentatus adversum specu-
lum ornetur, cuius supercilia radantur, qui barba vulsa
feminibusque subvulsis ambulet, qui in conviviis adulescentulus cum amatore cum chirodyta tunica interior[5] ac-
cubuerit, qui non modo vinosus, sed virosus quoque sit,
eumne quisquam dubitet, quin idem fecerit, quod cinaedi
facere solent?"

2 {in}decere *Gronovius*: indecere *vel* incedere *codd.*
3 indutus *codd.*: inbutus *Hertz*   4 Ga{u}lo *Münzer*: gaulo
codd.   5 interior *Lipsius*: inferior *codd.*

In His Defense Against Ti. Claudius Asellus
(F 18–22)

*During his censorship, Africanus took away the equestrian
status from Ti. Claudius Asellus and moved him to the
class of the* aerarii *(see F 13 n. 2); Asellus was later reinstated by Africanus' censorial colleague L. Mummius
Achaicus. Thereupon, Ti. Claudius Asellus prosecuted
Africanus (cf. Gell. NA 4.17.1 = Lucil. 394–95 Marx: Scipi-
adae magno improbus obiciebat Asellus / lustrum illo cen-*

was fitting for women only, to protect their arms and legs from sight. [3] But Roman men originally wore the toga alone without tunics; later, they had close and short tunics ending below one shoulder, the kind that the Greeks call *exomides*.[2] [4] Having adopted this older fashion, P. Africanus, Paulus' son, a man gifted with all worthy arts and every virtue, among many other things that he voiced as criticisms, reproached P. Sulpicius Galus, an effeminate man, also for wearing tunics covering his hands entirely. [5] These are Scipio's words: "For one who daily perfumes himself and dresses before a mirror, whose eyebrows are trimmed, who walks around with beard plucked out and thighs made smooth, who at banquets, as a young man, reclined in a long-sleeved tunic on the inner side of the couch with a lover,[3] who is fond not only of wine, but also of men, would anyone doubt that he has done the same thing that catamites commonly do?"

[2] *"Tunic with one sleeve*, leaving one shoulder bare" (*LSJ* s.v. ἐξωμίς), from ὦμος, "shoulder."   [3] A reference to the position of disreputable women at dinner parties (Liv. 39.43.3; Cic. *Fam.* 9.26.2).

In His Defense Against Ti. Claudius Asellus
(F 18–22)

sore malum infelixque fuisse), *perhaps when Tribune of the People in 140 BC (though this does not agree with Africanus' age given in F 18). Africanus defended himself (Astin: F 22, 26, 27, 28) in at least five orations; some of the transmitted comments would also suit the censorial* recognitio *(CCMR, App. A: 178; TLRR 6).*

F 18 Gell. *NA* 3.4.1–3

in libris, quos de vita P. Scipionis Africani compositos legimus, scriptum esse animadvertimus P. Scipioni, Pauli filio, postquam de Poenis triumphaverat censorque fuerat, diem dictum esse ad populum a Claudio Asello tribuno plebis, cui equum in censura ademerat, eumque, cum esset reus, neque barbam desisse radi neque non candida veste uti neque fuisse cultu solito reorum. [2] sed cum in eo tempore Scipionem minorem quadraginta annorum fuisse constaret, quod de barba rasa ita scriptum esset mirabamur. [3] comperimus autem ceteros quoque in isdem temporibus nobiles viros barbam in eiusmodi aetate rasitavisse, idcircoque plerasque imagines veterum, non admodum senum, sed in medio aetatis, ita factas videmus.

F 19 Gell. *NA* 6.11.9

P. Africanus pro se contra Tiberium Asellum de multa ad populum: "omnia mala, probra, flagitia, quae homines faciunt, in duabus rebus sunt, malitia atque nequitia.

F 18 Gellius, *Attic Nights*

In books that we read composed about the life of P. Scipio Africanus, we have noticed it written that P. Scipio, Paulus' son, after he had celebrated a triumph over the Carthaginians and had been censor [142 BC], was accused before the People by Claudius Asellus, a Tribune of the People, whom he had degraded from knighthood during his censorship; and that he [Scipio], although he was under accusation, neither ceased to shave his beard nor indeed not to wear white clothes, nor appeared in the usual garb of the accused. [2] But since it is certain that at that time Scipio was less than forty years old, we were surprised that this was written about shaving his beard. [3] We have learned, however, that other noblemen too in those same times were in the habit of shaving their beards at an age of that kind, and therefore we see that many portraits of the ancients, not only of old men, but in middle age, have been made in that way.[1]

[1] On the basis of conventions in his own time, Gellius notes that in Scipio's time men shaved their beards at his age: in that period it was common for men not to wear a beard after their first shaving until they had become older than Scipio was at that point (e.g., Cass. Dio 48.34.3); wearing a full beard became popular again under the emperor Hadrian (Cass. Dio 68.15.5; see Mau 1897).

F 19 Gellius, *Attic Nights*

P. Africanus [in the speech] in his own defense against Tiberius Asellus in the matter of a fine before the People [said]: "All the evils, shameful deeds, and crimes that men commit can be assigned to two things, malice and wicked-

utrum defendis, malitiam an nequitiam an utrumque simul? si nequitiam defendere vis, licet; si tu in uno scorto maiorem pecuniam absumpsisti, quam quanti omne instrumentum fundi Sabini in censum dedicavisti, si hoc ita est: qui spondet mille nummum? si tu plus tertia parte pecuniae paternae perdidisti atque absumpsisti in flagitiis, si hoc ita est: qui spondet mille nummum? non vis nequitiam. age malitiam saltem defende. si tu verbis conceptis coniuravisti sciens sciente animo tuo, si hoc ita est: qui spondet mille nummum?"

F 20 Gell. *NA* 2.20.4–6

"vivaria" autem quae nunc vulgus dicit, quos παραδείσους Graeci appellant, quae "leporaria" Varro dicit, haut usquam memini apud vetustiores scriptum. [5] sed quod apud Scipionem omnium aetatis suae purissime locutum legimus "roboraria," aliquot Romae doctos viros dicere audivi id significare, quod nos "vivaria" dicimus, appellataque esse a tabulis roboreis, quibus saepta essent; quod genus saeptorum vidimus in Italia locis plerisque. [6] verba ex oratione eius contra Claudium Asellum quinta haec sunt: "ubi agros optime cultos atque villas expolitis-

ness. Against which charge are you defending yourself,
malice or wickedness, or both at the same time? If you
wish to defend yourself against the charge of wickedness,
you may; if you have squandered more money on one
harlot than you reported for the census as the value of all
the equipment of your Sabine estate; if this is so, who
pledges a thousand sesterces? If you have wasted more
than a third of your paternal fortune and spent it on your
vices; if that is so, who pledges a thousand sesterces? You
do not care to defend yourself against the charge of wickedness. Come on, at least refute the charge of malice. If
you have sworn falsely in set terms knowingly and with a
conscious mind; if this is so, who pledges a thousand sesterces?"[1]

[1] The repeated questions allude to the practice of *sponsio*,
when a future creditor uses a set formula to request a binding
promise from the other party to pay a certain sum.

F 20 Gellius, *Attic Nights*

But as for *vivaria* ["animal enclosures"], as the common
people now say, which the Greeks call *paradeisoi* ["enclosed parks"] and which Varro terms *leporaria* ["enclosures for hares"], I do not recall it written anywhere in the
older writers. [5] But concerning *roboraria*, which we
read in Scipio, who used the purest diction of all men of
his time, I have heard several learned men at Rome assert
that this means what we call *vivaria* and that it was named
from the oaken planks [*tabulae roboreae*] by which they
were enclosed; this kind of enclosure we have seen in
many places in Italy. [6] These are the words from his
[Scipio's] fifth oration against Claudius Asellus: "Whenever he had seen very well cultivated fields and very well-

simas vidisset, in his regionibus excelsissimo loco grumam[1] statuere aiebat; inde corrigere[2] viam, aliis per vin-
eas medias, aliis per roborarium atque piscinam, aliis per
villam."

[1] loco grumam *Madvig*: locorum mu *vel* locorum *codd.*: loco
grumum *Hertz*   [2] derigere *Madvig*

F 21 Cic. *De or.* 2.258

[CAESAR STRABO:] in hoc genus coiciuntur etiam[1] prover-
bia, ut illud Scipionis, cum Asellus omnis se[2] provincias
stipendia merentem peragrasse gloriaretur: "agas asellum" et cetera.

[1] etiam *om. una familia codd.*: *del. Stangl, alii*   [2] se *om.*
una familia codd.

F 22 Cic. *De or.* 2.268 (= Lucil. 396 Marx)

[CAESAR STRABO:] arguta etiam significatio est, cum
parva re et saepe verbo res obscura et latens inlustratur;
ut cum . . . ut Asello Africanus obicienti lustrum illud infe-
lix: "noli" inquit "mirari; is enim, qui te ex aerariis exemit,
lustrum condidit et taurum immolavit."

kept farmhouses, he ordered a measuring rod to be set up on the highest spot in that district, he said, from there to construct a road in a straight line, in some places through the midst of vineyards, in others through a *roborarium* and a fishpond, in still others through a farmhouse."[1]

[1] On the structure of this passage, see Holford-Strevens 1983.

F 21 Cicero, *On the Orator*

[CAESAR STRABO:] Sayings too fall into this category [of established phrases inserted for comic effect], such as that comment by Scipio, when Asellus was bragging that he, when he was doing military service, had traveled through all provinces: "You may drive an ass," and the rest.[1]

[1] For an overview of the various interpretations and supplements proposed for this proverb, see Leeman, Pinkster, and Rabbie 1989, 281–82, *ad loc.*

F 22 Cicero, *On the Orator*

[CAESAR STRABO:] What is also clever is an allusion, when an obscure and hidden matter is illuminated by a small detail and often by a word, as when . . . as Africanus, when Asellus taxed him with that unfortunate censorial ceremony, said: "Do not be surprised; for he who removed you from the *aerarii* performed the final ceremony of the census and sacrificed the bull."[1]

[1] Scipio answers Asellus' criticism by recalling that the ritual, concluding the censorial *lustrum* after the census, had been conducted by his censorial colleague, who had reinstated Ti. Claudius Asellus (cf. Val. Max. 4.1.10. On the incident and problems in the sources, see Astin 1967, 325–31; on this passage and its difficulties, see Leeman, Pinkster, and Rabbie 1989, 300–302, *ad loc.*).

Against L. Aurelius Cotta (F 23–26)

In 138 BC (Liv. Epit. Ox. *55) or between 132 and 129 BC (Cic.* Mur. *58 [though Cicero may be inaccurate]), Africanus prosecuted (Astin: F 30) L. Aurelius Cotta (cos. 144*

F 23 Cic. *Mur.* 58

bis consul fuerat P. Africanus et duos terrores huius imperi, Carthaginem Numantiamque, deleverat cum accusavit L. Cottam. erat in eo[1] summa eloquentia, summa fides, summa integritas, auctoritas tanta quanta in imperio populi Romani quod illius opera tenebatur. saepe hoc maiores natu dicere audivi, hanc accusatoris eximiam vim et[2] dignitatem plurimum L. Cottae profuisse. noluerunt sapientissimi homines qui tum rem illam iudicabant ita quemquam cadere in iudicio ut nimiis adversarii viribus abiectus videretur.

[1] in eo *nonnulli codd.*: in *codd. cet.*: *fort.* ei *Clark*   [2] vim et *pauci codd. det.*: vim *codd. Clarki*: *om. ed. princ. Romae*

F 24 Liv. F Ox. LV 210–11

P. Africanus cum L. Cottam ⟨accu⟩sar⟨et, iudices ob⟩ magnitudinem nom⟨inis eum⟩ cad⟨ere noluerunt⟩.[1]

[1] *suppl. Grenfell-Hunt et Rossbach*: accusaret, propter magnitudinem nominis sui cadit in iudicio *Kornemann*: acc., p. m. nom. sui causam non tenuit *Luterbacher*

Against L. Aurelius Cotta (F 23–26)

*BC), presumably for extortion; Cotta was defended by Q. Caecilius Metellus Macedonicus (**18** F 1) and acquitted (TLRR 9).*

F 23 Cicero, *Pro Murena*

P. Africanus had been consul twice and had destroyed the two threats to this empire, Carthage and Numantia, when he accused L. Cotta. In him [Africanus] there was outstanding eloquence, outstanding loyalty, outstanding integrity, and authority as great as in the empire of the Roman People that was preserved by that man's service. I have often heard older men say the following, namely that this exceptional power and standing of the accuser was of the greatest advantage for L. Cotta. The very wise men who at that time were judging that case did not want any man to be condemned in court so that he appeared crushed by the excessive strength of his adversary.

F 24 Livy, *History of Rome*

When P. Africanus <accu>sed L. Cotta, <the judges did not want him to> fall because of the greatness of the famous na<me>.

F 25 Val. Max. 8.1.abs.11

sed quem ad modum splendor amplissimorum virorum in
protegendis reis plurimum valuit, ita in[1] opprimendis non
sane multum potuit: quin etiam evidenter noxiis, dum eos
acrius impugnat, profuit. P. Scipio Aemilianus Cottam
apud populum[2] accusavit. cuius causa, quamquam gravissimis criminibus erat confossa, septiens ampliata et ad
ultimum octavo iudicio absoluta est, quia homines vere-
bantur ne praecipuae accusatoris amplitudini damnatio
eius donata existimaretur.

[1] in *cod. corr.*: *om. codd. cett.*   [2] apud populum *codd.*:
apud iudices ad populum *cod. epit.*: apud praetorem *Pighi*

F 26 App. *B Civ.* 1.22.91–93
= **48** F 45.

On the Command of D. Brutus (F 27)

*Africanus may have delivered the speech on the command
of D. Iunius Brutus Callaicus (cos. 138 BC) in 136 BC
(Astin: F 31) during the discussion of an extension of that*

F 27 Fest., p. 277.7–8 L.

POTESTUR, Scipio Africanus in ea, quae est | de inperio D.
Bruti . . .

F 25 Valerius Maximus, *Memorable Doings and Sayings*

But, while the distinction of the most eminent men has been of the greatest influence in protecting the accused, it certainly has not achieved much in convicting them. Indeed, it has even been an advantage for the evidently guilty when it assaulted them too drastically. P. Scipio Aemilianus accused Cotta before the People. Although his case was riddled with the gravest charges, it was adjourned seven times and finally at the eighth hearing it was judged "not guilty," since people feared that his conviction might be thought to have been yielded to the exceptional prestige of the accuser.

F 26 Appian, *Civil Wars*

= **48** F 45.

On the Command of D. Brutus (F 27)

command. Brutus fought for several years in Hispania after his consulship.

F 27 Festus

potestur ["can"; unusual passive form], Scipio Africanus [used it] in that [speech] that exists on the command of D. Brutus . . .

Against Lex Papiria (F 28–29)

*In 131 or 130 BC, Africanus argued (Astin: F 52, 50d;
CCMR, App. A: 186) against a proposal of the Tribune of
the People C. Papirius Carbo (**35** F 7) that Tribunes of the*

F 28 Cic. *Amic.* 96

= **20** F 21.

F 29 Liv. *Epit.* 59.11–12

cum Carbo trib. plebi rogationem tulisset, ut eundem tribunum pleb., quotiens vellet, creare liceret, rogationem
eius P. Africanus gravissima oratione dissuasit; in qua dixit
Ti. Gracchum iure caesum videri. [12] ⟨C.⟩[1] Gracchus
contra suasit rogationem, sed Scipio tenuit.[2]

<hr>

[1] *add. Gronovius*   [2] tenuit *ed. Frobeniana*: censuit *codd.*

*Against a Law of Ti. Sempronius Gracchus
(F 30–31)*

*Africanus' intervention in the Senate recorded in F 31 and
dated to 129 BC seems to be linked to the judicial element
of Ti. Sempronius Gracchus' (**34**) second agrarian law
(LPPR, pp. 298–300; cf. Schol. Bob. ad Cic. Mil. 16*

F 30 Macrob. *Sat.* 3.14.6–8

nobilium vero filios et, quod dictu nefas est, filias quoque
virgines inter studiosa numerasse saltandi meditationem

Against Lex Papiria (F 28–29)

*People should be eligible for reelection; C. Laelius Sapiens also spoke against it (**20** F 21), while C. Sempronius Gracchus supported it (**48** F 16–20).*

F 28 Cicero, *On Friendship*

= **20** F 21.

F 29 Livy, *Epitome*

When Carbo, a Tribune of the People, had put forward a proposal that it should be allowed to elect the same man Tribune of the People, as often as he wished, P. Africanus argued against his proposal with a very stern speech; in that he said that Ti. Gracchus [Ti. Sempronius Gracchus (**34**)] seemed to have been killed justly. [12] <C.> Gracchus [C. Sempronius Gracchus (**48**), F 16–20], on the other hand, argued in favor of the proposal, but Scipio won the day.

Against a Law of Ti. Sempronius Gracchus (F 30–31)

[p. 118.6–9 St.]). Africanus' speech described as directed against a lex iudiciaria *of Gracchus in F 30 (Astin: F 53) may refer to the same law or to Gracchus'* Rogatio Sempronia iudiciaria *of 133 BC (LPPR, p. 301).*

F 30 Macrobius, *Saturnalia*

Indeed, for the fact that the sons of noblemen and, what is disgraceful to say, also unmarried daughters counted

145

testis est Scipio Africanus Aemilianus, qui in oratione contra legem iudiciariam Tib. Gracchi sic ait: [7] "docentur
praestigias inhonestas, cum cinaedulis et sambuca psalte-
rioque eunt in ludum histrionum, discunt cantare, quae
maiores nostri ingenuis probro ducier voluerunt. eunt,
inquam, in ludum saltatorium inter cinaedos virgines pue-
rique ingenui! haec cum mihi quisquam narrabat, non
poteram animum inducere ea liberos suos homines nobiles docere: sed cum ductus sum in ludum saltatorium,
plus medius fidius in eo ludo vidi pueris virginibusque
quinquaginta, in his unum—quo{d}[1] me rei publicae maxime miseritum est—puerum bullatum, petitoris filium
non minorem annis duodecim, cum crotalis saltare quam
saltationem {im}pudicus[2] servulus honeste saltare non
posset." [8] vides quem ad modum ingemuerit Africanus
quod vidisset cum crotalis saltantem filium petitoris, id est
candidati, quem ne tum quidem spes et ratio adipiscendi
magistratus, quo tempore se suosque ab omni probro
debuit vindicare, potuerit coercere quo minus faceret
quod scilicet turpe non habebatur.

[1] quo{d} *Courtney*: quod *codd.*   [2] {im}pudicus *Courtney*: impudicus *codd.*

F 31 App. *B Civ.* 1.19.78–80

ταῦτά τε δὴ καὶ τὰς ἐπὶ τούτοις τῶν δικαζόντων ἐπεί-
ξεις οὐ φέροντες οἱ Ἰταλιῶται Κορνήλιον Σκιπίωνα,
ὃς Καρχηδόνα ἐπόρθησεν, ἠξίουν προστάτην σφῶν
ἀδικουμένων γενέσθαι. [79] ὁ δ᾽ ἐς τοὺς πολέμους αὐ-

learning to dance among the worthwhile pursuits Scipio Africanus Aemilianus is a witness, who says as follows in the speech against the judicial law of Tib. Gracchus [Ti. Sempronius Gracchus (**34**)]: [7] "They are taught disreputable tricks, they go to acting school with catamites and with this and that kind of harp, they learn to sing, things our ancestors wished to be considered disgraceful for freeborn children. They go to dancing school, I say, freeborn maidens and boys, among catamites! When someone told me this, I could not believe that noble men were teaching their own children these things. But when I was taken to a dancing school, upon my word, I saw more than fifty boys and maidens in that school, and among these—wherefore I felt sorry for the Republic most of all—one boy wearing the amulet of the wellborn, the son of an office seeker, not less than twelve years old, doing a dance with castanets that an honorable little slave could not dance respectably." [8] You see how Africanus was aggrieved because he had seen dancing with castanets the son of an office seeker, that is, of a candidate for election, whose hopes and plans for winning a magistracy could not restrain him from doing something that evidently was not considered disgraceful, even at a time when he ought to keep himself and his family clear of any reproach.

F 31 Appian, *Civil Wars*

The Italians, who could not bear these [movements as a result of the agrarian law] and the haste of the lawsuits brought against them, chose Cornelius Scipio, who had destroyed Carthage, to become their defender against these grievances. [79] As he had made use of their very

τοῖς κεχρημένος προθυμοτάτοις ὑπεριδεῖν τε ὤκνησε
καὶ παρελθὼν εἰς τὸ βουλευτήριον τὸν μὲν Γράκχου
νόμον οὐκ ἔψεγε διὰ τὸν δῆμον σαφῶς, τὴν δὲ τοῦδε
δυσχέρειαν ἐπεξιὼν ἠξίου τὰς δίκας οὐκ ἐπὶ τῶν δι-
αιρούντων ὡς ὑπόπτων τοῖς δικαζομένοις, ἀλλ᾽ ἐφ᾽
ἑτέρων λέγεσθαι. [80] ᾧ δὴ καὶ μάλιστα ἔπεισεν, εἶναι
δοκοῦντι δικαίῳ· καὶ Τουδιτανὸς αὐτοῖς ὑπατεύων
ἐδόθη δικάζειν.

Unplaced Fragments (F 32–35)

F 32 Isid. *Orig.* 2.21.4

climax est gradatio, cum ab eo, quo sensus superior termi-
natur, inferior incipit, ac dehinc quasi per gradus dicendi
ordo servatur, ut est illud Africani: "ex innocentia nascitur
dignitas, ex dignitate honor, ex honore imperium, ex imperio libertas." hanc figuram nonnulli catenam appellant,
propter quod aliud in alio quasi nectitur nomine, atque ita
res plures in geminatione verborum trahuntur.

F 33 Isid. *Orig.* 2.21.4

fit autem hoc schema non solum in singulis verbis, sed
etiam in contexione verborum, ut apud Gracchum . . . sic
et apud Scipionem: "vi atque ingratis coactus cum illo

zealous support for the wars, he had scruples about disregarding their request. And when he came into the Senate, he did not openly criticize Gracchus' [Ti. Sempronius Gracchus (34)] law because of the People, but he pointed out its difficulties and urged that these cases should not be decided by those dividing the land, because they did not possess the confidence of the litigants, but should be assigned to others. [80] Thus he completely persuaded them of this, since it seemed just; and Tuditanus [C. Sempronius Tuditanus, cos. 129 BC], their consul, was appointed to give judgment.

Unplaced Fragments (F 32–35)

F 32 Isidore, *Origins*

A climax is a gradation, when with that by which the preceding phrase ends, the subsequent one begins, and then, as if through steps, the order of speaking is maintained, like that phrase of Africanus: "from innocence worthiness is produced, from worthiness esteem, from esteem command, from command liberty." Some call this figure a chain, for the reason that one noun is linked, as it were, with another, and thus many items are brought together in a doubling of words.

F 33 Isidore, *Origins*

And this figure [cf. F 32] does not occur only with individual words, but also with a sequence of words, as in Gracchus [C. Sempronius Gracchus (**48**), F 43] . . . So also in Scipio: "Compelled by force and ungrateful men, I ar-

sponsionem feci, facta sponsione ad iudicem adduxi, adductum primo coetu damnavi, damnatum ex voluntate dimisi."

F 34 Fest., p. 334.28–30 L.

REDARGUISSE per e | litteram Scipio Africanus Pauli filius dicitur enuntilasse, ut idem etiam pertisum.

F 35 Quint. *Inst.* 1.7.25

quid dicam "vortices" et "vorsus" ceteraque ad eundem modum, quae primus[1] Scipio Africanus in e litteram secundam vertisse dicitur?

[1] primus *vel* primo *codd.*

22 + 23 L. ET SP. MUMMII

L. Mummius (cos. 146, censor 142 BC; RE Mummius 7a) celebrated triumphs after the conquests of Achaea and Corinth.

His brother Sp. Mummius (RE Mummius 13) may have reached the praetorship; his attested political activities are his service as a legate to his brother in 146 BC and his involvement in an embassy in 139 BC. He was a learned man; Cicero mentions humorous verse epistles he sent

ranged a judicial wager[1] with him; with the wager arranged, I led him to the judge; led there, I had him sentenced at the first meeting; him being sentenced, I
voluntarily let him go."

[1] A *sponsio praeiudicialis*; cf. *OLD* s.v. *sponsio* 2 "(leg.) A sort
of wager whereby an intending litigant offered to pay a certain
sum of money in the event of his assertion being proved false in
the subsequent hearing of the case."

F 34 Festus

redarguisse ["to have refuted"], Scipio Africanus, Paulus'
son, is said to have pronounced it with the letter *e*, as the
same man also did with *pertisum* ["disgusted"; cf. Cic.
Orat. 159].

F 35 Quintilian, *The Orator's Education*

What shall I say about *vortices* ["whirls"] and *vorsus*
["turned"] and other instances of the same kind, with respect to which Scipio Africanus is said to have been the
first to turn the second letter into *e*?

22 + 23 L. ET SP. MUMMII

*back from Corinth (Cic. Att. 13.6.4) as well as his familiar-
ity with Stoic philosophy (T 1). Sp. Mummius is a partic-
ipant in Cicero's dialogue De re publica (Cic. Rep. 1.18,
3.46–48, 5.11).*

*Cicero attests that speeches of both brothers were extant
in his time; both of them are placed among the orators of
moderate ability, while Sp. Mummius is regarded as more
concise due to his Stoic training (T 1).*

T 1 Cic. *Brut.* 94

[CICERO:] fuerunt etiam in oratorum numero mediocrium L. et Sp. Mummii fratres, quorum exstant amborum orationes; simplex quidem Lucius et antiquus, Spurius autem nihilo ille quidem ornatior, sed tamen astrictior; fuit enim doctus ex disciplina Stoicorum.

24 SP. (POSTUMIUS) ALBINUS

T 1 Cic. *Brut.* 94

[CICERO:] multae sunt Sp. Albini orationes.

24A AP. CLAUDIUS PULCHER

Ap. Claudius Pulcher (cos. 143, censor 136 BC; RE Claudius 295) was a supporter of his son-in-law Ti. Sempronius Gracchus (34) and served on his agrarian commission (Plut. Ti. Gracch. 4, 9.1, 13.1).

T 1 Cic. *Brut.* 108

[CICERO:] Appi Claudi volubilis, sed paulo fervidior oratio.

T 1 Cicero, *Brutus*

[CICERO:] In the ranks of orators of moderate ability there were also the brothers L. and Sp. Mummius, from both of whom orations are extant; Lucius, certainly simple and archaic; and Spurius, in no way, in fact, more elaborate, yet more concise; for he had training from the school of the Stoics.

24 SP. (POSTUMIUS) ALBINUS

The existence of many orations by Sp. Albinus is recorded in Cicero (T 1). The orator is presumably Sp. Postumius Albinus Magnus (cos. 148 BC; RE Postumius 47).

T 1 Cicero, *Brutus*

[CICERO:] The orations of Sp. Albinus are numerous.

24A AP. CLAUDIUS PULCHER

In Cicero, Ap. Claudius Pulcher is described as a fluent and rather fervid speaker (T 1).

T 1 Cicero, *Brutus*

[CICERO:] Appius Claudius' manner of speaking was fluent, but a little too fervid.

On Public Land in the Senate (F 2)

F 2 Cic. *De or.* 2.284

[Caesar Strabo:] sed ex his omnibus nihil magis ridetur quam quod est praeter expectationem; cuius innumerabilia sunt exempla ut Appi maioris illius,[1] qui in senatu, cum ageretur de agris publicis et de lege Thoria et peteretur Lucullus[2] ab iis, qui a pecore eius depasci agros publicos dicerent, "non est" inquit "Luculli pecus illud; erratis"— defendere Lucullum videbatur—; "ego liberum puto esse; qua lubet, pascitur."

[1] illud *Badian*   [2] Lucullus *codd. plur.*: Lucilius *cod. unus*

25 M. AEMILIUS LEPIDUS PORCINA

M. Aemilius Lepidus Porcina (cos. 137 BC; RE Aemilius 83), after his consulship, fought in Hispania, where he suffered a severe defeat, as a result of which he lost his command (Liv. Epit. 56; App. Hisp. 80–83; Oros. 5.5.13) (TLRR 12). In 125 BC he was punished by the censors for extravagance (Vell. Pat. 2.10.1; Val. Max. 8.1.damn.7).

In Cicero, Porcina is described as a great orator and writer, notable for his style, as the first to use periodic

On Public Land in the Senate (F 2)

Ap. Claudius Pulcher is most likely the Appius who made
a comment in a discussion on the use and distribution of
public land.

F 2 Cicero, *On the Orator*

[CAESAR STRABO:] But out of all these [types of witty
remarks] nothing causes more amusement than what goes
against expectation; of this there are countless instances,
for example, the remark of that Appius the Elder, who, in
the Senate, when there was a debate about public lands
and the *Lex Thoria* [proposed by Sp. Thorius (**53A**)], and
Lucullus [or Lucilius?] was being attacked by those who
asserted that public lands were grazed down by his herd,
said "That herd is not that of Lucullus; you are making a
mistake"—he seemed to be defending Lucullus—; "I believe that it does not have an owner; it grazes where it
pleases."

25 M. AEMILIUS LEPIDUS PORCINA

structure, as extant speeches attest (T 1), and as an ex-
ample of archaic eloquence (T 2); elsewhere, it is men-
tioned that he, like other orators, did not know very much
about the law and the institutions of the ancestors (T 4).
In the Rhetorica ad Herennium *Porcina is listed as one of*
the writers from whom examples for students could be
drawn (T 5).

T 1 Cic. *Brut.* 95–96

[CICERO:] at vero M. Aemilius Lepidus, qui est Porcina dictus, isdem temporibus fere quibus Galba, sed paulo minor natu et summus orator est habitus et fuit, ut apparet ex orationibus, scriptor sane bonus. [96] hoc in oratore Latino primum mihi videtur et levitas apparuisse illa Graecorum et verborum comprensio et iam artifex, ut ita dicam, stilus.

T 2 Cic. *Brut.* 295

[ATTICUS:] probas Lepidi orationes. paulum hic tibi adsentior, modo ita laudes ut antiquas . . .

T 3 Cic. *Brut.* 333

= **19** T 4.

T 4 Cic. *De or.* 1.40

= **19** T 5.

T 5 *Rhet. Her.* 4.7

. . . nec mirum, cum ipse praeceptor artis omnia penes unum reperire non potuerit. allatis igitur exemplis a Catone, a Graccis, a Laelio, a Scipione, Galba Porcina,

T 1 Cicero, *Brutus*

[CICERO:] But, to be sure, M. Aemilius Lepidus, who was called Porcina, at about the same time as Galba [Ser. Sulpicius Galba (**19**)], though a little younger, was regarded as an outstanding orator, and, as appears from his speeches, was certainly a good writer. [96] In this Latin orator appears, I think, for the first time that smoothness and periodic sentence form characteristic of the Greeks, and, already, so to speak, the artistic pen.

T 2 Cicero, *Brutus*

[ATTICUS:] You approve of Lepidus' speeches. Here I give you some assent as long as you praise them as specimens of archaic eloquence . . .

T 3 Cicero, *Brutus*

= **19** T 4.

T 4 Cicero, *On the Orator*

= **19** T 5.

T 5 *Rhetorica ad Herennium*

. . . nor is it surprising, since the teacher of the art himself has been unable to find all the qualities in one author. Thus, when examples have been drawn from Cato [M. Porcius Cato (**8**)], from the Gracchi [Ti. Sempronius Gracchus (**34**) + C. Sempronius Gracchus (**48**)], from Laelius [C. Laelius Sapiens (**20**)], from Scipio [P. Cornelius Scipio Aemilianus Africanus minor (**21**)], Galba [Ser. Sulpicius Galba (**19**)], Porcina, Crassus [L. Licinius Crassus (**66**)],

Crasso, Antonio, ceteris, item sumptis aliis a poetis et historiarum scriptoribus necesse erit eum, qui discet, putare ab omnibus omnia, ab uno pauca vix potuisse sumi.

Against Lex Aemilia *(F 6)*

F 6 Prisc., *GL* II, p. 474.20–22

Aemilius Porcina orator in oratione, uti lex Aemilia abrogetur: "tempore adstiturum atque petiturum me esse."

Unplaced Fragment (F 7)

F 7 *De dub. nom.*, *GL* V, p. 590.3

situs loci generis masculini, ut Porcina: "ille[1] situs felix."

> [1] ille *Meyer*: illi *vel* illis *codd.*

26 L. FURIUS PHILUS

L. Furius Philus (cos. 136 BC; RE Furius 78) was known for his learning, authority, and moderation (T 2; Cic. Arch. 16; Mur. 66; Leg. agr. 2.64); he is one of the interlocutors in Cicero's De re publica. *In Cicero's works it is noted that*

Antonius [M. Antonius (**65**)], and others, and equally further ones have been taken from the poets and the writers
of history, the learner will necessarily believe that the to-
tality could have been taken only from them all and barely
a few examples from only one.

Against Lex Aemilia *(F 6)*

It is uncertain against which Lex Aemilia *Porcina's attested speech is directed: perhaps the* Leges Aemiliae *of
115 BC on luxury or voting rights of freedmen* (LPPR,
pp. 320–21).

F 6 Priscian

Aemilius Porcina, the orator, in the speech that the *Lex
Aemilia* should be repealed: "that betimes I will defend
and sue."

Unplaced Fragment *(F 7)*

F 7 Anonymous grammarian

situs ["site"], of a place, of masculine gender, as Porcina:
"that fortunate site."

26 L. FURIUS PHILUS

*Philus was regarded as a speaker of excellent and erudite
Latinity (T 1).*

   *As consul, Furius will have delivered public speeches
(cf.* **30** F 2).

T 1 Cic. *Brut.* 108

[CICERO:] . . . isdemque temporibus L. Furius Philus perbene Latine loqui putabatur litteratiusque quam ceteri . . .

T 2 Cic. *De or.* 2.154

= **20** T 6.

27 + 28 L. ET C. AURELII ORESTAE

Lucius Aurelius Orestes (cos. 126 BC; RE Aurelius 180) fought against the Sardinians as consul and celebrated a triumph over them in 122 BC (Liv. Epit. 60; Plut. C. Gracch. 22(1).4; Vir. ill. 72.3). Nothing is known about

T 1 Cic. *Brut.* 94

[CICERO:] sunt etiam L. et C. Aureliorum Orestarum, quos aliquo video in numero oratorum fuisse.

29 L. SCRIBONIUS LIBO

T 1 Cic. *Brut.* 90

[CICERO:] atque etiam ipsum Libonem non infantem video fuisse, ut ex orationibus eius intellegi potest.

T 1 Cicero, *Brutus*

[CICERO:] . . . and in the same period L. Furius Philus was considered to speak Latin very well and in a more erudite manner than others . . .

T 2 Cicero, *On the Orator*

= **20** T 6.

27 + 28 L. ET C. AURELII ORESTAE

Caius Aurelius Orestes (RE Aurelius 178), presumably a brother of the former. Cicero records the existence of orations by both (T 1).

T 1 Cicero, *Brutus*

[CICERO:] There are also [orations] of L. and C. Aurelius Orestes, who, I find, had some place among the orators.

29 L. SCRIBONIUS LIBO

L. Scribonius Libo (tr. pl. 149 BC; RE Scribonius 18) is described in Cicero as a not unskilled speaker, and there is a reference to extant speeches (T 1).

T 1 Cicero, *Brutus*

[CICERO:] And Libo himself as well was not, I note, an unskilled speaker, as may be gathered from his speeches.

Against Ser. Sulpicius Galba (F 2–4)

When Tribune of the People in 149 BC, Scribonius put forward a proposal, directed against Ser. Sulpicius Galba (**19**), that the Lusitanians, who had been sold into Gaul as a result of Galba's activities, should be restored to liberty. *M. Porcius Cato* (**8** ORF[4] F 196–99) *as well as L. Cornelius*

F 2 Cic. *Brut.* 89–90

= **19** F 13.

F 3 Liv. *Epit.* 49.17–20

= **19** F 12.

F 4 Val. Max. 8.1.abs.2

= **19** F 14.

30 Q. POMPEIUS

Q. Pompeius (cos. 141, censor 131 BC; RE Pompeius 12) was a homo novus *(Cic. Font. 23; Mur. 16) and formed, with Q. Caecilius Metellus Macedonicus (**18**), the first plebeian pair of censors (**18** F 4).*

T 1 Cic. *Brut.* 96

[Cicero:] Q. enim Pompeius non contemptus orator temporibus illis fuit, qui summos honores homo per se cognitus sine ulla commendatione maiorum est adeptus.

Against Ser. Sulpicius Galba (F 2–4)

*Cethegus argued in favor of the bill, but Ser. Sulpicius Galba (**19** F 12–14), supported by Q. Fulvius Nobilior (**19A** F 2), made an emotional plea and managed to get himself acquitted (TLRR 1; CCMR, App. A: 173).*

F 2 Cicero, *Brutus*

= **19** F 13.

F 3 Livy, *Epitome*

= **19** F 12.

F 4 Valerius Maximus, *Memorable Doings and Sayings*

= **19** F 14.

30 Q. POMPEIUS

In Cicero, Q. Pompeius is acknowledged as not a bad orator in his time, who gained recognition on his own merits (T 1).

T 1 Cicero, *Brutus*

[CICERO:] For Q. Pompeius was not a contemptible orator in those times, a man who, having gained recognition on his own merits, obtained the highest honors, without any recommendation of his ancestors.

In His Defense Concerning the Numantians
(F 2–4)

In his consular year and the subsequent one, Q. Pompeius
fought in Hispania. Having largely been unsuccessful, he
then arranged for a treaty with the Numantians without
authorization from the Senate. When the matter was in-

F 2 Cic. *Rep.* 3.28

[PHILUS:] consul ego quaesivi, cum vos mihi essetis in
consilio, de Numantino foedere. quis ignorabat Quintum
Pompeium fecisse foedus, eadem in causa esse Manci-
num? alter, vir optimus, etiam suasit rogationem, me ex
senatus consulto ferente, alter acerrime se defendit. si
pudor quaeritur, si probitas, si fides, Mancinus haec attu-
lit; si ratio, consilium, prudentia, Pompeius antistat.

F 3 Cic. *Off.* 3.109

quod idem multis annis post C. Mancinus, qui, ut Numan-
tinis, quibuscum sine senatus auctoritate foedus fecerat,
dederetur, rogationem suasit eam quam L. Furius Sex.
Atilius ex senatus consulto ferebant; qua accepta est hosti-

In His Defense Concerning the Numantians
(F 2–4)

vestigated, Q. Pompeius defended himself, and the Senate
ultimately decided to sanction his questionable behavior
and to continue the war (Cic. Rep. 3.28; Fin. 2.54; Vell.
Pat. 2.1.4–5).

F 2 Cicero, *On the Republic*

[PHILUS:] As consul [136 BC], when you [the interlocutors] were in my council, I consulted on the issue regarding the Numantian treaty. Who was not aware that Quintus Pompeius had made a treaty and that Mancinus [C. Hostilius Mancinus, cos. 137 BC] was in the same situation? The latter, an excellent man, even favored the bill that I proposed on the basis of a Senate decree; the former defended himself with great energy. If modesty, if probity, if honor is sought, Mancinus has brought these with him; if reason, wisdom, prudence [is sought], Pompeius is superior.

F 3 Cicero, *On Duties*

Many years later the same thing [as by Sp. Postumius Albinus, cos. II 321 BC] was done by C. Mancinus [C. Hostilius Mancinus, cos. 137 BC]: he supported that bill that L. Furius and Sex. Atilius [L. Furius Philus (**26**) and Sex. Atilius Serranus, cos. 136 BC] were putting forward on the basis of a Senate decree, namely that he should be delivered up to the Numantians, with whom he had made a treaty without the Senate's authorization; when the bill had been passed, he was delivered up to the enemy. He

bus deditus. honestius hic quam Q. Pompeius, quo, cum
in eadem causa esset, deprecante accepta lex non est. hic
ea quae videbatur utilitas plus valuit quam honestas, apud
superiores utilitatis species falsa ab honestatis auctoritate
superata est.

F 4 App. *Hisp.* 79.342–344

. . . ὁ δ᾽, ἀπηλλαγμένος μὲν τοῦ περὶ τοῦ πολέμου
δέους τῷ παρεῖναι τὸν διάδοχον, τὰς δὲ συνθήκας εἰ-
δὼς αἰσχράς τε καὶ ἄνευ Ῥωμαίων γενομένας, ἠρ-
νεῖτο μὴ συνθέσθαι τοῖς Νομαντίνοις. [343] καὶ οἱ μὲν
αὐτὸν ἤλεγχον ἐπὶ μάρτυσι τοῖς τότε παρατυχοῦσιν
ἀπό τε βουλῆς καὶ ἱππάρχοις καὶ χιλιάρχοις αὐτοῦ
Πομπηίου, ὁ δὲ Ποπίλιος αὐτοὺς ἐς Ῥώμην ἔπεμπε
δικασομένους τῷ Πομπηίῳ. [344] κρίσεως δ᾽ ἐν τῇ
βουλῇ γενομένης, Νομαντῖνοι μὲν καὶ Πομπήιος ἐς
ἀντιλογίαν ἦλθον, τῇ βουλῇ δ᾽ ἔδοξε πολεμεῖν Νομαντίνοις.

In His Defense Concerning Extortion (F 4A–B)

F 4A Cic. *Font.* 23

an vero vos id in testimoniis hominum barbarorum dubi-

acted more honorably than Q. Pompeius: he, when he was in the same situation, made entreaties, and the law was not passed. In this latter case what seemed to be expediency prevailed over moral rectitude; in the former cases, the false semblance of expediency was overcome by the weight of moral rectitude.

F 4 Appian, *Spanish Wars*

. . . and he [Pompeius], freed from the apprehension concerning the war by the presence of his successor [M. Popillius Laenas, cos. 139 BC] and knowing that the peace was disgraceful and made without the Romans, began to deny that he had come to any understanding with the Numantians. [343] And they refuted him by witnesses who had been present at the time, members of the Senate, prefects of horse, and military tribunes of Pompeius himself. Popillius sent them to Rome to carry on the controversy with Pompeius there. [344] When the case had been raised in the Senate, the Numantians and Pompeius entered into an argument; the Senate decided to continue the war with the Numantians.

In His Defense Concerning Extortion (F 4A–B)

After his proconsulship Q. Pompeius was accused of extortion; despite testimonies of eminent men against him, he was acquitted. It is likely that he spoke in his own defense (TLRR 8).

F 4A Cicero, *Pro Fonteio*

Or will you, as regards the evidence of barbarians, show hesitation in a matter [i.e., in rejecting the evidence], in

tabitis quod persaepe et nostra et patrum memoria sapientissimi iudices de clarissimis nostrae civitatis viris dubitandum non putaverunt? qui Cn. et Q. Caepionibus, L. et Q. Metellis testibus in Q. Pompeium, hominem novum, non crediderunt, quorum virtuti, generi, rebus gestis fidem et auctoritatem in testimonio cupiditatis atque inimicitiarum suspicio derogavit.

F 4B Val. Max. 8.5.1

Cn. et Q. Serviliis Caepionibus, iisdem parentibus natis et per omnes honorum gradus ad summam amplitudinem provectis, item fratribus Metellis Quinto et Lucio consularibus et censoriis, altero etiam triumphali, in Q. Pompeium A. f. repetundarum reum acerrime dicentibus testimonium non abrogata fides absoluto Pompeio, sed ne potentia inimicum oppressisse viderentur occursum est.

Against a Law of Ti. Sempronius Gracchus (F 5–7)

F 5 Plut. *Ti. Gracch.* 14.3
= **18** F 3.

which, within the recollection of both ourselves and our fathers, the wisest judges, with respect to the most eminent men of our community, very frequently thought that there should be no hesitation? They did not believe the witnesses Cn. and Q. Caepio [Cn. Servilius Caepio, cos. 141; Q. Servilius Caepio, cos. 140 BC] and L. and Q. Metellus [L. Caecilius Metellus Calvus, cos. 142 BC; Q. Caecilius Metellus Macedonicus (**18**)] against Q. Pompeius, a new man: a suspicion of ambition and enmity removed credibility and authority in giving evidence from their virtue, noble descent and great deeds.

F 4B Valerius Maximus, *Memorable Doings and Sayings*

Cn. and Q. Servilius Caepio, born of the same parents and advanced to the highest eminence through all stages of official rank, likewise the brothers Metelli, Quintus and Lucius, ex-consuls and ex-censors, one of them also a triumphator, spoke very strongly in evidence against Q. Pompeius, Aulus' son, accused of extortion. Their evidence was not denied belief when Pompeius was acquitted, but measures were taken so that they did not seem to have crushed an enemy by their influence.

Against a Law of Ti. Sempronius Gracchus (F 5–7)

*Q. Pompeius' opposition to a law put forward by Ti. Sempronius Gracchus (**34**) while in office and concerning the assets of King Attalus must date to the year of Gracchus' Tribunate and Attalus' death (133 BC).*

F 5 Plutarch, *Life of Tiberius Gracchus*
= **18** F 3.

F 6 Oros. *Hist*. 5.8.4

Gracchus gratiam populi pretio adpetens legem tulit uti pecunia quae fuisset Attali populo distribueretur. obsistente Nasica etiam Pompeius spopondit se Gracchum, cum primum magistratu abisset, accusaturum.

F 7 App. *B Civ*. 1.13.57

. . . οἱ δ᾽ ἡσσημένοι δυσφοροῦντες ἔτι παρέμενον καὶ ἐλογοποίουν οὐ χαιρήσειν Γράκχον, αὐτίκα ὅτε γένοιτο ἰδιώτης, ἀρχήν τε ὑβρίσαντα ἱερὰν καὶ ἄσυλον καὶ στάσεως τοσήνδε ἀφορμὴν ἐς τὴν Ἰταλίαν ἐμβαλόντα.

31 P. LICINIUS CRASSUS DIVES MUCIANUS

P. Licinius Crassus Dives Mucianus (cos. 131 BC; RE Licinius 72) had a successful public career (a biological son of P. Mucius Scaevola and later adopted). In 133 BC he supported the Tribune of the People Ti. Sempronius Gracchus (34) and, after the latter's death, was a member of the

F 6 Orosius, *Histories*

Gracchus [Ti. Sempronius Gracchus (**34**)], keen to win the favor of the People by a payment, put forward a law, that the money that had belonged to Attalus [king of Pergamum, d. 133 BC] was to be distributed among the People [see **17** F 3]. When Nasica [P. Cornelius Scipio Nasica Serapio (**38**)] opposed it, Pompeius too pledged that he would prosecute Gracchus as soon as he had resigned from office.

F 7 Appian, *Civil Wars*

. . . the defeated ones [citizens unhappy with Gracchus' agrarian law] still remained [in Rome], feeling aggrieved, and claimed that, as soon as Gracchus should become a private citizen, he would be sorry that he had insulted the sacred and inviolable office and had brought so great a source of strife into Italy.[1]

[1] The passage, placed here by Malcovati, shows dissatisfaction with Ti. Sempronius Gracchus' actions and implies plans to oppose him once this has become possible after he has stood down from office (as in Q. Pompeius' announcement). There is no mention of Q. Pompeius, however, and the dissatisfaction concerns the agrarian law rather than the funds from King Attalus.

31 P. LICINIUS CRASSUS DIVES MUCIANUS

*agrarian commission with C. Sempronius Gracchus (**48**) and Ap. Claudius Pulcher (**24A**) and later M. Fulvius Flaccus (**40**) to implement Tiberius' law (Plut. Ti. Gracch. 21.1–2).*

Crassus was not only famous for his wealth but also respected as a great orator and jurist (T 1–3; Cic. Brut. *127;* De or. *1.216, 1.239–40).*

T 1 Cic. *Brut.* 98

[CICERO:] P. Crassum valde probatum oratorem isdem fere temporibus accepimus, qui et ingenio valuit et studio et habuit quasdam etiam domesticas disciplinas. nam et cum summo illo oratore Ser. Galba, cuius Gaio filio filiam suam collocaverat, adfinitate sese devinxerat et cum esset P. Muci filius fratremque haberet P. Scaevolam, domi ius civile cognoverat. in eo industriam constat summam fuisse maximamque gratiam, cum et consuleretur plurimum et diceret.

T 2 Cic. *De or.* 1.170

[CRASSUS:] equidem propinquum nostrum P. Crassum illum Divitem et multis aliis rebus elegantem hominem et ornatum et praecipue in hoc ferendum[1] et laudandum puto, quod, cum P. Scaevola frater esset, solitus est ei persaepe dicere, neque illum in iure civili satis illi arti facere posse, nisi dicendi copiam adsumpsisset quod quidem

---

[1] ferendum *codd., Ernesti, Friedrich:* efferendum *codd. rec., sec. manus unius cod., ed. Veneta, Pearce, Wilkins, Courbaud*

One of his noteworthy acts was that, as consul and pontifex maximus, *he issued a penalty to his colleague L. Valerius Flaccus, the* flamen Martialis *(Cic.* Phil. *11.18) (TLRR 20).*

T 1 Cicero, *Brutus*

[CICERO:] P. Crassus was, we are told, a highly esteemed orator at about the same time: he was powerful through both talent and study, and he also possessed training in some areas through his family. For, on the one hand, he had established family ties with that famous orator Ser. Galba [Ser. Sulpicius Galba (**19**)], to whose son Gaius [C. Sulpicus Galba (**53**)] he had given his daughter in marriage, and on the other, as he was the son of P. Mucius [P. Mucius Scaevola, cos. 175 BC] and had P. Scaevola [P. Mucius Scaevola, cos. 133 BC] as his brother, he had learned civil law at home. It is evident that there was remarkable industry in him and extremely great popularity, as he both was consulted frequently for his legal advice and was active as a pleader.

T 2 Cicero, *On the Orator*

[CRASSUS:] Assuredly, I believe that our relative P. Crassus, that man called Dives, was in many other ways a man of taste and accomplishment and is particularly to be extolled and eulogized for this, that, although P. Scaevola was his brother, he used to tell him very often that neither, as to civil law, could he do justice to that art if he had not acquired a copious diction (which this son of his, who was

hic, qui mecum consul fuit, filius eius est consecutus, neque se ante causas amicorum tractare atque agere coepisse quam ius civile didicisset.

T 3 Gell. *NA* 1.13.9–10

. . . exemplum quoque P. Crassi Muciani, clari atque incluti viri . . . . [10] is Crassus a Sempronio Asellione et plerisque aliis historiae Romanae scriptoribus traditur habuisse quinque rerum bonarum maxima et praecipua: quod esset ditissimus, quod nobilissimus, quod eloquentissimus, quod iurisconsultissimus, quod pontifex maximus.

32 C. FANNIUS

C. Fannius (cos. 122 BC; RE Fannius 7) was supported by C. Sempronius Gracchus (48) in obtaining the consulship, but then turned against the latter's citizenship policy (Plut. C. Gracch. 29[8].1–3).

It is uncertain whether this C. Fannius is the same Fannius as the historian (FRHist 12)—probably not (for dis-

On the Italian Allies and Those Possessing the ius Latii *Against C. Sempronius Gracchus (F 1–5)*

F 1 Cic. *Brut.* 99–100

[CICERO:] ". . . horum aetatibus adiuncti duo C. Fannii C. et M.[1] filii fuerunt; quorum Gai filius, qui consul cum

---

[1] C. et M. *cod. corr.*: C. M. *cett.*

consul with me [Q. Mucius Scaevola, cos. 95 BC], certainly achieved), nor had he himself begun to handle and conduct the cases of friends before he had learned civil law.

T 3 Gellius, *Attic Nights*

. . . also the example of P. Crassus Mucianus, a distinguished and eminent man . . . [10] That Crassus is said by Sempronius Asellio [*FRHist* 20 F 13] and many other writers of Roman history to have had the five greatest and foremost of blessings: that he was very rich, was of the highest birth, was exceedingly eloquent, was most learned in the law, and was chief pontiff.

32 C. FANNIUS

cussion see FRHist *1:244–46). There is already confusion about the identity of the Fannii in Cicero (F 1; Cic. Att. 12.5b, 16.13a.2; Amic. 3).*

In Cicero, Fannius is credited with a single political speech (assigned to him), while it is noted that Fannius was an active pleader (F 1).

On the Italian Allies and Those Possessing the
ius Latii *Against C. Sempronius Gracchus (F 1–5)*

F 1 Cicero, *Brutus*

[CICERO:] ". . . Linked to the time of these [Q. Pompeius (**30**), P. Licinius Crassus Dives Mucianus (**31**) and others] were the two C. Fannii, Gaius' and Marcus' sons. Of these Gaius' son, who was consul with Domitius [122 BC], has

Domitio fuit, unam orationem de sociis et nomine Latino contra <C.>[2] Gracchum reliquit sane et bonam et nobilem." tum ATTICUS: "quid ergo? estne ista Fanni? nam varia opinio pueris nobis erat. alii a C. Persio litterato homine scriptam esse aiebant, illo quem significat valde doctum esse Lucilius; alii multos nobilis, quod quisque potuisset, in illam orationem contulisse." [100] tum ego [CICERO]: "audivi equidem ista," inquam, "de maioribus natu, sed nunquam sum adductus ut crederem; eamque suspicionem propter hanc causam credo fuisse, quod Fannius in mediocribus oratoribus habitus esset, oratio autem vel optima esset illo quidem tempore orationum omnium. sed nec eiusmodi est ut a pluribus confusa videatur—unus enim sonus est totius orationis et idem stilus—nec de Persio reticuisset Gracchus, cum ei[3] Fannius de Menelao Maratheno et de ceteris obiecisset; praesertim cum Fannius numquam sit habitus elinguis. nam et causas defensitavit et tribunatus eius arbitrio et auctoritate P. Africani gestus non obscurus fuit. . . ."

    [2] add. *Jahn*   [3] ei *Gruter*: et *codd.*

F 2 Cic. *De or.* 3.183

[CRASSUS:] est autem paean hic posterior non syllabarum numero sed aurium mensura, quod est acrius iudicium et certius, par fere cretico, qui est ex longa et brevi et longa: ut [Enn. *Trag.* 23.4 *TrRF / FRL*]: "quid petam praesidi aut

left a single oration concerning the allies and those possessing the *ius Latii* against <C.> Gracchus [C. Sempronius Gracchus (**48**)], which is indeed both good and well known." Here ATTICUS [said]: "What's that? Is that [speech] really by Fannius? For there were various opinions when we were boys. Some said that it was written by C. Persius [**33**], an educated man, the one whom Lucilius identifies as a man of vast learning; others that many noblemen contributed what each one could to that speech." [100] Then I [CICERO] said: "I have certainly heard that from our elders, but I never could be brought to believe it, and I assume that this suspicion existed for the reason that Fannius was regarded to be among the mediocre orators, yet the oration was certainly the best of all orations, at least in that time. But neither is it of such character that it seems to have been mixed together by many—for there is a single tone and the same style in the entire oration—nor would Gracchus have been silent about Persius, when Fannius reproached him concerning Menelaus of Marathus [Greek rhetorician] and others, especially since Fannius was never regarded as without a ready tongue. For he repeatedly defended cases in the courts, and his Tribunate [142 BC] too, conducted under the patronage and authority of P. Africanus [P. Cornelius Scipio Aemilianus Africanus minor (**21**)], was not undistinguished. . . ."

F 2 Cicero, *On the Orator*

[CRASSUS:] But this second [type of] paean [∪∪∪–] is almost the same, not in the number of syllables, but in the measurement of the ears, which is sharper and more reliable judgment, as the cretic [–∪–], which is made up of

exequar? quove nunc . . ." a quo numero exorsus est Fannius:[1] "sī, Quĭrītēs, mĭnās īllhǐūs . . ."

[1] Fannius *vel* Ennius *codd.*

F 3 Iulius Victor, *Ars* 6.4, *RLM*, p. 402.8–20

ab eventu in coniectura, quod Graeci ἀπὸ τῆς ἐκβάσεως dicunt: . . . et ut a Gaio Fannio adversus Gracchum dictum: "si Latinis civitatem dederitis, credo, existimatis vos ita, ut nunc constitistis,[1] in con{ten}tione[2] habituros locum aut ludis et festis diebus interfuturos. nonne illos omnia occupaturos putatis?" collegit enim non esse recipiendos in civitatem ex his, quae eventura sint. "prodere voluisse patriam arguor. quid ita? an ut eversa patria dignitatem a maioribus acceptam, fortunas optime constitutas amitterem, ut cui liceret beatissimo cum summa gloria vivere, idem hostium potestati subditus cum infamia degerem?"

[1] constitistis *Mommsen*: constitisse *cod.*: consuestis *Spengel*: constituitis (*vel* constituistis) *Dübner*   [2] con{ten}tione *Mai*: contentione *cod.*

long, short, long, for instance [Enn. *Trag.* 23.4 *TrRF* / *FRL*]:
"What protection could I seek or pursue? Or where
now . . ." With this rhythm Fannius started: "If, Romans,
the threats [acc.] of that person . . ."[1]

[1] This excerpt must come from a political speech; it is assigned
to the only one attested for Fannius and known to Cicero.

F 3 Iulius Victor

From the consequence in an inference, what the Greeks
call "from the outcome": . . . and as was said by Gaius
Fannius against Gracchus [C. Sempronius Gracchus
(**48**)]: "if you [i.e., the Romans] should give citizen rights
to the Latins, I believe, you suppose that you, in such a
way as you have assumed your place now, will have a place
in the public meeting or participate in games and festive
days. Don't you think that they [the Latins] will seize everything?" For he inferred that they [the Latins] should
not be received among the citizenry from what would happen. "I am condemned for having wished to betray the
country. What then? That, with the country ruined, I
should lose the status received from the ancestors, the
fortune set up extremely well, that I, for whom it was possible to live very happily with the greatest glory, should
spend my life in infamy, having been subjected to the
power of the enemy?"[1]

[1] The first excerpt is quoted as an extract from a speech by
Fannius. That the second example might be another fragment of
Fannius was suggested by Giomini (1978). But the sentence "For
. . . happen." sounds like a concluding comment on the passage
from Fannius' speech, and the next example seems to come from
the discussion of a different situation. Therefore, it is rather a
further example, for which the author is not mentioned.

F 4 Charis., *GL* I, p. 143.12–13 = p. 181.14–16 B.

senatuis ut fluctuis. "ita genetivum" inquit Plinius "decli-
nabant, ut G. Fannius cos. contra G. Gracchum: 'senatuis
consulta.'"

F 5 Prisc., *GL* II, p. 380.9

Gaius Fannius: "haec apiscuntur," ἐπιτυγχάνονται.

Unplaced Fragments (F 6–7)

*One of these passages (F 7) may come from a speech
against a Gracchus, but not necessarily from an oration by
Fannius. The first item (F 6) could have been taken from*

F 6 + 7 Iulius Victor, *Ars* 11, *RLM*, p. 413.2–11

paradigmaticon enthymema quamquam ad exemplum se
refert, hoc tamen differt ab exemplo, quod exemplum per
se positum probationem adiuvat, conversum autem in speciem argumenti formam accipit paradigmatis enthymema-
tici, ut sit exemplum: "non debetis largitionem permittere;
nam et Dionysius et Pisistratus cives largitione corrupe-
runt"; at vero, ut enthymema sit paradigmaticon, illo
modo corripitur et concluditur, ut: "si Phalaridi et Pisis-

F 4 Charisius

senatuis ["of the Senate"; unusual genitive], like *fluctuis* ["of a wave"]. "Thus they used to form the genitive," Pliny says, "like C. Fannius, the consul, against C. Gracchus: 'decrees of the Senate.'"

F 5 Priscian

Gaius Fannius: "these things are obtained,"[1] they are obtained [in Greek, explaining passive meaning of deponent].

[1] This fragment is also seen as a possible fragment of Fannius' *Annals* (*FRHist* 12 [F 7]).

Unplaced Fragments (F 6–7)

any speech or construed by the transmitting author for argumentative purposes; this latter option might also apply to the second item (F 7).

F 6 + 7 Iulius Victor

The *enthymema paradigmaticon* [syllogism providing a comparison], although it is linked to the example, still differs from the example in that the example, put on its own, supports the proof, but, turned into the shape of an argument, takes on the form of the *enthymema paradigmaticon*, so that this is an example: "You must not allow bribery; for both Dionysius and Pisistratus [Greek tyrants] corrupted the citizens by bribery": but indeed, so as to be an *enthymema paradigmaticon*, it is shortened and compressed in that way, like: "If for Phalaris and Pisistratus

trato et ceteris omnibus una res maxime, largitio, domina-
tionem conparavit, quid est, quod non idem Gracchum
affectare credatis, quem eadem quae illos facere videa-
tis?"

33 C. PERSIUS

C. Persius (RE *Persius 4*) *was a learned man in the time
of the satirist Lucilius* (*T 1–2; Cic.* Fin. *1.7; Plin.* HN praef.
7): *Lucilius said that he did not want his work to be read
by him, as Persius was too learned* (*Lucil. 592–96 Marx*).

T 1 Cic. *De or.* 2.25

[CRASSUS:] nam ut C. Lucilius homo doctus et perurbanus
dicere solebat ea quae scriberet neque se ab indoctissimis
neque a doctissimis legi velle, quod alteri nihil intelle-
gerent, alteri plus fortasse quam ipse—de quo etiam scripsit [Lucil. 593 Marx] "Persium non curo legere" (hic fuit
enim, ut noramus, omnium fere nostrorum hominum doc-
tissumus), "Laelium Decumum volo," quem cognovimus
virum bonum et non inlitteratum sed nihil ad Persium—
. . .

T 2 Cic. *Brut.* 99
= **32** F 1.

and all others [i.e., other tyrants] one thing in particular, bribery, procured absolute dominion, what reason is there that you don't believe that Gracchus is aiming for the same, since you see him doing the same things as those men?"

33 C. PERSIUS

Atticus and Cicero knew of some who used to attribute the one oration said to be left by C. Fannius (32 F 1–5) to C. Persius (T 2).

T 1 Cicero, *On the Orator*

[CRASSUS:] For just as C. Lucilius, a learned and highly accomplished man, used to say that he wished what he wrote to be read neither by the most ignorant nor by the most learned, since the former understood nothing and the latter possibly more than he himself—about this he also wrote [Lucil. 593 Marx]: "I do not desire Persius as a reader" (for he was, as we had learned, about the most erudite of all our fellow citizens), "I want Laelius Decumus," whom we have got to know as an excellent man and not without learning, but nothing compared to Persius—
. . .

T 2 Cicero, *Brutus*

= **32 F 1**.

34 TI. SEMPRONIUS GRACCHUS

Ti. Sempronius Gracchus (tr. pl. 133 BC; RE Sempronius 54) became Tribune of the People after a military career. As Tribune he tried to initiate a series of measures for the benefit of the People, in particular by an agrarian reform (Plut. Ti. Gracch. 8–13; App. B Civ. 1.9.35–13.57). His activities resulted in controversy, and Ti. Gracchus was killed at the end of his Tribunate (on his life see Plut. Ti. Gracch.; App. B Civ. 1.9.35–17.72; on the lives of the Gracchi, see Stockton 1979).

*After the early death of their father (**10**), the brothers Gracchi (**34** + **48**) had been carefully educated by their mother (T 2, 3, 8; Plut. Ti. Gracch. 1.7; Gracch. Comp. 1.1); they also studied with Greek teachers, including Diophanes of Mytilene (T 2). In Cicero it is acknowledged that Ti. Gracchus was a learned man and an outstanding orator in his precision of thought and style of speaking, with great potential cut short by an untimely death (T 2, 4, 5). Ti. Gracchus is said to have been an avid auditor of M. Ae-*

T 1 Cic. *Brut.* 96

[CICERO:] hunc studiose duo adulescentes ingeniosissimi et prope aequales C. Carbo et Ti. Gracchus audire soliti sunt . . .

T 2 Cic. *Brut.* 103–4 (cf. **35** T 2)

[CICERO:] utinam in Ti. Graccho Gaioque Carbone talis mens ad rem publicam bene gerendam fuisset, quale in-

34 TI. SEMPRONIUS GRACCHUS

milius Lepidus Porcina (**25**) (*T 1*). *Cicero's assessment of the political achievements of the Gracchi varies according to context; he frequently deplores that they did not use their intellectual and rhetorical faculties to the benefit of the Republic (T 2, 5). In the* Rhetorica ad Herennium *Ti. Gracchus is listed as one of the writers from whom examples for students could be drawn (Rhet. Her. 4.7:* **25** *T 5).*

Additonal speeches of Ti. Gracchus as Tribune of the People (beyond those attested below) are mentioned in ancient sources (see also **48** *F 68): on a treaty and arrangements with the Numantians (Vir. ill. 64.1–2); against his tribunician colleague M. Octavius (App. B Civ. 1.12.48–54; Plut. Ti. Gracch. 10.5–8); on the distribution of the inheritance of King Attalus (Plut. Ti. Gracch. 14; cf.* **17** *F 3;* **30** *F 6); on his own behalf when seeking reelection as Tribune (App. B Civ. 1.14.58–62; Plut. Ti. Gracch. 16.3).*

T 1 Cicero, *Brutus*

[CICERO:] Two young men of great talent and almost equal age, C. Carbo [C. Papirius Carbo (**35**)] and Ti. Gracchus, used to listen to him [M. Aemilius Lepidus Porcina (**25**)] eagerly . . .

T 2 Cicero, *Brutus* (cf. **35** T 2)

[CICERO:] Would that Ti. Gracchus and Gaius Carbo [C. Papirius Carbo (**35**)] had possessed such an attitude to running public affairs well as they possessed talent for

185

genium ad bene dicendum fuit: profecto nemo his viris
gloria praestitisset. sed eorum alter propter turbulentissi-
mum tribunatum, ad quem ex invidia foederis Numantini
bonis iratus accesserat, ab ipsa re publica est interfectus. . . . sed fuit uterque summus orator. [104] atque hoc
memoria patrum teste dicimus; nam et Carbonis et
Gracchi habemus orationes nondum satis splendidas verbis, sed acutas prudentiaeque plenissimas. fuit Gracchus
diligentia Corneliae matris a puero doctus et Graecis litteris eruditus. nam semper habuit exquisitos e Graecia
magistros, in eis iam adulescens Diophanem Mytilenaeum
Graeciae temporibus illis disertissimum. sed ei[1] breve
tempus ingeni augendi et declarandi fuit.

[1] ei *Lambinus*: et *codd.*

T 3 Cic. *Brut.* 211

[Cicero:] legimus epistulas Corneliae matris Gracchorum: apparet filios non tam in gremio educatos quam in
sermone matris.

T 4 Cic. *Brut.* 333

[Cicero:] . . . nam Gracchi in contionibus multo faciliore
et liberiore genere dicendi, quorum tamen ipsorum ad
aetatem laus eloquentiae perfecta nondum fuit . . .

186

speaking well: surely none would have surpassed these men in renown. But one of them [Ti. Gracchus], because of his very seditious Tribunate, to which he had come as a result of the resentment in relation to the treaty with the Numantians, full of anger at the nobility, was killed by the Republic itself. . . . But both were orators of the first rank. [104] And we say this with the recollection of our fathers as evidence; for we have orations of both Carbo and Gracchus not yet sufficiently brilliant in language, but acute and very full of sagacity. Gracchus, thanks to the careful attention of his mother Cornelia, had been trained from boyhood and thoroughly educated in Greek letters. For he always had carefully chosen teachers from Greece, including, when he was already a young man, Diophanes of Mytilene, the most eloquent speaker of Greece at that time. But he only had a brief period for developing and showing his talent.

T 3 Cicero, *Brutus*

[CICERO:] We have read the letters of Cornelia, the mother of the Gracchi: it is clear that her sons were raised not so much on their mother's lap as by her speech.

T 4 Cicero, *Brutus*

[CICERO:] . . . for the Gracchi, showing in their speeches to the People a much freer and more flexible style of speaking, though by their time the quality of eloquence had not yet been fully accomplished . . .

T 5 Cic. *De or.* 1.38

[SCAEVOLA:] . . . omnium mihi videor exceptis, Crasse, vobis duobus eloquentissimos audisse Ti. et C. Sempronios, quorum pater homo prudens et gravis haudquaquam eloquens, et saepe alias et maxime censor saluti rei publicae fuit. . . . at vero eius filii diserti et omnibus vel naturae vel doctrinae praesidiis ad dicendum parati cum civitatem vel paterno consilio vel avitis armis florentissimam accepissent, ista praeclara gubernatrice, ut ais, civitatum eloquentia rem publicam dissipaverunt.

T 6 Cic. *Har. resp.* 41

Ti. Gracchus convellit statum civitatis, qua gravitate vir, qua eloquentia, qua dignitate! nihil ut a patris avique Africani praestabili insignique virtute, praeterquam quod a senatu desciverat, deflexisset.

T 7 Diod. Sic. 34.5

ἐξ ἀμφοτέρων δὲ τῶν γονέων ἐπισημοτάτου γένους πεφυκώς, ἰδίᾳ πολὺ προεῖχε τῶν ἡλικιωτῶν συνέσει τε καὶ λόγου δεινότητι καὶ τὸ σύνολον πάσῃ παιδείᾳ, καὶ δυνάμενος παρρησίαν ἄγειν πρὸς τὴν ὑπεροχὴν τῶν ἀντιπραττόντων.

T 5 Cicero, *On the Orator*

[SCAEVOLA:] . . . of all men to whom I have listened except the two of you [M. Antonius (**65**) and L. Licinius Crassus (**66**)], Crassus, it seems to me that the most eloquent were Ti. and C. Sempronius, whose father [Ti. Sempronius Gracchus (**10**)], a sagacious and dignified man, but in no way eloquent, was often on other occasions and particularly when censor instrumental for the welfare of the Republic. . . . But his sons, accomplished speakers and equipped for speaking with all advantages of nature or training, after they had taken over a community flourishing exceedingly because of their father's counsels or their ancestors' military achievements, shattered the Republic by that outstanding guide of communities, as you call it, eloquence.

T 6 Cicero, *De Haruspicum Responsis*

Ti. Gracchus shattered the stability of the community, a man of what authority, what eloquence, what standing! So that he had not swerved at all from the eminent and remarkable qualities of his father [Ti. Sempronius Gracchus (**10**)] and his grandfather Africanus [P. Cornelius Scipio Africanus maior (**4**)], except for the fact that he had turned away from the Senate.

T 7 Diodorus Siculus, *Library of History*

Being descended from a distinguished family on both sides, in his own right he [Ti. Gracchus] towered above his contemporaries in sagacity, in skill as a speaker, and, in short, in every accomplishment; and he was able to maintain frankness of speech against the preeminence of his opponents.

189

T 8 Quint. *Inst.* 1.1.6

nec de patribus tantum loquor: nam Gracchorum eloquentiae multum contulisse accepimus Corneliam ma-
trem, cuius doctissimus sermo in posteros quoque est
epistulis traditus . . .

T 9 Quint. *Inst.* 2.5.21

duo autem genera maxime cavenda pueris puto: unum, ne
quis eos antiquitatis nimius admirator in Gracchorum
Catonisque et aliorum similium lectione durescere velit;
fient enim horridi atque ieiuni: nam neque vim eorum
adhuc intellectu consequentur et elocutione, quae tum
sine dubio erat optima, sed nostris temporibus aliena est,
contenti, quod est pessimum, similes sibi magnis viris vi-
debuntur.

T 10 Quint. *Inst.* 8.5.33

quo modo potest probare Ciceronem qui nihil putet ex
Catone Gracchisque mutandum? sed ante hos simplicior
adhuc ratio loquendi fuit.

T 11 Plut. *Ti. Gracch.* 2.2–3
= **48** T 7.

T 8 Quintilian, *The Orator's Education*

And I do not talk only of the fathers: for we have heard that the eloquence of the Gracchi received much support from their mother Cornelia, whose highly cultivated style is also transmitted to posterity by her letters . . .

T 9 Quintilian, *The Orator's Education*

But I believe that there are two types [of writing] one needs to guard against particularly in the interest of the boys: firstly, that no overzealous admirer of antiquity should wish them to become stiff by reading the Gracchi, Cato [M. Porcius Cato (**8**)], and other similar men; for they will only become uncouth and jejune: for, on the one hand, they will not yet be able to grasp these men's force with their understanding, and, on the other hand, content with the style that was doubtless excellent then, but is alien to our times, they will see themselves as similar to the great men, which is the worst thing.

T 10 Quintilian, *The Orator's Education*

How can someone approve of Cicero, if he thinks that nothing should be changed since Cato [M. Porcius Cato (**8**)] and the Gracchi? Yet before them, the pattern of speaking was even simpler.

T 11 Plutarch, *Life of Tiberius Gracchus*
= **48** T 7.

T 12 Plin. *HN* 13.83

Tiberi Gaique Gracchorum manus apud Pomponium Secundum vatem civemque clarissimum vidi annos fere post
ducentos . . .

On the Agrarian Law (F 13–15)

*When promoting his plans for agrarian reform during his
Tribunate, Ti. Gracchus seems to have delivered at least
two speeches (CCMR, App. A: 181), a more general one*

F 13 Plut. *Ti. Gracch.* 9.4–6

. . . ὁ γὰρ Τιβέριος πρὸς καλὴν ὑπόθεσιν καὶ δικαίαν
ἀγωνιζόμενος λόγῳ καὶ φαυλότερα κοσμῆσαι δυνα
μένῳ πράγματα, δεινὸς ἦν καὶ ἄμαχος, ὁπότε τοῦ δή
μου τῷ βήματι περικεχυμένου καταστὰς λέγοι περὶ
τῶν πενήτων, [5] ὡς τὰ μὲν θηρία τὰ τὴν Ἰταλίαν
νεμόμενα καὶ φωλεὸν ἔχει, καὶ κοιταῖόν ἐστιν αὐτῶν
ἑκάστῳ καὶ κατάδυσ{ε}ις,¹ τοῖς δ' ὑπὲρ τῆς Ἰταλίας
μαχομένοις καὶ ἀποθνήσκουσιν ἀέρος καὶ φωτός, ἄλ
λου δ' οὐδενὸς μέτεστιν, ἀλλ' ἄοικοι καὶ ἀνίδρυτοι
μετὰ τέκνων πλανῶνται καὶ γυναικῶν, οἱ δ' αὐτοκρά
τορες ψεύδονται τοὺς στρατιώτας ἐν ταῖς μάχαις
παρακαλοῦντες ὑπὲρ τάφων καὶ ἱερῶν ἀμύνεσθαι
τοὺς πολεμίους· [6] οὐδενὶ γάρ ἐστιν οὐ βωμὸς πα
τρῷος, οὐκ ἠρίον προγονικὸν τῶν τοσούτων Ῥωμαίων,
ἀλλ' ὑπὲρ ἀλλοτρίας τρυφῆς καὶ πλούτου πολεμοῦσι
καὶ ἀποθνήσκουσι, κύριοι τῆς οἰκουμένης εἶναι λεγό
μενοι, μίαν δὲ βῶλον ἰδίαν οὐκ ἔχοντες.

T 12 Pliny the Elder, *Natural History*

At the house of Pomponius Secundus, the poet and most distinguished citizen [cos. suff. 44 AD and playwright], I have seen the handwriting of Tiberius and Gaius Gracchus after almost two hundred years . . .

On the Agrarian Law (F 13–15)

earlier in the process (F 13–14) and a more specific one before the voting (F 15).

F 13 Plutarch, *Life of Tiberius Gracchus*

. . . for Tiberius, fighting for a good and just measure [his agrarian bill] with an eloquence able to adorn even worse causes, was formidable and invincible, whenever, with the People crowding around the Rostra, he rose and pleaded for the poor: [5] that the wild beasts roaming over Italy have even a den, and that there is a place to sleep and to hide for every one of them; but that the men who fight and die for Italy have a share of air and light, but nothing else; instead, houseless and homeless, they wander about with their children and wives. And the generals lie, when they exhort the soldiers in their battles to ward off the enemy from sepulchers and shrines; [6] for none of all these many Romans has a hereditary altar, none an ancestral tomb, but they fight and die for the wealth and luxury of others, and though they are said to be masters of the world, they have not a single clod of earth as their own.

---

¹ κατάδυσ{ε}ις Stephanus: καταδύσεις codd.

F 14 App. *B Civ.* 1.9.35–37

. . . μέχρι Τιβέριος Σεμπρώνιος Γράκχος, ἀνὴρ ἐπιφανὴς καὶ λαμπρὸς ἐς φιλοτιμίαν εἰπεῖν τε δυνατώτατος καὶ ἐκ τῶνδε ὁμοῦ πάντων γνωριμώτατος ἅπασι, δημαρχῶν ἐσεμνολόγησε περὶ τοῦ Ἰταλικοῦ γένους ὡς εὐπολεμωτάτου τε καὶ συγγενοῦς, φθειρομένου δὲ κατ᾽ ὀλίγον εἰς ἀπορίαν καὶ ὀλιγανδρίαν καὶ οὐδὲ ἐλπίδα ἔχοντος ἐς διόρθωσιν. [36] ἐπὶ δὲ τῷ δουλικῷ δυσχεράνας ὡς ἀστρατεύτῳ καὶ οὔποτε ἐς δεσπότας πιστῷ, τὸ ἔναγχος ἐπήνεγκεν ἐν Σικελίᾳ δεσποτῶν πάθος ὑπὸ θεραπόντων γενόμενον, ηὐξημένων κἀκείνων ἀπὸ γεωργίας, καὶ τὸν ἐπ᾽ αὐτοὺς Ῥωμαίων πόλεμον οὐ ῥᾴδιον οὐδὲ βραχύν, ἀλλὰ ἔς τε μῆκος χρόνου καὶ τροπὰς κινδύνων ποικίλας ἐκτραπέντα. [37] ταῦτα δὲ εἰπὼν ἀνεκαίνιζε τὸν νόμον μηδένα τῶν πεντακοσίων πλέθρων πλέον ἔχειν. παισὶ δ᾽ αὐτῶν ὑπὲρ τὸν παλαιὸν νόμον προσετίθει τὰ ἡμίσεα τούτων· καὶ τὴν λοιπὴν τρεῖς αἱρετοὺς ἄνδρας, ἐναλλασσομένους κατ᾽ ἔτος, διανέμειν τοῖς πένησι.

F 15 App. *B Civ.* 1.11.44–47

ἐνστάσης δὲ τῆς χειροτονίας πολλὰ μὲν ἄλλα προεῖπεν ἐπαγωγὰ καὶ μακρά, διηρώτα δ᾽ ἐπ᾽ ἐκείνοις, εἰ δίκαιον τὰ κοινὰ κοινῇ διανέμεσθαι καὶ εἰ γνησιώτερος αἰεὶ θεράποντος ὁ πολίτης καὶ χρησιμώτερος ὁ στρατιώτης ἀπολέμου καὶ τοῖς δημοσίοις εὐνούστερος

F 14 Appian, *Civil Wars*

. . . until Tiberius Sempronius Gracchus, an illustrious man, distinguished for his ambition, a most powerful speaker, and for all these reasons together well known to all, while serving as Tribune, delivered a fine speech about the Italian race, saying that they, so valiant in war and related in blood, were declining little by little into poverty and paucity of numbers and did not have any hope of remedy. [36] He expressed his disgust at the body of slaves as useless in war and never faithful to their masters, and adduced the recent calamity brought upon the masters by their slaves in Sicily [slave revolts], their numbers too having increased due to the demands of agriculture; recalling also the war of the Romans against them, neither easy nor short, but extended into a long period of time and many kinds of dangers. [37] After speaking thus, he again brought forward the law, providing that nobody should have more than those 500 *iugera* [ca. 125 ha]. But beyond the former law he added that their sons might each have half of that and that three elected commissioners, who should be changed annually, should divide the remainder among the poor.

F 15 Appian, *Civil Wars*

When the time for voting came, he [Ti. Gracchus] first mentioned many other matters, attractively and at considerable length, and then asked them [the People] whether it was just to divide the common property by common consent, whether a citizen was always worthy of more consideration than a slave, a soldier was more useful than a nonmilitary man, and one who had a share in the common

ὁ κοινωνός. [45] οὐκ ἐς πολὺ δὲ τὴν σύγκρισιν ὡς
ἄδοξον ἐπενεγκὼν αὖθις ἐπήει τὰς τῆς πατρίδος ἐλπίδας καὶ φόβους διεξιών, ὅτι πλείστης γῆς ἐκ πολέμου
βίᾳ κατέχοντες καὶ τὴν λοιπὴν τῆς οἰκουμένης χώραν
ἐν ἐλπίδι ἔχοντες κινδυνεύουσιν ἐν τῷδε περὶ ἁπάντων, ἢ κτήσασθαι καὶ τὰ λοιπὰ δι᾽ εὐανδρίαν ἢ καὶ
τάδε δι᾽ ἀσθένειαν καὶ φθόνον ὑπ᾽ ἐχθρῶν ἀφαιρεθῆ-
ναι. [46] ὧν τοῦ μὲν τὴν δόξαν καὶ εὐπορίαν, τοῦ δὲ
τὸν κίνδυνον καὶ φόβον ὑπερεπαίρων ἐκέλευε τοὺς
πλουσίους ἐνθυμουμένους ταῦτα ἐπιδόσιμον, εἰ δέοι,
παρὰ σφῶν αὐτῶν τήνδε τὴν γῆν εἰς τὰς μελλούσας
ἐλπίδας τοῖς παιδοτροφοῦσι χαρίσασθαι καὶ μή, ἐν
ᾧ περὶ μικρῶν διαφέρονται, τῶν πλεόνων ὑπεριδεῖν,
μισθὸν ἅμα τῆς πεπονημένης ἐξεργασίας αὐτάρκη
φερομένους τὴν ἐξαίρετον ἄνευ τιμῆς κτῆσιν ἐς αἰεὶ
βέβαιον ἑκάστῳ πεντακοσίων πλέθρων, καὶ παισίν,
οἷς εἰσὶ παῖδες, ἑκάστῳ καὶ τούτων τὰ ἡμίσεα. [47]
τοιαῦτα πολλὰ ὁ Γράκχος εἰπὼν τούς τε πένητας
καὶ ὅσοι ἄλλοι λογισμῷ μᾶλλον ἢ πόθῳ κτήσεως
ἐχρῶντο, ἐρεθίσας ἐκέλευε τῷ γραμματεῖ τὸν νόμον
ἀναγνῶναι.

On M. Octavius Before the People (F 16)

property was more likely to be devoted to the public interests. [45] He did not dwell long on this comparison, considering it degrading, but proceeded again to a review of their hopes and fears for the country, saying that they possessed most of their territory by the force of war and had hopes of occupying the rest of the habitable world; but the danger for them lay, above all, in the question of whether they should gain the rest by an abundance of men or, through weakness and mutual jealousy, be deprived of their current possessions by their enemies. [46] After exaggerating the glory and riches on the one side and the danger and fear on the other, he admonished the rich to consider these things and, for the realization of these hopes, to bestow this land as a free gift from them, if necessary, on men who would rear children, and not, by contending about small things, overlook larger ones, especially since, as adequate reward for the high state of cultivation [of the lands to be given up], they were receiving the special ownership, without cost, of 500 *iugera* [ca. 125 ha] each fixed for ever, and for their sons, those who had sons, half of that in addition for each. [47] After saying many things of this kind and exciting the poor as well as all others who were moved by reason rather than by the desire for gain, Gracchus ordered the clerk to read the proposed law.

On M. Octavius Before the People (F 16)

In another speech to the People (CCMR, App. A: 182, 184), Ti. Gracchus defended his treatment of his colleague M. Octavius, whom, being opposed to him, he had removed from office (Plut. Ti. Gracch. 12; Cic. Nat. D. 1.106).

F 16 Plut. *Ti. Gracch.* 15.1–16.1

αἰσθανόμενος δὲ τῶν πολιτευμάτων τὸ περὶ τὸν Ὀκτά-
βιον οὐ τοῖς δυνατοῖς μόνον, ἀλλὰ καὶ τοῖς πολλοῖς
ἐπαχθέστερον[1] ‹ὂν›[2]—μέγα γάρ τι καὶ καλὸν ἐδόκει
τὸ τῶν δημάρχων ἀξίωμα μέχρι τῆς ἡμέρας ἐκείνης
διατετηρημένον ἀνῃρῆσθαι καὶ καθυβρίσθαι—λόγον
ἐν τῷ δήμῳ διεξῆλθεν, οὗ μικρὰ παραθέσθαι τῶν
ἐπιχειρημάτων οὐκ ἄτοπον ἦν, ὥσθ᾽ ὑπονοηθῆναι τὴν
πιθανότητα καὶ πυκνότητα τοῦ ἀνδρός. [2–9] . . . [16.1]
τοιαῦτα μὲν ἦν τὰ κεφάλαια τῆς τοῦ Τιβερίου δικαιο-
λογίας.

[1] ἐπαχθέστερον Wyttenbach: ἐκπαθέστερον codd.
[2] add. Coraes

35 C. PAPIRIUS CARBO

*C. Papirius Carbo (tr. pl. 131 or 130, cos. 120 BC; RE
Papirius 33), the father of C. Papirius Carbo Arvina (**87**),
was originally a supporter of the* populares *and was appointed to serve on the agrarian commission for the imple-
mentation of Ti. Sempronius Gracchus' (**34**) agrarian law,
to replace one of the original members (cf. F 8). As consul,
however, Carbo defended L. Opimius (cos. 121 BC), who
had killed C. Sempronius Gracchus (**48**). Then Carbo was*

F 16 Plutarch, *Life of Tiberius Gracchus*

Perceiving that of his political measures that concerning Octavius [M. Octavius, tr. pl. 133 BC] ⟨was⟩ very displeasing, not only to the nobles, but also to the multitude—for it was thought that the great and worthy dignity of the Tribunate, so carefully guarded up to that day, had been destroyed and insulted—he [Ti. Gracchus] made a lengthy speech before the People, a few of the arguments of which it will not be out of place to lay before the readers, so that they may get an idea of the man's persuasiveness and subtlety.

[2–9] *Gracchus is said to argue that a Tribune is sacred and inviolable; yet, if he does wrong to the People, he deprives himself of this office by not doing what he is supposed to do. The People should have the right to remove the Tribunate from such men by a unanimous vote. Gracchus illustrates this view with some examples and parallels.*

[16.1] Such were the chief points in Tiberius' justification.

35 C. PAPIRIUS CARBO

*prosecuted by the young L. Licinius Crassus (**66** F 13–14) and avoided punishment by suicide (Cic. Verr. 2.3.3; Brut. 103; De or. 1.40, 1.154; Fam. 9.2.1; Leg. 3.35; Tac. Dial. 34.7) (TLRR 30). Carbo was also suspected of involvement in the death of P. Cornelius Scipio Aemilianus Africanus minor (**21**) (Cic. De or. 2.170; Fam. 9.21.3).*

*As in the case of Ti. Sempronius Gracchus (**34**), it is regretted in Cicero's works that Carbo did not use his*

abilities for the benefit of the Republic, while it is acknowledged that he was an industrious, charming, and precise speaker, well known as a frequent pleader in court cases,

T 1 Cic. *Brut.* 96

= **34** T 1.

T 2 Cic. *Brut.* 103–6 (cf. **34** T 2)

[CICERO:] utinam in Ti. Graccho Gaioque Carbone talis mens ad rem publicam bene gerendam fuisset, quale ingenium ad bene dicendum fuit: profecto nemo his viris gloria praestitisset. . . . alter propter perpetuam in populari ratione levitatem morte voluntaria se a severitate iudicum vindicavit. sed fuit uterque summus orator. [104] atque hoc memoria patrum teste dicimus; nam et Carbonis et Gracchi habemus orationes nondum satis splendidas verbis, sed acutas prudentiaeque plenissimas. . . . [105] Carbo, quoi[1] vita suppeditavit, est in multis iudiciis causisque cognitus. hunc qui audierant prudentes homines, in quibus familiaris noster L. Gellius, qui se illi contubernalem in consulatu fuisse narrat, canorum oratorem et volubilem et satis acrem atque eundem et vehementem et valde dulcem et perfacetum fuisse dicebat; addebat industrium etiam et diligentem et in exercitationibus commentationibusque[2] multum operae solitum esse ponere. [106] hic optimus illis temporibus est patronus habitus eoque forum tenente plura fieri iudicia coeperunt.

---

[1] quoi *Friedrich*: cui *Aldus*: quo *codd.*: quod *edd.*: quoad *Lambinus*   [2] commentationibusque *edd.*: commendationibusque *codd.*

though elsewhere his knowledge of the law is described as limited (T 2–6; Cic. Tusc. 1.5; cf. Quint. Inst. 10.7.27; Vell. Pat. 2.9.1).

T 1 Cicero, *Brutus*

= **34** T 1.

T 2 Cicero, *Brutus* (cf. **34** T 2)

[CICERO:] Would that Ti. Gracchus [Ti. Sempronius Gracchus (**34**)] and Gaius Carbo had possessed such an attitude to running public affairs well as they possessed talent for speaking well: surely none would have surpassed these men in renown. . . . the other [Carbo], as a result of constant fickleness in policies appealing to the People, saved himself by a voluntary death from the severity of the judges. But both were orators of the first rank. [104] And we say this with the recollection of our fathers as evidence; for we have orations of both Carbo and Gracchus not yet sufficiently brilliant in language, but acute and very full of sagacity. . . . [105] Carbo, for whom life lasted long enough, came to be known by many public trials and civil suits. Those who had heard him were competent men; among them was our friend L. Gellius [L. Gellius Poplicola (**101**)], who used to comment that he had been his assistant during the consulship and said that he had been an orator of good voice, fluent, rather sharp, and likewise vehement, very charming, and with much wit; he added that he had been also industrious, painstaking, and in the habit of devoting much attention to declamatory exercises and compositions. [106] He was regarded as the best advocate in that time, and, while he was in control of the Forum, trials began to become more numerous.

T 3 Cic. *Brut.* 296

[ATTICUS:] Carbonem in summis oratoribus habitum scio; sed cum in ceteris rebus tum in dicendo semper, quo iam[1] nihil est melius, id laudari,[2] qualecumque est, solet.

[1] quo iam *Jahn*: quoniam *codd.*: quo *edd.*   [2] laudari *edd.*: laudare *codd.*

T 4 Cic. *Brut.* 333
= **19** T 4.

T 5 Cic. *De or.* 1.40
= **19** T 5.

T 6 Cic. *De or.* 3.28
= **19** T 6.

On the Bill for the Reelection of Tribunes of the People (F 7)

*As Tribune of the People, Carbo proposed, among other things, a bill to allow the reelection of Tribunes of the People (*CCMR*, *App. A: 186;* Rogatio Papiria de tribunis*

F 7 Cic. *Amic.* 96
= **20** F 21.

T 3 Cicero, *Brutus*

[ATTICUS:] As for Carbo, I know that he was accounted among the greatest orators; but as in other things so also in oratory it is customary always to praise whatever is not yet surpassed, whatever its value.

T 4 Cicero, *Brutus*
= **19** T 4.

T 5 Cicero, *On the Orator*
= **19** T 5.

T 6 Cicero, *On the Orator*
= **19** T 6.

On the Bill for the Reelection of Tribunes
of the People (F 7)

plebis reficiendis: LPPR, *p. 302), opposed by C. Laelius Sapiens (***20** F 21) and P. Cornelius Scipio Aemilianus Africanus minor (***21** F 28–29).

F 7 Cicero, *On Friendship*
= **20** F 21.

On Behalf of L. Opimius (F 8–11)

As consul in 120 BC, Carbo defended L. Opimius (cos. 121 BC), who had killed C. Sempronius Gracchus (48), when he was prosecuted by P. Decius, Tribune of the People in that year (36 F 2–3), and managed to have him acquitted (Cic. Brut. 128; Sest. 140; De or. 2.170; Part. 104–6)

F 8 Cic. *De or.* 2.106

[ANTONIUS:] saepe etiam res non sit necne, sed qualis sit quaeritur: ut cum L. Opimi causam defendebat apud populum audiente me C. Carbo cos. nihil de C. Gracchi nece negabat, sed id iure pro salute patriae factum esse dicebat; ut eidem Carboni tribuno plebis alia tum mente rem publicam capessenti P. Africanus de Ti. Graccho interroganti responderat iure caesum videri.

F 9 Cic. *De or.* 2.135

[ANTONIUS:] quin etiam in iis ipsis, ubi de facto ambigitur, ceperitne pecunias contra leges {P.}[1] Decius,[2] argumenta et criminum et defensionis revocentur oportet et ad genus et ad naturam universam . . .

---

[1] P. *om. una familia codd.: del. Stangl*   [2] Decius *vel* de cuius *codd.*

On Behalf of L. Opimius (F 8–11)

(TLRR 27). *An earlier verbal exchange about Ti. Sempro-*
nius Gracchus (34), with P. Cornelius Scipio Aemilianus
Africanus minor (21), can be inferred (F 8; Cic. Mil. 8;
Vell. Pat. 2.4.4; Val. Max. 6.2.3; Liv. Epit. 59; CCMR, App.
A: 189).

F 8 Cicero, *On the Orator*

[ANTONIUS:] Often too the question is not whether or not
something is a fact, but what is its nature; as, when the
consul C. Carbo defended the case of L. Opimius before
the People, while I was in the audience, he denied nothing
concerning the killing of C. Gracchus [C. Sempronius
Gracchus (48)], but argued that it was done justly for the
welfare of the country; or as, when P. Africanus [P. Cornelius Scipio Aemilianus Africanus minor (21)] had replied
to that very Carbo (a Tribune of the People, then approaching public affairs with a different attitude), asking
about Ti. Gracchus [Ti. Sempronius Gracchus (34)], that
he seemed to have been killed justly.

F 9 Cicero, *On the Orator*

[ANTONIUS:] Indeed, even in those very cases where there
is a dispute about the facts, such as whether {P.} Decius
took moneys against the law, the arguments of both the
prosecution and the defense must have reference both to
the particular category and to universal nature . . .[1]

[1] Because Decius is mentioned, the statement is attributed to
this speech of C. Papirius Carbo. Since, however, it seems to refer
to another issue concerning Decius, it might rather come from a
different trial, which may not have involved C. Papirius Carbo.

F 10 Cic. *De or.* 2.165

[ANTONIUS:] si ex vocabulo, ut Carbo: "si consul est qui consulit patriae, quid aliud fecit Opimius?"

F 11 Cic. *De or.* 2.169

[ANTONIUS:] iam ex contrario: "si Gracchus nefarie, prae-clare Opimius."

36 P. DECIUS

P. Decius (tr. pl. 120, praet. 115 BC; RE Decius 9), when Tribune of the People, charged (F 2–3) L. Opimius (cos. 121 BC) with his action against C. Sempronius Gracchus (48); L. Opimius was defended by C. Papirius Carbo (35 F 8–11), and Decius was unsuccessful (TLRR 27). As prae-

T 1 Cic. *Brut.* 108

[CICERO:] Flacci autem aemulus P. Decius fuit, non infans ille quidem, sed ut vita sic oratione etiam turbulentus.

F 10 Cicero, *On the Orator*

[ANTONIUS:] If [the argument turns] on a word, like Carbo: "If he is a consul who looks after the country, what else did Opimius do?"

F 11 Cicero, *On the Orator*

[ANTONIUS:] Again, [as a deduction] from a contrast: "If Gracchus [acted] wickedly, Opimius [acted] nobly."[1]

---

[1] Because of the reference to Gracchus and Opimius, the fragment has been assigned to this speech of C. Papirius Carbo.

36 P. DECIUS

tor, Decius clashed with M. Aemilius Scaurus, one of the consuls, again without success (Vir. ill. 72.6).

In Cicero's works Decius is described as a gifted orator, but undisciplined both in his life and in his oratory (T 1).

T 1 Cicero, *Brutus*

[CICERO:] And Flaccus' [M. Fulvius Flaccus (**40**)] rival was P. Decius: he was certainly not without some eloquence, but as in his life so also in his speech unruly.

Against L. Opimius (F 2–3)

F 2 Liv. *Epit.* 61.9

L. Opimius accusatus apud populum a Q. Decio trib. pl., quod indemnatos cives in carcerem coniecisset, absolutus est.

F 3 Cic. *De or.* 2.132

[ANTONIUS:] . . . deinde quid veniat in iudicium, quod isti sic iubent quaerere: interfecit Opimius Gracchum. quid facit causam? quod rei p(ublicae) causa, cum ex s(enatus) c(onsulto) ad arma vocasset. hoc tolle, causa non erit. at id ipsum negat contra leges licuisse Decius. veniet igitur in iudicium: licueritne ex senatus consulto servandae rei p(ublicae) causa?

37 L. CALPURNIUS PISO FRUGI

L. Calpurnius Piso Frugi (cos. 133, censor 120 [or 108] BC; RE Calpurnius 96) was probably named for his prudent and self-controlled manner (Cic. Tusc. 3.16; Sest. 21; Font. 39; on his life see FRHist 1:230–33).

As Tribune of the People in 149 BC, Piso initiated the introduction of Rome's first quaestio perpetua *on the recovery of extorted money* (de repetundis) *(T 1; Cic. Verr.*

Against L. Opimius (F 2–3)

F 2 Livy, *Epitome*

L. Opimius, accused before the People by Q. Decius,[1] a Tribune of the People, on the grounds that he had thrown uncondemned citizens into jail, was acquitted.

> [1] Livy gives the *praenomen* as *Q.*, while it is *P.* in Cicero and in *De viris illustribus* (72.6). *P.* is regarded as the correct version.

F 3 Cicero, *On the Orator*

[ANTONIUS:] . . . next, what will come before the court, which those men [teachers] order to investigate as follows: Opimius killed Gracchus. What is the issue of the case? That he did so in the interest of the country, after he had issued a call to arms on the basis of a Senate decree. Remove this [proposition], and there will be no case. Decius, however, denies that this very matter was allowed, as being against the laws. So this will come before the court: was it allowed on the basis of a Senate decree for the sake of saving the Republic?

37 L. CALPURNIUS PISO FRUGI

2.3.195, 2.4.56; Off. 2.75; Schol. Bob. ad Cic. Flacc. *[p. 96.28 St.]).*

According to Cicero, Piso was active in the courts and supported or opposed many laws (T 1). Cicero knew speeches and a historical work by Piso Frugi (FRHist 9), even though the speeches were getting forgotten in his time; the style of Piso's historical work is described as plain (T 1; Cic. De or. 2.53; Leg. 1.6; Gell. NA 11.14.1).

T 1 Cic. *Brut.* 106

[CICERO:] . . . L. enim Piso tribunus plebis legem primus de pecuniis repetundis Censorino et Manilio consulibus tulit—ipse etiam Piso et causas egit et multarum legum aut auctor aut dissuasor fuit, isque et orationes reliquit, quae iam evanuerunt, et annalis sane exiliter scriptos—. . .

Against C. Sempronius Gracchus'
Grain Law (F 2)

F 2 Cic. *Tusc.* 3.48

= **48** F 41.

38 P. CORNELIUS SCIPIO NASICA SERAPIO

P. Cornelius Scipio Nasica Serapio (cos. 138 BC; RE Cornelius 354) was an opponent of Ti. Sempronius Gracchus (34). For instance, Nasica Serapio disapproved of a proposal by Ti. Sempronius Gracchus that the money of King Attalus should be distributed among the People (cf. 30 F 6).

T 1 Cicero, *Brutus*

[CICERO:] . . . for L. Piso, as Tribune of the People, was the first to propose a law on the recovery of extorted money, in the consulship of Censorinus and Manilius [149 BC]—Piso himself, too, both was active as a pleader and was the supporter or opponent of many laws, and he left both orations, which have now faded away, and *Annals* [FRHist 9], written in a rather plain style— . . .

Against C. Sempronius Gracchus'
Grain Law (F 2)

*In 123 BC Piso Frugi vehemently opposed a grain law proposed by C. Sempronius Gracchus (**48**) (CCMR, App. A: 194; Schol. Bob. ad Cic.* Flacc. *[p. 96.28–29 St.]).*

F 2 Cicero, *Tusculan Disputations*
= **48** F 41.

38 P. CORNELIUS SCIPIO
NASICA SERAPIO

*In his consular year, Nasica Serapio, along with his colleague D. Iunius Brutus Callaicus (**39**), was asked by the Senate to investigate the crimes in the Silan forest (cf. **19** F 16) (TLRR 10).*

In Cicero, Nasica Serapio is described as a forceful and sharp speaker (T 1–2).

T 1 Cic. *Brut.* 107

[CICERO:] . . . et vero ante Maximum illum Scipionem, quo duce privato Ti. Gracchus occisus esset, cum omnibus in rebus vehementem tum acrem aiebat in dicendo fuisse.

T 2 Cic. *Off.* 1.109

audivi ex maioribus natu hoc idem fuisse in P. Scipione Nasica, contraque patrem eius, illum qui Ti. Gracchi conatus perditos vindicavit, nullam comitatem habuisse sermonis {ne Xenocratem quidem, severissimum philosophorum}[1] ob eamque rem ipsam magnum et clarum fuisse.

[1] *del. Heumann*

On the Grain Supply Before the People (F 3)

F 3 Val. Max. 3.7.3

in quamcumque memorabilium partem exemplorum convertor, velim nolimve, in cognomine Scipionum haeream necesse est: qui enim licet hoc loci Nasicam praeterire, fidentis animi dicti{que}[1] clarissimum auctorem? annonae caritate increbrescente C. Curiatius tribunus plebis pro-

[1] *del. Gertz*

T 1 Cicero, *Brutus*

[CICERO:] . . . and earlier than Maximus [Q. Fabius Maximus Allobrogicus (**49**)], that Scipio, under whose leadership as a private person Ti. Gracchus [Ti. Sempronius Gracchus (**34**)] was killed, was, he [Accius] used to say, in all matters forceful and particularly sharp in speaking.

T 2 Cicero, *On Duties*

I have heard from older people that this quality [graciousness] was equally present in P. Scipio Nasica, and that his father, on the other hand, the man who punished the reckless ventures of Ti. Gracchus [Ti. Sempronius Gracchus (**34**)], had no graciousness in conversation {not even Xenocrates, the most severe of philosophers} and because of that very fact was great and famous.

On the Grain Supply Before the People (F 3)

When Nasica Serapio was consul (138 BC), he was forced by a Tribune of the People to explain his policies concerning the grain supply in front of the People (CCMR, *App. A: 180*).

F 3 Valerius Maximus, *Memorable Doings and Sayings*

To whatever quarter of memorable examples I turn, whether or not I like it, I must stick fast to the *cognomen* of the Scipios. For how at this point can I pass over Nasica, the very famous author of a statement expressing a confident spirit? When the price of grain was rising, C. Curiatius, a Tribune of the People [138 BC], brought the con-

ductos in contionem consules compellebat ut de frumento emendo adque[2] id negotium explicandum mittendis legatis in curia referrent. cuius instituti minime utilis interpellandi gratia Nasica contrariam actionem ordiri coepit. obstrepente deinde plebe "tacete, quaeso, Quirites," inquit, "plus ego enim quam vos quid rei publicae expediat intellego." qua voce audita omnes pleno venerationis silentio maiorem auctoritatis eius quam suorum alimentorum respectum egerunt.

[2] adque *vel* atque *codd.*: atque ‹ad› *Novák*

On Ti. Sempronius Gracchus in the Senate (F 4)

In 133 BC, when the consul P. Mucius Scaevola was reluctant to intervene, Nasica Serapio was a leading figure in the movement that caused Ti. Sempronius Gracchus' (34) death (Cic. Brut. 107; Off. 1.109; Tusc. 4.51; Vell. Pat.

F 4 Val. Max. 3.2.17

cum Ti. Gracchus in tribunatu, profusissimis largitionibus favore populi occupato, rem publicam oppressam teneret palamque dictitaret interempto senatu omnia per plebem agi debere, in aedem Fidei Publicae convocati patres conscripti a consule Mucio Scaevola quidnam in tali tempestate faciendum esset deliberabant, cunctisque censentibus ut consul armis rem publicam tueretur, Scaevola negavit se quicquam vi esse acturum. tum Scipio Nasica, "quoniam" inquit "consul, dum iuris ordinem sequitur, id

suls before a public meeting and urged them to consult in the Senate house about buying grain and sending envoys to arrange that matter. In order to obstruct this highly inexpedient course of action, Nasica began to speak in a contrary sense. Then, when the People shouted in protest, he said: "Be silent, Romans, if you please. For I understand better than you what is expedient for the Republic." When this comment had been heard, all fell reverently silent and paid more regard to his authority than to their own nutriment.

On Ti. Sempronius Gracchus in the Senate (F 4)

2.3.1–2; Liv. Epit. 58; Plut. Ti. Gracch. 19.3–5; App. B Civ. 1.16.68–69; Vir. ill. 64.7; Diod. Sic. 34.33.7), announcing his intention in the Senate and defending it afterward (Diod. Sic. 34.33.7).

F 4 Valerius Maximus, Memorable Doings and Sayings

Ti. Gracchus [Ti. Sempronius Gracchus (**34**)], in his Tribunate [133 BC], had won the favor of the People by the most lavish handouts and held the Republic oppressed; he kept on saying openly that the Senate should be killed and everything handled through the commons. Thereupon the senators were called together by consul Mucius Scaevola [P. Mucius Scaevola, cos. 133 BC] in the Temple of Fides Publica and deliberated on what should be done in such a crisis. And while everybody thought the consul should protect the Republic by armed force, Scaevola refused to do anything with violence. Then Scipio Nasica said: "Since the consul, following legal process, is bringing it about that

agit ut cum omnibus legibus Romanum imperium corruat, egomet me privatus voluntati vestrae ducem offero," ac deinde laevam manum ‹im›a parte[1] togae circumdedit sublataque dextra proclamavit "qui rem publicam salvam esse volunt me sequantur," eaque voce cunctatione bonorum civium discussa Gracchum cum scelerata factione quas merebatur poenas persolvere coegit.

[1] manum ‹im›a parte *Kempf*: manum aparte *vel* manum aperte *vel* manum parte *codd.*: ima parte *Stanger*

Against M. Fulvius Flaccus (F 5)

F 5 Cic. *De or.* 2.285

[CAESAR STRABO:] placet mihi illud etiam Scipionis illius, qui Ti. Gracchum perculit. cum ei M. Flaccus[1] multis probris obiectis P. Mucium iudicem tulisset: "eiero"[2] inquit "iniquus est." cum esset admurmuratum: "a" inquit "P. C. non ego mihi illum iniquum eiero, verum omnibus."

[1] Flaccus *vel* Crassus *codd.*   [2] eiero *ed. Cratandrina*: eiuro *vel* vero *vel* eiuero *codd.*

the Roman empire collapses along with all laws, I, a private individual, offer myself as a leader for your wishes." And then he wrapped the hem of his toga around his left hand and, with his right hand raised, shouted: "Let those who want the Republic safe follow me." And with that call he dissipated the hesitation of the loyal citizens and forced Gracchus, along with his criminal retinue, to pay the penalties they deserved.

Against M. Fulvius Flaccus (F 5)

Cicero reports a witty remark of Scipio Nasica against M. Fulvius Flaccus (40), his opponent in a forthcoming trial (TLRR 18).

F 5 Cicero, *On the Orator*

[CAESAR STRABO:] I also like that remark of that famous Scipio who struck down Ti. Gracchus [Ti. Sempronius Gracchus (34)]. When, after hurling many insults, M. Flaccus [M. Fulvius Flaccus (40)] had proposed P. Mucius [P. Mucius Scaevola, cos. 133 BC] as a judge to him, he [Scipio] said: "I challenge him on oath; he is prejudiced." When there had been a murmur, he said: "Ah, Members of the Senate, I do not challenge him as prejudiced against myself, but against everybody."

39 D. IUNIUS BRUTUS CALLAICUS

D. Iunius Brutus Callaicus (cos. 138 BC; RE Iunius 57)
was a friend of the poet Accius and a successful general,
fighting against the Lusitanians and the Callaici and then
celebrating a triumph (Cic. Arch. *27; Val. Max. 8.14.2).*
    Cicero records that he heard from Accius that Brutus

T 1 Cic. *Brut.* 107

[CICERO:] vester etiam D. Brutus M. filius, ut ex familiari
eius L. Accio poeta sum audire solitus, et dicere non in-
culte solebat et erat cum litteris Latinis tum etiam Graecis
ut temporibus illis eruditus. quae tribuebat idem Accius
etiam Q. Maximo L. Paulli nepoti . . .

40 M. FULVIUS FLACCUS

M. Fulvius Flaccus (cos. 125, tr. pl. 122 BC; RE Fulvius
*58) was a supporter of the brothers Gracchi (**34** + **48**)*
and served on the committee to implement the Gracchan
agrarian laws; he died in 121 BC in the conflict with con-
sul L. Opimius in the aftermath of the Gracchan initia-

T 1 Cic. *Brut.* 108

[CICERO:] erat in aliquo numero etiam M. Fulvius Flaccus
et C. Cato, Africani sororis filius, mediocres oratores; etsi
Flacci scripta sunt, sed ut studiosi litterarum.

39 D. IUNIUS BRUTUS CALLAICUS

*was a refined speaker and learned in both Greek and Latin
literature (T 1). As consul, along with his colleague P. Cornelius Scipio Nasica Serapio (38), Brutus was asked by the
Senate to investigate the crimes in the Silan forest (cf. **19**
F 16) (TLRR 10).*

T 1 Cicero, *Brutus*

[CICERO:] Your D. Brutus, Marcus' son, too, as I used to
hear from his friend L. Accius the poet, used to speak not
without refinement and was, for that time, well versed in
both Latin and even Greek letters. That praise the same
Accius also assigned to Q. Maximus [Q. Fabius Maximus
Allobrogicus (**49**)], L. Paullus' [L. Aemilius Paullus (**12**)]
grandson . . .

40 M. FULVIUS FLACCUS

*tives. Fulvius prosecuted P. Cornelius Scipio Nasica Sera-
pio (**38** F 5) (TLRR 18).*

*Writings of Fulvius were extant in Cicero's time: it is
acknowledged that they show his devotion to literature,
while he is regarded as an orator of moderate quality (T 1).*

T 1 Cicero, *Brutus*

[CICERO:] There were held of some account also M. Fulvius Flaccus and C. Cato [C. Porcius Cato, cos. 114 BC],
son of Africanus' sister, orators of moderate quality. And
yet writings of Flaccus are extant, but they are those of a
student of letters.

41 M. PORCIUS CATO

M. Porcius Cato (cos. 118 BC; RE Porcius 10), a grandson of M. Porcius Cato (8), fought as consul in Africa and died in that province (T 1).

Cato is not mentioned in Cicero, but Gellius describes him as a rather impressive orator and notes that he left written versions of his speeches (T 1).

T 1 Gell. *NA* 13.20.9–10

ex maiore autem Catonis filio, qui praetor designatus patre vivo mortuus est, et egregios de iuris disciplina libros reliquit, nascitur hic, de quo quaeritur, M. Cato M. filius M. nepos. [10] is satis vehemens orator fuit multasque orationes ad exemplum avi scriptas reliquit et consul cum Q. Marcio Rege fuit inque eo consulatu in Africam profectus in ea provincia mortem obit.

In Defense of His Law Before the People (F 2)

F 2 Prisc., *GL* II, p. 90.11–16

a "saepe" adverbio positivum vel comparativum nomen non legi, superlativum posuit Cato nepos de actionibus ad populum, ne lex sua abrogetur: "facite vobis in mentem

41 M. PORCIUS CATO

As a young man, Cato may have delivered the funeral oration for his father on the latter's death in 152 BC (Gell. NA 13.20; see Malcovati 1981).

T 1 Gellius, *Attic Nights*

But from Cato's elder son, who died when praetor-elect, while his father was still alive, and left admirable books on the study of law, the offspring is the man with whom the inquiry is concerned, M. Cato, Marcus' son and Marcus' grandson. [10] He was an orator of some power and left many speeches written according to the example of his grandfather [M. Porcius Cato (**8**)], and he was consul with Q. Marcius Rex [118 BC], and, having gone to Africa during that consulship, died in that province.

In Defense of His Law Before the People (F 2)

The nature of the law that Cato, possibly when consul, defended in a speech to the People is uncertain (LPPR, p. 320).

F 2 Priscian

An adjective in the positive or comparative derived from the adverb *saepe* ["often"] I have not read; Cato the grandson [of M. Porcius Cato (**8**)] used the superlative before the People [in the speech] about legal processes, so that his law would not be annulled: "Make an effort to recall in

221

veniat, Quirites, ex aere alieno in hac civitate et in aliis omnibus propter diem atque fenus saepissimam discordiam fuisse."

Unplaced Fragment (F 3)

F 3 Fest., p. 142.4–12 L.

MAGNI‖|FICIUS pro magnificentius usurp⌋avit[1] Cato . . . at nepos eius, | in ea [– – –][2] tamen," ait, "cum aedilis | [– – –] tris ludos magni | [– – –]"[3]

    [1] *suppl. Ursinus ex Epit.*   [2] ⟨quam scripsit⟩ *suppl. Ursinus*   [3] ⟨Magnae Ma⟩tris ludos magni⟨ficentius⟩ *suppl. Ursinus*

42 M. LIVIUS DRUSUS

*M. Livius Drusus (cos. 112, censor 109 BC; RE Livius 17), the father of M. Livius Drusus (**72**), fought in Macedonia and Thrace as consul and proconsul and celebrated a triumph upon his return; he died while censor.*

T 1 Cic. *Brut.* 109

[CICERO:] M. Drusus C. f., qui in tribunatu C. Gracchum conlegam iterum tribunum fregit,[1] vir et oratione gravis et auctoritate . . .

    [1] fregit *Victor Pisanus*: fecit *codd.*

T 2 Plut. *C. Gracch.* 29(8).5

ἦν γὰρ εἷς τῶν τοῦ Γαΐου συναρχόντων Λίβιος Δροῦ-

your minds, Romans, that, on account of debt, in this community and in all others, because of a fixed date for interest [payments], there has been the most frequent discord."

Unplaced Fragment (F 3)

F 3 Festus

magnificius ["more splendidly"; old form of comparative], ⟨instead of *magnificentius* [usual form of comparative],⟩ was what Cato [M. Porcius Cato (**8**)] used . . . but his grandson in that [speech] . . . said: ". . . still, when the aedile . . . [organized] the games of ⟨Magna Ma⟩ter more ⟨splendidly⟩ [?] . . ."

42 M. LIVIUS DRUSUS

Drusus is described as a respected orator and personality (T 1–2; Diod. Sic. 37.10.1).

T 1 Cicero, *Brutus*

[CICERO:] M. Drusus, Gaius' son, who, in his Tribunate [122 BC], crushed C. Gracchus [C. Sempronius Gracchus (**48**)], his colleague, Tribune for a second time, was a respected man as regards both eloquence and prestige . . .

T 2 Plutarch, *Life of Gaius Gracchus*

For one of the colleagues of Gaius [C. Sempronius Gracchus (**48**)] was Livius Drusus, a man not inferior to any

σος, ἀνὴρ οὔτε γεγονὼς τινος Ῥωμαίων οὔτε τεθραμ-
μένος χεῖρον, ἤθει δὲ καὶ λόγῳ καὶ πλούτῳ {ἐν}[1]
τοῖς μάλιστα τιμωμένοις καὶ δυναμένοις ἀπὸ τούτων
ἐνάμιλλος.

[1] del. *Stephanus*

Speeches (F 3–6)

As Tribune of the People in 122 BC, Drusus was a colleague of C. Sempronius Gracchus (**48**) and opposed some
of the latter's schemes; he criticized him and justified measures against him (F 4–5).

F 3 Cic. *Orat.* 213–14

me stante C. Carbo C. f. tr. pl. in contione dixit his verbis:
"o M. Druse, patrem appello"—haec quidem duo binis
pedibus incisim; dein membratim: "tu dicere solebas sa-
cram esse rem publicam"—haec item membra ternis;
[214] post ambitus: "quicunque eam violavissent, ab omnibus esse ei poenas persolutas"—dichoreus (nihil enim ad
rem, extrema illa longa sit an brevis), deinde: "patris dictum sapiens temeritas filii comprobavit"—hoc dichoreo
tantus clamor contionis excitatus est, ut admirabile esset.
quaero nonne id numerus effecerit. verborum ordinem

Cf. Rufin. *GL* VI, p. 576.8–18; Non., p. 130.13–14 M. = 189 L.;
Arist. *Rh.* 3.8 (1409a3–21).

---

[1] Each of the two commata consists of two trochees or spon-
dees ([o] Mārcĕ | Drūsĕ ‖ pātr(em) āp|pēllō).   [2] Two *cola* of
three feet each (tū dī|cĕrĕ sŏl|lēbās ‖ sācr(am) ēs|sĕ rēm |

Roman in either birth or rearing, and in character, eloquence, and wealth in an equal contest with those who
were most honored and influential as a result of these
[features].

Speeches (F 3–6)

*Cicero's report of what C. Papirius Carbo Arvina (87
F 4) claimed that Drusus had said (F 3) may not represent
the original wording.*

F 3 Cicero, *Orator*

While I was standing by, C. Carbo, Gaius' son [C. Papirius
Carbo Arvina (87), F 4], a Tribune of the People [90 BC],
spoke at a meeting of the People in these words: "Marcus
Drusus, I mean the father"—these are in fact two *commata*, each consisting of two feet;[1] then in *cola*: "you were
accustomed to say that the Republic is sacred"—these are
likewise *cola* of three feet each;[2] [214] then the period:
"that all who had violated her, paid a penalty to her"—a
ditrochee[3] (for it does not make a difference whether that
final [syllable] is long or short); then: "the father's wise
statement the son's rashness proved"—at this ditrochee
such a cry was raised from the crowd that it was amazing.
I ask whether it was not the rhythm that produced this.
Change the order of the words, arrange them this way:

pūblǐcăm).   [3] The clausulae at the end of the phrases
(pērsŏ‖lūtās / cōmbrŏ‖bāvǐt).

immuta, fac sic: "comprobavit filii temeritas": iam nihil erit, etsi temeritas ex tribus brevibus et longa est, quem Aristoteles ut optimum probat (a quo dissentio).

F 4 Plut. *C. Gracch.* 30(9).6

καὶ μέντοι καὶ αὐτὸς ὁ Λίβιος ἀεὶ δημηγορῶν ἔλεγεν, ὡς γράφοι ταῦτα τῇ βουλῇ δοκοῦντα κηδομένῃ τῶν πολλῶν. ὃ δὴ καὶ μόνον ἀπὸ τῶν πολιτευμάτων αὐτοῦ χρήσιμον ὑπῆρχεν.

F 5 Plut. *C. Gracch.* 31(10).2

ἐπεὶ δὲ Ῥουβρίου τῶν συναρχόντων ἑνὸς οἰκίζεσθαι Καρχηδόνα γράψαντος ἀνῃρημένην ὑπὸ Σκηπίωνος, κλήρῳ λαχὼν ὁ Γάιος ἐξέπλευσεν εἰς Λιβύην ἐπὶ τὸν κατοικισμόν, ἔτι μᾶλλον ἐπιβὰς ὁ Δροῦσος ἀπόντος αὐτοῦ τὸν δῆμον ὑπελάμβανε καὶ προσήγετο, μάλιστα ταῖς κατὰ τοῦ Φουλβίου διαβολαῖς.

F 6 Plut. *Ti. Gracch.* 2.4

. . . ὡς οἱ περὶ Δροῦσον ἤλεγχον ὅτι δελφῖνας ἀργυροῦς ἐπρίατο τιμῆς εἰς ἑκάστην λίτραν δραχμῶν χιλίων καὶ διακοσίων πεντήκοντα.

---

1 M. Livius Drusus presumably shared this view, but the passage does not reveal whether he voiced it in any context.

"proved the son's rashness." There will not be any effect, although *temeritas* ["rashness"] consists of three shorts and a long [syllable], the foot [paeon] that Aristotle [cf. Cic. *Orat.* 192–93; *De or.* 3.182–83] regards as the best (with whom I disagree).

F 4 Plutarch, *Life of Gaius Gracchus*

And indeed Livius himself, in his public speeches, always said that he drafted these [bills on settlement, opposed to C. Sempronius Gracchus (**48**)] as approved by the Senate, being concerned for the common people. And this in fact was the only advantage that resulted from his political measures.

F 5 Plutarch, *Life of Gaius Gracchus*

And when Rubrius [C.(?) Rubrius, tr. pl. 122 BC], one of his colleagues, had brought in a bill for the founding of a colony in Carthage, which had been destroyed by Scipio [P. Cornelius Scipio Aemilianus Africanus minor (**21**)], Gaius [C. Sempronius Gracchus (**48**)], selected by lot, sailed off to Africa for the foundation. In his [Gaius'] absence, Drusus assaulted him even more, made the People defect [from Gaius], and attached them to himself, particularly through his slanders against Fulvius [M. Fulvius Flaccus (**40**)].

F 6 Plutarch, *Life of Tiberius Gracchus*

. . . hence the followers of Drusus found fault with him [C. Sempronius Gracchus (**48**)] because he bought silver dolphins at a price of twelve hundred and fifty drachmas for each pound.[1]

43 M. AEMILIUS SCAURUS
PRINCEPS SENATUS

M. Aemilius Scaurus (cos. 115, censor 109 BC; RE Aemilius 140) was a respected and dominant figure in Roman political life. He was princeps senatus *from about the time of his consulship until his death (T 1) and was a supporter of the* optimates. *He was involved in military action, embassies, building projects, the drafting of laws, and many court cases (on his life see* FRHist 1:267–68; Bates 1986).

In Cicero it is recorded that Scaurus' oratory was weighty, dignified, and trustworthy, suited to appearances

T 1 Cic. *Brut.* 110–16 (cf. **44** T 1)

[CICERO:] de Scauro et Rutilio breviter licet dicere, quorum neuter summi oratoris habuit laudem, et ‹est› uterque[1] in multis causis versatus. erat in quibusdam laudandis viris, etiam si maximi ingeni non essent, probabilis tamen industria;[2] quamquam his quidem non omnino ingenium, sed oratorium ingenium defuit. . . . [111] . . . in Scauri oratione, sapientis hominis et recti, gravitas summa et naturalis quaedam inerat auctoritas, non ut causam, sed ut testimonium dicere putares cum pro reo diceret. [112] hoc dicendi genus ad patrocinia mediocriter aptum vide-

---

[1] et ‹est› uterque *Stangl:* et uterque *codd.:* at uterque . . . versatus est *Martha*   [2] erat in quibusdam laudandis viris . . . probabilis tamen industria *Peter:* erat. in quibusdam laudandis viris etiamsi . . . probabiles *codd.:* erant . . . laudandi viri et, vel si . . . probabiles *Stangl:* erat: in quibusdam laudandi viri . . . probabiles *Orelli*

43 M. AEMILIUS SCAURUS
PRINCEPS SENATUS

in the Senate (T 1–2). Some of Scaurus' speeches were available to Cicero (T 1). Scaurus also produced an autobiography in three books (FRHist 18; cf. T 1).

*Scaurus was an advocate for L. Calpurnius Bestia (cos. 111 BC) at a trial in 109 BC, when he was prosecuted by C. Memmius (**60** F 5) (TLRR 54). Scaurus himself was prosecuted by Cn. Domitius Ahenobarbus (**69** F 3–4) for failure to look after cult practices properly (TLRR 68).*

T 1 Cicero, *Brutus* (cf. **44** T 1)

[CICERO:] Concerning Scaurus and Rutilius [P. Rutilius Rufus (**44**)] one may speak briefly: neither of them had the reputation of being an orator of the first rank, and both ⟨were⟩ active in many court cases. Some men of high reputation, even though they did not have the greatest talent, still possessed commendable industry; yet these men lacked not any talent at all, but talent for oratory. . . . [111] . . . In the oratory of Scaurus, a wise and upright man, there was the greatest dignity and a certain innate authority, so that, when he spoke for a client, you would think not that he pleaded a case, but that he gave testimony. [112] This manner of speaking seemed suited for appearing as a patron in court merely to some extent, but

batur, ad senatoriam vero sententiam, cuius erat ille princeps, vel maxime; significabat enim non prudentiam solum, sed quod maxime rem continebat, fidem. habebat
hoc a natura ipsa, quod a doctrina non facile posset; quamquam huius quoque ipsius rei, quem ad modum scis, prae-
cepta sunt. huius et orationes sunt et tres ad L. Fufidium
libri scripti de vita ipsius acta sane utiles, quos nemo legit;
at Cyri vitam et disciplinam legunt, praeclaram illam quidem, sed neque tam nostris rebus aptam nec tamen Scauri
laudibus anteponendam. [113] . . . e‹ra›t³ uterque natura
vehemens et acer . . . [F 3] . . . [116] habemus igitur in
Stoicis oratoribus Rutilium, Scaurum in antiquis; utrumque tamen laudemus, quoniam per illos ne haec quidem
in civitate genera hac oratoria laude caruerunt.

³ e‹ra›t *Jahn:* et *codd.*

T 2 Cic. *De or.* 1.214

[Antonius:] M. vero Scaurus . . . vir regendae rei publicae scientissimus, si audierit hanc auctoritatem gravitatis
et consilii sui vindicari a te, Crasse, quod eam oratoris
propriam esse dicas, iam, credo, huc veniat et hanc loqua-
citatem nostram vultu ipso aspectuque conterreat; qui
quamquam est in dicendo minime contemnendus, prudentia tamen rerum magnarum magis quam dicendi arte
nititur.

for the expression of an opinion in the Senate, where he was the leader, even particularly well. For it demonstrated not only wisdom, but, since he very much kept to the matter at issue, trustworthiness. Thus he possessed from nature herself what he could not easily have from learning, although, as you know, there are rules for this very matter too. There are extant from him orations as well as three books addressed to L. Fufidius written about the course of his own life [*FRHist* 18], certainly useful, which nobody reads. Instead, they read Cyrus' life and training [i.e., Xenophon's *Cyropaedia*], certainly splendid, but neither so suited to our conditions nor yet to be preferred to Scaurus' eulogy. [113] . . . Both men were by nature forceful and sharp. . . . [F 3] . . . [116] Thus we have Rutilius among the Stoic orators, Scaurus among the old-fashioned ones; still, let us praise both since through them not even these types of oratory have been without distinction in this community.

T 2 Cicero, *On the Orator*

[ANTONIUS:] Indeed, if M. Scaurus . . . a most knowledgeable man in running political affairs, happened to hear that this influence of his own worth and wisdom was claimed by you, Crassus, because you say that it is the particular feature of an orator, he would, I believe, instantly come here and frighten this chatting of ours by the very look on his face; he, though by no means to be despised as a speaker, still relies on his knowledge of higher politics rather than on the art of oratory.

Against P. Rutilius Rufus (F 3–4)

*In 116 BC, when both Scaurus and P. Rutilius Rufus (**44**) were candidates for the consulship (with only Scaurus being successful), the latter accused the former of* ambitus,

F 3 Cic. *Brut.* 113

[CICERO:] e⟨ra⟩t[1] uterque natura vehemens et acer; itaque cum una consulatum petivissent, non ille solum, qui repulsam tulerat, accusavit ambitus designatum competitorem, sed Scaurus etiam absolutus Rutilium in iudicium vocavit.

[1] e⟨ra⟩t *Jahn*: et *codd.*

F 4 Cic. *De or.* 2.280

[CAESAR STRABO:] movent illa etiam, quae coniectura explanantur longe aliter atque sunt, sed acute atque concinne; ut cum Scaurus accusaret Rutilium ambitus, cum ipse consul esset factus, ille repulsam tulisset, et in eius tabulis ostenderet litteras A. F. P. R. idque diceret esse: "actum fide P. Rutili," Rutilius autem: "ante factum post relatum," C. Canius eques Romanus, cum Rufo adesset, exclamat neutrum illis litteris declarari. "quid ergo?" inquit Scaurus;—"Aemilius fecit, plectitur Rutilius."

Against P. Rutilius Rufus (F 3–4)

and Scaurus then prosecuted Rutilius (cf. Tac. Ann. *3.66.2)*
(TLRR 34, 35).

F 3 Cicero, *Brutus*

[CICERO:] Both men [Rutilius and Scaurus] were by nature forceful and sharp. Thus, when they had been candidates for the consulship at the same time [in 116 BC], not
only did that one who had experienced a defeat accuse his
rival, the consul designate, of bribery, but even Scaurus,
on acquittal, took Rutilius to court.

F 4 Cicero, *On the Orator*

[CAESAR STRABO:] Also effective are those comments
that, by conjecture, explain matters in a completely different way from what they are, but sharply and wittily; as,
when Scaurus prosecuted Rutilius for bribery, when he
himself had been elected consul and the other had experienced a defeat, and pointed out the letters A. F. P. R. in
the other's account books, and said that this meant "trans-
acted on credit for Publius Rutilius," whereas Rutilius
[said] "first done, then registered," C. Canius, a Roman
knight, who supported Rufus, called out that none of these
was expressed by those letters. "What then?" said Scaurus;—"Aemilius did it, punished is Rutilius."[1]

---

[1] In the interest of a more precise rendering of the meaning
of the three versions, the play with different expansions of the
same abbreviation in the Latin has not been fully recreated.

In His Defense Concerning Extortion (F 5–7)

When Scaurus was prosecuted for extortion by M. Iunius
Brutus (**56** F 2), presumably after Scaurus' consulship
(114 BC; TLRR 37), rather than later in support of a

F 5 Cic. *Font.* 38

M. Aemilium Scaurum, summum nostrae civitatis virum,
scimus accusatum a M. Bruto. exstant orationes, ex quibus
intellegi potest multa in illum ipsum Scaurum esse dicta
(falso; quis negat?), verum tamen ab inimico dicta et
obiecta.

F 6 Charis., *GL* I, p. 129.10–12 = p. 164.10–13 B.

fabrum pro fabrorum . . . M. Scaurus contra Brutum de
pecuniis repetundis "praefecti fabrum."

F 7 Charis., *GL* I, p. 210.3–4 = p. 272.3–5 B.

M. Scaurus ⌊de pe⌋cuniis[1] repetundis ⌊in⌋[2] M. Brutum:
"ita officiose atque observanter ⌊imperi⌋[3] milites trium-
phavere."

---

[1] ⌊de pe⌋cuniis (⌊de pe⌋ *in cod. unico non iam legibile*)   [2] ⌊in⌋
ex deperdito cod.: <contra> *Meyer*   [3] ⌊imperi⌋ *suppl. secun-*
dum Cauchii ex deperdito cod. excerpta

In His Defense Concerning Extortion (F 5–7)

charge by Q. Servilius Caepio (**85**; TLRR 96; cf. F 8–10), he spoke in his defense.

F 5 Cicero, *Pro Fonteio*

We know that M. Aemilius Scaurus, a most eminent man in our community, was accused by M. Brutus [M. Iunius Brutus (**56**), F 2]. The speeches are extant; from these it may be gathered that many charges were leveled against that Scaurus himself (falsely; who denies it?), yet leveled and alleged by his opponent they were.

F 6 Charisius

fabrum ["of craftsmen"; old form of genitive plural], instead of *fabrorum* [standard form] . . . M. Scaurus [in the speech] against Brutus about the recovery of extorted money: "the overseers of the craftsmen."

F 7 Charisius

M. Scaurus [in the speech] about the recovery of extorted money ⟨against⟩ M. Brutus: "so dutifully and respectfully ⟨toward the empire⟩ the soldiers have triumphed."[1]

[1] Malcovati suggests that another comment about the army attested for Scaurus might belong to the same context (Frontin. *Str.* 4.3.13 = *FRHist* 18 F 5).

Against Q. Servilius Caepio (F 8–10)

F 8 Asc. in Cic. *Scaur.* I.2 (p. 19 KS = 21.18–24 C.)

Q. Servilius Caepio Scaurum ob legationis Asiaticae invidiam {et}[1] adversus leges pecuniarum captarum reum
fecit repetundarum lege quam tulit Servilius Glaucia.[2]
Scaurus tanta fuit continentia animi et magnitudine ut
Caepionem contra reum[3] detulerit et breviore die inqui-
sitionis accepta effecerit ut ille prior causam diceret; M.
quoque Drusum tribunum plebis cohortatus est[4] ut iudicia commutaret.

[1] *del. Mommsen*   [2] Glaucia *Lodoicus*: claudia gracchia
codd.   [3] contra reum *Manutius*: contrarium *codd.*   [4] est
Mommsen: sit *vel* fuit *codd.*

F 9 Charis., *GL* I, p. 147.10–11 = pp. 186.30–87.1 B.

vulturius M. Aemilius Scaurus contra Quintum Caepionem actione II, "nefarius vulturius, patriae parricida"
. . .

F 10 Charis., *GL* I, p. 147.12–13 = p. 187.2–3 B.

. . . idem in eadem Scaurus: "vulturius rei publicae."

Against Q. Servilius Caepio (F 8–10)

*In late 92 or early 91 BC Scaurus was accused of financial malpractice by Q. Servilius Caepio (**85** F 3) (TLRR 96; Cic. Scaur. F I[d]; Flor. 2.5.5). In turn, Scaurus took Caepio to court, presumably also for extortion (TLRR 97).*

F 8 Asconius on Cicero, *Pro Scauro*

Q. Servilius Caepio [**85** F 3] took Scaurus to court, because of the resentment on account of the Asian embassy, for taking money against the law, under the law on the recovery of extorted money that Servilius Glaucia [C. Servilius Glaucia (**58b**)] put forward [*Lex Servilia repetundarum: LPPR*, p. 322]. Scaurus was of such self-control and greatness of mind that, in return, he charged Caepio and, having obtained an earlier date for the investigation, achieved that the other should plead his case first; he also urged M. Drusus, the Tribune of the People [M. Livius Drusus (**72**), tr. pl. 91 BC], to modify the courts [i.e., change the composition of juries].

F 9 Charisius

vulturius ["vulture"], M. Aemilius Scaurus against Quintus Caepio in the second hearing: "abominable vulture, assassin of the fatherland" . . .

F 10 Charisius

. . . the same Scaurus in the same [speech]: "vulture of the Republic."

In His Defense Against Q. Varius Hybrida (F 11)

*In 90 BC, in old age, Scaurus was challenged by the Tri-
bune of the People Q. Varius Hybrida (**88**), cooperating
with Q. Servilius Caepio (**85** F 4–7), to defend himself (cf.
Cic. Sest. 101; Scaur. F I[e]; slightly different versions in*

F 11 Asc. in Cic. in *Scaur.* I.3 (pp. 19–20 KS = 22.5–
20 C.)

non multo ante, Italico bello exorto, cum ob sociis nega-
tam civitatem nobilitas in invidia esset, Q. Varius tr. pl.
legem tulit ut quaereretur de iis quorum ope consiliove
socii contra populum Romanum arma sumpsissent. tum
Q. Caepio vetus inimicus Scauri sperans se invenisse occasionem[1] opprimendi eius egit[2] ut Q. Varius tribunus plebis
belli concitati crimine adesse apud se Scaurum iuberet
anno LXXII. ille per viatorem arcessitus, cum iam ex
morbo male solveretur, dissuadentibus amicis ne se in illa
valetudine et aetate invidiae populi obiceret, innixus nobi-
lissimis iuvenibus, processit in forum, deinde accepto respondendi loco dixit: "Q. Varius Hispanus M. Scaurum
principem senatus socios in arma ait convocasse; M. Scaurus princeps senatus negat; testis nemo est: utri vos, Qui-

---

[1] se invenisse occasionem *Manutius*: se inuenisse se questi-
onem *vel* inuenisse se (se) quaestionem *codd.*   [2] egit *suppl.*
unus cod., Poggius: om. cett.

In His Defense Against Q. Varius Hybrida (F 11)

Val. Max. 3.7.8; Quint. Inst. 5.12.10; Vir. ill. 72.11; cf.
Gruen 1965, 62–63); presumably, the Tribune first denounced him in a contio, which was followed by charges
under the Lex Varia de maiestate (see 88) (TLRR 100).

F 11 Asconius on Cicero, *Pro Scauro*

Not much earlier, after the Italic War had broken out,
when, because of having denied the citizenship to the allies, the nobility was experiencing unpopularity, Q. Varius
[Q. Varius Hybrida (**88**)], a Tribune of the People, put
forward a law that there should be an investigation about
those through whose help or advice allies had taken up
arms against the Roman People [*Lex Varia de maiestate*].
Then Q. Caepio [Q. Servilius Caepio (**85**), F 4–7], an old
enemy of Scaurus, hoping that he had found a chance to
overwhelm him, arranged it so that Q. Varius, the Tribune
of the People, ordered Scaurus, in his seventy-second
year, to appear in front of him on the charge of having
stirred up war. He [Scaurus], summoned by an officer,
when he was just barely freed from an illness, while his
friends argued against him putting himself against the ill
will of the People in such a state of health and age, leaning
upon very noble young men, proceeded into the Forum;
then, having accepted the position of respondent, he said:
"Q. Varius the Spaniard[1] says that M. Scaurus, the leader
of the Senate, has called the allies to arms; M. Scaurus,
the leader of the Senate, denies it; there is no witness:

---

[1] Here, employed as a term of abuse.

239

rites, convenit credere?" qua voce ita omnium commutavit animos ut ab ipso etiam tribuno dimitteretur.

44 P. RUTILIUS RUFUS

P. Rutilius Rufus (cos. 105 BC; RE Rutilius 34) was known for his outstandingly upright character (on his life see FRHist 1:278–79; on his oratory see Aubert-Baillot 2014).

*Rutilius was a recognized and active legal expert, educated in Greek literature, and a follower of the Stoics and Panaetius in particular (T 1; Cic. De or. 1.226; Off. 2.47, 3.10); he was in close contact with other educated Romans, such as C. Laelius Sapiens (**20**) and P. Mucius Scaevola*

T 1 Cic. *Brut.* 110–16 (cf. **43** T 1)

[CICERO:] de Scauro et Rutilio breviter licet dicere, quorum neuter summi oratoris habuit laudem, et ‹est› uterque[1] in multis causis versatus. erat in quibusdam laudandis viris, etiam si maximi ingeni non essent, probabilis tamen industria;[2] quamquam his quidem non omnino ingenium, sed oratorium ingenium defuit. . . . [113] . . . Rutilius autem in quodam tristi et severo genere dicendi versatus est. e‹ra›t[3] uterque natura vehemens et acer. . . .

---

[1] et ‹est› uterque *Stangl*: et uterque *codd.*: at uterque versatus est *Martha*   [2] erat in quibusdam laudandis viris . . . probabilis tamen industria *Peter*: erat. in quibusdam laudandis viris etiamsi . . . probabiles *codd.*: erant . . . laudandi viri et, vel si . . . probabiles *Stangl*: erat: in quibusdam laudandi viri . . . probabiles *Orelli*   [3] e‹ra›t *Jahn*: et *codd.*

which of the two, Romans, is it appropriate for you to believe?" With this utterance he changed the minds of all to such an extent that he was released even by the Tribune himself.

44 P. RUTILIUS RUFUS

(Cic. Off. 2.47; Amic. 101). Presumably while in exile, Rutilius wrote a historical work in Greek and a description of his life in Latin in at least five books (FRHist 21).

In Cicero, Rutilius' speeches are described as severe, sharp, and unembellished, as was to be expected from a Stoic (T 1; Cic. Brut. 118; De or. 1.227–29). Some of Rutilius' speeches seem to have survived until the time of the emperor Augustus (F 2).

T 1 Cicero, *Brutus* (cf. **43** T 1)

[CICERO:] Concerning Scaurus [M. Aemilius Scaurus (**43**)] and Rutilius one may speak briefly: neither of them had the reputation of being an orator of the first rank, and both ⟨were⟩ active in many court cases. Some men of high reputation, even though they did not have the greatest talent, still possessed commendable industry; yet these men lacked not any talent at all, but talent for oratory. . . . [113] . . . Rutilius, on the other hand, kept to a somber and severe style of speaking. Both men were by nature forceful

multaque opera multaque industria Rutilius fuit, quae
erat propterea gratior, quod idem magnum munus de iure
respondendi sustinebat. [114] sunt eius orationes ieiunae;
multa praeclara de iure; doctus vir et Graecis litteris eruditus, Panaeti auditor, prope perfectus in Stoicis; . . . [F 3]
. . . [116] habemus igitur in Stoicis oratoribus Rutilium,
Scaurum in antiquis; utrumque tamen laudemus, quoniam per illos ne haec quidem in civitate genera hac oratoria laude caruerunt.

Against M. Aemilius Scaurus (F 2A)

F 2A Cic. *Brut.* 113; Cic. *De or.* 2.280
= **43** F 3–4.

On the Size of Buildings (F 2)

F 2 Suet. *Aug.* 89.2
= **18** F 5.

and sharp. . . . Rutilius was a man of much activity and much industry, which was the more appreciated because he also shouldered an extensive service of responding to questions of law. [114] His orations are jejune; [there are] many admirable passages on questions of law; [he was] a man of learning and educated in Greek letters, a pupil of Panaetius, almost perfectly trained in Stoic matters. . . . [F 3] . . . [116] Thus we have Rutilius among the Stoic orators, Scaurus among the old-fashioned ones; still, let us praise both since through them not even these types of oratory have been without distinction in this community.

Against M. Aemilius Scaurus (F 2A)

*After his first (unsuccessful) candidacy for the consulship in 116 BC, Rutilius accused his successful rival M. Aemilius Scaurus (**43**) of ambitus; he was prosecuted on the same charge by the latter (**43** F 3–4) (TLRR 34, 35).*

F 2A Cicero, *Brutus*; Cicero, *On the Orator*
= **43** F 3–4.

On the Size of Buildings (F 2)

F 2 Suetonius, *Life of Augustus*
= **18** F 5.

FRL III: ORATORY, PART 1

In His Defense Concerning Extortion (F 3–6)

*After a military career, Rutilius went to Asia in the 90s BC and supported the local population against the abuses of tax collectors; thereupon, after his return to Rome, he was prosecuted on a charge of extortion, mainly by Apicius; he defended himself, supported by Q. Mucius Scaevola (**67** F 7–8) and C. Aurelius Cotta (**80** F 8–9). Due to the perjury of the judges, Rutilius was found guilty and went into*

F 3 Cic. *Brut.* 115

[CICERO:] qui cum innocentissimus[1] in iudicium vocatus esset, quo iudicio convulsam penitus scimus esse rem publicam, cum essent eo tempore eloquentissimi viri L. Crassus et M. Antonius consulares, eorum adhibere neutrum voluit. dixit ipse pro sese et pauca C. Cotta, quod sororis erat filius . . . et Q.[2] Mucius enucleate ille quidem et polite, ut solebat, nequaquam autem ea vi atque copia quam genus illud iudici et magnitudo causae postulabat.

[1] cum innocentissimus *edd.*: quam innocentissimus *codd.*: quamquam innocentissimus *Lambinus*   [2] et Q. *Bake*: sed Q. *codd.*

In His Defense Concerning Extortion (F 3–6)

exile in Asia (TLRR 94; Posid. FGrHist 87 F 27; Ath. 4, p. 168d). The trial came to be seen as an example of a wrongful condemnation of a virtuous and innocent person (Cic. Font. 38; Val. Max. 6.4.4; Vell. Pat. 2.13.2). Cicero visited Rutilius in Smyrna in 78 BC and allegedly learned from him stories about orators and politicians of an earlier generation (Cic. Rep. 1.13; Brut. 85 [19 F 16]).

F 3 Cicero, *Brutus*

[CICERO:] When he [Rutilius], though perfectly innocent, had been brought to that trial by which, as we know, the Republic was profoundly rent asunder, while at that time L. Crassus [L. Licinius Crassus (**66**)] and M. Antonius [**65**], ex-consuls, most eloquent men, were around, he did not wish to invoke the aid of either of them. He spoke himself in his own defense, and C. Cotta [C. Aurelius Cotta (**80**), F 8–9], since he was the son of his sister, added a few words . . . and Q. Mucius [Q. Mucius Scaevola (**67**), F 7–8] spoke, precisely indeed and in a carefully finished manner, as he was accustomed to, but in no way with that fire and fullness that this kind of trial and the significance of the case demanded.

F 4 Liv. *Epit*. 70.8

P. Rutilius, vir summae innocentiae, quoniam legatus C. Muci procos. a publicanorum iniuriis Asiam defenderat, invisus equestri ordini, penes quem iudicia erant, repetundarum damnatus in exilium missus est.

F 5 Cass. Dio 28, F 97.1–2 Boissevain

ὅτι τοῦ Ῥουτιλίου ἀγαθοῦ ὄντος ἀνδρὸς ἀδικώτατα κατεψηφίσαντο· ἐσήχθη γὰρ ἐς δικαστήριον ἐκ κατασκευασμοῦ τῶν ἱππέων ὡς δωροδοκή<σας . . .>[1] . . . [2] ὅτι ὁ Ῥουτίλιος ἀπελογήσατο μὲν γενναιότατα, καὶ οὐδὲν ὅ τι οὐκ εἶπεν ὧν <ἂν>[2] ἀνὴρ ἀγαθὸς συκοφαντούμενος καὶ πολὺ πλεῖον τὰ τῶν κοινῶν ἢ τὰ ἑαυτοῦ ὀδυρόμενος φθέγξαιτο, ἑάλω δέ, καὶ τῆς γε οὐσίας εὐθὺς ἐξέστη.

[1] *post* δωροδοκή *lac. statuit Boissevain, quam e.g. suppl.*: δωροδοκή<σας ὑποστρατηγῶν ἐν τῇ Ἀσίᾳ τῷ> [2] *add. Bekker*

F 6 Oros. *Hist*. 5.17.12–13

Rutilius quoque vir integerrimus adeo fidei atque innocentiae constantia usus est ut die sibi ab accusatoribus dicta usque ad cognitionem neque capillum barbamve

F 4 Livy, *Epitome*

P. Rutilius, a man of the highest integrity, since, as legate of the proconsul C.[1] Mucius, he had defended Asia from the injustices of the tax collectors, was hated by the equestrian order, who were in charge of the courts; thus, he was found guilty of extortion and sent into exile.[2]

[1] Apparently a mistake for *Q.*: Q. Mucius Scaevola (**67**) was proconsul in Asia after his consulship and administered the province in an exemplary way (e.g., Cic. *Div. Caec.* 57; *Verr.* 2.3.209). [2] This passage provides information about the trial but does not confirm that P. Rutilius Rufus delivered a speech.

F 5 Cassius Dio, *Roman History*

They condemned Rutilius, an upright man, most unjustly; for he was brought into court by a fabricated plan of the knights on the charge of having received bri‹bes . . .› . . . [2] Rutilius defended himself very nobly; and there was nothing that he did not say of what an upright man would say, being falsely accused and grieving far more for the fate of the community than for his own; he was convicted, however, and immediately stripped of his property.

F 6 Orosius, *Histories*

Rutilius too, a most upright man, maintained honesty and blamelessness to such an extent that, after the date had been announced to him by his accusers, until the trial he

promiserit, neque sordida veste humilive habitu suffraga-
tores conciliarit, inimicos permulserit, iudices temperarit,
orationem quoque a praetore concessam nihilo summis-
siorem quam animum habuerit. [13] cum evidenti op-
pugnaretur calumnia et opinione bonorum omnium iure
absolvendus putaretur, peiurio iudicum condemnatus est.

45 Q. AELIUS TUBERO

According to Cicero, Q. Aelius Tubero (tr. pl. 129 BC; RE
*Aelius 155), a grandson of L. Aemilius Paullus (**12**) and a*
nephew of P. Cornelius Scipio Aemilianus Africanus minor
*(**21**), was a mediocre orator with rough language, though*
skilled argument. Besides, he is described as a good and
steadfast citizen; he followed the Stoics and is the ad-
dressee of works by the Stoic philosophers Panaetius and

T 1 Cic. *Brut.* 117–18

[CICERO:] "et quoniam Stoicorum est facta mentio, Q.
Aelius Tubero fuit illo tempore, L. Paulli nepos; nullo in
oratorum numero, sed vita severus et congruens cum ea
disciplina quam colebat, paulo etiam durior . . . sed ut vita
sic oratione durus, incultus, horridus; itaque honoribus
maiorum respondere non potuit. fuit autem constans civis
et fortis et in primis Graccho molestus, quod indicat

neither let his hair or beard grow nor procured the favor
of supporters by filthy dress or lowly attire [i.e., as the accused typically did], nor appeased his enemies, nor influenced the judges, and even delivered a speech, as granted
by the praetor, in no way more submissive than his mind.
[13] When he was attacked by obvious false accusation and
was believed as justly due for release in the view of all good
men, he was found guilty due to perjury of the judges.

45 Q. AELIUS TUBERO

his pupil Hecaton of Rhodes (T 1; Cic. Tusc. *4.4;* Fin. *4.23;*
Off. *3.63;* De or. *3.87;* Acad. *2.135).*

    Cicero mentions speeches by Tubero against C. Sempro-
nius Gracchus (48) (T 1; Cic. Amic. *37). Tubero is a*
speaker in Cicero's treatise De re publica *(on the funeral*
eulogy of P. Cornelius Scipio Aemilianus Africanus minor
[21], see C. Laelius Sapiens [20], F 22–23).

T 1 Cicero, *Brutus*

[CICERO:] "And since mention of the Stoics has been
made [cf. **43** T 1; **44** T 1], Q. Aelius Tubero, L. Paullus'
[L. Aemilius Paullus (**12**)] grandson, was around in that
same period, of no account among the orators, but severe
in his way of life and congruent with that philosophy that
he practiced, even somewhat more rigid . . . but as in life,
so in his oratory he was harsh, unrefined, and rough; therefore, he was not able to match the ranks of offices of his
ancestors. He was, however, a steadfast and courageous
citizen, and, in particular, troublesome to Gracchus, as
Gracchus' speech against him shows [C. Sempronius

Gracchi in eum oratio. sunt etiam in Gracchum Tuberonis;
is fuit mediocris in dicendo, doctissimus in disputando."
[118] tum BRUTUS: "quam hoc idem in nostris contingere
intellego quod in Graecis, ut omnes fere Stoici prudentis-
simi in disserendo sint et id arte faciant sintque architecti
paene verborum, idem traducti a disputando ad dicendum
inopes reperiantur. unum excipio Catonem, in quo per-
fectissimo Stoico summam eloquentiam non desiderem,
quam exiguam in Fannio, ne in Rutilio quidem magnam,
in Tuberone nullam video fuisse."

46 M. IUNIUS PENNUS

*M. Iunius Pennus (RE Iunius 123) was a Tribune of the
People in 126 BC; his career was cut short by an untimely
death after his aedileship (T 1). As Tribune of the People,
Pennus proposed a law arranging for the expulsion of for-*

T 1 Cic. *Brut.* 109

[CICERO:] tuus etiam gentilis, Brute, M. Pennus facete[1]
agitavit in tribunatu C. Gracchum, paulum[2] aetate antecedens. fuit enim M.[3] Lepido et L. Oreste consulibus quaestor Gracchus, tribunus Pennus, illius Marci filius, qui cum
Q. Aelio consul fuit; sed is omnia summa sperans aedili-
cius est mortuus.

---

[1] facete *Lambinus*: facile *codd.*
edd.: paulum C. Gracchum *codd.*

[2] C. Gracchum paulum
[3] M. *vel* L. *codd.*

Gracchus (**48**), F 54–55]. There are also [speeches] of
Tubero against Gracchus; he was mediocre in speaking,
but very skilled in debating." [118] Thereupon BRUTUS
[said]: "Remarkable: I see the same thing applying to our
countrymen as to the Greeks, that practically all Stoics are
very able in precise exposition, and they do that with art
and are almost architects of words; but when the same
people are transferred from debating to speaking, they are
found to be deficient. One exception I make for Cato [M.
Porcius Cato (**126**), T 1], in whom, though a most accomplished Stoic, I feel no desire for the most perfect eloquence, which I regard as slight in Fannius, even in Rutilius [P. Rutilius Rufus (**44**)] as not great, in Tubero as
nonexistent."

46 M. IUNIUS PENNUS

*eigners from Rome (MRR I 508; Cic. Off. 3.47; Lex Iunia
de peregrinis: LPPR, p. 304). C. Sempronius Gracchus
(**48** F 21–22) spoke against the bill, but it was approved.*

T 1 Cicero, *Brutus*

[CICERO:] Your kinsman too, Brutus, M. Pennus, in his
Tribunate, wittily harassed C. Gracchus [C. Sempronius
Gracchus (**48**)], Pennus being a little more advanced in
age. For in the consulship of M. Lepidus and L. Orestes
[126 BC] Gracchus was quaestor, and Pennus, son of that
Marcus who was consul with Q. Aelius [167 BC], was Tribune; but he, hoping for all the highest honors, died after
his aedileship.

47 C. SCRIBONIUS CURIO AVUS

C. Scribonius Curio (praet. ca. 121 BC; RE Scribonius 9)
was the father and then the grandfather of two politicians
and orators of the same name (86 + 170; cf. T 4; F 7; on
these three orators see Rosillo López 2013).

T 1 Cic. *Brut.* 122–24 (cf. F 6)

[CICERO:] "Curio fuit igitur eiusdem aetatis fere sane in-
lustris orator, cuius de ingenio ex orationibus eius existimari potest: sunt enim et aliae et pro Ser. Fulvio de incestu
nobilis oratio. . . ." [123] . . . [124] ". . . scripsit etiam alia
non nulla et multa dixit et illustria et[1] in numero patronorum fuit, ut eum mirer, cum et vita suppeditavisset et
splendor ei non defuisset, consulem non fuisse. . . ."

[1] et illustria et *edd.*: illustri et in *codd.*: et illustri in numero
{patronum} *Martha*

T 2 Cic. *De or.* 2.98

[ANTONIUS:] . . . vester aequalis Curio, patre mea sententia vel eloquentissimo temporibus illis . . .

T 3 Sen. *Ep.* 114.13
= **1** T 1.

47 C. SCRIBONIUS CURIO AVUS

*In Cicero's works Curio is described as an active and
highly regarded orator in his time. Some of his speeches
survived into the age of Cicero; by then they were hardly
read any more and were regarded as not too sophisticated
(T 1–2; F 6).*

T 1 Cicero, *Brutus* (cf. F 6)

[CICERO:] "Curio, then, was quite a distinguished orator
of about the same time [of the Gracchi]; his talent can be
judged from his orations: for there are others and in particular the well-known speech for Ser. Fulvius on the
charge of sexual impurity. . . ." [123] . . . [124] ". . . He
wrote several other things, he gave many distinguished
speeches, and he was prominent among the pleaders; accordingly, I am wondering, since his life lasted for a long
time and also personal distinction was not lacking, that he
never was consul. . . ."

T 2 Cicero, *On the Orator*

[ANTONIUS:] . . . Curio [C. Scribonius Curio (**86**)], your
contemporary, whose father, in my view, was even the
most eloquent in that period . . .

T 3 Seneca, *Epistles*

= **1** T 1.

T 4 Plin. *HN* 7.133

. . . una familia Curionum, in qua tres continua serie oratores exstiterint . . .

T 5 Tac. *Dial.* 37.2–3

[CURIATIUS MATERNUS:] nescio an venerint in manus vestras haec vetera, quae et in antiqu⟨ari⟩orum[1] bibliothecis adhuc manent et cum maxime a Muciano contrahuntur, ac iam undecim, ut opinor, Actorum libris et tribus Epistularum composita et edita sunt. [3] ex his intellegi potest Cn. Pompeium et M. Crassum non viribus modo et armis, sed ingenio quoque et oratione valuisse; Lentulos et Metellos et Lucullos et Curiones et ceteram procerum manum multum in his studiis operae curaeque posuisse, nec quemquam illis temporibus magnam potentiam sine aliqua eloquentia consecutum.

1 antiqu⟨ari⟩orum *Schurzfleisch*: antiquorum *codd.*

On Behalf of Ser. Fulvius Concerning
Sexual Impurity (F 6–8)

The identity of the Ser. Fulvius defended by Curio on a charge of unchastity is uncertain (TLRR 44). It has been suggested that Ser. Fulvius was accused of sexual relations

F 6 Cic. *Brut.* 122–24 (cf. T 1)

[CICERO:] ". . . sunt enim et aliae et pro Ser. Fulvio de

T 4 Pliny the Elder, *Natural History*

. . . a single family, the Curiones, where three orators in unbroken series have emerged . . .

T 5 Tacitus, *Dialogue on Oratory*

[CURIATIUS MATERNUS:] I wonder whether these ancient records have come into your hands, the records that are still extant in the libraries of students of the past and at this very moment are being collected by Mucianus [C. Licinius Mucianus, cos. suff. ca. 64, 70 AD and author] and have already been arranged and edited in eleven volumes, I believe, of Proceedings and three of Letters. [3] From these it can be concluded that Pompey [Cn. Pompeius Magnus (**111**)] and Crassus [M. Licinius Crassus Dives (**102**)] were powerful not only by force and arms, but also by natural ability and oratory, that the Lentuli and the Metelli and the Luculli and the Curiones and the rest of the group of noblemen devoted a lot of care and attention to these pursuits, and that in that period nobody achieved great influence without some kind of eloquence.

On Behalf of Ser. Fulvius Concerning
Sexual Impurity (F 6–8)

with a Vestal Virgin and that this case was the same as the
*one in which M. Antonius (**65**) and L. Licinius Crassus*
*(**66**) were involved (114/13 BC).*

F 6 Cicero, *Brutus* (cf. T 1)

[CICERO:] ". . . for there are others and in particular the well-known speech for Ser. Fulvius on the charge of sexual

incestu nobilis oratio. nobis quidem pueris haec omnium optima putabatur, quae vix iam comparet in hac turba novorum voluminum." [123] . . . [124] "atqui haec," inquam, "de incestu laudata oratio puerilis est locis multis: de amore, de tormentis, de rumore loci sane inanes, verum tamen nondum tritis nostrorum hominum auribus nec erudita civitate tolerabiles. . . ."

F 7 Schol. Bob. ad Cic. *Clod. et Cur.* (p. 85.17–19 Stangl)

nam tres illis temporibus Curiones inlustri nomine extiterunt atque ita in libris adhuc feruntur: Curio avus qui Servium Fulvium incesti reum defendit . . .

F 8 Cic. *Inv. rhet.* 1.80

quod pro credibili sumptum erit, infirmabitur si . . . id, quod raro fit, fieri omnino negatur, ut Curio pro Fulvio: "nemo potest uno aspectu neque praeteriens in amorem incidere."

Cf. *Rhet. Her.* 2.33.

48 C. SEMPRONIUS GRACCHUS

C. Sempronius Gracchus (trib. pl. 123, 122 BC; RE Sempronius 47) was the younger brother of Ti. Sempronius Gracchus (34) and the son of Ti. Sempronius Gracchus (10). In 133 BC C. Gracchus was a member of his brother's agrarian commission; later, he became quaestor and

impurity. When we were boys, this was considered the best of all; now it is hardly visible in this mass of new volumes." [123] . . . [124] "But this much praised oration on sexual impurity," I [CICERO] said, "is puerile in many places: about love, about torture, about rumor, worthless passages indeed, and yet, when the ears of our people were not yet practiced and the public untrained, they were tolerable. . . ."

F 7 Scholia Bobiensia to Cicero, *Against Clodius and Curio*

For in those times there were three men called Curio with an illustrious name, and they are still referred to in the books thus: Curio the grandfather, who defended Servius Fulvius accused of sexual impurity . . .

F 8 Cicero, *On Invention*

What is adduced as credible will be weakened if . . . what rarely happens is declared never to happen at all, as Curio [does in the speech] on behalf of Fulvius: "No one can fall in love at first sight or as he is passing by."

48 C. SEMPRONIUS GRACCHUS

then Tribune of the People for 123 and 122 BC. As Tribune, he proposed a number of "popular" laws and died in the struggle with the nobility in 121 BC (on his life, see Plut. C. Gracch.; on the lives of the Gracchi, see Stockton 1979, on C. Gracchus' speeches, pp. 217–25; Sciarrino 2007,

60–64; on his career and oratory, van der Blom 2016,
69–112, on his speeches, pp. 290–95; for testimonia and
fragments with commentary, see Häpke 1915; for a selec-
tion of fragments with commentary, see Courtney 1999,
124–33; on his style, see von Albrecht 1989, 33–53 [esp. on
F 48]).

Like his brother, C. Gracchus enjoyed a thorough edu-
*cation (see **34**). In Cicero's works C. Gracchus' rhetorical*
brilliance, especially in delivery, style, and ideas, is high-
lighted, while it is regretted that he did not apply his
abilities to better purposes, that their development was cut
short by an untimely death, and that he neglected to give
his writings the final polish (T 1–3; Cic. Brut. 296; De or.
1.38, 1.154, 3.225; Font. 39 [F 39]; cf. T 8, 9, 10; Val. Max.
8.10.1; Apul. Apol. 95.5; Fronto, Ad Ant. 3.1.3 [p. 105.13–
15 van den Hout]; for further characteristics of C. Grac-
*chus' speeches, see, e.g., T 7, 13, 14; Plin. Ep. 1.20.4: **121***
T 9). Ancient authorities regard C. Gracchus' eloquence
highly and rate it above that of his brother (T 4–5; Rhet.
Her. 4.2; Quint. Inst. 1.10.27; Plut. C. Gracch. 24[3].4;

T 1 Cic. *Brut.* 125–26

[Cicero:] ". . . sed ecce in manibus vir et praestantissimo
ingenio et flagranti studio et doctus a puero C. Gracchus.
noli enim putare quemquam, Brute, pleniorem aut ube-
riorem ad dicendum fuisse." . . . ". . . damnum enim illius
immaturo interitu res Romanae Latinaeque litterae fece-
runt. [126] utinam non tam fratri pietatem quam patriae
praestare voluisset! quam ille facile tali ingenio, diutius si
vixisset, vel paternam esset vel avitam gloriam consecutus!

Cass. Dio 25.85.1; but cf. T 13); modern scholars therefore
generally assign utterances attributed to "Gracchus" to
him. In the Rhetorica ad Herennium *C. Gracchus is listed*
as one of the writers from whom examples for students
could be drawn (Rhet. Her. 4.7: **25** *T 5).*

Written versions of some speeches of C. Gracchus ex-
isted, and some were available in writing after his death
(T 1, 12; F 22, 41, 59). C. Gracchus may also have com-
posed a historical work (FRHist 11; cf. Cic. Div. 1.36, 2.62;
Plut. Ti. Gracch. *8.9).*

Further occasions (beyond those attested below) on
which C. Gracchus must have spoken are known, even if
details of these orations have not been preserved: speeches
to the People (Diod. Sic. 34.25.1); proposal of a grain law
(Cic. Sest. 103); explanation that M. Octavius was released
upon the request of C. Gracchus' mother, Cornelia (Plut.
C. Gracch. 25(4).3; Diod. Sic. 34.25.2); speech to prompt
the Senate to sell the grain sent to Rome from Hispania by
the propraetor Fabius and transfer the money back (Plut.
C. Gracch. 27(6).2).

T 1 Cicero, *Brutus*

[CICERO:] ". . . But now there is at hand a man of preeminent talent, of intense application, of careful training
from boyhood, C. Gracchus. For do not imagine, Brutus,
that anyone was ever more completely or more richly en-
dowed for speaking." . . . ". . . For by his untimely death
the Roman state and Latin letters suffered a loss. [126]
Would that he had wished to show loyalty not so much to
his brother as to his country! How easily with such talent
would he have achieved the glory of his father or his

eloquentia quidem nescio an habuisset parem neminem. grandis est verbis, sapiens sententiis, genere toto gravis. manus extrema non accessit operibus eius; praeclare incohata multa, perfecta non plane. legendus, inquam, est hic orator, Brute, si quisquam alius, iuventuti; non enim solum acuere sed etiam alere ingenium potest. . . ."

T 2 Cic. *Brut.* 333

= **34** T 4.

T 3 Cic. *Har. resp.* 41

secutus est C. Gracchus, quo ingenio, qua eloquentia, quanta vi, quanta gravitate dicendi! ut dolerent boni non illa tanta ornamenta ad meliorem mentem voluntatemque esse conversa.

T 4 Liv. *Epit.* 60.7

⟨C.⟩[1] Gracchus, Tiberi frater, trib. plebis, eloquentior quam frater . . .

   [1] *add. ed. Frobeniana*

T 5 Vell. Pat. 2.6.1

decem deinde interpositis annis, qui Ti. Gracchum, idem Gaium fratrem eius occupavit furor, tam virtutibus eius omnibus quam huic errori similem, ingenio etiam eloquentiaque longe praestantiorem.

T 6 Sen. *Ep.* 114.13

= **1** T 1.

grandfather had he lived longer! In eloquence at least, he would probably not have had any equal. He is elevated in diction, thoughtful in ideas, in his whole style impressive. The final touch has not come to his works; there is much brilliantly begun, not absolutely finished to perfection. This orator, I say, is to be read, Brutus, he if anyone, by our youth; for he can not only sharpen, but also nourish the mind. . . ."

T 2 Cicero, *Brutus*

= **34** T 4.

T 3 Cicero, *De Haruspicum Responsis*

C. Gracchus followed, of what talent, what eloquence, what great force, what great impressiveness of speaking! Therefore, the loyal men regretted that those great endowments were not turned to better purposes and ambitions.

T 4 Livy, *Epitome*

⟨C.⟩ Gracchus, Tiberius' brother, a Tribune of the People, more eloquent than his brother . . .

T 5 Velleius Paterculus, *Compendium of Roman History*

Then, after an interval of ten years, the same madness that [had possessed] Ti. Gracchus seized upon his brother Gaius, in all the former's virtues as well as in this error similar, yet in talent and eloquence far superior.

T 6 Seneca, *Epistles*

= **1** T 1.

T 7 Plut. *Ti. Gracch.* 2.2–6

πρῶτον μὲν οὖν ἰδέᾳ προσώπου καὶ βλέμματι καὶ κι-
νήματι πρᾷος καὶ καταστηματικὸς ἦν ὁ Τιβέριος,
ἔντονος δὲ καὶ σφοδρὸς ὁ Γάιος, ὥστε καὶ δημηγορεῖν
τὸν μὲν ἐν μιᾷ χώρᾳ βεβηκότα κοσμίως, τὸν δὲ Ῥωμαίων πρῶτον ἐπὶ τοῦ βήματος περιπάτῳ τε χρή-
σασθαι καὶ περισπάσαι τὴν τήβεννον ἐξ ὤμου λέ-
γοντα . . . [3] ἔπειθ' ὁ λόγος τοῦ μὲν Γαΐου φοβερὸς
καὶ περιπαθὴς εἰς δείνωσιν, ἡδίων δ' ὁ τοῦ Τιβερίου
καὶ μᾶλλον ἐπαγωγὸς οἴκτου· τῇ δὲ λέξει καθαρὸς καὶ
διαπεπονημένος ἀκριβῶς ἐκεῖνος, ὁ δὲ Γαΐου πιθανὸς
καὶ γεγανωμένος. [4] . . . [5] τῷ δὲ ἤθει κατὰ τὴν τοῦ
λόγου διαφορὰν ὁ μὲν ἐπιεικὴς καὶ πρᾷος, ὁ δὲ τρα-
χὺς καὶ θυμοειδής, ὥστε καὶ παρὰ γνώμην ἐν τῷ λέγειν ἐκφερόμενον πολλάκις ὑπ' ὀργῆς τήν τε φωνὴν
ἀποξύνειν καὶ βλασφημεῖν καὶ συνταράττειν τὸν λόγον. [6] ὅθεν καὶ βοήθημα τῆς ἐκτροπῆς ταύτης
ἐποιήσατο {τὸν}[1] Λικίννιον οἰκέτην οὐκ ἀνόητον, ὃς
ἔχων φωνασκικὸν ὄργανον, ᾧ τοὺς φθόγγους ἀναβι-
βάζουσιν, ὄπισθεν ἑστὼς τοῦ Γαΐου λέγοντος, ὁπη-
νίκα τραχυνόμενον αἴσθοιτο τῇ φωνῇ καὶ παραρρη-
γνύμενον δι' ὀργήν, ἐνεδίδου τόνον μαλακόν, ᾧ τὸ
σφοδρὸν εὐθὺς ἐκεῖνος ἅμα τοῦ πάθους καὶ τῆς φωνῆς
ἀνιεὶς ἐπραΰνετο καὶ παρεῖχεν ἑαυτὸν εὐανάκλητον.

[1] del. Ziegler

Cf. Cic. *De or.* 3.225–27; Val. Max. 8.10.1; Quint. *Inst.* 1.10.27;
Gell. *NA* 1.11.10; Amm. Marc. 30.4.19; Plut. *Mor.* 456A.

T 7 Plutarch, *Life of Tiberius Gracchus*

In the first place, then, as regards cast of features and look and bearing, Tiberius was gentle and sedate, while Gaius was high-strung and vehement, so that, even when speaking to the People, the one stood composedly in one spot, while the other was the first Roman to walk around on the Rostra and pull his toga off his shoulder as he spoke . . . [3] In the second place, the speech of Gaius was awe-inspiring and passionate to exaggeration, while that of Tiberius was more agreeable and more conducive to pity. And that man's style was pure and carefully elaborated, while that of Gaius was persuasive and ornate. [4] . . . [5] And in their tempers they were different as in their speech: the one [Tiberius] was reasonable and gentle, the other [Gaius] harsh and fiery, so that against his better judgment he was often carried away by anger when speaking, raised his voice to a high pitch, uttered abuse, and threw the oration into disorder. [6] Therefore, he even created a remedy against such digressions: Licinius, a not-unintelligent slave, who stood behind Gaius when he was speaking, with a sounding instrument by which one gives the tones of the voice their pitch; whenever he noticed that he [Gaius] was getting harsh and broken in his voice because of anger, he would give out a soft note, whereupon he would at once remit the vehemence of his passion and of his speech, grow gentle, and show himself easily reined in.

T 8 Plut. *C. Gracch.* 25(4).1

τοιούτοις λόγοις προανασείσας τὸν δῆμον—ἦν δὲ καὶ
μεγαλοφωνότατος καὶ ῥωμαλεώτατος ἐν τῷ λέγειν—
δύο νόμους εἰσέφερε . . .

T 9 Tac. *Dial.* 18.2

[APER:] . . . si illud ante praedixero, mutari cum temporibus formas quoque et genera dicendi. sic Catoni seni com-
paratus C. Gracchus plenior et uberior, sic Graccho poli-
tior et ornatior Crassus, sic utroque distinctior et urbanior
et altior Cicero, Cicerone mitior Corvinus et dulcior et in
verbis magis elaboratus.

T 10 Tac. *Dial.* 26.1

[MESSALLA:] ceterum si omisso optimo illo et perfectis-
simo genere eloquentiae eligenda sit forma dicendi, malim hercule C. Gracchi impetum aut L. Crassi maturita-
tem quam calamistros Maecenatis aut tinnitus Gallionis:
adeo melius est orationem vel hirta toga induere quam
fucatis et meretriciis vestibus insignire.

T 11 Fronto, *Ad M. Antoninum de eloquentia* 1.2
(p. 134.3–5 van den Hout)

[FRONTO:] contionatur . . . Gracchus turbulente, . . . iam
in iudiciis . . . tumultuatur Gracchus . . . [cf. **165 T 12**]

T 8 Plutarch, *Life of Gaius Gracchus*

Having first stirred up the People with such words—and he was both extremely loud-voiced and most vigorous in his speaking—he [C. Gracchus] proposed two laws . . .

T 9 Tacitus, *Dialogue on Oratory*

[APER:] . . . if I have first said this, that the forms and types of oratory also change with the times. Thus, compared with the old Cato [M. Porcius Cato (**8**)], C. Gracchus is fuller and richer; thus Crassus [L. Licinius Crassus (**66**)] is more finished and ornate than Gracchus; thus Cicero is more lucid, more elegant, and more profound than either of them; compared with Cicero, Corvinus [M. Valerius Messalla Corvinus (**176**)] is mellower, sweeter, and more elaborate in the choice of words.

T 10 Tacitus, *Dialogue on Oratory*

[MESSALLA:] Moreover, if, with that supreme and perfect form of eloquence discounted, a style of speaking were to be chosen, I should indeed prefer the vigor of C. Gracchus or the maturity of L. Crassus [L. Licinius Crassus (**66**)] to the curling tongs of Maecenas or the jangling sound of Gallio [L. Iunius Gallio, senator and friend of Seneca the Elder]: for it is so much better to clothe the speech even in a shaggy toga than to adorn it with the gay-colored garments of a courtesan.

T 11 Fronto, *Correspondence*

[FRONTO:] Gracchus delivers speeches to the People in a riotous way . . . further, in the courts . . . Gracchus creates a confused uproar . . . [cf. **165** T 12]

T 12 Fronto, *Ad M. Caes.* 3.19.1 (p. 51.2–4 van den Hout)

[M. AURELIUS ad Frontonem:] in quantum me iuverit lectio orationum istarum Gracchi, non opus est me dicere, quom tu scias optime, qui me ut eas legerem doctissimo iudicio ac benignissimo tuo animo hortatus es.

T 13 Gell. *NA* 10.3.1, 4, 6

fortis ac vehemens orator existimatur esse C. Gracchus. nemo id negat. sed quod nonnullis videtur severior, acrior ampliorque esse M. Tullio, ferri id qui potest? [2] . . . [F 48] . . . [4] in tam atroci re ac tam misera atque maesta iniuriae publicae contestatione ecquid est, quod aut ampliter insigniterque aut lacrimose atque miseranter aut multa copiosaque invidia gravique et penetrabili querimonia dixerit? brevitas sane et venustas et mundities orationis est, qualis haberi ferme in comoediarum festivitatibus solet. [5] . . . [6] haec quidem oratio super tam violento atque crudeli facinore nihil profecto abest a cotidianis sermonibus.

T 14 Serv. ad Verg. *Aen.* 11.301

"praefatus divos more antiquo": nam maiores nullam orationem nisi invocatis numinibus inchoabant, sicut sunt omnes orationes Catonis et Gracchi; nam generale caput in omnibus legimus.

T 12 Fronto, *Correspondence*

[M. AURELIUS to Fronto:] To what extent reading those orations of Gracchus has pleased me is not necessary for me to say, since you know it very well, as you have encouraged me to read these with your very experienced judgment and very kind mind.

T 13 Gellius, *Attic Nights*

C. Gracchus is regarded as a powerful and vigorous speaker. No one denies this. But how can this be tolerated that to some he seems to be more austere, more spirited, and more copious than M. Tullius [Cicero]? [2] ... [F 48] ... [4] With respect to such an atrocious matter, such a lamentable and sad manifestation of injustice committed by a public body, is there anything that he said either copiously and brilliantly, or in such a way as to arouse tears and pity, or with abundant and plentiful expression of indignation, and with an impressive and penetrating protest? Brevity there is, to be sure, and grace, and purity of speech, such as is usually found in the gaiety of comedies. [5] ... [6] Now this passage about such a violent and cruel misdeed certainly does not differ in the least from ordinary conversation.

T 14 Servius, *Commentary on Virgil*

"having addressed the gods in prayer beforehand according to ancient custom": For the ancestors did not open any speech without invoking the divinities, as is the case for all orations of Cato [M. Porcius Cato (**8**)] and Gracchus; for we read a generic beginning in all of them.

On Behalf of Vettius (F 15)

F 15 Plut. *C. Gracch.* 22(1).3

ἐπεὶ δὲ προϊόντος τοῦ χρόνου τόν τε τρόπον ἡσυχῇ
διέφαινεν ἀργίας καὶ μαλακίας καὶ πότων καὶ χρημα-
τισμῶν ἀλλότριον ὄντα, καὶ τὸν λόγον ὥσπερ ὠκύ-
πτερα κατασκευαζόμενος ἐπὶ τὴν πολιτείαν δῆλος ἦν
οὐκ ἠρεμήσων, δίκην τέ τινι τῶν φίλων φεύγοντι Βετ-
τίῳ συνειπών, τοῦ δήμου συνενθουσιῶντος ὑφ᾽ ἡδο-
νῆς καὶ βακχεύοντος περὶ αὐτόν, ἀπέδειξε τοὺς ἄλλους ῥήτορας παίδων μηδὲν διαφέροντας, εἰς φόβον
αὖθις οἱ δυνατοὶ καθίσταντο, καὶ πολὺς ἦν ἐν αὐτοῖς
λόγος, ὡς οὐκ ἐάσουσιν ἐπὶ δημαρχίαν τὸν Γάιον
προελθεῖν.

In Support of Lex Papiria (F 16–20)

*In 131 or 130 BC the Tribune of the People C. Papirius
Carbo (**35** F 7) proposed a bill to enable the reelection of
tribunes; this initiative was supported by C. Gracchus, but*

F 16 Liv. *Epit.* 59.11–12
= **21** F 29.

F 17 Charis., *GL* I, p. 240.16–20 = p. 313.18–23 B.

em G. Gracchus ut lex Papiria accipiatur: "pessimi Tiberium fratrem meum optimum interfecerunt. em! videte

On Behalf of Vettius (F 15)

C. Gracchus defended a friend called Vettius in an early speech, preceding his Tribunate (TLRR 19).

F 15 Plutarch, *Life of Gaius Gracchus*

But as time went on, he [C. Gracchus] gradually showed a disposition averse to idleness, effeminacy, drinking, and moneymaking; and by preparing his oratory like swift wings to public life, he made it clear that he was not going to remain quiet; and in defending Vettius, a friend of his who was prosecuted, he made the other orators appear to be no different from children while the People were inspired and frantic with sympathetic delight around him. Once more, therefore, the nobles began to be alarmed, and there was much talk among them that they should not permit Gaius to proceed to the Tribunate.

In Support of Lex Papiria *(F 16–20)*

*opposed by P. Cornelius Scipio Aemilianus Africanus minor (**21** F 28–29) and C. Laelius Sapiens (**20** F 21; CCMR, App. A: 186).*

F 16 Livy, *Epitome*

= **21** F 29.

F 17 Charisius

em ["look at this"], C. Gracchus [in the speech] that the *Lex Papiria* should be accepted: "The most villainous men have killed my brother Tiberius, an excellent man. *em*

quam par pari sim." at[1] quidam em pro en volunt esse. sed
decet commemorationi fraternae mortis ingemescere. itaque mora distinctionis par est ostendere adfectus.

[1] pari sim at *Keil*: pari si ṅ I at *cod.*: pari si non ut *Cauchii ex
deperdito cod. excerpta*

F 18 Charis., *GL* I, p. 196.25–27 = pp. 255.29–56.3 B.

communiter G. Gracchus ut lex Papiria accipiatur: "qui
sapientem cum faciet, qui et vobis et rei puplicae et sibi
communiter prospiciat, non qui pro sylla humanum[1] tru-
cidet."

[1] prospiciat o non qui prosullam humanam *Cauchii ex deperdito cod. excerpta*

F 19 Charis., *GL* I, p. 202.9–10 = p. 262.18–20 B.

iniuriose G. Gracchus uti lex Papiria accipiatur: "nequaquam iniuriose nobis contumeliam imponi sinatis."

F 20 Charis., *GL* I, p. 223.5–8 = p. 287.22–26 B.

usquequaque . . . G. Gracchus uti lex Papiria accipiatur:
"usquequaque curavit."

270

['look at this']! See how similar I am to him in a similar position."[1] But some want *em* to be in place of *en* ["come on"]. Yet it is fitting to sigh for the recollection of a brother's death. Therefore, the pause resulting from the distinction is appropriate for showing emotions.

[1] This expression makes use of a standard phrase in an unusual construction and thus emphasizes the similarity in the political situation of the two brothers.

F 18 Charisius

communiter ["jointly"], C. Gracchus [in the speech] that the *Lex Papiria* should be accepted: "when he will appoint a wise man who looks out for you [pl.] and the Republic and himself jointly, not one who kills a human being for Sulla."[1]

[1] The reading is uncertain. If the text is correct, this must either be a mistake by the quoting author or refer to one of the ancestors of the dictator L. Cornelius Sulla.

F 19 Charisius

iniuriose ["unjustly"], C. Gracchus [in the speech] that the *Lex Papiria* should be accepted: "not at all should you [pl.] let insult be inflicted upon us unjustly."

F 20 Charisius

usquequaque ["always / everywhere"], . . . C. Gracchus [in the speech] that the *Lex Papiria* should be accepted: "he took care always / everywhere."

On Pennus' Law (F 21–22)

*In 126 BC the Tribune of the People M. Iunius Pennus (**46**) proposed a bill that foreigners should be expelled from the city of Rome, as they had congregated there as a result of the Gracchan measures; C. Gracchus argued against this proposal, but the People approved it* (Lex Iunia de pere-

F 21 Cic. *Brut.* 109

= **46** T 1.

F 22 Fest., pp. 362.33–64.1 L.

RESPUBLICA multa|rum civitatum pluraliter dixit C. Gracchus in ea, | quam conscripsit de lege Penni et peregri|nis, cum ait: "eae nationes, cum aliis rebus, per ava|ritiam atque stultitiam, res publicas suas ami|serunt."

In 126 BC C. Gracchus took up a quaestorship in Sardinia, which was extended; he returned of his own accord in 124 BC (Vir. ill. 65.1). Thereupon, the censors Cn. Servilius Caepio and L. Cassius Longinus intended to take away his equestrian status, but he defended himself before

On Pennus' Law (F 21–22)

grinis: LPPR, *p. 304). According to Festus (F 22), a written
version of the speech existed (cf. F 59); the wording has
been interpreted as pointing to a written missive, since C.
Gracchus might have been away in Sardinia at the time.*

F 21 Cicero, *Brutus*

= **46** T 1.[1]

[1] This passage attests a conflict between M. Iunius Pennus
(**46**) and C. Sempronius Gracchus, while it does not confirm that
the latter delivered a speech against this particular bill.

F 22 Festus

respublica ["republic / state"], C. Gracchus used it in the
plural of many communities in that [speech] that he wrote
about the law of Pennus and the foreigners, when he says:
"those nations have lost their states [i.e., functioning political systems], along wih other matters, through avarice
and stupidity."

*them (F 23–25) and justified his behavior in front of the
People (F 26–28; CCMR, App. A: 191). The sources report
similar statements for both speeches (F 23, 28): there may
be overlap between the orations or confusion in the
sources.*

On His Return from Sardinia Before the Censors
(F 23–25)

F 23 Plut. *C. Gracch.* 23(2).6–10

ἔπειτα δόγμα ποιοῦνται τοῖς μὲν στρατιώταις διαδο-
χὴν ἀποσταλῆναι, τὸν δ᾽ Ὀρέστην ἐπιμένειν, ὡς δὴ
καὶ τοῦ Γαΐου διὰ τὴν ἀρχὴν παραμενοῦντος. [7] ὁ δὲ
τούτων αὐτῷ προσπεσόντων εὐθὺς ἐξέπλευσε πρὸς
ὀργήν, καὶ φανεὶς ἐν Ῥώμῃ παρ᾽ ἐλπίδας οὐ μόνον
ὑπὸ τῶν ἐχθρῶν αἰτίαν εἶχεν, ἀλλὰ καὶ τοῖς πολλοῖς
ἀλλόκοτον ἐδόκει τὸ ταμίαν ὄντα προαποστῆναι τοῦ
ἄρχοντος. [8] οὐ μὴν ἀλλὰ κατηγορίας αὐτῷ γενομένης ἐπὶ τῶν τιμητῶν, αἰτησάμενος λόγον οὕτω μετ-
έστησε τὰς γνώμας τῶν ἀκουσάντων, ὡς ἀπελθεῖν
ἠδικῆσθαι τὰ μέγιστα δόξας. [9] ἐστρατεῦσθαι μὲν
γὰρ ἔφη δώδεκα ἔτη, τῶν ἄλλων δέκα στρατευομένων
ἐν ἀνάγκαις, ταμιεύων δὲ τῷ στρατηγῷ παραμεμενη-
κέναι τριετίαν, τοῦ νόμου μετ᾽ ἐνιαυτὸν ἐπανελθεῖν
διδόντος· [10] μόνος δὲ τῶν στρατευσαμένων πλῆρες
τὸ βαλλάντιον ἐξενηνοχὼς κενὸν εἰσενηνοχέναι, τοὺς
δ᾽ ἄλλους ἐκπιόντας ὃν εἰσήνεγκαν οἶνον, ἀργυρίου
καὶ χρυσίου μεστοὺς δεῦρο τοὺς ἀμφορεῖς ἥκειν κο-
μίζοντας.

F 24 Cic. *Orat.* 233

age sume de Gracchi apud censores illud: "abesse non
potest quin eiusdem hominis sit probos improbare, qui

On His Return from Sardinia Before the Censors
(F 23–25)

F 23 Plutarch, *Life of Gaius Gracchus*

Then they passed a decree that relief should be sent to the soldiers, but that Orestes [L. Aurelius Orestes (**27**)] should remain [in Sardinia], assuming that Gaius too would remain because of his office. [7] But when that came to his ears, he [C. Gracchus] straightaway sailed off in anger, and, unexpectedly appearing in Rome, he not only attracted criticism from his enemies, but also made the commons think it strange that he, being quaestor, had left his post before his commander. [8] Yet, when he was denounced before the censors, he demanded the chance to speak and wrought such a change in the opinions of the hearers that he left the court believed to have been greatly wronged. [9] For he said that he had served in the army twelve years, while the others served ten by compulsion, and that he had continued to serve as quaestor under his commander into a third year, although the law permitted coming back after a year. [10] He was the only man in the army, he said, who had brought a full purse and taken away an empty one; the others had drunk up the wine that they had brought and had come back here carrying wine jars full of gold and silver. [continued by F 29]

F 24 Cicero, *Orator*

Come, take this example from [the speech] of Gracchus before the censors: "it cannot be otherwise than that it is a characteristic of the same person to disapprove of the good [men] when he approves of the bad"; how much

improbos probet"; quanto aptius, si ita dixisset: "quin eiusdem hominis sit qui improbos probet probos improbare."

F 25 Charis., *GL* I, p. 80.5–9 = p. 101.1–6 B.

galeros Vergilius masculino genere dixit [Verg. *Aen.* 7.688]
. . . sed C. Gracchus apud censores "cum galera † ursici †"[1]
dixit . . .

[1] cum galera *ed. princ.*: cum galere *cod.*: cum galeare
Keil   ursici *cod.*: ursi cum *ed. princ.*: versicolori *Keil*

On His Return from Sardinia Before the People
(F 26–28)

F 26–28 Gell. *NA* 15.12.1–4

C. Gracchus, cum ex Sardinia rediit, orationem ad populum in contione habuit. [2] ea verba haec sunt: "versatus
sum" inquit "in provincia, quomodo ex usu vestro existi-
mabam esse, non quomodo ambitioni meae conducere
arbitrabar. nulla apud me fuit popina, neque pueri eximia
facie stabant, sed in convivio liberi vestri modestius erant
quam apud principia." [3] post deinde haec dicit: "ita ver-

more elegant if he had said it as follows: "that it is a characteristic of the same person who approves of the bad to disapprove of the good."[1]

[1] Cicero suggests changing the word order, which places the words from the same stem next to each other and modifies the clausula: his version gives a combination of cretic and ditrochee rather than of trochee and cretic (hypodochmiac).

F 25 Charisius

Virgil used *galerus* ["cap"; masculine; also *galerum*, neuter] in the masculine gender [Verg. *Aen.* 7.688] . . . but C. Gracchus said before the censors: "with a cap [*galera*; feminine][1] of . . . [?]"

[1] The feminine form, *galera*, is not attested elsewhere, but the point must be that in C. Gracchus the same word is used with an unusual gender, rather than a different word.

On His Return from Sardinia Before the People
(F 26–28)

F 26–28 Gellius, *Attic Nights*

When C. Gracchus returned from Sardinia, he delivered a speech to the People at a public meeting. [2] Its words are as follows: "I conducted myself in the province," he said, "as I thought would be to your advantage, not as I believed would contribute to my own ambitions. There was no tavern at my establishment, nor were slaves of conspicuous beauty in attendance; instead, at an entertainment of mine your sons were treated more modestly than at the general's tent." [3] Later on he speaks as fol-

satus sum in provincia, uti nemo posset vere dicere assem aut eo plus in muneribus me accepisse aut mea opera quemquam sumptum fecisse. biennium fui in provincia; si ulla meretrix domum meam introivit aut cuiusquam servulus propter me sollicitatus est, omnium nationum postremissimum nequissimumque existimatote. cum a servis eorum tam caste me habuerim, inde poteritis considerare, quomodo me putetis cum liberis vestris vixisse." [4] atque ibi ex intervallo: "itaque," inquit "Quirites, cum Romam profectus sum, zonas, quas plenas argenti extuli, eas ex provincia inanes retuli; alii vini amphoras quas plenas tulerunt, eas argento repletas domum reportaverunt."

On His Own Behalf (F 29–30)

Later in 124 BC C. Gracchus defended himself against charges of involvement in the conspiracy at Fregellae in Latium (cf. Vir. ill. 65.2) (TLRR 24). It is uncertain whether the speech on his own behalf (F 30) is the same as

F 29 Plut. *C. Gracch.* 24(3).1–2

ἐκ τούτου πάλιν ἄλλας αἰτίας αὐτῷ καὶ δίκας ἐπῆγον, ὡς τοὺς συμμάχους ἀφιστάντι καὶ κεκοινωνηκότι τῆς περὶ Φρέγελλαν ἐνδειχθείσης συνωμοσίας. [2] ὁ δὲ πᾶσαν ὑποψίαν ἀπολυσάμενος καὶ φανεὶς καθαρός, εὐθὺς ἐπὶ δημαρχίαν ὥρμησε . . .

lows: "I so conducted myself in the province that no one could truly say that I received an *as* or more than that by way of presents or that anyone was put to expense on my account. I spent a period of two years in the province; if any courtesan entered my house or anyone's slave boy was seduced because of me, consider me the lowest and basest of all nations. Since I conducted myself so chastely toward their slaves, you will be able to infer from that how you should believe me having lived with your sons." [4] And then after an interval he says: "Accordingly, Romans, when I left for Rome, I brought back empty from the province the purses that I took there full of money; others have brought home overflowing with silver the wine jars that they took there filled with wine."

On His Own Behalf (F 29–30)

the one in defense against the charge of involvement in the conspiracy at Fregellae (F 29). The first testimonium does not mention a speech, but only thereby can C. Gracchus have proved his innocence.

F 29 Plutarch, *Life of Gaius Gracchus*

[continued from F 23] After this [the defense of the return from Sardinia], they brought again other charges and indictments against him [C. Gracchus], on the grounds that he had caused the allies to revolt and had been privy to the conspiracy at Fregellae [125 BC], which had been revealed. [2] But having cleared himself of all suspicion and established his innocence, he immediately began a canvass for the Tribunate . . .

FRL III: ORATORY, PART 1

F 30 Prisc., *GL* II, p. 513.16–18

. . . "nanciscor" vero a "nancio" est, quod in usu fuit vetustissimis. Gracchus pro se: "si nanciam populi desiderium, conprobabo rei publicae commoda."

As Tribune to the People (F 31)

F 31 Plut. *C. Gracch.* 24(3).4–7

παραλαβὼν δὲ τὴν ἀρχὴν εὐθὺς ἦν ἁπάντων πρῶτος, ἰσχύων τε τῷ λέγειν ὡς ἄλλος οὐδείς, καὶ τοῦ πάθους αὐτῷ παρρησίαν πολλὴν διδόντος, ἀνακλαιομένῳ τὸν ἀδελφόν. [5] ἐνταῦτα γὰρ ἐξ ἁπάσης προφάσεως περιῆγε τὸν δῆμον, ἀναμιμνήσκων τῶν γεγονότων καὶ παρατιθεὶς τὰ τῶν προγόνων, ὡς ἐκεῖνοι μὲν καὶ Φαλίσκοις ἐπολέμησαν ὑπὲρ Γενυκίου τινὸς δημάρχου λοιδορηθέντος, καὶ Γαΐου Βετουρίου θάνατον κατέγνωσαν, ὅτι δημάρχῳ πορευομένῳ δι᾽ ἀγορᾶς οὐχ ὑπεξέστη μόνος· [6] "ὑμῶν δ᾽ ὁρώντων" ἔφη "Τιβέριον ξύλοις συνέκοπτον οὗτοι, καὶ διὰ μέσης τῆς πόλεως ἐσύρετο νεκρὸς ἐκ Καπετωλίου, ῥιφησόμενος εἰς τὸν ποταμόν· οἱ δ᾽ ἁλισκόμενοι τῶν φίλων ἀπέθνησκον ἄκριτοι. [7] καίτοι πάτριόν ἐστιν ἡμῖν, εἴ τις ἔχων δίκην θανατικὴν μὴ ὑπακούει, τούτου πρὸς τὰς θύρας

280

F 30 Priscian

... but *nanciscor* ["obtain"] comes from *nancio*, which was in use among the most ancient writers. Gracchus [in the speech] on his own behalf: "if I obtain the wishes of the People, I will confirm benefits for the Republic."

As Tribune to the People (F 31)

The speeches of C. Gracchus as Tribune of the People to meetings of the People seem to date to 123 BC (CCMR, App. A: 192).

F 31 Plutarch, *Life of Gaius Gracchus*

And as soon as he had taken up office [as Tribune of the People], he [C. Gracchus] was the first of all, being powerful in oratory like nobody else, and his affliction gave him great boldness of speech in bewailing his brother. [5] For to this subject he would bring the People round on every pretext, reminding them of what had happened and comparing the conduct of their ancestors, since those went to war against the Falisci on behalf of Genucius [Cn. Genucius Augurinus, consular tribune 399, 396 BC], a Tribune, when he had been insulted, and condemned Gaius Veturius [patrician, not otherwise known] to death because he was the only one not to make way for a Tribune passing through the Forum. [6] "But before your eyes," he said, "those men beat Tiberius to death with clubs, and his dead body was dragged from the Capitol through the midst of the city to be thrown into the river; moreover, those of his friends who were caught were put to death without trial. [7] And yet it is an ancient custom among us that, if anyone who is arraigned on a capital charge does not answer, a

ἔωθεν ἐλθόντα σαλπιγκτὴν ἀνακαλεῖσθαι τῇ σάλ-
πιγγι, καὶ μὴ πρότερον ἐπιφέρειν ψῆφον αὐτῷ τοὺς
δικαστάς· οὕτως εὐλαβεῖς καὶ πεφυλαγμένοι περὶ τὰς
κρίσεις ἦσαν."

In C. Gracchus' first year as Tribune, P. Popillius Laenas
(cos. 132 BC) was taken to court because he had been involved in trials against supporters of Ti. Sempronius Gracchus (**34**). P. Popillius Laenas went into exile, possibly
before the trial; he was recalled after C. Gracchus' death
(TLRR 25; Cic. Brut. 128; Dom. 82, 87; Vell. Pat. 2.7.4;
Plut. C. Gracch. 25(4).2–3; Schol. Bob. ad Cic. Red. pop. 6

Against P. Popillius Laenas from the Rostra
(F 32–33)

F 32 Gell. NA 11.13.1–3

apud Titum Castricium, disciplinae rhetoricae doctorem,
gravi atque firmo iudicio virum, legebatur oratio C.
Gracchi in P. Popilium. [2] in eius orationis principio
conlocata verba sunt accuratius modulatiusque quam veterum oratorum consuetudo fert. [3] ea verba sicuti dixi
conposita haec sunt: "quae vos cupide per hosce annos
adpetistis atque voluistis, ea, si temere repudiaritis, abesse
non potest, quin aut olim cupide adpetisse aut nunc temere repudiasse dicamini."

trumpeter shall go to the door of that man's house in the morning and summon him forth with the trumpet, and not before that shall the judges vote on his case. So careful and guarded were they in the judgments [of capital cases]."

[p. 111.18–20 St.]). The sources mention two speeches by C. Gracchus against P. Popillius Laenas (F 36), distinguished by the venue and sometimes merely identified by the venue (F 32–33, 34–37), delivered from the Rostra and around the places of assembly in hamlets outside Rome, which, therefore, cannot be connected directly with the court case.

Against P. Popillius Laena from the Rostra
(F 32–33)

F 32 Gellius, *Attic Nights*

Before Titus Castricius, a teacher of the art of rhetoric and a man of authoritative and well-founded judgment, the speech of C. Gracchus against P. Popilius was read. [2] At the beginning of that speech the words were put together with more care and regard for rhythm than was the custom of the early orators. [3] These words, arranged as I have said, are as follows: "As for those things that for all these years you have eagerly sought and longed for, if you should now reject those rashly, it cannot be otherwise than that one would say either that in the past you sought them eagerly or that now you rejected them rashly."[1]

[1] The testimonium does not identify from which of the two speeches against P. Popillius Laenas this excerpt comes; the context suggests the oration delivered from the Rostra.

F 33 Fest., pp. 218.32–20.2 L.

OCCISITANTUR, saepe occiduntur. sic | C. Gracchus pro rostris in P. Popillium: "homines li|lberi nunc in oppido occisitantur."

On P. Popillius Laenas Around the Places of Assembly (F 34–37)

F 34 Gell. *NA* 1.7.6–8

"nam 'futurum' " inquit "non refertur ad rem, sicut legentibus temere et incuriose videtur, neque pro participio positum est, set verbum est indefinitum, quod Graeci appellant ἀπαρέμφατον, neque numeris neque generibus praeserviens, set liberum undique et inpromiscum, quali C. Gracchus verbo usus est in oratione, [7] cuius titulus est de P. Popilio circum conciliabula, in qua ita scriptum est: 'credo ego inimicos meos hoc dicturum.' 'inimicos dicturum' inquit, non 'dicturos'; [8] videturne ea ratione positum esse aput Gracchum 'dicturum,' qua est aput Ciceronem 'futurum'? . . ."

F 35 Fest., p. 277.8–9 L.

. . . et POTERATUR, C. Gracchus | in ea qua usus est, cum circum conciliabula iret.

F 33 Festus

occisitantur ["they are killed"], often *occiduntur* [usual form]. Thus C. Gracchus, [speaking] from the front of the Rostra against P. Popillius: "free men are now being killed in the town."

On P. Popillius Laenas Around the Places of Assembly (F 34–37)

F 34 Gellius, *Attic Nights*

"For *futurum* does not," he [an expert] said, "refer to *rem*,[1] as it seems to hasty and careless readers, nor is it used as a participle; rather, it is an infinitive, what the Greeks call *aparemphaton* ['infinitive mood'], not subject to either number or gender, but altogether free and not integrated, such a word as C. Gracchus used in the speech, [7] whose title is *On P. Popilius around the places of assembly*, in which it is written as follows: 'I believe that my enemies will say this.' *inimicos dicturum*," he said, "not *dicturos* [agreeing in case, number and gender with *inimicos*]; [8] doesn't *dicturum* in Gracchus seem to be used according to the same principle as *futurum* in Cicero? . . ."

[1] The discussion concerns the structure of the phrase *hanc sibi rem praesidio sperant futurum* at Cic. *Verr.* 2.5.167, where the Ciceronian manuscripts have *futuram*. Gellius notes what is probably a syntactic archaism in infinitive constructions.

F 35 Festus

. . . and *poteratur* ["could"; unusual passive form], C. Gracchus in that [speech] that he used when he went round the places of assembly.

F 36 Fest., p. 136.12–15 L.

MALO CRUCE, masculino genere cum dixit Gracchus | in ea oratione quae est in P. Popillium, posteriore, tam | repraesentavit antiquam consuetudinem, quam hunc | frontem . . .

F 37 Diom., *GL* I, p. 374.17–20

excello legimus crebro apud veteres, ut Cicero . . . Gracchus praeterea similiter cohortatione circum conciliabula "antecellant" . . .

Against P. Po{m}pil<l>ius and Married Women
(F 38)

F 36 Festus

malo cruce ["by painful torment"; usually feminine], of masculine gender, when Gracchus said it in that speech that exists against P. Popillius, the second one,[1] it represented an ancient custom in the same way as *hunc frontem* ["this forehead"; usually feminine rather than masculine] . . .

[1] None of the testimonia specifies that the speech given around the places of assembly is the second one against P. Popillius Laenas, but this is generally assumed.

F 37 Diomedes

excello ["I am eminent"; mostly only participle used] we read frequently in the ancients, like Cicero . . . Gracchus, moreover, in a similar way [uses] *antecellant* ["they may be prominent"; another compound] in the exhortation [delivered] around the places of assembly[1] . . .

[1] Unless there is another, otherwise unattested, speech by C. Gracchus given *circum conciliabula*, this excerpt must come from the speech against P. Popillius Laenas, although the name is not mentioned.

Against P. Po{m}pil<l>ius and Married Women
(F 38)

During P. Popillius Laenas' absence in exile, C. Gracchus may have made another speech against him and married women, who were presumably asking for his return (cf. Cic. Red. sen. 37; Red. pop. 6).

F 38 Fest., p. 136.16–19 L.

item I cum idem in Po{m}pil‹l›ium[1] et matronas ait: "eo I exemplo instituto dignus fuit, qui malo cruce I periret."

1 Po{m}pil‹l›ium *Ant. Augustinus*: Pompilium *cod.*

Abuse Against L. Calpurnius Piso Frugi (F 39–43)

F 39 Cic. *Font.* 39

exstat oratio hominis, ut opinio mea fert, nostrorum hominum longe ingeniosissimi atque eloquentissimi, C. Gracchi; qua in oratione permulta in L. Pisonem turpia ac flagitiosa dicuntur. at in quem virum! qui tanta virtute atque integritate fuit ut etiam illis optimis temporibus, cum hominem invenire nequam neminem posses, solus tamen Frugi nominaretur. quem cum in contionem Gracchus vocari iuberet et viator quaereret, quem Pisonem, quod erant plures: "cogis me," inquit, "dicere inimicum meum Frugi." is igitur vir quem ne inimicus quidem satis in appellando significare poterat, nisi ante laudasset, qui uno cognomine declarabatur non modo quis esset sed etiam qualis esset, tamen in falsam atque iniquam probrorum insimulationem vocabatur . . .

F 38 Festus

Likewise [cf. F 36], when the same [C. Gracchus] says [in the speech] against Po{m}pil<l>ius and married women: "Having instituted this example, he was worthy to perish by painful torment."

Abuse Against L. Calpurnius Piso Frugi (F 39–43)

As Tribune of the People, C. Gracchus delivered (CCMR, App. A: 193) an abusive speech (F 39–40) against L. Calpurnius Piso Frugi (37), who opposed C. Gracchus' grain law (37 F 2).

F 39 Cicero, *Pro Fonteio*

There is extant a speech delivered by a man who was, in my opinion, by far the ablest and most eloquent of our countrymen, C. Gracchus; in that speech very many repulsive and scandalous things are said against L. Piso. But against what a man! A man who had such virtue and integrity that, even in those great days, when you could not find a worthless person, still, he alone was called Frugi ["Honest"]. When Gracchus ordered that he should be summoned to a meeting of the People, and the attendant asked which Piso, since there were several, he said: "You force me to say: my enemy Frugi." Thus, the man whom not even his enemy could sufficiently indicate in naming him without first having praised him, who by a single *cognomen* was declared not only who he was, but also what he was like, was yet called upon to meet a false and unjust charge of offenses . . .

F 40 Schol. Bob. ad Cic. *Flacc.* 5 (p. 96.26–29 Stangl)

verum quod ad Pisonem pertineat: plurimi quidem ex hac
familia cognomentum frugalitatis habuerunt, sed enim
primus hoc meruit L. Piso qui legem de pecuniis repetundis tulit et fuit C. Graccho capitalis inimicus; in quem
ipsius Gracchi exstat oratio maledictorum magis plena
quam criminum.

F 41 Cic. *Tusc.* 3.48

[M.:] "at laudat saepe virtutem." et quidem C. Gracchus,
cum largitiones maximas fecisset et effudisset aerarium,
verbis tamen defendebat aerarium. quid verba audiam,
cum facta videam? L. Piso ille Frugi semper contra legem
frumentariam dixerat. is lege lata consularis ad frumentum accipiundum venerat. animum advertit Gracchus in
contione Pisonem stantem; quaerit audiente populo Romano qui sibi constet, cum ea lege frumentum petat quam
dissuaserit. "nolim" inquit "mea bona, Gracche, tibi viri-
tim dividere libeat, sed, si facias, partem petam." parumne
declaravit vir gravis et sapiens lege Sempronia patrimonium publicum dissupari? lege orationes Gracchi: patro-
num aerari esse dices.

F 40 Scholia Bobiensia to Cicero, *Pro Flacco*

But what concerns Piso: many of this family bore the *cognomen* relating to worthiness, but L. Piso was the first to have deserved it, he who proposed the law on the recovery of extorted money and was the archenemy of C. Gracchus; against him there is a speech of Gracchus himself, full of abuse rather than charges.

F 41 Cicero, *Tusculan Disputations*

[M.:] "But he [Epicurus] often praises virtue." [comment by a fictitious interlocutor] And so did C. Gracchus indeed: after he had handed out huge gifts and poured out the funds of the treasury, still, in his words, he was the protector of the treasury. Why should I listen to words when I can see the deeds? L. Piso, that well-known Frugi, had always spoken against the grain law. When the law had been passed, he, despite being a consular, had turned up to receive grain. Gracchus notices Piso standing in the throng; he asks him in the hearing of the Roman People how he acted consistently when he sought grain under that law that he had opposed. "I would not like it, Gracchus," he said, "that you feel like dividing up my property among all citizens; but, should you do so, I should seek my share." Did this serious and sagacious man show insufficiently that the public inheritance was squandered by the *Lex Sempronia*? Read Gracchus' speeches: you will say he was the patron of the treasury.[1]

---

[1] This passage reports a verbal exchange between Piso and C. Gracchus, but it seems to have taken place on an occasion separate from the confrontation in the *contio* (F 39). The reference to Gracchus' speeches at the end is not limited to those directed against Piso.

F 42 Prisc., *GL* II, p. 386.3–4

Gaius Gracchus: "aerarium delargitur Romano populo," "delargitur" passive protulit.

F 43 Isid. *Orig.* 2.21.4

fit autem hoc schema [i.e., climax] non solum in singulis verbis, sed etiam in contexione verborum, ut apud Gracchum: "pueritia tua adulescentiae tuae inhonestamentum fuit, adulescentia senectuti dedecoramentum, senectus reipublicae flagitium." sic et apud Scipionem . . .

Against Lex Aufeia *(F 44)*

As Tribune of the People, C. Gracchus spoke (CCMR, App. A: 195) against the Lex Aufeia *(if the transmission is correct), which seems to have dealt with Roman arrange-*

F 44 Gell. *NA* 11.10.1–6

quod in capite superiore a Critolao scriptum esse diximus super Demosthene, id C. Gracchus in oratione, qua legem Aufeiam[1] dissuasit, in Demaden contulit verbis hisce: [2]

---

[1] Aufeiam *vel* aufegam *vel* auferam *codd.*: Saufeiam *Gronovius*: Aquiliam *Hill*

F 42 Priscian

Gaius Gracchus: "the treasury is lavished upon the Roman People," *delargitur* ["is lavished"] he used in the passive [usually deponent].[1]

[1] This fragment might come from a discussion about the grain law, but need not belong to the speech against Piso.

F 43 Isidore, *Origins*

And this figure [climax] does not occur only with individual words, but also with a sequence of words, as in Gracchus: "Your childhood was a dishonor to your youth, your youth a disgrace to your old age, your old age an outrage to the Republic."[1] So also in Scipio [P. Cornelius Scipio Aemilianus Africanus minor (**21**), F 33] . . .

[1] This fragment is part of an abusive speech, which could, but need not, be the one against Piso. It has also been attributed to a speech against M. Octavius.

Against Lex Aufeia *(F 44)*

ments for Asia and thus affected Rome's relationship with kings in the east (Rogatio Aufeia de provincia Asia: LPPR, p. 309).

F 44 Gellius, *Attic Nights*

What we said in the preceding chapter was written by Critolaus [Greek Peripatetic philosopher, 2nd cent. BC] about Demosthenes, this was transferred by C. Gracchus, in the speech by which he argued against the *Lex Aufeia*, to Demades [Greek orator, 4th cent. BC] in the following

"nam vos, Quirites, si velitis sapientia atque virtute uti, etsi quaeritis, neminem nostrum invenietis sine pretio huc prodire. omnes nos, qui verba facimus, aliquid petimus, neque ullius rei causa quisquam ad vos prodit, nisi ut aliquid auferat. [3] ego ipse, qui aput vos verba facio, uti vectigalia vestra augeatis, quo facilius vestra commoda et rempublicam administrare possitis, non gratis prodeo; verum peto a vobis non pecuniam, sed bonam existimationem atque honorem. [4] qui prodeunt dissuasuri, ne hanc legem accipiatis, petunt non honorem a vobis, verum a Nicomede pecuniam; qui suadent, ut accipiatis, hi quoque petunt non a vobis bonam existimationem, verum a Mitridate rei familiari{s}[2] suae pretium et praemium; qui autem ex eodem loco atque ordine tacent, hi vel acerrimi sunt; nam ab omnibus pretium accipiunt et omnis fallunt. [5] vos, cum putatis eos ab his rebus remotos esse, inpertitis bonam existimationem; [6] legationes autem a regibus, cum putant eos sua causa reticere, sumptus atque pecunias maximas praebent, item uti in terra Graecia, quo in tempore tragoedus gloriae sibi ducebat talentum magnum ob unam fabulam datum esse, homo eloquentissimus civitatis suae Demades ei respondisse dicitur: 'mirum tibi videtur, si tu loquendo talentum quaesisti? ego, ut tacerem, decem talenta a rege accepi.' item nunc isti pretia maxima ob tacendum accipiunt."

[2] familiari{s} *Madvig*: familiaris *codd.*

---

[1] See *OLD* s.v. *talentum* 2, "A talent of silver as a unit of currency; *-um magnum* (app.) an Attic talent, so called to distinguish it from currencies of lower value."

294

words: [2] "For, Romans, if you wish to apply wisdom and virtue, even if you inquire into it, you will find that none of us comes forward here without a reward. All of us who deliver speeches are seeking something, and no one appears before you for any purpose except to carry something away. [3] I myself, who am now delivering a speech before you, arguing that you increase taxes, so that you may serve your own advantage and the Republic more easily, do not come here for nothing; but I ask of you, not money, but good reputation and honor. [4] Those who come forward to persuade you not to accept this law, do not seek honor from you, but money from Nicomedes [Nicomedes II, king of Bithynia]; those who advise you to accept it are not seeking good reputation from you either, but from Mithridates [Mithridates V Euergetes, king of Pontus] a reward and an increase of their possessions; those, however, of the same rank and order who are silent, these are even the fiercest, for they are taking money from all and deceiving all. [5] You, since you believe that they are removed from such matters, impart good reputation to them; [6] but the embassies from the kings, since they believe that it is for their sake that they are silent, offer them resources and very large amounts of money, in the same way as in the land of Greece, when a tragic actor regarded it as an honor for himself that he had received an Attic talent[1] for a single play, Demades, the most eloquent man of his country, is said to have replied to him: 'Does it seem wonderful to you that you have gained a talent by speaking? I have received ten talents from the king [of Macedon] for being silent.' Just so, those men now receive very high rewards because of being silent."

On lex iudiciaria (*F 45*)

F 45 App. *B Civ.* 1.22.91–93

ὁ μὲν δὴ Γάιος Γράκχος οὕτως ἐδημάρχει τὸ δεύτε-
ρον· . . . [92] τὰ δικαστήρια, ἀδοξοῦντα ἐπὶ δωροδοκί-
αις, ἐς τοὺς ἱππέας ἀπὸ τῶν βουλευτῶν μετέφερε, τὰ
ὑπόγυα μάλιστα αὐτοῖς ὀνειδίζων, ὅτι Αὐρήλιος Κότ-
τας καὶ Σαλινάτωρ καὶ τρίτος ἐπὶ τούτοις Μάνιος
Ἀκύλιος, ὁ τὴν Ἀσίαν ἑλών, σαφῶς δεδωροδοκηκότες
ἀφεῖντο ὑπὸ τῶν δικασάντων, οἵ τε πρέσβεις οἱ κατ'
αὐτῶν ἔτι παρόντες σὺν φθόνῳ ταῦτα περιόντες ἐκε-
κράγεσαν. ἅπερ ἡ βουλὴ μάλιστα αἰδουμένη ἐς τὸν
νόμον ἐνεδίδου· καὶ ὁ δῆμος αὐτὸν ἐκύρου. [93] καὶ
μετηνέχθη μὲν ὧδε ἐς τοὺς ἱππέας ἀπὸ τῆς βουλῆς
τὰ δικαστήρια· φασὶ δὲ κυρωθέντος μὲν ἄρτι τοῦ νόμου τὸν Γράκχον εἰπεῖν, ὅτι ἀθρόως τὴν βουλὴν καθ-
ῃρήκοι, τοῦ δ' ἔργου προϊόντος ἐς πεῖραν μειζόνως ἔτι
ἐκφανῆναι τὸ ἔπος τὸ Γράκχου.

On lex iudiciaria *(F 45)*

C. Gracchus argued for a lex iudiciaria, *which was to en-hance the role of the knights in the courts at the expense of that of the senators* (Lex Sempronia iudiciaria: LPPR, pp. 313–14; see Diod. Sic. 37.9; Plut. C. Gracch. 26(5).2–4).

F 45 Appian, *Civil Wars*

And so Gaius Gracchus was Tribune a second time [122 BC]. . . . [92] He transferred the courts of justice, which had become discredited through bribery, to the knights from the senators, reproaching them especially with the recent examples, namely that Aurelius Cotta [L. Aurelius Cotta, cos. 144 BC; cf. P. Cornelius Scipio Aemilianus Africanus minor (**21**), F 23–26], Salinator [otherwise un-known, ca. 130 BC], and, the third after them, Manius Aquillius [cos. 129 BC; cf. P. Cornelius Lentulus (**15**), F 2], who conquered Asia, manifest bribe-takers, had been acquitted by the judges, while ambassadors sent to complain about them were still present and, going round, uttered bitter accusations. The Senate was extremely ashamed of these things and yielded to the law, and the People ratified it. [93] And in this way the courts were transferred to the knights from the Senate. They say that soon after the passage of this law Gracchus remarked that he had broken the power of the Senate completely, and the statement of Gracchus came to the test more strongly as events progressed.

Again as Tribune to the People (F 46)

F 46 Plut. *C. Gracch.* 29(8).1–2

ἐπὶ τούτοις τοῦ δήμου μεγαλύνοντος αὐτὸν καὶ πᾶν
ὁτιοῦν ἑτοίμως ἔχοντος ἐνδείκνυσθαι πρὸς εὔνοιαν,
ἔφη ποτὲ δημηγορῶν αὐτὸς αἰτήσειν χάριν, ἣν λα-
βὼν μὲν ἀντὶ παντὸς ἕξειν, εἰ δ' ἀποτύχοι, μηδὲν ἐκείνοις μεμψιμοιρήσειν. τοῦτο ῥηθὲν ἔδοξεν αἴτησις
ὑπατείας εἶναι, καὶ προσδοκίαν πᾶσιν ὡς ἅμα μὲν
ὑπατείαν, ἅμα δὲ δημαρχίαν μετιὼν παρέσχεν. [2] ἐν-
στάντων δὲ τῶν ὑπατικῶν ἀρχαιρεσιῶν καὶ μετεώρων
ὄντων ἁπάντων, ὤφθη Γάιον Φάννιον κατάγων εἰς τὸ
πεδίον καὶ συναρχαιρεσιάζων ἐκείνῳ μετὰ τῶν φίλων.

On Promulgated Laws (F 47–52)

F 47 Schol. Bob. ad Cic. *Sull.* 26 (p. 81.18–24 Stangl)

et hic, quantum mea opinio est, imitatus est C. Gracchum:
sic enim et ille de legibus promulgatis, ut ipsius etiam
verborum faciam mentionem: "si vellem," inquit, "aput

Again as Tribune to the People (F 46)

Another tribunician contio *(CCMR, App. A: 197) seems to date to a period shortly before the elections for offices in 122 BC.*

F 46 Plutarch, *Life of Gaius Gracchus*

Since the People extolled him [C. Gracchus] for these [political, social, and infrastructure measures, mentioned in what precedes] and were ready to show him any token whatsoever of their goodwill, he said once in a public speech that he was going to ask a favor of them, which, if granted, he should value above everything, but if he would not gain it, he should find no fault with them. This utterance was thought to be a request for a consulship and created the expectation for all that he would sue for a consulship and a tribuneship at the same time. [2] But when the consular elections were at hand and everybody was in suspense, he was seen leading Gaius Fannius [cos. 122 BC] down into the Campus and joining in the canvass for him along with his friends.

On Promulgated Laws (F 47–52)

The speech refers to laws proposed by C. Gracchus (F 52), presumably during his Tribunate.

F 47 Scholia Bobiensia to Cicero, *Pro Sulla*

And here, according to my opinion at least, he has imitated C. Gracchus: for thus he too said [in the speech] on promulgated laws, so that I even make mention of his very

vos verba facere et a vobis postulare, cum genere summo
ortus essem et cum fratrem propter vos amisissem, nec
quisquam de P. Africani et Tiberi Gracchi familia nisi ego
et puer restaremus, ut pateremini hoc tempore me quies-
cere, ne a stirpe genus nostrum interiret et uti aliqua pro-
pago generis nostri reliqua esset: haud ‹scio›[1] an lubenti-
bus a vobis impetrassem."

[1] haud ‹scio› *ed. Romana 1828*: haud *cod.*

F 48 Gell. *NA* 10.3.2–3, 11

legebamus adeo nuper orationem Gracchi de legibus promulgatis, in qua M. Marium et quosdam ex municipiis
Italicis honestos viros virgis per iniuriam caesos a magi-
stratibus populi Romani, quanta maxima invidia potest,
conqueritur. [3] verba haec sunt, quae super ea re fecit:
"nuper Teanum Sidicinum consul venit. uxor eius dixit se
in balneis virilibus lavari velle. quaestori Sidicino M.[1]
Mario datum est negotium, uti balneis exigerentur qui
lavabantur. uxor renuntiat viro parum cito sibi balneas tra-
ditas esse et parum lautas fuisse. idcirco palus destitutus
est in foro, eoque adductus suae civitatis nobilissimus
homo M. Marius. vestimenta detracta sunt, virgis caesus
est. Caleni, ubi id audierunt, edixerunt, ne quis in balneis

[1] Sidicino M. *Mommsen*: sidicino (-icioni / -ici omi) a m. *vel*
sidicinam *codd.*

words: "If I wished," he said, "to deliver a speech in front of you and to demand from you, since I had been born into a very noble family and since I had lost a brother because of you, and nobody from the family of P. Africanus [P. Cornelius Scipio Africanus maior (**4**), his maternal grandfather] and Tiberius Gracchus [Ti. Sempronius Gracchus (**10**), his father] remained except myself and a boy, that you would bear me at this point to abstain from politics, so that our family would not perish at the root and that some offspring of our family was left: I do not ⟨know⟩ whether I would have obtained this from you in line with your wishes."

F 48 Gellius, *Attic Nights*

Indeed, we recently read the speech of Gracchus on promulgated laws, in which he complains that M. Marius [quaestor of the Latin colony Teanum Sidicinum] and certain other distinguished men from the Italic free towns were unlawfully beaten with rods by magistrates of the Roman People, with the greatest indignation possible. [3] These are the words that he pronounced on that matter: "The consul recently came to Teanum Sidicinum. His wife said that she wished to bathe in the male baths. M. Marius, the quaestor of Sidicinum, was given the task of removing the bathers from the baths. The wife tells her husband that the baths were not given up to her quickly enough and were not sufficiently clean. Therefore, a stake was planted in the Forum, and M. Marius, the most illustrious man of his community, was led to it. His clothing was stripped off; he was beaten with rods. The people of Cales, when they had heard of this, passed a decree that no one should plan

lavisse vellet, cum magistratus Romanus ibi esset. Ferentini ob eandem causam praetor noster quaestores arripi iussit: alter se de muro deiecit, alter prensus et virgis caesus est." . . . [11] Gracchus autem non querentis neque implorantis, sed nuntiantis vicem: "palus" inquit "in foro destitutus est, vestimenta detracta sunt, virgis caesus est."

F 49 Gell. *NA* 10.3.5

item Gracchus alio in loco ita dicit: "quanta libido quantaque intemperantia sit hominum adulescentium, unum exemplum vobis ostendam. his annis paucis ex Asia[1] missus est, qui per id tempus magistratum non ceperat, homo adulescens pro legato. is in lectica ferebatur. ei obviam bubulcus de plebe Venusina advenit et per iocum, cum ignoraret, qui ferretur, rogavit, num mortuum ferrent. ubi id audivit, lecticam iussit deponi; st<r>uppis,[2] quibus lectica deligata erat, usque adeo verberari iussit, dum animam efflavit."

[1] ex Asia *codd.*: in Asiam *Lipsius*: Venusiam *Jordan*: ex <s.c. in> Asia<m> *Hertz*   [2] st<r>uppis *Scioppius*: stuppis *vel* suppis *codd.*

F 50 + 51 Gell. *NA* 9.14.16–17

C. Gracchus de legibus promulgatis: "ea luxurii causa aiunt institui"; [17] et ibidem infra ita scriptum est: "non est ea luxuries, quae necessario parentur vitae causa," per quod

to bathe in the public baths when a Roman magistrate was there. At Ferentinum, for the same reason, our praetor ordered the quaestors to be arrested: one threw himself from the wall, the other was caught and beaten with rods." . . . [11] But Gracchus plays the part, not of one who complains or implores, but of one who reports: "A stake," he says, "was planted in the Forum; his clothing was stripped off; he was beaten with rods."

F 49 Gellius, *Attic Nights*

Likewise, Gracchus in another place [of the same speech; cf. F 48] speaks as follows: "How great the lawlessness and how great the lack of self-control of young men is, of this I will show you a single example. Within the last few years a young man who, at that time, had not yet held a magisterial office, was sent in the capacity of an envoy from Asia. He was carried in a litter. A herdsman, from the folk of Venusia [modern Venosa, in southern Italy], came across him, and, jokingly, since he did not know who was being carried, asked whether they were carrying a corpse. As soon as he heard this, he [the young man] ordered that the litter be set down; and he ordered that the peasant be beaten, until he breathed his last, with the thongs by which the litter was fastened."

F 50 + 51 Gellius, *Attic Nights*

C. Gracchus [says in the speech] on promulgated laws: "they say that those measures are being introduced for the sake of luxury [*luxurii causa*]"; [17] and further on in the same speech it is written as follows: "that is not luxury [*luxuries*] that is necessarily provided for the sake of life";

apparet eum ab eo, quod est "luxuries," "luxurii" patrio casu dixisse.

F 52 Fest., p. 218.27–32 L.

OSTENTUM, quo nunc | utimur interdum prodigii vice, quin participiali|ter quoque dici solitum sit, non dubium facit eti|am C. Gracchus de legibus a se promulgatis, cum | ait: "quod unum nobis inostentum, ipsis inusum | adportatur."

On Lex Minucia *(F 53)*

The speech on the Lex Minucia *is directed against a bill put forward by the Tribune of the People M.(?) Minucius Rufus (tr. pl. 121 BC), at the instigation of the* optimates, *proposing the repeal of the* Lex Rubria, *the basis for the*

F 53 Fest., p. 220.2–5 L.

OSI SUNT, ab odio | declinasse antiquos testis est C. Gracchus in ea, quae | est de lege Minucia, cum ait: "mirum si quid | his iniuriae fit; semper eos osi sunt."

Against Q. Aelius Tubero (F 54–55)

F 54 Cic. *Brut.* 117
= **45** T 1.

thereby it is evident that he formed *luxurii* from *luxuries* in the genitive case [instead of *luxuriei*].

F 52 Festus

ostentum ["prodigy, wonder"], which we now sometimes use instead of *prodigium* [different word with same meaning]; that it was also commonly used as a participle [of *ostendo*], is proved beyond doubt even by C. Gracchus [in the speech] on laws promulgated by him, when he says: "which is the only thing conveyed not shown to us [negation + participle of *ostendo*] and not used by them."

On Lex Minucia *(F 53)*

colonization program of C. Gracchus and M. Fulvius Flaccus (**40**) *(Lex Minucia de colonia Carthaginem deducenda = de lege Rubria abroganda; LPPR, p. 316).*

F 53 Festus

osi sunt ["they have hated"; rare form of perfect], for the fact that the ancients formed this from *odio* ["I hate"; rare form of present] C. Gracchus is a witness in that [speech] that exists on the *Lex Minucia*, when he says: "It would be remarkable if any injury happens to these people; they have always hated those people."

Against Q. Aelius Tubero (F 54–55)

F 54 Cicero, *Brutus*
= **45** T 1.

F 55 Prisc., *GL* II, p. 88.4–6

C. Gracchus contra Q. Aelium Tuberonem: "utrum inimicorum meorum factio an magis sollicitudo te impulit, ut in me industriior sis quam in te?"

Against L. Metellus (F 56)

F 56 Diom., *GL* I, p. 311.16–24

verba genitivis casibus sic iunguntur: memor sum bonorum, obliviscor iniuriae . . . sed et dativo dixerunt, ut Gracchus in L. Metellum: "usque adeo pertaesum vos mihi esse."

Against Furnius (F 57)

F 57 Diom., *GL* I, p. 401.2–3

item auxilio ait Gracchus adversus Furnium: "quibus ego primus quo modo auxiliem."[1]

   [1] primum cum auxilio *edd. vet.*   auxiliem *vel* auxilii est *codd.*

Against Maevius (F 58)

F 58 Isid. *Orig.* 19.32.4

apud veteres ultra unum anulum uti infame habitum viro. Gracchus in Mevium: "considerate, Quirites, sinistram eius; en cuius auctoritatem sequimini, qui propter mulierum cupiditatem ut mulier est ornatus."

F 55 Priscian

C. Gracchus [in the speech] against Q. Aelius Tubero: "Has the faction of my enemies or rather anxiety provoked you to be more active for me than for you?"

Against L. Metellus (F 56)

F 56 Diomedes

Verbs are combined with genitive cases in the following way: I remember good things, I forget injustice . . . but they used them also with the dative, as Gracchus [in the speech] against L. Metellus: "that you [pl.] were so disgusted at me."

Against Furnius (F 57)

F 57 Diomedes

In the same way Gracchus uses *auxilio* ["I help"; rare active form] [in the speech] against Furnius: "for them I [am] the first [to consider] how to help."

Against Maevius (F 58)

F 58 Isidore, *Origins*

Among the ancients, wearing more than one ring was regarded as disreputable attire for a man. Gracchus [in the speech] against M<a>evius: "Consider, Romans, his left hand; look, he whose authority you follow, who, because of his desire for women, is adorned like a woman."

Against Plautius (F 59)

F 59 Val. Max. 9.5.ext.4

insolentiae vero inter Carthaginiensem et Campanum senatum quasi aemulatio fuit: ille enim separato a plebe balneo lavabatur, hic diverso foro utebatur. quem morem Capuae aliquamdiu retentum C. quoque Gracchi oratione in Plautium scripta patet.

On the Bill of Cn. Marcius Censorinus (F 60)

F 60 Charis., *GL* I, p. 208.19–22 = p. 270.11–15 B.

necessario M. Cato [**8** *ORF*⁴ F 100] . . . G. Gracchus in rogatione Cn. Marci Censorini: "si vobis probati essent homines adulescentes, tamen necessario vobis tribuni militares veteres faciundi essent."

An Emotional Speech (F 61)

F 61 Cic. *De or.* 3.214

[CRASSUS:] quid fuit in Graccho, quem tu melius, Catule, meministi, quod me puero tanto opere ferretur? "quo me miser conferam? quo vertam? in Capitoliumne? at fratris

Against Plautius (F 59)

F 59 Valerius Maximus, *Memorable Doings and Sayings*

There was a kind of competition in insolence between the Carthaginian and the Campanian Senate: for the former bathed in a bath separated from the common people, the latter used a different Forum. That this practice was retained in Capua for some time is evident also from C. Gracchus' speech written against Plautius.

On the Bill of Cn. Marcius Censorinus (F 60)

The speech apparently concerns a Rogatio Marcia de tribunis militum? *(LPPR, p. 311), proposed by Cn. Marcius Censorinus, perhaps praetor in 123 BC (LPPR, p. 311) or Tribune of the People in 122 BC (MRR I 517).*

F 60 Charisius

necessario ["necessarily"; adverb], M. Cato [M. Porcius Cato (**8**) *ORF*[4] F 100] . . . C. Gracchus [in the speech] concerning the bill of Cn. Marcius Censorinus: "If young men had been approved by you, still, necessarily, old men would have to be made military tribunes by you."

An Emotional Speech (F 61)

F 61 Cicero, *On the Orator*

[CRASSUS:] What was there in Gracchus, whom you, Catulus [Q. Lutatius Catulus (**63**)], remember better, that was to be so highly extolled, when I was a boy? "Where am I to go, wretch that I am? Where am I to turn? To the

sanguine redundat, an domum? matremne ut miseram
lamentantem videam et abiectam?" quae sic ab illo esse
acta constabat oculis, voce, gestu, inimici ut lacrimas te-
nere non possent.

Cf. Cic. *Mur.* 88; Quint. *Inst.* 11.3.115; Iulius Victor, *RLM*,
p. 443.3–4.

Unplaced Fragments (F 62–69)

F 62 *De dub. nom.*, *GL* V, p. 577.30

diadema generis neutri, ut Gracchus: "purpura⟨m⟩[1] et
diadema."

   [1] purpura⟨m⟩ *Haupt*: purpura *codd.*

F 63 Charis., *GL* I, p. 107.19–24 = p. 137.15–22 B.

nam familia est ut plebs, et posset pater familiae dici ut
tribunus plebis. . . . et ideo etiam "matres familiae" Varro
dixit de scaenicis originibus primo et tertio [Varro, F 71,
74 *GRF*], et Gracchus "patres familiae," non familiarum.

F 64 Gell. *NA* 20.6.9–11

"mei" enim Plautus hoc in loco [Plaut. *Pseud.* 3–6] non ab
eo dixit, quod est "meus," sed ab eo, quod est "ego." [10]
itaque si dicere velis "patrem mei" pro "patrem meum,"

310

Capitol? But it drips with my brother's blood. Or to my home? To see my unhappy mother lamenting and despondent?" This was delivered by him, as was known, with such glances, tone of voice, and gestures that even his enemies could not restrain their tears.

Unplaced Fragments (F 62–69)

F 62 Anonymous grammarian

diadema ["diadem"; originally Greek word], of neuter gender, like Gracchus: "purple and diadem [acc.]."[1]

[1] This fragment may come from a reaction to accusations of Ti. Sempronius Gracchus (**34**) having received a diadem and purple robe from the king of Pergamum (cf. **18** F 3).

F 63 Charisius

For "family" [*familia*] is like "people" [*plebs*], and "father of the family" could be said like "tribune of the people." . . . And therefore Varro also said "mothers of the family" in the first and third [books] on the origins of drama [Varro, F 71, 74 *GRF*] and Gracchus "fathers of the family," not "of families" [genitive singular instead of genitive plural, as these expressions are understood as distributive noun phrases].

F 64 Gellius, *Attic Nights*

For in this passage [Plaut. *Pseud.* 3–6] Plautus used *mei*, not from *meus*, but from *ego*. [10] Therefore, if you should choose to say *patrem mei* ["the father of me"] instead of

quo Graeci modo τὸν πατέρα μου dicunt, inusitate quidem, sed recte profecto eaque ratione dices, qua Plautus
dixit "labori mei" pro "labori meo." [11] haec autem ipsa
ratio est in numero plurativo, qua Gracchus "misereri vestrum" dixit et . . .

F 65a Sen. *Dial.* 12.16.6

Corneliam ex duodecim liberis ad duos fortuna redegerat:
si numerare funera Corneliae velles, amiserat decem, si
aestimare, amiserat Gracchos. flentibus tamen circa se et
fatum eius execrantibus interdixit, ne fortunam accu-
sarent, quae sibi filios Gracchos dedisset. ex hac femina
debuit nasci qui diceret in contione: "tu matri meae male-
dicas, quae me peperit?"

F 65b + 66 Plut. *C. Gracch.* 25(4).5–6

ἀπομνημονεύεται δὲ καὶ τοῦ Γαΐου πολλὰ ῥητορικῶς
καὶ ἀγοραίως ὑπὲρ αὐτῆς εἰρημένα πρός τινα τῶν

patrem meum ["my father"], as the Greeks say τὸν πατέρα μου ["the father of me"], you will say it in an unusual, but surely correct way and on the same principle according to which Plautus said *labori mei* ["for the trouble of me"] instead of *labori meo* ["for my trouble"]. [11] And this very principle applies in the plural number, according to which Gracchus said *misereri vestrum* ["to have pity on you"][1] and . . .

[1] Here, the genitive of a personal pronoun (in the plural) is an object of a verb and does not indicate a possessive relationship to a noun, as in the examples up to this point.

F 65a Seneca, *Dialogues. De Consolatione ad Helviam*

Fortune had reduced Cornelia [the mother of the Gracchi] from having twelve children to two; if you wished to count Cornelia's funerals, she had lost ten, if to assess them, she had lost the Gracchi. Nevertheless, when her friends were weeping around her and cursing her fate, she forbade them to criticize Fortune, who had given her the Gracchi as sons. It was appropriate that he was born from such a woman, he who said at a meeting of the People: "Do you dare to revile my mother who gave birth to me?"[1]

[1] The following testimonium (F 65b + 66) suggests that this is an utterance of C. Sempronius Gracchus rather than of his brother Tiberius (**34**).

F 65b + 66 Plutarch, *Life of Gaius Gracchus*

There are on record also many utterances of Gaius about her [Cornelia, his mother] in the rhetorical style of forensic speech, directed toward one of his enemies: "What,"

ἐχθρῶν "σὺ γάρ" ἔφη "Κορνηλίαν λοιδορεῖς τὴν Τιβέριον τεκοῦσαν;" [6] ἐπεὶ δὲ διαβεβλημένος ἦν εἰς
μαλακίαν ὁ λοιδορηθείς, "τίνα δ᾽ " εἶπεν "ἔχων παρρησίαν συγκρίνεις Κορνηλίᾳ σεαυτόν; ἔτεκες γὰρ ὡς
ἐκείνη; καὶ μὴν πάντες ἴσασι Ῥωμαῖοι πλείω χρόνον
ἐκείνην ἀπ᾽ ἀνδρὸς οὖσαν ἢ σὲ τὸν ἄνδρα." τοιαύτη
μὲν ἡ πικρία τῶν λόγων ἦν αὐτοῦ, καὶ πολλὰ λαβεῖν
ἐκ τῶν γεγραμμένων ἔστιν ὅμοια.

F 67 Charis., *GL* I, p. 102.20–103.1 = pp. 130.19–31.2 B.

heres parens homo, etsi in communi sexu intellegantur,
tamen masculino genere semper dicuntur. nemo enim aut
secundam heredem dicit aut bonam parentem aut malam
hominem, sed masculine, tametsi de femina sermo habea-
tur. . . . sed Gracchus "suos parentes amat" cum dicit in
significatione matris ‹. . .›[1] et in alia epistula "tuus parens
sum"[2] ait, cum de se loqueretur.

[1] *post* matris *certe quaedam excidisse neque tamen reliqua quo
pertineant aut quemadmodum corrigenda sint constare monet
Keil*   [2] sum *cod.*: tuum *Cauchii ex deperdito cod. excerpta*

F 68 Serv. ad Verg. *Aen.* 7.715

"frigida misit / Nursia": Piceni civitas, "frigida" autem aut
re vera, aut certe venenosa, nocens: Gracchi namque ubi-
que in contionibus suis Nursinos sceleratos appellaverunt,
et scimus amare Vergilium historiarum rem per transitum
tangere.

---

[1] These statements are attributed to both Gracchi.

he said, "do you abuse Cornelia, who gave birth to Tiberius?" [6] And since the one who had uttered the abuse was charged with effeminate practices, "With what effrontery," he said, "can you compare yourself with Cornelia? Have you borne such children as she did? And verily all Romans know that she refrained from associating with men longer than you, the man." Such was the bitterness of his language, and many similar examples are there to be taken from his writings.

F 67 Charisius

"Heir," "parent," "human," although they are understood for both genders, are still always said in the masculine gender. For nobody says "second heiress" or "good female parent" or "bad female human," but in the masculine form, even if the statement is made about a woman. . . . But when Gracchus says "he loves his parents [masc. pl.]" in the sense of mother ⟨. . .⟩[1] and in another letter she says "I am your parent [masc. sg.]," when she talked about herself.

[1] What follows after the gap in the text are quotations from letters of the mother, Cornelia, rather than from texts by one of her sons.

F 68 Servius, *Commentary on Virgil*

"cold Nursia sent them": a community of Picenum [area in Italy between the Adriatic Sea and the Apennines], and "cold" either in fact or certainly full of poison, damaging: for the Gracchi called the Nursini wicked everywhere in their speeches before the People,[1] and we know that Virgil loved to touch on matters of history in passing.

F 69 Terent. Maur., vv. 985–88, *GL* VI, p. 354

nempe et esse[1] litterarum syllaba una sex potest, / Graeca cum duplex duabus solvitur nostratibus, / dixerit si forte quidam "scrobs abunde fossa erit,"[2] / "stirps" velut dixit disertus Gracchus alter Gaius.

[1] nempe et esse *Lachmann*: nec monet esse *ed. princ.*
[2] fossa erit *Lachmann*: fossa est *ed. princ.*

49 Q. FABIUS MAXIMUS ALLOBROGICUS

Q. Fabius Maximus Allobrogicus (cos. 121 BC; RE Fabius 110) fought against the Allobroges during his consulship; he then celebrated a triumph and received the cognomen *Allobrogicus.*

T 1 Cic. *Brut.* 107
= **39** T 1.

*Funeral Eulogy of P. Cornelius Scipio Aemilianus
Africanus Minor (F 2–3)*

F 2 Schol. Bob. ad Cic. *Mil.* 16 (p. 118.11–12 Stangl)
= **20** F 22.

F 69 Terentianus Maurus

And in fact a single syllable can consist of six letters, when a double Greek letter [i.e., a double consonant like $\psi = ps$] is resolved by two of ours, as when by chance someone would say "a pit [*scrobs*] of big dimensions will be a trench," [or] as for example the eloquent second Gracchus, Gaius, said "stem" [*stirps*].[1]

---

[1] Servius (Serv. ad Verg. *G.* 2.288) misinterprets Terentianus Maurus and ascribes *abunde fossa scrobis est* also to C. Gracchus, while Terentianus assigns only *stirps* to him.

49 Q. FABIUS MAXIMUS ALLOBROGICUS

According to the view of the poet Accius, reported in Cicero, Allobrogicus was a learned man and a decent speaker (T 1).

T 1 Cicero, *Brutus*

= **39** T 1.

Funeral Eulogy of P. Cornelius Scipio Aemilianus Africanus Minor (F 2–3)

*Upon the death of his uncle P. Cornelius Scipio Aemilianus Africanus minor (**21**) in 129 BC, Allobrogicus delivered the funeral speech (CCMR, App. A: 190), composed by C. Laelius Sapiens (**20** F 22–23).*

F 2 Scholia Bobiensia to Cicero, *Pro Milone*

= **20** F 22.

F 3 Cic. *Mur.* 75

= **20** F 23.

50 Q. MUCIUS SCAEVOLA AUGUR

Q. Mucius Scaevola (cos. 117 BC; RE Mucius 21) was augur from 129 BC until his death; he was called "augur" because he held this office for a long period and to distinguish him from relatives of the same name.

Scaevola was a well-respected and frequently consulted lawyer and a man familiar with philosophy, particularly Stoicism (T 1–4, 6; Cic. De or. 1.45, 1.75, 3.68; Brut. 212).

T 1 Cic. *Brut.* 102

[CICERO:] Mucius autem augur, quod pro se opus erat, ipse dicebat, ut de pecuniis repetundis contra T. Albucium. is oratorum in numero non fuit, iuris civilis intellegentia atque omni prudentiae genere praestitit.

T 2 Cic. *Brut.* 306

[CICERO:] ego autem ⟨in⟩[1] iuris civilis studio multum operae dabam Q. Scaevolae Q. f., qui quamquam nemini ⟨se⟩[2] ad docendum dabat, tamen consulentibus respondendo studiosos audiendi docebat.

[1] *add. Müller*   [2] *add. edd.*

F 3 Cicero, *Pro Murena*

= **20** F 23.

50 Q. MUCIUS SCAEVOLA AUGUR

Cicero trained with Scaevola (T 2; Cic. Amic. 1); Scaevola is an interlocutor in Cicero's De re publica (Cic. Rep. 1.18) and in the first book of De oratore (Cic. Att. 4.16.3).

In Cicero, Scaevola is said not to have been an outstanding orator and to have often obtained the Senate's approval in important matters when he spoke briefly and in a fairly unpolished way (T 1, 5).

T 1 Cicero, *Brutus*

[CICERO:] And Mucius the augur used to speak himself as far as was necessary on his own behalf, as with regard to a charge of extortion of money against T. Albucius [**64**]. He was not reckoned among the orators; but in understanding of civil law and in all kinds of knowledge he was supreme.

T 2 Cicero, *Brutus*

[CICERO:] In the study of civil law, however, I devoted much attention to Q. Scaevola, Quintus' son, who, though he offered himself to nobody as a teacher, still, by the legal replies given to people consulting him, taught those eager to listen to him.

T 3 Cic. *De or.* 1.39

[SCAEVOLA:] quid? haec iura civilia quae iam pridem in nostra familia sine ulla eloquentiae laude versantur, num aut inventa sunt aut cognita aut omnino ab oratorum genere tractata?

T 4 Cic. *De or.* 1.200

[CRASSUS:] est enim sine dubio domus iuris consulti totius oraculum civitatis. testis est huiusce Q. Muci ianua et vestibulum, quod in eius infirmissima valetudine adfectaque iam aetate maxima cotidie frequentia civium ac summorum hominum splendore celebratur.

T 5 Cic. *De or.* 1.214

[ANTONIUS:] Crassus vero mihi noster visus est oratoris facultatem non illius artis terminis, sed ingenii sui finibus immensis paene describere. nam et civitatum regendarum oratori gubernacula sententia sua tradidit, in quo per mihi mirum visum est, Scaevola, te hoc illi concedere, cum saepissime tibi senatus breviter impoliteque dicenti maximis sit de rebus adsensus.

T 6 Vell. Pat. 2.9.2

. . . nam Q. Mucius iuris scientia quam proprie[1] eloquentiae nomine celebrior fuit.

> [1] proprie *Lipsius*: propriae *cod.*

T 3 Cicero, *On the Orator*

[SCAEVOLA:] What? As regards those rules of civil law that have long made their home in our family without any reputation for eloquence, were they ever invented or investigated or dealt with in any way by the tribe of orators?

T 4 Cicero, *On the Orator*

[CRASSUS:] For the house of a jurist is undoubtedly an oracle of the whole community. Evidence for this is the gateway and the forecourt of our friend here, Q. Mucius, since, notwithstanding his very poor health and already advanced age, they are thronged daily by a great crowd of citizens and the splendor of most distinguished men.

T 5 Cicero, *On the Orator*

[ANTONIUS:] Now our friend Crassus [L. Licinius Crassus (**66**)] seemed to me to mark out the scope of the orator, not by the bounds of that art, but by the almost infinite extent of his own talent. For by his verdict he even handed over to the orator the helm of running the community; and in that it seemed most amazing to me, Scaevola, that you should grant him this point, since the Senate has very often agreed with you on very important matters, when you spoke briefly and without ornament.

T 6 Velleius Paterculus, *Compendium of Roman History*

. . . for Q. Mucius[1] was more famous for his knowledge of jurisprudence than, strictly speaking, on account of his eloquence.

---

[1] Which Q. Mucius is referred to is uncertain: this may be a comment on Q. Mucius Scaevola (**67**).

On His Own Behalf Concerning Extortion (F 7A)

The only oration by Scaevola for which occasion and content are known is a speech in self-defense against the charge of extortion, delivered against T. Albucius. T. Albucius (**64**) accused Scaevola when the latter returned from

F 7A Cic. *Brut.* 102

= T 1.

51 C. TITIUS

*C. Titius (RE Titius 7) was an orator of the second century BC (Fronto, Ad M. Caes. 1.7 [p. 15.12 van den Hout]). Cicero associates him with the period of M. Antonius (**65**) and L. Licinius Crassus (**66**) (T 1) and notes that the playwright L. Afranius (fl. ca. 160–120 BC) imitated Titius (Cic. Brut. 167), while Macrobius describes him as a man of the time of the satirist Lucilius (F 2). Thus, Titius presumably was an older contemporary of Antonius and Crassus, and active around the middle of the second cen-*

T 1 Cic. *Brut.* 167

[CICERO:] eiusdem fere temporis fuit eques Romanus C. Titius, qui meo iudicio eo pervenisse videtur quo potuit fere Latinus orator sine Graecis litteris et sine multo usu pervenire. huius orationes tantum argutiarum, tantum exemplorum, tantum urbanitatis habent, ut paene Attico

51 C. TITIUS

On His Own Behalf Concerning Extortion (F 7A)

his praetorship in Asia in 119 BC; Scaevola was not found guilty (Cic. De or. 2.281; cf. **65** *F 15) (TLRR 32). The satirist Lucilius composed a parody of this incident (Lucil. book 2; cf. Cic. Orat. 149; Fin. 1.9).*

F 7A Cicero, *Brutus*

= T 1.

51 C. TITIUS

tury BC (for a recent discussion of Titius' dates and the time of the attested speech, see Cavarzere 2018; on the fragments and ways of approaching them, see Dugan 2018).

Titius is described as an impressive orator in Cicero because of his refined style, particularly in view of his lack of Greek education and of practice (T 1). Titius also composed tragedies (T 1; cf. TrRF 1:139).

T 1 Cicero, *Brutus*

[CICERO:] Of about the same time [roughly the period of M. Antonius (**65**) and L. Licinius Crassus (**66**)] was the Roman knight C. Titius, who, in my judgment, seems to have achieved as much as a Latin orator could generally achieve without acquaintance with Greek letters and without much practical experience. His orations have such an amount of refinements of expression, such a wealth of examples, such a great deal of urbanity that they seem

stilo scriptae esse videantur. easdem argutias in tragoedias
satis ille quidem acute, sed parum tragice transtulit.

On Lex Fannia (F 2–3)

Titius is said to have spoken in support of the Lex Fannia,
*a sumptuary law proposed by the consul C. Fannius in 161
BC* (Lex Fannia cibaria: LPPR, pp. 287–88). *Because Titius' main period of activity is likely to be somewhat later,
and in view of the procedural legal details mentioned in*

F 2 Macrob. *Sat.* 3.16.13–17

haec Varro [Varro, *Rer. hum.* 11, F 1 Mirsch] de omnibus
scilicet huius fluminis piscibus sed inter eos, ut supra dixi,
praecipuum locum lupus tenuit, et quidem is qui inter
duos pontes captus esset. [14] id ostendunt cum multi alii
tum etiam Titius, vir aetatis Lucilianae, in oratione qua
legem Fanniam suasit. cuius verba ideo pono quia non
solum de lupo inter duos pontes capto erunt testimonio,
sed etiam mores quibus plerique tunc vivebant facile pu-
blicabunt. describens enim homines prodigos in forum ad
iudicandum ebrios commeantes quaeque soleant inter se
sermocinari sic ait: [15] "ludunt alea studiose, delibuti
unguentis, scortis stipati. ubi horae decem sunt, iubent
puerum vocari ut comitium eat percontatum quid in foro

almost to have been written by an Attic pen. These same refinements he carried over into his tragedies, rather cleverly certainly, but in a scarcely tragic way.

On Lex Fannia (F 2–3)

the sources, it is widely believed that the speech does not belong to the year in which the law was first proposed, but was rather given at a later date in connection with discussions about its extension or abolition.

F 2 Macrobius, *Saturnalia*

This is what Varro [Varro, *Rer. hum.* 11, F 1 Mirsch] says about all the fish of this river [Tiber], of course, but among them, as I said earlier, the wolffish had pride of place, and in particular that caught between the two bridges [Aemilian and Fabrician bridges]. [14] This is demonstrated by many others and particularly also by Titius, a man of Lucilius' [the satirist's] time, in the speech in which he argued for the *Lex Fannia*. I put down his words for the reason that they will not only provide evidence about the wolffish caught between the two bridges, but also easily reveal the habits according to which many people then used to live. For, describing wastrels wandering drunk into the Forum to serve as judges and what they were accustomed to talk about among themselves, he says as follows: [15] "They play dice enthusiastically, smeared with scented oils, closely surrounded by their whores. When it is the tenth hour [i.e., late afternoon], they order that a slave be summoned to go to the *comitium* [place in the Forum for

gestum sit, qui suaserint, qui dissuaserint, quot tribus ius-
serint, quot vetuerint. inde ad comitium vadunt ne litem
suam faciant. dum eunt, nulla est in angiporto amphora
quam non impleant, quippe qui vesicam plenam vini ha-
beant. [16] veniunt in comitium, tristes iubent dicere.
quorum negotium est narrant, iudex testes poscit, ipsus it
minctum. ubi redit, ait se omnia audivisse, tabulas poscit,
litteras inspicit: vix prae vino sustinet palpebras. eunt in
consilium. ibi haec oratio: 'quid mihi negotii est cum istis
nugatoribus? quin potius[1] potamus mulsum mixtum vino
Graeco, edimus turdum pinguem bonumque piscem, lu-
pum germanum qui inter duos pontes captus fuit?'" [17]
haec Titius.

[1] quin potius *Madvig*: potius quam *codd.*

F 3 Macrob. *Sat.* 3.13.13

ubi iam luxuria tunc accusaretur quando tot rebus farta
fuit cena pontificum? ipsa vero edulium genera quam
dictu turpia? nam Titius in suasione legis Fanniae obicit
saeculo suo quod porcum Troianum mensis inferant,
quem illi ideo sic vocabant, quasi aliis inclusis animalibus
gravidum, ut ille Troianus "equus gravidus armatis" [cf.
Enn. *Trag.* F 22 *TrRF / FRL*] fuit.

legislative and judicial matters] and ask what business was
conducted in the Forum, who spoke in favor, who against
a bill, how many tribes voted for, how many voted against.
Then they make their way to the *comitium*, so that they
will not be held liable for dereliction of duty.[1] On their way
there is not a single pot in an alleyway that they do not fill,
since they have their bladders full of wine. [16] They come
to the *comitium*; grumpy, they call for the speeches. Those
whose duty it is state their cases, the judge calls for the
witnesses, while he himself goes to pee. When he comes
back, he says he has heard everything, calls for the accounts, inspects the writing: he is scarcely able to keep his
eyelids open due to the wine. They withdraw to deliberate.
There the discussion runs like this: 'What have I to do with
those fools? Why don't we rather drink some mead mixed
with Greek wine, eat a nice fat thrush and a good piece of
fish, a real wolffish that was caught between the two
bridges?'" [17] Thus Titius.

[1] The phrase literally means "to cause one's own lawsuit" and
is particularly applied to negligent judges.

F 3 Macrobius, *Saturnalia*

Where else could luxury then be criticized when a meal of
pontiffs was stuffed with so many things [as just de-
scribed]? How disgusting indeed just to mention the sorts
of food! For Titius, in the speech supporting the *Lex Fannia*, reproaches his contemporaries because they put Trojan pig on the tables, which they called thus for the reason
that it was "pregnant" as it were with other animals enclosed within, as the famous Trojan "horse [was] 'pregnant' with armed men" [cf. Enn. *Trag.* F 22 *TrRF / FRL*].

327

52 [FAVORINUS]

*[Favorinus] is given as the name of the orator from whose speech the antiquarian Gellius quotes. An orator of this name is not attested elsewhere, and it is not a typical Roman name. Therefore, an error in Gellius' text is often assumed, and this orator is frequently identified with M. Favonius (**166**). It is not impossible, though, that another orator called Favorinus existed.*

On Lex Licinia (F 1)

F 1 Gell. *NA* 15.8.1–2

Locus ex oratione Favorini,[1] veteris oratoris, de cenarum atque luxuriae obprobratione, qua usus est, cum legem Liciniam de sumptu minuendo suasit.—[1] cum legeremus orationem veterem Favorini,[2] non indiserti viri, qua oratione ‹. . .›[3] totum, ut meminisse possemus odio esse hercle istiusmodi sumptus atque victus, perdidicimus. [2] verba haec, quae adposuimus, Favorini[4] sunt: "praefecti popinae atque luxuriae negant cenam lautam esse, nisi, cum lubentissime edis, tum auferatur et alia esca melior atque amplior succenturietur. is nunc flos cenae habetur inter istos, quibus sumptus et fastidium pro facetiis procedit, qui negant ullam avem praeter ficedulam totam comesse oportere; ceterarum avium atque altilium nisi tantum adponatur, ut a cluniculis inferiore parte saturi fiant, convivium putant inopia sordere, superiorem par-

---

1-2, 4 Favorini *codd.*: Favonii *vir doctus ap. Gronovium*: Fannii *Pithoeus*   3 *lac. statuit Hertz*

52 [FAVORINUS]

A sumptuary Lex Licinia *was proposed apparently shortly before 103 BC (*Gell*. NA 2.24.7, 20.1.23; *Macrob*. Sat. 3.17.7–9; *Paul*. Fest., p. 47.5–7 L.; Lex Licinia sumptuaria: LPPR, pp. 327–28). [Favorinus] spoke in its support either when it was first proposed or at a later date.*

On Lex Licinia *(F 1)*

F 1 Gellius, *Attic Nights*

Chapter title: A passage from the oration of Favorinus, an old orator, about criticism of feasts and luxury, which he used when he spoke in support of the *Lex Licinia* on reducing expenditure.—[1] When we were reading an old speech of Favorinus, not an ineloquent man, in which speech < . . . > we learned the whole of it by heart, in order to be able to remember that extravagant living of that kind, by Hercules, is hateful. [2] These words, which we have appended, are those of Favorinus: "The leaders in gluttony and luxury declare that a feast is not elegant, unless, at the point when you are eating with the greatest relish, the dish is cleared and another better and richer dainty is supplied. This is now thought the very flower of a feast among those for whom extravagance and fastidiousness come forward in place of elegance, who say that no bird ought to be eaten whole except a fig pecker, who believe that a dinner is soiled by stinginess unless so many of the other birds and fatted fowl are provided that they [the guests] may be satisfied with the rumps and hinder parts,

329

tem avium atque altilium qui edint, eos palatum ⟨non⟩[5]
habere. si proportione pergit luxuria crescere, quid relin-
quitur, nisi uti delibari sibi cenas iubeant, ne edendo defe-
tigentur, quando stratus auro, argento, purpura amplior
aliquot hominibus quam dis inmortalibus adornatur?"

[5] *add. codd. rec.*: ⟨parum delicatum⟩ *Hertz*

53 C. SULPICIUS GALBA

*C. Sulpicius Galba (RE Sulpicius 51), a son of Ser. Sulpi-
cius Galba (19), became a member of the Gracchan land
commission in 121 BC after the deaths of C. Sempronius
Gracchus (48) and M. Fulvius Flaccus (40).*

Under the Lex Mamilia de coniuratione Iugurthina

On His Own Behalf (F 1)

F 1 Cic. *Brut.* 127

[CICERO:] huic successit aetati C. Galba,[1] Servi illius[2] eloquentissimi viri filius, P. Crassi eloquentis et iuris periti
gener. laudabant hunc patres nostri, favebant etiam propter patris memoriam, sed cecidit in cursu. nam rogatione
Mamilia, Iugurthinae coniurationis invidia, cum pro sese
ipse dixisset, oppressus est. exstat eius peroratio, qui epi-
logus dicitur; qui tanto in honore pueris nobis erat ut eum
etiam edisceremus. hic, qui in conlegio sacerdotum esset,
primus post Romam conditam iudicio publico est condemnatus.

[1] C. Galba *edd.*: p. Galba *codd. plerique*   [2] Seruilius *vel*
Serulius *codd.*

that those who eat the upper parts of such birds and fatted fowl have <no> taste. If luxury continues to increase in this proportion, what remains but that men should ask for part of their feasts to be removed, so that they may not fatigue themselves by feeding, when the couch is more profusely adorned with gold, silver, and purple for some mortals than for the immortal gods?"

53 C. SULPICIUS GALBA

(LPPR, p. 324), put forward by the Tribune of the People C. Mamilius Limetanus in 109 BC (Sall. Iug. 40), Galba was accused of having accepted money from King Jugurtha; despite the speech in his own defense, he was found guilty and went into exile (TLRR 52).

On His Own Behalf (F 1)

F 1 Cicero, *Brutus*

[CICERO:] Upon this period followed C. Galba, son of Servius [Ser. Sulpicius Galba (**19**)], that very eloquent man, and son-in-law of P. Crassus [P. Licinius Crassus Dives Mucianus (**31**)], also eloquent and an expert in law. Our fathers praised him [Galba]; they liked him too for the memory of his father, but he fell on the path. For he was convicted as a result of the proposal of Mamilius, through odium aroused in relation to a conspiracy with Jugurtha, though he had spoken in his own defense. His peroration, which is called epilogue, is extant; it was held in such honor when we were boys that we even learned it by heart. He was the first man since the foundation of Rome, though belonging to a priestly college, to be found guilty by a public court of law.

53A SP. THORIUS

*Sp. Thorius (tr. pl. end of 2nd cent. BC; RE Thorius 2),
when Tribune of the People (F 3), proposed a Lex Thoria
agraria (LPPR, p. 318) concerning public land; details and
the identification of the law with any of those mentioned*

On Lex Thoria agraria *(F 1–3)*

F 1 Cic. *Brut.* 136

[CICERO:] Sp. Thorius satis valuit in populari genere dicendi, is qui agrum publicum vitiosa et inutili lege vectigali[1] levavit.

> [1] vectigali *cod. det.*: vectigale *codd.*

F 2 Cic. *De or.* 2.284
= **24A** F 2.

F 3 App. *B Civ.* 1.27.122

καὶ περιῆν ἐς χεῖρον ἔτι τοῖς πένησι, μέχρι Σπούριος[1]
Θόριος[2] δημαρχῶν εἰσηγήσατο νόμον, τὴν μὲν γῆν
μηκέτι διανέμειν, ἀλλ᾽ εἶναι τῶν ἐχόντων, καὶ φόρους
ὑπὲρ αὐτῆς τῷ δήμῳ κατατίθεσθαι καὶ τάδε τὰ χρή-
ματα χωρεῖν ἐς διανομάς. ὅπερ ἦν μέν τις τοῖς πένησι
παρηγορία διὰ τὰς διανομάς, ὄφελος δ᾽ οὐδὲν ἐς πο-
λυπληθίαν.

> [1] Σπόριος *cum uno cod. scr. Mendelssohnius*
> [2] Θόριος *Hotmanus:* βόριος *vel* βούριος *codd.*

53A SP. THORIUS

in Appian and with the inscriptionally preserved Lex agraria *of 111 BC are uncertain and controversial (on the difficulties see, e.g., Badian 1965).*

On Lex Thoria agraria *(F 1–3)*

F 1 Cicero, *Brutus*

[CICERO:] Sp. Thorius had considerable proficiency in the kind of speaking appealing to the People, he who freed the public land from tax payment by a flawed and inexpedient law.[1]

[1] Various translations and emendations for the second half of this passage have been proposed, since its interpretation is crucial for addressing the problems surrounding the *Lex Thoria*.

F 2 Cicero, *On the Orator*

= **24A** F 2.

F 3 Appian, *Civil Wars*

And there was even less available for the poor, until Spurius Thorius, a Tribune of the People, brought forward a law, providing that the land should no longer be distributed, but should belong to those in possession of it, and they should pay rent for it to the People, and that this money should go to distributions. Thus, there was some consolation for the poor through the distributions, but no positive effect for increasing the population.

54 M. GRATIDIUS

*M. Gratidius (d. 102 BC; RE Gratidius 2), a great-uncle
of Cicero, served as a prefect of M. Antonius (65) in Cilicia
and died in the war against the pirates there (T 1).*

Gratidius proposed a bill on voting by ballot for Arpi-

T 1 Cic. *Brut.* 168

[CICERO:] doctus autem Graecis litteris propinquus noster, factus ad dicendum, M. Gratidius M. Antoni perfami-
liaris, cuius praefectus cum esset in Cilicia est interfectus;
⟨is⟩ qui[1] accusavit C. Fimbriam, M. Mari Gratidiani pater.[2]

    [1] ⟨is⟩ qui *Jahn*   [2] pater *edd.*: patrem *codd.*

55 C. FLAVIUS FIMBRIA

C. Flavius Fimbria (cos. 104 BC; RE Flavius 87), a homo
novus *(Wiseman 1971, 231, no. 180), is praised in Cicero
for his diligence and strength of mind, while there are
mixed reactions to his harsh, abusive, and fervid style of
speaking (T 1–2; Cic. Planc. 12).*

*Fimbria was accused of extortion by M. Gratidius (54
T 1), with M. Aemilius Scaurus (43) appearing as a witness*

T 1 Cic. *Brut.* 129

[CICERO:] C. Fimbria temporibus isdem fere, sed longius
aetate provectus, habitus est sane, ut ita dicam, lutulen-

54 M. GRATIDIUS

*num, which was opposed by Cicero's grandfather (Cic.
Leg. 3.36), and he (unsuccessfully) prosecuted C. Flavius
Fimbria (55) for extortion (T 1; cf. Val. Max. 8.5.2) (TLRR
61).*

T 1 Cicero, *Brutus*

[CICERO:] And a man educated in Greek letters and born
to speak was our kinsman M. Gratidius, an intimate friend
of M. Antonius [**65**]; when he was the latter's prefect in
Cilicia, he was killed. ⟨He⟩ [is the one] who brought an
accusation against C. Fimbria [C. Flavius Fimbria (**55**)]
and was the father of M. Marius Gratidianus.

55 C. FLAVIUS FIMBRIA

*against the defendant, but he was not found guilty (Cic.
Font. 24, 26; Val. Max. 8.5.2) (TLRR 61).*

*Cicero's report indicates that Fimbria delivered speeches
in the Senate and in law courts. Some of these must have
been published since Cicero was able to read them when
he was young; yet already at the end of Cicero's life they
were hard to find (T 1).*

T 1 Cicero, *Brutus*

[CICERO:] C. Fimbria, at about the same time [as other
orators of the late second century BC just mentioned],
though more advanced in age, was certainly regarded as,

tus,[1] {patronus}[2] asper, maledicus; genere toto paulo fervidior atque commotior, diligentia tamen et virtute animi atque vita bonus auctor in senatu; idem tolerabilis patronus nec rudis in iure civili et cum virtute tum etiam ipso orationis genere liber; cuius orationes pueri legebamus, quas iam reperire vix possumus.

[1] lutulentus *Jahn*: luculentus *codd.*: truculentus *Ernesti*
[2] *del. Jahn*

T 2 Cic. *De or.* 2.91

[Antonius:] nihil est facilius quam amictum imitari alicuius aut statum aut motum. si vero etiam vitiosi[1] aliquid est, id sumere {et in eo vitiosum esse}[2] non magnum est, ut ille, qui nunc etiam amissa voce furit in re publica, Fufius nervos in dicendo C. Fimbriae, quos tamen habuit ille, non adsequitur, oris pravitatem et verborum latitudinem imitatur.

[1] vitiosi *Manutius*: vitiose *codd.*: paene vitiosi *Muther*: insigne *Schuetz*   [2] *del. Herthel*: et in eo vitiosum esse *codd.*   in eo vitio totum *Müller ed.*: in eo socium *Müller*: in eo ipso vitiosum *Ellendt*: in eo ipso vitio vitiosum *Bake*: in eo ambitiosum *Lachmann*: in eo vitii similem *Adler*: in eo vitio summum *aut* vitiosissimum *Orelli*: in eo vitio suum *Polster*

56 M. IUNIUS BRUTUS

M. Iunius Brutus (RE *Iunius* 50) *was the son of the eminent lawyer and jurist M. Iunius Brutus and was regarded as a disgrace to the family (T 1; Cic. De or. 2.125): he did not aim for political office (T 1) or a military career (Cic.*

if I may say so, muddy, harsh, and abusive; in his whole style a little too fervid and too excited; yet because of his diligence, and the vigor of his mind and his life, a good counselor in the Senate; likewise a tolerable pleader, and not unlearned in civil law; and as in his excellent nature, so also in his very style of speaking, open; when we were boys we used to read his orations, which we can now scarcely find.

T 2 Cicero, *On the Orator*

[ANTONIUS:] Nothing is easier than to imitate someone's style of dress, pose, or movement. Moreover, if there is even something faulty, it is not a big deal to appropriate that {and be faulty in that}, just as that man, who even now, though having lost his voice, is raving in the Republic, Fufius [L. Fufius (**75**)], fails to attain the energy in speaking of C. Fimbria, which the latter at least possessed, but imitates the distortion of his face in speaking and his broad pronunciation of the words.

56 M. IUNIUS BRUTUS

De or. 2.126); *instead he sold his paternal wealth (Cic. De or. 2.126) and was active as a sharp-tongued professional prosecutor (T 1; Cic. Off. 2.50).*

T 1 Cic. *Brut.* 130

[CICERO:] isdem temporibus M. Brutus, in quo magnum fuit, Brute, dedecus generi vestro, qui, cum tanto nomine esset patremque optimum virum habuisset et iuris peritissimum, accusationem factitaverit, ut Athenis Lycurgus. is magistratus non petivit, sed fuit accusator vehemens et molestus, ut facile cerneres naturale quoddam stirpis bonum degeneravisse vitio depravatae voluntatis.

Against M. Aemilius Scaurus (F 2)

F 2 Cic. *Font.* 38
= **43** F 5.

Against C. Plancus (F 3–5)

T 1 Cicero, *Brutus*

[CICERO:] To the same time [as C. Sextius Calvinus (**70A**) and other orators of the late 2nd century BC] belonged M. Brutus, who was a great stain on your family, Brutus, in that, although he had such a distinguished name and a father who was a very good man and a most knowledge-able legal expert, he regularly undertook prosecutions, like Lycurgus at Athens.[1] He did not seek public office, but was a vehement and annoying prosecution lawyer, so that you could readily see how a certain natural gift de-rived from his stock had degenerated through the vice of depraved intention.

[1] A one-sided characterization of the Athenian statesman (ca. 390–324 BC), ignoring patriotic activities.

Against M. Aemilius Scaurus (F 2)

*Brutus took M. Aemilius Scaurus (**43** F 5–7) to court for extortion, perhaps in 114 BC after the latter's consulship; the speech was still extant in Cicero's time (TLRR 37, 96).*

F 2 Cicero, *Pro Fonteio*

= **43** F 5.

Against C. Plancus (F 3–5)

*Brutus prosecuted C. Plancus (different versions of name transmitted), defended by L. Licinius Crassus (**66** F 45–47), presumably shortly before 91 BC (TLRR 98).*

F 3 Cic. *Clu.* 140–41

= **66** F 46.

F 4 Cic. *De or.* 2.220–23

= **66** F 45.

F 5 Plin. *HN* 36.7

iam L. Crassum oratorem illum qui primus peregrini mar-
moris columnas habuit in eodem Palatio, Hymettias tamen nec pluris sex aut longiores duodenum pedum, M.
Brutus in iurgiis ob id Venerem Palatinam appellaverat.

57 L. CAESULENUS

*Cicero notes that he heard L. Caesulenus (*RE *Caesulenus
1), then an old man, speak when he was suing "Sabellius"
(name uncertain) under a* Lex Aquilia, *perhaps in the early*

T 1 Cic. *Brut.* 131

[CICERO:] atque eodem tempore accusator de plebe L.
Caesulenus fuit, quem ego audivi iam senem, cum ab L.

F 3 Cicero, *Pro Cluentio*

= **66** F 46.

F 4 Cicero, *On the Orator*

= **66** F 45.

F 5 Pliny the Elder, *Natural History*

Already that orator L. Crassus [L. Licinius Crassus (**66**)], he who was the first to have columns of foreign marble also on the Palatine, yet of Hymettus marble [from Mount Hymettus near Athens], and no more than six or taller than twelve feet, had been called "Venus Palatina" by M. Brutus because of this in their quarrels.[1]

[1] The testimonium does not mention a connection with the case of C. Plancus and talks of "quarrels" more generally. Because of the opposition of L. Licinius Crassus (**66**) and M. Iunius Brutus, it could refer to an exchange between the two pleaders during this lawsuit.

57 L. CAESULENUS

80s BC (F 2A) (TLRR 111). L. Caesulenus' skill as an accuser is highlighted (T 1).

T 1 Cicero, *Brutus*

[CICERO:] And at the same time [as M. Iunius Brutus (**56**) and other orators of the late 2nd cent. BC] there was a prosecutor of plebeian origin, L. Caesulenus, whom I heard when he was already an old man, when he sought

Sabellio[1] multam lege Aquilia † de iustitia †[2] petivisset.
non fecissem hominis paene infimi mentionem, nisi iudi-
carem qui suspiciosius aut criminosius diceret audivisse
me neminem.

[1] Sabellio *edd.*: Savelio *codd.*: Saufeio *Martha*   [2] † de
iustitia † *Barwick*: de iustitia *codd.*: *del. Friedrich*: damni iniuria
Hotomann: . . . sestertia *Martha*

Against L. Sabellius? (F 2A)

F 2A Cic. *Brut.* 131

= T 1.

58 Q. CAECILIUS METELLUS NUMIDICUS

*Q. Caecilius Metellus Numidicus (cos. 109, censor 102 BC;
RE Caecilius 97) acquired his* cognomen *(and celebrated
a triumph) after waging war in Numidia and defeating
Jugurtha (Sall.* Iug. *43–86; Liv.* Epit. *65). When the Tribune of the People L. Appuleius Saturninus (**64A**) proposed a land law requiring senators to swear allegiance or
accept a penalty, Numidicus refused the oath and apparently was then challenged (TLRR 77; details unclear). He
left Rome for exile on Rhodes and later in Tralles (in modern Turkey); he was recalled and returned to Rome in
99 BC.*

Numidicus studied with the Greek philosopher Car-

to exact a penalty from L. Sabellius [?] under the *Lex Aquilia* † on justice †.[1] I would not have made mention of a man almost at the very bottom if I did not feel that I never heard anyone who spoke in a manner more designed to awake suspicion or in a more accusatory fashion.

[1] Probably a reference to the *Lex Aquilia de damno* (*LPPR*, pp. 241–42), though the description is nontechnical and the text is uncertain.

Against L. Sabellius? (F 2A)

F 2A Cicero, *Brutus*

= T 1.

58 Q. CAECILIUS METELLUS NUMIDICUS

neades (Cic. De or. 3.68) and was friends with the poet Archias and the scholar L. Aelius Stilo Praeconinus (74 T 2; Cic. Arch. 6), who may have composed orations for him (T 2–3). Numidicus was regarded as a worthy orator (T 1; Cic. De or. 1.215; Vell. Pat. 2.9.1) and singled out for the purity of his Latin (Gell. NA 17.2.7). Fragments of letters written by him while in exile have been preserved (Gell. NA 15.13.6, 17.2.7).

Unless there is confusion in the sources, Numidicus, when censor, may have delivered a speech encouraging the People to enter marriages (18 F 6–7, with note).

T 1 Cic. *Brut.* 135

[CICERO:] Q. Metellus Numidicus et eius conlega M. Silanus dicebant de re publica quod esset illis viris et consulari dignitati satis.

T 2 Suet. *Gram. et rhet.* 3.2

Aelius cognomine duplici fuit: nam et Praeconinus,[1] quod pater eius praeconium fecerat, vocabatur et Stilo, quod orationes nobilissimo cuique scribere solebat, tantus[2] optimatium fautor ut Metellum[3] Numidicum in exilium comitatus sit.

[1] Praeconinus *Beroaldus*: pr(a)econius *codd.* [2] tantus *unus cod.*: tantum *codd. plerique* [3] Metellum *unus cod.*: M. Metellum *codd. plerique*: Q. Metellum *Aldus*

T 3 Cic. *Brut.* 206

[CICERO:] scribebat tamen orationes, quas alii dicerent; ut Q. Metello ‹. . .› f.,[1] . . .

[1] ‹L.› f. *Martha*: Balearici filio *Lambinus*

T 1 Cicero, *Brutus*

[CICERO:] Q. Metellus Numidicus and his colleague M. Silanus [as consul in 109 BC], in deliberations on public affairs, spoke in a manner that was appropriate to the personalities of those men and the dignity of the consular rank.

T 2 Suetonius, *Lives of Illustrious Men. Grammarians and Rhetoricians*

Aelius [L. Aelius Stilo Praeconinus (**74**)] had two *cognomina*: for he was called both Praeconinus, since his father had done the job of a public announcer [*praeconium*], and Stilo, since he was in the habit of writing orations for the most noble men in particular [*stilus* = "pen"]; he was such a supporter of the *optimates* that he accompanied Metellus Numidicus into exile.

T 3 Cicero, *Brutus*

[CICERO:] Yet he [L. Aelius Stilo Praeconinus (**74**), F 3] wrote orations for others to deliver, as, for example, for Q. Metellus,[1] son of ⟨. . .⟩, . . .

---

[1] Owing to textual difficulties the identity of Q. Metellus is not certain. Because of the close familiarity of L. Aelius Stilo Praeconinus and Q. Caecilius Metellus Numidicus indicated by T 2, this Q. Metellus could be Numidicus; or the passage might refer to Q. Caecilius Metellus Nepos (cos. 98 BC).

On His Own Behalf (F 4)

F 4 Cic. *Balb.* 11

audivi hoc de parente meo puer, cum Q. Metellus Luci filius causam de pecuniis repetundis diceret, ille, ille vir, cui patriae salus dulcior quam conspectus fuit, qui de civitate decedere quam de sententia maluit—hoc igitur causam dicente, cum ipsius tabulae circumferrentur inspiciendi nominis causa, fuisse iudicem ex illis equitibus Romanis gravissimis viris neminem quin removeret oculos ‹et›[1] se totum averteret, ne forte, quod ille in tabulas publicas rettulisset, dubitasse quisquam verumne an falsum esset videretur . . .

   [1] *om. codd.* (sed *vel* seque *codd. recc.*)

Against C. (T.) Manlius Before the People (F 5–6)

The Tribune of the People against whom Numidicus delivered a speech may have been T. Manlius Mancinus (tr. pl. 107 BC; thus in Sallust, while the praenomen is C. in other

F 5 Prisc., *GL* II, p. 382.6–9

Metellus Numidicus in oratione, qua apud populum G. Manlio tribuno plebis respondit: "nam ut aliis plerumque

On His Own Behalf (F 4)

Numidicus' defense of himself in a case of extortion will have taken place after one of his provincial governorships in around 112/11 BC or 106 BC (Cic. Att. 1.16.4; Val. Max. 2.10.1) (TLRR 51).

F 4 Cicero, *Pro Balbo*

When I was a boy, I heard this from my father: when Q. Metellus, Lucius' son, was defending himself concerning the recovery of extorted money, that great man, to whom the welfare of his country was dearer than the sight of it, who preferred to depart from his country rather than his principles—well, when he was pleading his case and when his accounts were being handed round for the purpose of examining an entry, not a single judge among those Roman knights, much respected men, failed to avert his gaze ⟨and⟩ turn completely away, lest by chance anyone might seem to have any doubt whether what that man had entered in the public records was true or false . . .

Against C. (T.) Manlius Before the People (F 5–6)

sources), who intended to remove the command over Numidia from him (Sall. Iug. 73.7).

F 5 Priscian

Metellus Numidicus, in the speech with which he replied to C. Manlius, a Tribune of the People, before the People: "for as to others frequently, to the magistrate, upon arrival,

advenienti[1] magistratu ob metum statuae polliceantur,"
passive, ἐπαγγελθῶσιν.

[1] advenienti *Meyer dub.*: obvenienti *vel* obvenienienti *codd.*

F 6 Gell. *NA* 7.11.1–3

cum inquinatissimis hominibus non esse convicio decer-
tandum neque maledictis adversum inpudentes et inpro-
bos velitandum, quia tantisper similis et compar eorum
fias, dum paria et consimilia dicas atque audias, non minus
ex oratione Q. Metelli Numidici, sapientis viri, cognosci
potest quam ex libris et disciplinis philosophorum. [2]
verba haec sunt Metelli adversus C. Manlium tribunum
plebis, a quo apud populum in contione lacessitus iactatus-
que fuerat dictis petulantibus: [3] "nunc quod ad illum
attinet, Quirites, quoniam se ampliorem putat esse, si se
mihi inimicum dictitarit, quem ego mihi neque amicum
recipio neque inimicum respicio, in eum ego non sum
plura dicturus. nam cum indignissimum arbitror, cui a
viris bonis benedicatur, tum ne idoneum quidem, cui a
probis maledicatur. nam si in eo tempore huiusmodi ho-
munculum nomines, in quo punire non possis, maiore
honore quam contumelia adficias."

On His Triumph (F 7)

statues may be promised out of fear," in the passive, "they may be promised" [in Greek; *polliceor*, usually deponent, here with passive sense].

F 6 Gellius, *Attic Nights*

That one should not vie with the basest men in abusive language nor have skirmishes of foul words against the shameless and wicked, since you become similar and equal to them for as long as you say identical and similar things to what you hear: this may be perceived no less from a speech by Q. Metellus Numidicus, a wise man, than from the books and teachings of the philosophers. [2] These are the words of Metellus against C. Manlius, a Tribune of the People, by whom he had been assailed and taunted with aggressive words in a speech before the People: [3] "Now, as far as that man is concerned, Romans, since he thinks that he will be a greater man if he keeps calling me his enemy, I, who neither count him as my friend nor take account of him as an enemy, I will not say anything further against him. For I consider him not only wholly unworthy to be well spoken of by good men, but unfit even to be reproached by the upright. For if you should name an insignificant fellow of his kind at a time when you cannot punish him, you would confer more honor upon him than ignominy."

On His Triumph (F 7)

On the occasion of his triumph over Numidia in 106 BC (Vell. Pat. 2.11.2; Eutr. 4.27.4; Vir. ill. 62.1), Numidicus delivered a speech, also commenting on his opponents.

F 7 Gell. *NA* 12.9.3–6

sed "honorem" quoque mediam vocem fuisse et ita appel-
latum, ut etiam malus honos diceretur et significaret iniuriam, id profecto rarissimum est. [4] Quintus autem Metellus Numidicus in oratione, quam de triumpho suo dixit,
his verbis usus est: "qua in re quanto universi me unum
antistatis, tanto vobis quam mihi maiorem iniuriam atque
contumeliam facit, Quirites, et quanto probi iniuriam facilius accipiunt, quam alteri tradunt, tanto ille vobis quam
mihi peiorem honorem habuit; nam me iniuriam ferre, vos
facere vult, Quirites, ut hic conquestio, istic vituperatio
relinquatur." [5] "honorem" inquit "peiorem vobis habuit
quam {gratiam}[1] mihi"; cuius verbi sententia est, quam
ipse quoque supra dicit: "maiore vos adfecit iniuria et
contumelia quam me." [6] praeter huius autem verbi no-
tionem adscribendam esse hanc sententiam ex oratione
Quinti Metelli existimavi, ut designaremus Socratis[2] decretum [cf. Plat. *Gorg.* 473a5, 489a3–4, 508b8–9]: κάκιον
εἶναι τὸ ἀδικεῖν ἢ τὸ ἀδικεῖσθαι.

---

[1] {gratiam} *Carrio*: gratiam *codd.*   [2] designaremus Socratis
Vogel: desineremus Socratis esse *codd.*: definiremus Socratis esse
codd. rec.: depingeremus Socratis *Marshall*

Against Valerius Messalla (F 8)

F 7 Gellius, *Attic Nights*

But that "honor" was also a neutral word and was used as such, so that people even spoke of "bad honor," thereby signifying "injury," is indeed very rare. [4] Quintus Metellus Numidicus, however, in the speech that he delivered on his triumph, used these words: "In this affair, by as much as the whole of you are more important than I alone, by so much he [probably C. Marius; cf. Sall. *Iug.* 73.2–7, 84.1] inflicts upon you greater insult and injury than on me, Romans; and by as much as honest men are more willing to suffer wrong than to do it to another, by so much has he shown 'worse honor' to you than to me; for he wishes me to suffer injustice and you to inflict it, Romans, so that on the one side there will be complaint and on the other reproach." [5] He says, "he has shown 'worse honor' {favor} to you than to me," and the meaning of this expression is as he himself too says earlier: "he has afflicted you with a greater injury and insult than me." [6] Besides the meaning of this word, I thought I ought to quote this statement from the speech of Quintus Metellus, so as to mark out a precept of Socrates [cf. Plat. *Gorg.* 473a5, 489a3–4, 508b8–9]: "that it is worse to be unjust than to suffer injustice."

Against Valerius Messalla (F 8)

The identity of the Valerius Messalla against whom Numidicus seems to have delivered several orations, accusing him of extortion, is uncertain, as is the date of the trial (TLRR 29).

F 8 Gell. *NA* 15.14.1–4

aput Q. Metellum Numidicum in libro accusationis in Valerium Messalam tertio nove dictum esse adnotavimus. [2] verba ex oratione eius haec sunt: "cum sese sciret in tantum crimen venisse atque socios ad senatum questum flentes venisse sese pecunias maximas exactos esse." [3] "<sese>[1] pecunias" inquit "<maximas>[2] exactos esse" pro eo, quod est "pecunias a se esse[3] maximas exactas." [4] id nobis videbatur Graeca figura dictum; Graeci enim dicunt: εἰσεπράξατό με ἀργύριον, id significat "exegit me pecuniam." quod si id dici potest, etiam "exactus esse aliqui pecuniam" dici potest . . .

[1] *add. Hertz*   [2] *add. Carrio*   [3] a se esse *Hertz*: a se *codd. plerique*: esse *cod. unus*

58b C. SERVILIUS GLAUCIA

C. Servilius Glaucia (tr. pl. ca. 101, praet. 100 BC; RE Servilius 65) collaborated with L. Appuleius Saturninus (64A) on "popular" policies. For instance, he proposed a law according to which juries in trials for the recovery of extorted money would consist entirely of knights and which would introduce procedural reforms (MRR I 571–72; Lex Servilia repetundarum: LPPR, p. 322). When Glaucia tried to gain the consulship for 99 BC illegally, assuming that L. Appuleius Saturninus would win a third

F 8 Gellius, *Attic Nights*

In Q. Metellus Numidicus, in the third book of his accusation of Valerius Messalla, we have noted something said in a novel way. [2] The words from his speech are as follows: "when he knew that he had incurred so grave an accusation and that the allies had come to the Senate in tears, to complain that they had been exacted enormous sums of money." [3] He says "that ⟨they⟩ had been exacted ⟨enormous⟩ sums of money," instead of "that enormous sums of money had been exacted from them." [4] This seemed to us said with a Greek construction; for the Greeks say: εἰσεπράξατό με ἀργύριον; this means "he exacted me money." If this can be said, it can also be said "someone to have been exacted money"[1] . . .

[1] Gellius comments on the rare use of *exigere* transitively with double accusative; he notes that such a phrase may be turned into a personal passive construction with one accusative retained (cf. Non., p. 106.21 M. = 152 L.: *EXIGOR: pro "a me exigitur."*—"'I am exacted' for 'it is exacted from me.'") and compares it to the construction of the Greek verb with similar meaning.

58b C. SERVILIUS GLAUCIA

Tribunate, the two men were killed by the consuls on the basis of a senatus consultum ultimum *(T 1; Liv. Epit. 69).*

In Cicero Glaucia's morals and policies are condemned; it is acknowledged, however, that he was clever and an expert in provoking laughter (T 1).

Examples of witty comments by Glaucia, not necessarily coming from proper speeches, have been preserved (F 3–4), as has a characteristic remark made before the People (F 5).

T 1 Cic. *Brut.* 224

[CICERO:] longe autem post natos homines improbissimus C. Servilius Glaucia, sed peracutus et callidus cum primisque ridiculus. is ex summis et fortunae et vitae sordibus in praetura consul factus esset, si rationem eius haberi licere iudicatum esset. nam et plebem tenebat et equestrem ordinem beneficio legis devinxerat. is praetor eodem die quo Saturninus tribunus plebis Mario et Flacco consulibus publice est interfectus; homo simillimus Atheniensis Hyperboli, cuius improbitatem veteres Atticorum comoediae notaverunt.

T 2 Cic. *De or.* 3.164

[CRASSUS:] nolo dici morte Africani "castratam" esse rem publicam, nolo "stercus curiae" dici Glauciam; quamvis sit simile, tamen est in utroque deformis cogitatio similitudinis.

Cf. Quint. *Inst.* 8.6.15; Mart. Cap., *RLM*, p. 473.26–28: Clodium [*vel* Claudium] stercus senatus.

T 1 Cicero, *Brutus*

[CICERO:] But by far the greatest rascal in the memory of mankind was C. Servilius Glaucia, yet very shrewd and clever, and particularly good at provoking laughter. Rising from the lowest condition of fortune and circumstances of life, he would have been made consul while still praetor if it had been held that his candidacy could be legally considered. For he both held sway over the People and had the equestrian order bound to him through the benefits resulting from the law. While praetor, he was put to death in the name of the state, on the same day as Saturninus [L. Appuleius Saturninus (**64A**)], the Tribune of the People, in the consulship of Marius and Flaccus [100 BC]. [He was] a man very similar to the Athenian Hyperbolus [Athenian politician, ostracized in 416 or 415 BC], whose shamelessness old Attic comedies have branded [e.g., Ar. *Eq.* 1304, 1362–63; *Nub.* 551–62, 623–26, 1065–66; *Pax* 681–92, 921, 1319; *Ach.* 845; *Ran.* 570; *Vesp.* 1007].

T 2 Cicero, *On the Orator*

[CRASSUS:] I do not approve of it being said that by Africanus' [P. Cornelius Scipio Aemilianus Africanus minor's (**21**)] death the Republic was "castrated," I do not approve of Glaucia being called "the excrement of the Senate house" [cf. F 4]: however much of a similarity there is, still, in both cases, the thought of the similarity is unseemly.

On Calvinus (F 3)

F 3 Cic. *De or.* 2.249

[CAESAR STRABO:] . . . quod Calvino Glaucia claudicanti: "ubi est vetus illud: num claudicat? at hic clodicat," hoc ridiculum est . . .

On Metellus (F 4)

F 4 Cic. *De or.* 2.263

[CAESAR STRABO:] . . . ornant igitur in primis orationem verba relata contrarie; quod idem genus est saepe etiam facetum; ut . . . a quo genere ne illud quidem plurimum distat, quod Glaucia Metello: "villam in Tiburti habes, cohortem in Palatio."

On Calvinus (F 3)

F 3 Cicero, *On the Orator*

[CAESAR STRABO:] . . . but what Glaucia said to Calvinus [presumably C. Sextius Calvinus (**70A**)], who was limping, "Where is that old saying: surely he is not limping [*claudicat*]? But he is wavering [*clodicat*]"—this is funny[1] . . .

[1] *clodicare* is a plebeian form of *claudicare*; the Sextii were a plebeian family.

On Metellus (F 4)

F 4 Cicero, *On the Orator*

[CAESAR STRABO:] . . . thus words linked by contrast embellish diction in particular; and this same device is often witty as well, as . . . From this type [of pleasantry] not even what Glaucia said to Metellus [Q. Caecilius Metellus Numidicus (**58**)] is very different: "You have a country house at Tibur [modern Tivoli in Latium], a farmyard[1] on the Palatine [in Rome]."

[1] A play on different meanings of *cohors* (see also Varro, *Ling.* 5.88), "farmyard" (*OLD* 1) and "group of people" (*OLD* 6), alluding to a "herd" of followers in Rome, more appropriate in the countryside.—Gwyn Morgan (1974) suggests that this remark might be a response to Metellus (as censor in 102 BC) having called Glaucia *stercus curiae* (**T 2**) when he tried to expel Glaucia from the Senate (App. *B Civ.* 1.28.126).

To the People (F 5)

F 5 Cic. *Rab. Post.* 14

Glaucia solebat, homo impurus, sed tamen acutus, populum monere ut, cum lex aliqua recitaretur, primum versum attenderet. si esset "dictator, consul, praetor, magister equitum," ne laboraret; sciret nihil ad se pertinere; sin esset "quicumque post hanc legem," videret ne qua nova quaestione adligaretur.

59 M. AURELIUS SCAURUS

T 1 Cic. *Brut.* 135

[CICERO:] M. Aurelius Scaurus non saepe dicebat sed polite; Latine vero in primis est eleganter locutus.

In the Council of the Cimbri (F 2)

Scaurus was defeated and captured by the Cimbri (Germanic tribe) in 105 BC as a legate of consul Cn. Manlius; after he had delivered a speech in their council, he was killed (Vell. Pat. 2.12.2; Tac. Germ. 37.5; Oros. 5.16.2;

To the People (F 5)

F 5 Cicero, *Pro Rabirio Postumo*

Glaucia, an abominable man, but shrewd nevertheless, used to warn the People, when some law was being read out, to pay attention to the opening phrase. If it was "dictator, consul, praetor, master of the horse," they should not worry; for they would know that it did not affect them; but if it was "whosoever after the passing of this law," then they were to see to it that they were not made liable to any new form of inquiry.

59 M. AURELIUS SCAURUS

M. Aurelius Scaurus (cos. suff. 108 BC; RE Aurelius 215) is singled out in Cicero for his polished and elegant speeches (T 1).

T 1 Cicero, *Brutus*

[CICERO:] M. Aurelius Scaurus did not speak often, but in a polished manner; indeed, for speaking in pure Latin and elegantly he was in the first rank.

In the Council of the Cimbri (F 2)

Gran. Lic. 33.2–4 [pp. 9.13–10.2 Criniti]). This "speech" is atypical since it was not delivered in Rome in one of the usual venues for public speaking.

F 2 Liv. *Epit.* 67.1

M. Aurelius Scaurus, legatus consulis, a Cimbris fuso exercitu captus est, et cum in consilium ab his advocatus deterreret eos ne Alpes transirent Italiam petituri, eo quod dicere{n}t[1] Romanos vinci non posse, a Boiorige,[2] feroci iuvene, occisus est.

[1] dicere{n}t *edd.*: dicerent *codd.* [2] a Boiorige *Freinshemius*: a bolo rege *codd.*

60 C. MEMMIUS

C. Memmius (tr. pl. 111, praet. ca. 104 BC; RE Memmius 5), probably a brother of L. Memmius (61), was killed while running for the consulship in 100 BC (e.g., Cic. Cat. 4.4; Liv. Epit. 69; Oros. 5.17.5).

C. Memmius is described as a passionate man hostile to the nobility (F 2–3; Oros. 5.17.5). Sallust mentions that the

T 1 Cic. *Brut.* 136

[CICERO:] tum etiam C. L. Memmii fuerunt oratores mediocres, accusatores acres atque acerbi; itaque in iudicium capitis multos vocaverunt, pro reis non saepe dixerunt.

Concerning Jugurtha to the People (F 2–4)

As Tribune of the People designate in 112 BC, Memmius provided information to the People about the activities of supporters of Jugurtha (F 2). In 111 BC, as Tribune of the People, Memmius talked to the People about the reduction of their freedom as well as the corruption and licentious-

F 2 Livy, *Epitome*

M. Aurelius Scaurus, a legate of the consul, was captured
by the Cimbri after the army had been routed, and when
he, called into council by them, deterred them from going
over the Alps to aim for Italy, for the reason that he said
that the Romans could not be defeated, he was killed by
Boiorix, a ferocious young man.

60 C. MEMMIUS

*oratory of C. Memmius was highly regarded (F 3); in Cic-
ero, C. and L. Memmius are said to be mediocre orators,
focusing on prosecutions (T 1).*

*C. Memmius was mocked by L. Licinius Crassus (**66
F 20–21**). He was prosecuted by M. Aemilius Scaurus (**43**)
for extortion (Cic. Font. 24; Val. Max. 8.5.2) (TLRR 60).*

T 1 Cicero, *Brutus*

[CICERO:] Of this time [late 2nd / early 1st cent. BC] too
were C. and L. Memmius, mediocre orators, vigorous and
harsh prosecutors; thus, they brought to trial many on
capital charges. For defendants they did not speak often.

Concerning Jugurtha to the People (F 2–4)

*ness of the nobility (F 3; CCMR, App. A: 201; TLRR 49).
After Jugurtha had come to Rome, he spoke about the
king's misdeeds and invited the king to reveal further details (F 4; CCMR, App. A: 202).*

F 2 Sall. *Iug.* 27.2

ac ni C. Memmius tribunus plebis designatus, vir acer et infestus potentiae nobilitatis, populum Romanum edocuisset id agi ut per paucos factiosos Iugurthae scelus condonaretur, profecto omnis invidia prolatandis consultationibus dilapsa foret: tanta vis gratiae atque pecuniae regis erat.

F 3 Sall. *Iug.* 30.3–32.1

at C. Memmius, quoius de libertate ingeni et odio potentiae nobilitatis supra diximus, inter dubitationem et moras senatus contionibus populum ad vindicandum hortari, monere ne rem publicam, ne libertatem suam desererent, multa superba et crudelia facinora nobilitatis ostendere; prorsus intentus omni modo plebis animum accendebat. [4] sed quoniam ea tempestate Romae Memmi facundia clara pollensque fuit, decere existumavi unam ex tam multis orationem eius perscribere, ac potissimum ea dicam quae in contione post reditum Bestiae huiusce modi verbis disseruit: [31.1–29] . . . [32.1] haec atque alia huiusce

F 2 Sallust, *The War with Jugurtha*

And if C. Memmius, a Tribune of the People designate, a passionate man and hostile to the power of the nobility, had not informed the Roman People that this was being brought about, that by the activities of a few intriguers [cf. Sall. *Iug.* 27.1] Jugurtha's crime was to be pardoned, undoubtedly all indignation would indeed have faded with the protracted deliberations: so great was the power of the king's influence and money.

F 3 Sallust, *The War with Jugurtha*

But C. Memmius, of whose independence of mind and hatred of the power of the nobility we have spoken above, in the midst of the Senate's hesitation and delay, urged the People in public meetings to take vengeance; he warned them not to forsake the Republic and their own liberty; he pointed out the many arrogant and cruel deeds of the nobility: in short, he earnestly tried in every way to inflame the minds of the commons. [4] But since Memmius' eloquence was famous and potent in Rome at that time, I have thought it fitting to reproduce a single one of his numerous speeches, and I shall mention as a prime example what he said at a public meeting after Bestia's [L. Calpurnius Besta, cos. 111 BC] return in words of this kind:

[31.1–29] *In a long speech Memmius outlines the deterioration of the Republic, the maltreatment of the People, who accept this situation silently, and the insolent and irresponsible behavior of those in power; thereby he encourages the People to take action, remembering their ancestors.*

[32.1] By repeatedly saying such things and others of

modi saepe in contione dicundo Memmius populo persua-
det uti L. Cassius, qui tum praetor erat, ad Iugurtham
mitteretur eumque interposita fide publica Romam duce-
ret, quo facilius indicio regis Scauri et relicuorum, quos
pecuniae captae arcessebat, delicta patefierent.

F 4 Sall. *Iug.* 33.3–4

at C. Memmius advocata contione, quamquam regi infesta
plebes erat et pars in vincula duci iubebat, pars, nisi socios
sceleris sui aperiret, more maiorum de hoste supplicium
sumi, dignitati quam irae magis consulens sedare motus
et animos eorum mollire, postremo confirmare fidem
publicam per sese inviolatam fore. [4] post, ubi silentium
coepit, producto Iugurtha verba facit, Romae Numidiae-
que facinora eius memorat, scelera in patrem fratresque
ostendit. quibus iuvantibus quibusque ministris ea egerit,
quamquam intellegat populus Romanus, tamen velle
manufesta magis ex illo habere: si verum aperiat, in fide
et clementia populi Romani magnam spem illi sitam; sin
reticeat, non sociis saluti fore, sed se suasque spes corrup-
turum.

this kind at a meeting of the People, Memmius induced the People to send L. Cassius [L. Cassius Longinus, pr. 111, cos. 107 BC], who was praetor at the time, to Jugurtha and to have him bring the king to Rome under pledge of public protection, so that through the king's testimony the offenses of Scaurus [M. Aemilius Scaurus (**43**)] and the rest whom he was accusing of having accepted money might the more readily be disclosed.

F 4 Sallust, *The War with Jugurtha*

But when C. Memmius had called a public meeting, while the commons were hostile to the king (some demanding that he be imprisoned, others that he be punished by death as a public enemy after the custom of the ancestors, if he did not reveal the accomplices in his crime), he, taking thought for worthy behavior rather than anger, quieted their outbursts of feelings and soothed their spirits; finally he confirmed that the pledge of public protection would be inviolate as far as he was concerned. [4] Afterward, as soon as silence had set in and after Jugurtha had been brought before the meeting, he [Memmius] gave a speech, recalled his [the king's] actions at Rome and in Numidia, and pointed out his crimes against his father and his brothers. He said that, although the Roman People knew by whose aid and by whose complicity he had done these things, they nevertheless wanted to have clearer signs from him; that, if he revealed the truth, he could place much hope in the good faith and mercy of the Roman People; but if he kept silence, he would not save his accomplices, but would ruin himself and his hopes.

Against L. Calpurnius Bestia (F 5)

*In 109 BC C. Memmius prosecuted L. Calpurnius Bestia (cos. 111 BC), defended by M. Aemilius Scaurus (**43**), according to the* Lex Mamilia *(cf. **53**), since Bestia was said to have accepted money from Jugurtha (TLRR 54). The*

F 5 Cic. *De or.* 2.283

[CAESAR STRABO:] bellum etiam est, cum quid cuique sit consentaneum dicitur, ut cum Scaurus non nullam haberet invidiam ex eo, quod Phrygionis Pompei locupletis hominis bona sine testamento possederat, sederetque advocatus reo Bestiae, cum funus quoddam duceretur, accusator C.[1] Memmius "vide," inquit, "Scaure, mortuus rapitur, si potes esse possessor."

[1] C. *om. una familia codd.*: *del. Friedrich*

61 L. MEMMIUS

*L. Memmius (RE Memmius 12) was presumably a brother of C. Memmius (**60**); in Cicero both of them are said to be mediocre orators, focusing on prosecutions (T 1). A L. Memmius (RE Memmius 14) defended himself in 90 BC*

T 1 Cic. *Brut.* 136
= **60** T 1.

Against L. Calpurnius Bestia (F 5)

transmitted phrase looks like an impromptu remark directed against the advocate rather than part of a set speech.

F 5 Cicero, *On the Orator*

[CAESAR STRABO:] It is also nice when it is pointed out what goes with each one's individual characteristics, as when Scaurus [M. Aemilius Scaurus (**43**)] was incurring considerable resentment for the reason that he had taken possession of the estate of Pompeius Phrygio, a wealthy man, without a will, and he was sitting in court as an advocate for a defendant named Bestia, when some funeral happened to pass by, the prosecutor C. Memmius said: "Scaurus, a dead man is being carried past; see if you might be nominated heir."

61 L. MEMMIUS

(F 2) when charged under the Lex Varia de maiestate *(see* **88***), but it is regarded as unlikely that he is the same L. Memmius.*

T 1 Cicero, *Brutus*
= **60** T 1.

On His Own Behalf (F 2)

F 2 Cic. *Brut.* 304

[CICERO:] . . . exercebatur una lege iudicium Varia, ceteris propter bellum intermissis; cui[1] frequens aderam, quamquam[2] pro se ipsi dicebant oratores non illi quidem principes, L. Memmius et Q. Pompeius, sed oratores tamen teste diserto utique[3] Philippo, cuius in testimonio contentio et vim accusatoris habebat et copiam.

[1] cui *edd.*: qui *codd.*   [2] quamquam *codd.*: cum *edd.*: quoque *Madvig*   [3] utique *Jahn*: uterque *codd.*: utentes uterque *Buttmann*

62 Q. SERVILIUS CAEPIO

Q. Servilius Caepio (cos. 106 BC; RE Servilius 49) fought successfully in Hispania as praetor and later, after his consulship, in Gaul, where he conquered Tolosa (modern Toulouse). After the money captured there was lost on its way to Massilia (modern Marseille), he was regarded as being responsible. Caepio was then defeated in the fighting against the Cimbri and Teutoni (Germanic tribes) at Arausio (modern Orange, France). Subsequently, he was taken to court because of the loss of the gold from Tolosa and because of the defeat (TLRR 65, 66; T 1; Cic. De or. 2.199–200: 65 F 29; Oros. 5.15.25; cf. LPPR, pp. 325–26, 327). In defense, Caepio spoke before the Tribunes of the People to explain the loss of his army (F 2). He was unsuccessful, and his property was confiscated (Liv. Epit. 67). Accord-

On His Own Behalf (F 2)

F 2 Cicero, *Brutus*

[CICERO:] . . . the court was kept busy by cases under a single law, the *Lex Varia*; the others were suspended because of the war [Social War, 91–88 BC]. At its hearings I was present regularly, although those speaking in their own defense were surely not orators of the first rank, L. Memmius and Q. Pompeius [Q. Pompeius Rufus (**83**), F 2], but orators nevertheless, according to the undoubtedly eloquent witness Philippus [L. Marcius Philippus (**70**), F 11], whose vehemence in testimony had both the force and the oratorical fullness of a prosecutor.

62 Q. SERVILIUS CAEPIO

ing to Valerius Maximus, Caepio died in prison (Val. Max. 6.9.13) or was freed by another Tribune of the People and led into exile (Val. Max. 4.7.3); the latter version is supported by Cicero (Cic. Balb. 28). The Tribune of the People who prosecuted Caepio, C. Norbanus (tr. pl. prob. 103 BC; cf. MRR I 565–66 n. 7), was later charged with maiestas minuta *(see* **65** F 22–30).

As consul, Caepio had proposed a law according to which senators would again have a decisive role in the courts (Cic. De or. 2.199–200: **65** F 29; Inv. rhet. 1.92; Lex Servilia iudiciaria: LPPR, p. 325).

In Cicero, Caepio is introduced as an eloquent speaker (T 1).

T 1 Cic. *Brut.* 135

[CICERO:] Q. etiam Caepio, vir acer et fortis, cui fortuna belli crimini, invidia populi calamitati fuit.

Before the Tribunes of the People on the Loss of His Army (F 2)

F 2 *Rhet. Her.* 1.24

concessio est, cum reus postulat ignosci. ea dividitur in purgationem et deprecationem. purgatio est, cum consulto negat se reus fecisse. ea dividitur in inprudentiam, fortunam, necessitatem: fortunam, ut Caepio ad tr. pl. de exercitus amissione . . .

63 Q. LUTATIUS CATULUS

Q. Lutatius Catulus (cos. 102 BC; RE Lutatius 7), who became consul at the fourth attempt (with C. Marius), fought against the Cimbri (Germanic tribe), celebrating a triumph afterward (on his life see FRHist 1:271–72). He first cooperated with C. Marius; later, however, the two men fell out. During the civil war in 87 BC, Catulus was prosecuted on a capital charge by M. Marius Gratidianus (tr. pl. 87 BC) and took his own life under pressure from C. Marius (TLRR 115; Val. Max. 9.12.4; Vell. Pat. 2.22.3–4; Cic. Tusc. 5.56; De or. 3.9; Brut. 307; Nat. D. 3.80; Diod. Sic. 39.4.2–3; Plut. Mar. 44.8; App. B Civ. 1.74.341–42; Flor. 2.9.15; August. De civ. D. 3.27).

T 1 Cicero, *Brutus*

[CICERO:] Also Q. Caepio [was held to be among the eloquent speakers], an energetic and brave man, for whom
the fortunes of war resulted in a charge and odium of the
People in ruin.

> *Before the Tribunes of the People on the Loss of*
> *His Army (F 2)*

F 2 *Rhetorica ad Herennium*

The acknowledgment is when the defendant asks for par-
don. It is divided into the exculpation and the plea for
mercy. The exculpation is when the defendant denies that
he acted with intent. It is divided into ignorance, chance,
and necessity: chance, like Caepio before the Tribunes of
the People on the loss of his army . . .

63 Q. LUTATIUS CATULUS

*Catulus is described as a learned and upright man and
a well-regarded speaker (T 1–2; Cic.* Rab. perd. *26; Mur.
36; Planc. 12; De or. 2.234); he is praised in Cicero for his
education, pure Latinity, elegant diction, occasional ar-
chaisms, and pleasant tone of voice (T 1–4; Cic.* De or.
3.42, 3.153; Off. 1.133; cf. Quint. Inst. *11.3.35). He is made
to say that he achieved successes by soothing the judges
(Cic.* De or. *2.74). Catulus was familiar with Greek literature (Cic.* De or. *2.19–20, 2.151, 3.187); he was a follower
of the Greek philosopher Carneades (Cic.* Acad. *2.148)
and a friend of the poets Antipater of Sidon, Archias, and
A. Furius (T 1; Cic.* De or. *3.194; Arch. 6); he had educated*

Greek slaves (Suet. Gram. et rhet. 3.5) and was a connoisseur of the arts (Plin. HN 34.54). He is a speaker in Cicero's De oratore. Catulus also wrote poetry (Plin. Ep. 5.3.5; Cic. Nat. D. 1.79; Gell. NA 19.9.14) and a historical work, probably an account of his military activities (FRHist 19).

T 1 Cic. *Brut.* 132–34

[CICERO:] "iam Q. Catulus non antiquo illo more, sed hoc nostro, nisi quid fieri potest perfectius, eruditus. multae litterae, summa non vitae solum atque naturae sed orationis etiam comitas, incorrupta quaedam Latini sermonis integritas; quae perspici cum ex orationibus eius potest tum facillime ex eo libro quem de consulatu et de rebus gestis suis conscriptum molli et Xenophontio genere sermonis misit ad A. Furium poetam, familiarem suum [*FRHist* 19 T 1]; qui liber nihilo notior est quam illi tres, de quibus ante dixi, Scauri libri." [133] . . . "fuit igitur in Catulo sermo Latinus; quae laus dicendi non mediocris ab oratoribus plerisque neglecta est. nam de sono vocis et suavitate appellandarum litterarum, quoniam filium cognovisti, noli exspectare quid dicam. . . . [134] nec habitus est tamen pater ipse Catulus princeps in numero patronorum, sed erat talis ut, cum quosdam audires qui tum erant praestantes, videretur esse inferior, cum autem ipsum audires sine comparatione, non modo contentus esses, sed melius non quaereres."

*Catulus delivered the funeral eulogy of his mother Po-
pilia (F 5; CCMR, App. A: 209). In addition, brief witty
remarks have been transmitted (Cic. De or. 2.220, 2.233,
2.255; Quint. Inst. 6.3.81).*

T 1 Cicero, *Brutus*

[CICERO:] "Now Q. Catulus, a man accomplished, not in
that old style, but in our modern fashion, unless anything
can be more perfect. Wide reading, a courtesy, not only in
life and nature, but also in speech, a certain untainted
purity of Latin diction: this can be seen both from his orations and most easily from that book that he wrote on his
consulship and his own deeds, in a smooth and Xeno-
phontic style of expression, and dedicated to the poet A.
Furius, his friend [*FRHist* 19 T 1]; this book is no better
known than those three of Scaurus about which I have
spoken before [M. Aemilius Scaurus (**43**), T 1]." [133] ...
"Indeed, Catulus had a pure Latin diction; such a not in-
considerable merit of style is neglected by most orators.
For about the sound of his voice and the charm of his
pronouncing the letters, do not expect me to say anything,
since you knew his son [Q. Lutatius Catulus (**96**), T 1]. . . .
[134] Nor was the father, Catulus himself, in spite of that
[his qualities as a speaker], regarded as the first among the
pleaders either; instead, he was such a one that, when you
heard some speak who were outstanding at the time, he
seemed to be inferior, but when you heard him alone without comparison, you would not only be satisfied, but would
not seek anything better."

T 2 Cic. *Brut.* 259

[Atticus:] Catulus erat ille quidem minime indoctus, ut a te paulo est ante dictum, sed tamen suavitas vocis et lenis appellatio litterarum bene loquendi famam confecerat.

T 3 Cic. *De or.* 2.28

[Antonius:] et eo quidem loquar confidentius, quod Catulus auditor accessit, cui non solum nos Latini sermonis sed etiam Graeci ipsi solent suae linguae subtilitatem elegantiamque concedere.

T 4 Cic. *De or.* 3.29

[Crassus:] quid iucundius auribus nostris umquam accidit huius oratione Catuli? quae est pura sic ut Latine loqui paene solus videatur, sic autem gravis ut in singulari dignitate omnis tamen adsit humanitas ac lepos. quid multa? istum audiens equidem sic iudicare soleo, quidquid aut addideris aut mutaveris aut detraxeris, vitiosius et deterius futurum.

Funeral Eulogy of His Mother Popilia (F 5)

F 5 Cic. *De or.* 2.44

"ita," inquit Antonius "et in eo quidem genere scio et me et omnes qui adfuerunt delectatos esse vehementer, cum

T 2 Cicero, *Brutus*

[ATTICUS:] This Catulus was certainly by no means uneducated, as you mentioned a little earlier [T 1]; yet, nevertheless, it was the charm of his voice and the smooth pronunciation of letters that gave him the reputation of speaking well.

T 3 Cicero, *On the Orator*

[ANTONIUS:] And I shall indeed speak more confidently for that reason that Catulus has joined us as a listener, to whom not only we, concerning the Latin language, but also the Greeks themselves, concerning their language, are accustomed to concede accuracy and elegance.

T 4 Cicero, *On the Orator*

[CRASSUS:] Has anything more pleasant ever happened to our ears than the speech of our friend Catulus? It is so pure that he seems almost the only person to speak Latin, and so weighty that in its unique dignity there is nevertheless complete urbanity and charm. What else? For my own part, when listening to him, I usually decide that whatever you add or alter or subtract would make it worse and inferior.

Funeral Eulogy of His Mother Popilia (F 5)

F 5 Cicero, *On the Orator*

"Precisely so," said ANTONIUS, "and, with regard to that type of oratory, I know that I myself and all who were present were highly delighted when your mother Popilia

a te est Popilia mater vestra laudata, cui primum mulieri
hunc honorem in nostra civitate tributum puto. . . ."

64 T. ALBUCIUS

*T. Albucius (RE Albucius 2) was praetor in about 107 BC
and then propraetor in Sardinia. Upon his return from the
province, he was charged with extortion by C. Iulius Caesar Strabo (73 F 7–10); found guilty, he went into exile in
Athens (Cic. Off. 2.50; Scaur. 40; Tusc. 5.108; Pis. 92)
(TLRR 67). Albucius had accused Q. Mucius Scaevola*

T 1 Cic. *Brut.* 131

[CICERO:] doctus etiam Graecis T. Albucius vel potius
paene Graecus. loquor ut opinor; sed licet ex orationibus
iudicare. fuit autem Athenis adulescens, perfectus Epicu-
rius evaserat, minime aptum ad dicendum genus.

64A L. APPULEIUS SATURNINUS

*L. Appuleius Saturninus (tr. pl. 103, 100 BC; RE Appu-
leius 29) was a well-known, "popular" politician (T 2), who
proposed a number of laws as Tribune of the People. Eventually, Saturninus and his supporters were cornered in
Rome and killed as a result of a senatus consultum ultimum in 100 BC (Cic. Brut. 224; Liv. Epit. 69; App. B*

[of Q. Lutatius Catulus and of C. Iulius Caesar Strabo (**73**)] was eulogized by you; she was, I think, the woman to whom this honor was first rendered in our community. . . ."

64 T. ALBUCIUS

(**50**) *of extortion, though unsuccessfully (Cic.* Brut. *102;* De or. *2.281; cf.* **65** *F 15) (TLRR 32).*

*Albucius was learned in Greek matters and was a follower of Epicurus (T 1). His fondness for all things Greek was ridiculed by Q. Mucius Scaevola (**50**), as described by the satirist Lucilius (Cic.* Fin. *1.9:* Lucil. *88–94 Marx). Speeches by Albucius were extant in Cicero's time (T 1).*

T 1 Cicero, *Brutus*

[CICERO:] T. Albucius was actually learned in Greek matters, or rather, almost a Greek. I speak as I feel; but a judgment may be made on the basis of his orations. He was in Athens as a young man and had emerged as a complete Epicurean, a species not at all suited to public speaking.

64A L. APPULEIUS SATURNINUS

Civ. *1.32.143–45; Vir. ill. 73.9–12; on the date see* MRR Suppl. *21–23).*

In Cicero, Saturninus is characterized as the most eloquent of all seditious politicians after the Gracchi, while it is noted that this assessment is based more on his appearance and behavior than on his abilities as an orator (T 1).

T 1 Cic. *Brut.* 224

[CICERO:] et quoniam huius generis facta mentio est, seditiosorum omnium post Gracchos L. Appuleius Saturninus eloquentissimus visus est; magis specie tamen et motu atque ipso amictu capiebat homines quam aut dicendi copia aut mediocritate prudentiae.

T 2 Cic. *Sest.* 37

. . . res erat cum L. Saturnino, iterum tribuno plebis, vigilante homine, et in causa populari si non moderate at certe populariter abstinenterque versato.

On His Laws (F 3–4)

During his second Tribunate, Saturninus probably pushed through a grain law, with the support of the praetor C. Servilius Glaucia (58b), and a land law on the establishment of settlements in Gallia cisalpina (Lex Appuleia frumentaria: LPPR, p. 332; Lex Appuleia agraria: LPPR,

F 3 *Rhet. Her.* 1.21
= **85** F 2.

T 1 Cicero, *Brutus*

[CICERO:] And since mention has been made [of speakers] of this type, of all seditious men after the Gracchi [Ti. Sempronius Gracchus (**34**) and C. Sempronius Gracchus (**48**)], L. Appuleius Saturninus appeared as the most eloquent; yet he caught the public rather by appearance, movement, and even dress than by the fullness of his eloquence or his mediocre possession of good sense.

T 2 Cicero, *Pro Sestio*

. . . he had to deal with L. Saturninus, Tribune of the People for the second time, a man fully alert and one who, in supporting the popular cause, behaved, if not with moderation, at least in the interest of the People and without self-seeking.

On His Laws (F 3–4)

*p. 331). Senators were meant to swear an oath on the land law, but Q. Caecilius Metellus Numidicus (**58**) refused to do so (App.* B Civ. *1.29.130–31.140; Plut.* Mar. *29; Liv.* Epit. *69; Vir. ill. 73.1; TLRR 77).*

F 3 *Rhetorica ad Herennium*
= **85** F 2.

F 4 [Aurel. Vict.] *Vir. ill.* 73.6–8

aqua et igni interdixit ei, qui in leges suas non iurasset. [7] huic legi multi nobiles obrogantes,[1] cum tonuisset, clamarunt:[2] "iam," inquit, "nisi quiescetis, grandinabit." [8] Metellus Numidicus exulare quam iurare maluit.

[1] multi nobiles obrogantes *codd., Klotz*: multi nobiles ab- (*vel* ad-) rogantes *vel* multi volentibus arrogantiam *vel* multis nobilibus ab- (*vel* ar-) rogantibus *codd. rel.*   [2] clamarunt *Opitz*: et clamarent *vel* acclamavit *vel* clamavit *codd.*: reclamarunt *Klotz*: tonuisse clamarent *Damsté*

65 M. ANTONIUS

M. Antonius (cos. 99, censor 97 BC; RE Antonius 28) fought in Cilicia (as propraetor) against pirates and celebrated a triumph after his victory (Liv. Epit. 68). In the civil war he was killed by the faction of C. Marius and L. Cornelius Cinna in 87 BC (b. 143 BC). In relation to the election campaign for the censorship, Antonius had been unsuccessfully charged by M. Duronius (68) with ambitus (TLRR 83).

Antonius was regarded as an excellent and naturally gifted orator (T 1–2, 5; Cic. Brut. 296; Orat. 18; Vell. Pat. 2.22.3). Along with L. Licinius Crassus (66), with whom he is often compared as the two of them are regarded as the major orators of the period (T 4–5, 12; Cic. Brut. 186, 189; Orat. 18–19, 106; Div. Caec. 25; Vell. Pat. 2.9), he is one of the main speakers in Cicero's De oratore. In Cicero, Antonius is praised for his varied oratory, well-prepared, energetic, and adapted to the respective situations, his

F 4 [Aurelius Victor], *On Famous Men*

He [Saturninus] excluded from water and fire [i.e., banished] that man who had not sworn the oath on his laws. [7] Many noblemen, opposing this law, cried out when it had thundered: "Soon," he [Saturninus] said, "if you will not be quiet, it will hail." [8] Metellus Numidicus [Q. Caecilius Metellus Numidicus (**58**)] preferred to go into exile rather than swear the oath.[1]

[1] On the meaning of and the confusion in this passage, see Linderski 1983.

65 M. ANTONIUS

well-arranged and well-delivered speeches, and his well-chosen language; he was noted for his sharp mind, logical presentation of material, and extraordinary memory (T 3–6; Cic. De or. 2.124–25). Antonius had made the acquaintance of Greek intellectuals; yet he did not choose to admit his familiarity with Greek learning (T 7–8; Cic. De or. 1.82–93, 2.153, 2.360). He allegedly had little formal legal knowledge (T 3; Cic. De or. 2.248). Quintilian claims that Antonius preferred to conceal the artfulness of his accomplished eloquence (T 10; Quint. Inst. 12.9.5).

*Antonius is said to have claimed never to have written down any speeches (T 9; F 37; cf. Cic. Orat. 132: **80** T 6), but others may have produced summaries. In the* Rhetorica ad Herennium *Antonius is listed as one of the writers from whom examples for students could be drawn (Rhet. Her. 4.7: **25** T 5). Antonius produced a brief work on the art of speaking (F 37–40).*

T 1 Cic. *Tusc.* 5.55

[M.:] . . . M. Antoni, omnium eloquentissimi quos ego audierim . . .

T 2 Cic. *De or.* 3.16

[CICERO:] . . . quo in genere orationis utrumque oratorem cognoveramus, id ipsum sumus in eorum sermone adumbrare conati. quod si quis erit, qui ductus opinione vulgi aut Antonium ieiuniorem aut Crassum pleniorem fuisse putet, quam quomodo a nobis uterque inductus est, is erit ex iis, qui aut illos non audierint aut iudicare non possint. nam fuit uterque, ut exposui antea, cum studio et ingenio et doctrina praestans omnibus, tum in suo genere perfectus, ut neque in Antonio deesset hic ornatus orationis neque in Crasso redundaret.

T 3 Cic. *De or.* 1.172

[CRASSUS:] Antoni incredibilis quaedam et prope singularis et divina vis ingenii videtur, etiam si hac scientia iuris nudata sit, posse se facile ceteris armis prudentiae tueri atque defendere.

T 4 Cic. *De or.* 3.32

[CRASSUS:] ad nosmet ipsos iam revertor, quoniam sic fuimus semper comparati, ut hominum sermonibus quasi in

T 1 Cicero, *Tusculan Disputations*

[M.:] . . . of M. Antonius, the most eloquent of all [the speakers] I have heard . . .

T 2 Cicero, *On the Orator*

[CICERO:] . . . we have attempted to indicate in their discourses the precise type of oratory for which we had gotten to know each of these two orators. And if there will be anybody who, led by the view of the masses, thinks that either Antonius was plainer or Crassus [L. Licinius Crassus (**66**)] more abundant than how each of the two has been represented by us, that man will belong to those who either have not heard those speakers or are unable to judge them. For each of the two, as I have explained earlier, exceeded everyone in zeal, natural talent, and learning, and, moreover, was also a master in his own type, so that these oratorical embellishments were neither wanting in the case of Antonius nor superabundant in that of Crassus.

T 3 Cicero, *On the Orator*

[CRASSUS:] Antonius' particular power of genius, marvelous and almost unique and godlike, seems, even though it is bereft of this legal knowledge, to be able easily to guard and defend itself with other weapons derived from practical wisdom.

T 4 Cicero, *On the Orator*

[CRASSUS:] I now come back to ourselves, since we have always been compared in such a way that we are almost summoned by the talk of people to appear in some court

aliquod contentionis iudicium vocaremur; quid tam dissi-
mile quam ego in dicendo et Antonius? cum ille is sit
orator, ut nihil eo possit esse praestantius, ego autem,
quamquam memet mei paenitet, cum hoc maxime tamen
in comparatione coniungar. videtisne, genus hoc quod sit
Antoni? forte, vehemens, commotum in agendo, praemu-
nitum et ex omni parte causae saeptum, acre, acutum,
enucleatum, in una quaque re commorans, honeste ce-
dens, acriter insequens, terrens, supplicans, summa orationis varietate, nulla nostrarum aurium satietate.

T 5 Cic. *Brut.* 138–44, 165 (cf. **66** T 2)

[CICERO:] . . . sic nunc ad Antonium Crassumque perve-
nimus! nam ego sic existimo, hos oratores fuisse maximos
et in his primum cum Graecorum gloria Latine dicendi
copiam aequatam. [139] omnia veniebant Antonio in mentem; eaque suo quaeque loco, ubi plurimum proficere et
valere possent, ut ab imperatore equites pedites levis ar-
matura, sic ab illo in maxime opportunis orationis partibus
conlocabantur. erat memoria summa, nulla meditationis
suspicio; imparatus semper aggredi ad dicendum videbatur, sed ita erat paratus ut iudices illo dicente non numquam viderentur non satis parati ad cavendum fuisse.
[140] verba ipsa non illa quidem elegantissimo sermone,
itaque diligenter loquendi laude caruit; neque tamen est

for competition. What is so dissimilar as I [L. Licinius Crassus (**66**)] and Antonius in speaking? While he is such an orator that nothing could be more outstanding than him, I, although I am dissatisfied with myself, am nevertheless especially coupled with him for comparison. Do you see what this style of Antonius is? Bold, vehement, vigorous in delivery, carefully prepared and safeguarded in respect of every aspect of the case, sharp, penetrating, precise, dwelling upon each separate point, making courteous concessions, offering sharp attacks, intimidating, imploring, with a vast variety of styles, never filling our ears to satiety.

T 5 Cicero, *Brutus* (cf. **66** T 2)

[CICERO:] . . . so now we come to Antonius and Crassus [L. Licinius Crassus (**66**)]! For I am of the opinion that these men were the greatest orators and that in them for the first time oratorical fullness in speaking Latin was put on a level with the glory of the Greeks. [139] Everything [that was relevant] came to be noticed by Antonius; and each thing was set by him in its own place, where it could be most effective and be most powerful, like cavalry, infantry, and skirmishers by a general, in the most opportune parts of the oration. His memory was outstanding, there was no suggestion of previous rehearsal; he always gave the appearance of coming forward to speak without preparation, but he was so well prepared that, when he spoke, the judges sometimes seemed not sufficiently prepared to maintain their guard. [140] The words themselves, admittedly, were not of the most elegant diction; therefore, he lacked the distinction of speaking painstak-

admodum inquinate locutus, sed illa, quae proprie[1] laus oratoris est in verbis. . . . sed tamen Antonius in verbis et eligendis, neque id ipsum tam leporis causa quam ponderis, et conlocandis et comprehensione devinciendis nihil non ad rationem et tamquam ad artem dirigebat; verum multo magis hoc idem in sententiarum ornamentis et conformationibus. [141] . . . sed cum haec magna in Antonio tum actio singularis; quae si partienda est in gestum atque vocem, gestus erat non verba exprimens, sed cum sententiis congruens: manus, umeri, latera, supplosio pedis, status, incessus, omnisque motus cum verbis sententiisque consentiens; vox permanens, verum subrauca natura. sed hoc vitium huic uni in bonum convertebat. [142] habebat enim flebile quiddam in questionibus aptumque cum ad fidem faciendam tum ad misericordiam commovendam . . . [144] nam ut Antonius coniectura movenda aut sedanda suspicione aut excitanda incredibilem vim habebat: sic in interpretando, in definiendo, in explicanda aequitate nihil erat Crasso copiosius . . . [165] et vero fuit in hoc etiam popularis dictio excellens; Antoni genus dicendi multo aptius iudiciis quam contionibus.

[1] proprie *codd.*: propria *Lambinus*

ingly. Still, he did not speak in a completely impure way, but [he lacked] that distinction that is specifically that of the orator in the use of words. . . . But, still, in choosing words (and indeed not so much for charm as for weight) and placing them and binding them together in periods, Antonius controlled everything by purpose and by art, as it were; and the same quality was still more noticeable in the embellishment and figurative expression of his sentiments. [141] . . . But while in these respects Antonius was great, his delivery was outstanding; if this is to be divided into gesture and voice, his gesture was not expressive of [single] words, but agreed with the course of his thought: hands, shoulders, chest, stamp of the foot, posture, pacing about, and all movement were in harmony with his words and thoughts; [his] voice [was] remaining steady, though of a somewhat hoarse nature. But for him alone this defect turned to an advantage. [142] For in complaints it had something plaintive and well-suited to winning confidence and also to stirring compassion . . . [144] For as Antonius possessed incredible skill in creating an inference, in provoking or allaying a suspicion, so in interpretation, in definition, in unfolding the implications of equity nothing was more resourceful than Crassus . . . [165] And, indeed, he [Crassus] was also outstanding in the manner of speaking for addressing the People; Antonius' manner of speaking was much better suited to the courts than to popular assemblies.

T 6 Cic. *Brut.* 215

[CICERO:] reperiebat quid dici opus esset et quo modo
praeparari et quo loco locari, memoriaque ea comprehen-
debat Antonius; excellebat autem actione. erant[1] ei quaedam ex his paria cum Crasso, quaedam etiam superiora; at
Crassi magis nitebat oratio.

   [1] erant *vel* erantque *codd.*

T 7 Cic. *De or.* 1.82

[ANTONIUS:] namque egomet, qui sero ac leviter Graecas
litteras attigissem, tamen cum pro consule in Ciliciam proficiscens venissem Athenas, complures tum ibi dies sum
propter navigandi difficultatem commoratus; sed, cum
cotidie mecum haberem homines doctissimos—eos fere
ipsos qui abs te modo sunt nominati—cumque[1] hoc nescio
quo modo apud eos increbruisset me in causis maioribus
sicuti te solere versari, pro se quisque eorum quantum
quisque poterat[2] de officio et ratione oratoris disputabat.

   [1] cumque *vel* cum *vel* quom *codd.*   [2] quisque eorum
quantum quisque poterat *vel* quisque poterat *vel* quisque ut poterat *vel* quisque quae poterat *codd. plerique*: quae quisque poterat *codd. Lambini*

T 8 Cic. *De or.* 2.3–4

[CICERO:] de Antonio vero quamquam saepe ex humanis-
simo homine patruo nostro acceperamus quem ad modum
ille vel Athenis vel Rhodi se doctissimorum hominum sermonibus dedisset, tamen ipse adulescentulus, quantum

T 6 Cicero, *Brutus*

[CICERO:] Antonius found what needed to be said, how it was to be prepared, and at which points it was to be placed, and he grasped that with his memory; but he excelled in delivery. In some of these respects he was the equal of Crassus [L. Licinius Crassus (**66**)], in some even superior; but Crassus' language was the more brilliant.

T 7 Cicero, *On the Orator*

[ANTONIUS:] For I, who had touched Greek letters late in life and lightly, still, at the time when on my journey to Cilicia as proconsul [102 BC] I had come to Athens, I stayed there for several days because of the difficulty in putting to sea; but, as I had about me daily the most learned men—almost the very people who have just been mentioned by you [L. Licinius Crassus (**66**)]—and as a rumor had somehow spread among them that I, like yourself, was usually engaged in the more important cases, every one of them, according to their respective ability, contributed what each of them could to a discussion on the task and method of an orator.

T 8 Cicero, *On the Orator*

[CICERO:] But as for Antonius, although we had frequently understood from a highly accomplished man, our paternal uncle [L. Tullius Cicero], how, be it at Athens or at Rhodes, he had devoted himself to conversation with the most learned men, yet I myself, as a very young man, went as far as the modesty of that young age permitted in

illius ineuntis aetatis meae patiebatur pudor, multa ex eo saepe quaesivi. non erit profecto tibi, quod scribo, hoc novum; nam iam tum ex me audiebas mihi illum ex multis variisque sermonibus nullius rei, quae quidem esset in his artibus de quibus aliquid existimare possem, rudem aut ignarum esse visum. [4] sed fuit hoc in utroque eorum, ut Crassus non tam existimari vellet non didicisse quam illa despicere et nostrorum hominum in omni genere prudentiam Graecis anteferre; Antonius autem probabiliorem hoc populo orationem fore censebat suam, si omnino didicisse numquam putaretur; atque ita se uterque graviorem fore, si alter contemnere alter ne nosse quidem Graecos videretur.

T 9

a Cic. *Clu.* 140

hominem ingeniosum, M. Antonium, aiunt solitum esse dicere idcirco se nullam umquam orationem scripsisse ut, si quid aliquando non opus esset ab se esse dictum, posset negare dixisse . . .

b Val. Max. 7.3.5

nam M. Antonio remittendum convicium est, qui idcirco se aiebat nullam orationem scripsisse, ut si quid superiore iudicio actum ei quem postea defensurus esset nociturum foret, non dictum a se adfirmare posset, quia facti vix

questioning him frequently on many subjects. What I am writing will assuredly not be new to you [Cicero's brother Quintus], for you heard from me even then that, as the result of many conversations on various subjects, there was nothing, at least in any studies about which I could form some opinion, about which he seemed to be inexperienced or ignorant. [4] There was this feature in each of the two, that Crassus [L. Licinius Crassus (**66**)] did not so much wish to be thought to have learned nothing as to be despising those things and placing the knowledge of our countrymen above that of the Greeks in all departments; Antonius, however, believed that his speech would be more acceptable to the people in this country, if he was thought never to have learned anything at all; and so both of them believed that they would be more authoritative, one, if he appeared to look down upon the Greeks, the other, if he appeared not even to know them.

T 9

a Cicero, *Pro Cluentio*

They report that the talented man, M. Antonius, used to say that he had never written down any speech with the intention that, if at some point anything should not have been said by him, he would be able to deny having said it
. . .

b Valerius Maximus, *Memorable Doings and Sayings*

For one should forgo censure of M. Antonius, who used to say that he had not written down any speech with the intention that, if something delivered at an earlier trial would harm someone whom he was to defend later, he could claim that it had not been said by him, because he

pudentis causam tolerabilem habuit: pro periclitantium enim capite non solum eloquentia sua uti, sed etiam verecundia abuti erat paratus.

T 10 Quint. *Inst.* 2.17.5–6

quidam naturalem esse rhetoricen volunt et tamen adiuvari exercitatione non diffitentur, ut in libris Ciceronis de oratore [cf. Cic. *De or.* 2.232] dicit Antonius observationem quandam esse, non artem. [6] quod non ideo ut pro vero accipiamus est positum, sed ut Antoni persona servetur, qui dissimulator artis fuit . . .

T 11 Diom., *GL* I, p. 472.4–7

si in paenultimo tribrachys fuerit vel dactylus vel pyrrichius, et successerit vel tribrachys vel molossus vel pyrrichius vel anapaestus, erit structura quae vel delumbis vel fluxa vel mollis dicitur; qua usus dicitur Antonius maior.

T 12 Macrob. *Sat.* 5.1.16–17

sunt praeterea stili dicendi duo dispari moralitate diversi. unus est maturus et gravis, qualis Crasso assignatur. . . . [17] alter huic contrarius ardens et erectus et infensus, quali est usus Antonius.

had a tolerable excuse for a scarcely honorable proceeding: for on behalf of people with their lives at risk he was ready not only to use his eloquence but even to abuse his sense of decency.

T 10 Quintilian, *The Orator's Education*

Some want rhetoric to be something innate and yet do not deny that it is supported by practice, as in Cicero's books on the orator [cf. Cic. *De or.* 2.232] Antonius says that it is a kind of observation, not an art. [6] This statement is not put there for us to accept it as true, but to maintain Antonius' character, as he was a man who concealed his art . . .

T 11 Diomedes

If in the penultimate [position] there is a tribrach or a dactyl or a pyrrhic, and there follows a tribrach or a molossus or a pyrrhic or an anapest, there will be a structure that is called lame or loose or soft; Antonius the Elder is said to have used that.

T 12 Macrobius, *Saturnalia*

There are, moreover, two styles of speaking contrasting by their different character. One is mature and serious, like that associated with Crassus [L. Licinius Crassus (**66**)]. . . . [17] The other is the opposite to this: fiery, confident, and aggressive, such as Antonius used.

On His Own Behalf (F 13–14)

Probably in early 113 BC Antonius spoke in his own defense, having been charged with sexual relations with a Vestal Virgin (TLRR 43). This step of the proceedings was instigated by the Tribune of the People Sex. Peducaeus (113 BC; Lex Peducaea de incestu virginum Vestalium:

F 13 Val. Max. 3.7.9

contra M. Antonius ille disertus—non enim respuendo sed amplectendo causae dictionem quam innocens esset testatus est—quaestor proficiscens in Asiam, Brundisium iam pervenerat; ubi litteris certior incesti se postulatum apud L. Cassium praetorem, cuius tribunal propter nimiam severitatem "scopulus reorum" dicebatur, cum id vitare beneficio legis Memmiae liceret, quae eorum qui rei publicae causa abessent recipi nomina vetabat, in urbem tamen recurrit. quo tam pleno fiduciae bonae consilio cum absolutionem celerem tum profectionem honestiorem consecutus est.

F 14 Val. Max. 6.8.1

M. Antonius, avorum nostrorum temporibus clarissimus orator, incesti reus agebatur. cuius in iudicio accusatores

On His Own Behalf (F 13–14)

LPPR, *p. 321), after three Vestal Virgins initially accused had not all been found guilty (Asc. in Cic.* Mil. *32 [pp. 45.22–46.6 C.]; Cic.* Nat. D. *3.74; Liv.* Epit. *63; Oros. 5.15.22; Iul. Obs. 37; Plut.* Quaest. Rom. *83; Cass. Dio 26, F 87; see Bätz 2012, 236–38, with further references).*

F 13 Valerius Maximus, *Memorable Doings and Sayings*

By contrast [to M. Aemilius Scaurus (**43**)], that eloquent M. Antonius—for he attested how innocent he was not by indignantly refusing to plead his case, but by welcoming it—on his way to Asia as quaestor [113 BC], had already got to Brundisium; when he was informed by letter that he had been accused of sexual impurity before the praetor L. Cassius,[1] whose tribunal was called "the reef of defendants" because of the excessive severity, although he could have avoided it thanks to the *Lex Memmia*, which forbade the prosecution of those who were absent on public business [*LPPR*, pp. 321–22], he nevertheless hastened back to city [of Rome]. By that decision steeped in honest confidence, he won a quick acquittal and also a more respectable departure.

[1] L. Cassius Longinus Ravilla (cos. 127 BC) was *quaesitor* (*MRR* I 537), rather than praetor, but Valerius Maximus may use terminology influenced by post-Sullan conventions (Gruen 1968b).

F 14 Valerius Maximus, *Memorable Doings and Sayings*

M. Antonius, a very famous orator in the time of our ancestors, was accused of sexual impurity. In his trial the

servum in quaestionem perseverantissime postulabant, quod ab eo, cum ad stuprum iret,[1] lanternam praelatam contenderent. erat autem is etiam tum imberbis, et stabat <in> corona,[2] videbatque rem ad suos cruciatus pertinere, nec tamen eos fugitavit. ille vero, ut domum quoque ventum est, Antonium hoc nomine vehementius confusum et sollicitum ultro est hortatus ut se iudicibus torquendum traderet, adfirmans nullum ore suo verbum exiturum quo causa eius laederetur, ac promissi fidem mira patientia praestitit: plurimis etenim[3] laceratus verberibus eculeoque impositus, candentibus etiam lamminis ustus, omnem vim accusationis custodita rei salute subvertit. argui fortuna merito potest quod tam pium et tam fortem spiritum servili nomine inclusit.

[1] iret *vel* irent *codd.* 　　[2] <in> corona *Becker*: coronam *vel* corona *vel* coram *codd.* 　　[3] etenim *Lipsius*: etiam *codd.*: enim *codd. dett.*

Against Cn. Papirius Carbo (F 15–16)

F 15 Apul. *Apol.* 66.4

neque autem gloriae causa me accusat, ut M. Antonius Cn. Carbonem, C. Mucius A. Albucium,[1] P. Sulpicius Cn.

[1] C. Iulius T. Albucium *Sauppe*　　mutius *cod.*　　albutiū *cod.*

prosecutors very insistently demanded a slave for inter-
rogation, since they asserted that he had carried a lantern
in front when he [Antonius] went to the defilement. And
he [the slave] was still beardless at the time and stood
there ⟨among⟩ the spectators, and he realized that the
matter pertained to his own torture; yet he did not run
away from it. Indeed, as soon as they had got home, he
spontaneously urged Antonius, who was rather upset and
worried on this account, to hand him over to the judges
for torture, affirming that no word would pass his lips
whereby the other's case might be weakened, and he kept
faith with his promise with marvelous endurance: for lac-
erated with very many lashes, put on the rack, burned
even with hot plates, he guarded the defendant's safety
and destroyed all the force of the prosecution. Fortune
can deservedly be blamed that it enclosed so loyal and so
brave a spirit in the body of a slave.[1]

[1] The passage provides further information about the trial but
does not offer details on Antonius' speech.

Against Cn. Papirius Carbo (F 15–16)

*In ca. 112 BC Antonius prosecuted Cn. Papirius Carbo
(cos. 113 BC) on account of the latter's behavior in the war
against the Cimbri (Cic. Fam. 9.21.3; App. Gall. 13–14;
Liv. Epit. 68; Vell. Pat. 2.12.2) (TLRR 47).*

F 15 Apuleius, *Apologia*

And he does not accuse me for the sake of glory, as M.
Antonius Cn. Carbo, C. Mucius A. Albucius, P. Sulpicius

Norbanum,[2] C. Furius[3] M' Aquillium, C. Curio Q. Metellum. quippe homines eruditissimi iuvenes laudis gratia primum hoc rudimentum forensis operae subibant, ut aliquo insigni iudicio civibus suis noscerentur.

[2] C. Norbanum *Kroll*   [3] L. Fufius *Kroll*

F 16 Cic. *Off.* 2.49

sed cum sint plura causarum genera quae eloquentiam desiderent, multique in nostra republica adulescentes et apud iudices et apud populum et apud senatum dicendo laudem adsecuti sint, maxima est admiratio in iudiciis. quorum ratio duplex est; nam ex accusatione et ex defensione constat. quarum etsi laudabilior est defensio, tamen etiam accusatio probata persaepe est. dixi paulo ante de Crasso. idem fecit adulescens M. Antonius.

Cn. Norbanus, C. Furius M'. Aquillius, C. Curio Q. Metellus.[1] Indeed, very learned young men undertook this first piece of forensic work for the sake of glory, so that they might become known to their fellow citizens by some illustrious trial.

[1] With some confusion of names (some of which might have to be emended) and of the roles of accuser and accused, the list seems to refer also to the following trials: Q. Mucius Scaevola (**50**) or (with emendation) C. Iulius Caesar Strabo (**73**) vs. T. Albucius (**64**), P. Sulpicius Rufus (**76**) vs C. Norbanus, L. Fufius (**75**) vs. M'. Aquillius, C. Scribonius Curio (**86**) vs. Q. Caecilius Metellus Nepos Balearici filius.

F 16 Cicero, *On Duties*

But while there are many types of cases that call for eloquence, and many young men in our Republic have obtained distinction by speaking before the judges, before the People, and before the Senate, admiration is highest in the courts. Their pattern is twofold; for it consists of the prosecution and the defense. While of those the defense is more honorable, still the prosecution also has very often won approval. I spoke of Crassus [L. Licinius Crassus (**66**)] a moment ago; M. Antonius, when a youth, did the same.[1]

[1] Because the prosecution of Cn. Papirius Carbo appears to have been famous in antiquity (F 15) and dates to an early period of Antonius' career, the passage has been assigned to that speech. Yet it sounds more like a general statement about Antonius' activities in his youth than a reference to a particular trial.

On Cn. Mallius (F 17)

*In 103 BC Antonius may have defended the ex-consul Cn.
Mallius Maximus (cos. 105 BC), who was charged on account of activities in the Cimbrian war (see **62**) and sent*

F 17 Cic. *De or.* 2.125

[CRASSUS:] quid ego de Cn. Malli,[1] quid de Q. Regis
commiseratione dicam? quid de aliis innumerabilibus? in
quibus hoc non maxime enituit quod tibi omnes dant, acumen quoddam singulare, sed haec ipsa, quae nunc ad me
delegare vis, ea semper in te eximia et praestantia fuerunt.

[1] Gn. Manlii *vel* Gn. Manili Malli *vel* Gn. Manili *vel* Gn. Manilii Mallii *vel* Gn. Manlii *vel* Gn. Manilii *codd.*: Cn. Manli *Kumaniecki*

Evidence Against Sex. Titius (F 18)

*When Sex. Titius (**67C**) was prosecuted, probably for treason, after his Tribunate and Antonius' consulship (99 BC),
Antonius acted as a witness in the trial (TLRR 80), in*

F 18 Cic. *De or.* 2.48

[ANTONIUS:] nam et testimonium saepe dicendum est ac
nonnumquam etiam accuratius, ut mihi etiam necesse fuit
in Sex.[1] Titium seditiosum civem et turbulentum: explicavi
in eo testimonio dicendo omnia consilia consulatus mei,
quibus illi tr(ibuno) pl(ebis) pro re publica restitissem,
quaeque ab eo contra rem publicam facta arbitrarer exposui; diu retentus sum, multa audivi, multa respondi.

[1] Sex. *vel* Sextum *codd.*: *del. Orelli*

On Cn. Mallius (F 17)

into exile (Liv. Epit. *67; TLRR 64), or he may have mentioned him in the context of another case.*

F 17 Cicero, *On the Orator*

[CRASSUS:] What shall I say of the rousing of pity over Cn.
Mallius, what of that over Q. Rex [F 31]? What of countless other cases? In those that unique acuteness, which all
attribute to you, was not the most brilliant feature, but
those very matters that you now wish to delegate to me
[rhetorical embellishment and passionate delivery] were
consistently displayed as outstanding and excellent in you.

Evidence Against Sex. Titius (F 18)

which Sex. Titius was condemned (Cic. Rab. perd. *24–25;
Val. Max. 8.1.damn.3; cf. also F 36).*

F 18 Cicero, *On the Orator*

[ANTONIUS:] For evidence also often has to be given, and
sometimes even rather precisely, as it was necessary also
for me to do against Sex. Titius, a factious and troublesome
citizen: in giving that evidence I revealed all the measures
of my consulship whereby, in defense of the Republic, I
had withstood that Tribune of the People, and I pointed
out all his actions that I considered inimical to the Republic; I was kept for a long time, had to listen to a great deal,
and provided many replies.

On Behalf of M'. Aquillius (F 19–21)

*When M'. Aquillius (cos. 101 BC) had successfully con-
cluded the servile war in Sicily after his consulship and
was charged with extortion by L. Fufius (**75** F 4–6) upon*

F 19 Liv. *Epit.* 70.1–3

cum M'.[1] Aquillius de pecuniis repetundis causam diceret,
ipse iudices rogare noluit; M. Antonius, qui pro eo pero-
rabat, tunicam a pectore eius discidit, ut honestas cicatrices ostenderet. [2] indubitate absolutus est. [3] Cicero
eius rei solus auctor.

[1] M'. *Sigonius*: M. *codd.*

F 20 Cic. *De or.* 2.124

[Crassus:] quod enim ornamentum, quae vis, qui animus,
quae dignitas illi oratori defuit, qui in causa peroranda non
dubitavit excitare reum consularem et eius diloricare tunicam et iudicibus cicatrices adversas senis imperatoris
ostendere?

F 21 Cic. *De or.* 2.194–196

[Antonius:] saepe enim audivi poetam bonum neminem
. . . sine inflammatione animorum existere posse et sine
quodam adflatu quasi furoris. quare nolite existimare me
ipsum, qui non heroum veteres casus fictosque luctus
velim imitari atque adumbrare dicendo—neque actor
sum alienae personae, sed auctor meae—cum mihi M'.
Aquillius in civitate retinendus esset, quae in illa causa

On Behalf of M'. Aquillius (F 19–21)

, *Antonius managed to have him acquitted by an
₩ plea* (TLRR *84; Cic.* De or. *2.188;* Verr. *2.5.3;
; Quint.* Inst. *2.15.7).*

✓   ͷy, *Epitome*

Μ'. Aquillius defended his case concerning the ex-
of money, he did not wish to appeal to the judges
.f; M. Antonius, who delivered the peroration for
., cut the tunic from the former's breast, so that he
ᴅsplayed the honorable scars. [2] Indisputably he was acquitted. [3] Cicero is the only witness of that matter.

F 20 Cicero, *On the Orator*

[CRASSUS:] For what ornament, what force, what passion,
what standing did that orator [i.e., Antonius] lack, who in
closing the case did not hesitate to call forward the defendant of consular rank, tear open his tunic, and display to
the judges the scars on the old general's breast?

F 21 Cicero, *On the Orator*

[ANTONIUS:] For I have often heard that no good poet . . .
can exist without a passionate fire of the mind and without
some inspiration of something like frenzy. Do not suppose
then that I myself, who do not wish to portray and sketch
in language the bygone misfortunes and made-up instances of grief of heroes—and who am not the actor of
another's personality, but the spokesman of my own—did
without enormous distress what I did when concluding

peroranda fecerim, sine magno dolore fecisse. [19.
enim ego consulem fuisse, imperatorem, ornatun
natu, ovantem in Capitolium ascendisse memin
hunc cum adflictum, debilitatum, maerentem, in ‹
mum discrimen adductum viderem, non prius sum cc
tus misericordiam aliis commovere quam misericor‹
sum ipse captus. sensi equidem tum magno opere mov‹
iudices, cum excitavi maestum ac sordidatum senem ‹
cum ista feci, quae tu, Crasse, laudas, non arte de qua quid
loquar nescio sed motu magno animi ac dolore, ut discin-
derem tunicam, ut cicatrices ostenderem. [196] cum C.
Marius maerorem orationis meae praesens ac sedens multum lacrimis suis adiuvaret cumque ego illum crebro ap-
pellans collegam ei suum commendarem atque ipsum
advocatum ad communem imperatorum fortunam de-
fendendam invocarem, non fuit haec sine meis lacrimis,
non sine dolore magno miseratio omniumque deorum et
hominum et civium et sociorum imploratio. quibus omnibus verbis, quae a me tum sunt habita, si dolor afuisset
meus, non modo non miserabilis, sed etiam inridenda fuisset oratio mea. quam ob rem hoc vos doceo, Sulpici, bonus
ego videlicet atque eruditus magister, ut in dicendo irasci,
ut dolere, ut flere possitis.

that famous case, when I had to retain M'. Aquillius as a member of the community. [195] For when I saw a man, whom I remembered having been consul, general, honored by the Senate, and mounting in an ovation up to the Capitol, now cast down, crippled, sorrowing, brought to the greatest crisis, I did not try to arouse compassion in others before I myself was overcome by compassion. I certainly felt that the judges were deeply moved when I called forward the unhappy old man in his garb of woe and when I did those things that you, Crassus, praise, not by way of an art, about which I do not know what to say, but out of a great movement of passion and distress, namely that I tore open his tunic to expose his scars. [196] When C. Marius, present and sitting in court, was strongly reinforcing, by his tears, the pathos of my speech, and I, repeatedly naming him, was committing his colleague to his care and calling upon him to speak himself in support of the common interests of generals, this lamentation, as well as the invocation of all gods and men, citizens and allies, was not without my tears, not without enormous distress. Had my distress been missing from all the words that I uttered on that occasion, my speech would not only not have inspired compassion, but would even have deserved ridicule. That is why I am telling you this, Sulpicius [P. Sulpicius Rufus (**76**)], the decent and accomplished teacher, obviously, that I am, so that you all can be wrathful, be indignant, and be tearful when speaking.

On Behalf of C. Norbanus (F 22–30)

*After his censorship in 97 BC (F 22), Antonius defended
C. Norbanus (prob. tr. pl. 103, cos. 83 BC), who had been
his praetor in Cilicia, and managed to get him acquitted
(TLRR 86; cf. Cic. De or. 2.124). Norbanus was charged
with* maiestas minuta *(according to the* Lex Appuleia de

F 22 Cic. *De or.* 2.197–98

[ANTONIUS:] quamquam te quidem quid hoc doceam, qui
in accusando sodali[1] meo tantum incendium non oratione
solum, sed multo etiam magis vi et dolore et ardore animi
concitaras, ut ego ad id restinguendum vix conarer acce-
dere? habueras enim tu omnia in causa superiora: vim,
fugam, lapidationem, crudelitatem tribuniciam in Caepionis gravi miserabilique casu in iudicium vocabas; deinde
principem et senatus et civitatis, M. Aemilium, lapide
percussum esse constabat; vi pulsum e templo L. Cottam
et T. Didium, cum intercedere vellent rogationi, nemo
poterat negare. [198] accedebat, ut haec tu adulescens pro
re publica queri summa cum dignitate existimarere, ego,
homo censorius, vix satis honeste viderer seditiosum civem et in hominis consularis calamitate crudelem posse
defendere. erant optimi cives iudices, bonorum virorum
plenum forum, vix ut mihi tenuis quaedam venia daretur

[1] sodali (*edd.*) *vel* sodali et quaestore *codd.*: quaestore *Courbaud*

On Behalf of C. Norbanus (F 22–30)

maiestate minuta; LPPR, *pp. 329–30) by P. Sulpicius Rufus (**76** F 12–15), since Norbanus, in his year as Tribune of the People, had prosecuted Q. Servilus Caepio (**62**), when the proceedings included tumultuous and violent incidents.*

F 22 Cicero, *On the Orator*

[ANTONIUS:] But why indeed should I teach this to you [P. Sulpicius Rufus (**76**), F 12–15], who, in prosecuting my comrade [Norbanus], had kindled such a blaze, not only by eloquence, but far more even by vehemence, distress, and fiery enthusiasm, that I hardly ventured to draw near and put it out? For you had all the advantages in that case: you were citing to the court the violence, the flight, the stone-throwing, and the Tribunes' cruelty in the disastrous and lamentable affair of Caepio [Q. Servilius Caepio (**62**)]; then it was known that M. Aemilius [M. Aemilius Scaurus (**43**)], foremost in the Senate and the community, had been struck by a stone; nobody could deny that L. Cotta [L. Aurelius Cotta, tr. pl. 103 BC] and T. Didius [tr. pl. 103 BC], when they wished to veto the bill, had been forcibly driven from the sanctuary. [198] It was the case, moreover, that you, a young man, were thought to be protesting at this on behalf of the Republic with the greatest distinction, while I, a former censor, was seen to be hardly able to defend honorably a citizen who was factious and cruel in the distress of a former consul. The best citizens were the judges, the Forum was full of loyal men, so that some sort of tenuous acceptance was hardly given to my justifi-

excusationis, quod tamen eum defenderem, qui mihi quaestor[2] fuisset. hic ego quid dicam me artem aliquam adhibuisse? quid fecerim narrabo; si placuerit, vos meam defensionem in aliquo artis loco reponetis.

[2] quaestor *vel* legatus *codd.*: sodalis *Nonius, Friedrich*

F 23 Cic. *De or.* 2.202–3

hic SULPICIUS, "vere hercle" inquit, "Antoni, ista commemoras. nam ego nihil umquam vidi quod tam e manibus elaberetur, quam mihi tum est elapsa illa causa. cum enim, quem ad modum dixisti, tibi ego non iudicium, sed incendium tradidissem, quod tuum principium, di immortales, fuit! qui timor, quae dubitatio, quanta haesitatio tractusque verborum! ut tu illud initio, quod tibi unum ad ignoscendum homines dabant, tenuisti, te pro homine pernecessario, quaestore tuo, dicere! quam tibi primum munisti ad te audiendum viam! [203] ecce autem, cum te nihil aliud profecisse arbitrarer, nisi ut homines tibi civem improbum defendenti ignoscendum propter necessitudinem arbitrarentur, serpere occulte coepisti, nihil dum aliis suspicantibus, me vero iam pertimescente, ut illam non Norbani seditionem, sed populi Romani iracundiam neque eam iniustam, sed meritam ac debitam fuisse defenderes. . . ."

cation, namely that, at any rate, I defended him who had been my quaestor. Here, how can I say I used any particular technique? What I did I will relate; if you please, you will put my line of defense in some place in the system.

F 23 Cicero, *On the Orator*

Here SULPICIUS said: "By Hercules, Antonius, you are recounting those matters truthfully. For never did I see anything slip through the fingers in the way in which that case then slipped through mine. For when, as you said [F 22], I had handed over to you not a court case, but a conflagration, by god, what was your opening like! What fear, what hesitation, how much stammering and drawing out of words! How you clung at the outset to the single excuse that everyone granted you, that you were defending a very close friend, your quaestor! How, at first, did you pave the way toward getting a hearing! [203] But look, when I was thinking that you had achieved nothing else other than that people thought you should be pardoned for defending a wicked citizen because of your close relationship, while other people suspected nothing as yet, but I was already in great fear, you began to sneak in imperceptibly that you were defending that incident not as an insurrection of Norbanus, but as a result of anger of the Roman People, which was not unjustified, but just and appropriate. . . ."

F 24 Cic. *De or.* 2.199

[ANTONIUS:] omnium seditionum genera, vitia, pericula collegi eamque orationem ex omni rei publicae nostrae temporum varietate repetivi conclusique ita, ut dicerem, etsi omnes molestae semper seditiones fuissent, iustas tamen fuisse non nullas et prope necessarias. tum illa, quae modo Crassus commemorabat, egi: neque reges ex hac civitate exigi neque tribunos plebis creari neque plebiscitis totiens consularem potestatem minui neque provocationem, patronam illam civitatis ac vindicem libertatis, populo Romano dari sine nobilium dissensione potuisse; ac si illae seditiones saluti huic civitati fuissent, non continuo, si qui motus populi factus esset, id C. Norbano in nefario crimine atque in fraude capitali esse ponendum. quod si umquam populo Romano concessum esset, ut iure incitatus videretur, id quod docebam saepe esse concessum, nullam illa causa iustiorem fuisse.

F 25 Cic. *De or.* 2.107–9

[ANTONIUS:] iam quid vocetur quaeritur, cum quo verbo quid appellandum sit contenditur: ut mihi ipsi cum hoc Sulpicio fuit in Norbani causa summa contentio. pleraque enim de iis quae ab isto obiciebantur cum confiterer, ta-

F 24 Cicero, *On the Orator*

[ANTONIUS:] I collected the types, faults, and dangers of all civil discords, and I derived that part of my speech from all the vicissitudes of our Republic over time, and I concluded in such a way that I said that, even though all civil discords had always been troublesome, still some had been justifiable and almost necessary. Next I discussed what Crassus [L. Licinius Crassus (**66**)] has just recalled [Cic. *De or.* 2.124]: that neither the expulsion of kings from this community, nor the establishment of Tribunes of the People, nor the frequent restriction of the consuls' power by plebiscites, nor the bestowal upon the Roman People of the right of appeal, that famous patron of the community and defense of freedom, could have happened without disagreement with the nobility; and that, if those civil discords had been beneficial to this community, not without further evidence, if some uprising of the People had been caused, ought this to be counted against C. Norbanus as heinous wickedness and a capital offense. That, if it had ever been conceded to the Roman People that it seemed to have been justly aroused, which, as I showed, was often conceded, no cause had been more just than that one.

F 25 Cicero, *On the Orator*

[ANTONIUS:] Again the question is one of terminology, when the term by which something should be called is in dispute, as the great argument was between myself and Sulpicius here [P. Sulpicius Rufus (**76**), F 12–15] at the trial of Norbanus. For, while I admitted most of what was charged by him, I still denied that the defendant was guilty

411

men ab illo maiestatem minutam negabam; ex quo verbo
lege Apuleia tota illa causa pendebat. [108] . . . [109] quod
quidem in illa causa neque Sulpicius fecit neque ego facere conatus sum. nam quantum uterque nostrum potuit,
omni copia dicendi dilatavit, quid esset maiestatem mi-
nuere.

F 26 Cic. *De or.* 2.167

[ANTONIUS:] ex coniunctis sic argumenta ducuntur: . . . ex
genere autem: "si magistratus in populi Romani esse pot-
estate debent, quid Norbanum accusas, cuius tribunatus
voluntati paruit civitatis?"

F 27 Cic. *De or.* 2.164

[ANTONIUS:] si res tota quaeritur, definitione universa vis
explicanda est sic: si maiestas est amplitudo ac dignitas
civitatis, is eam minuit, qui exercitum hostibus populi
Romani tradidit, non qui eum qui id fecisset populi Romani potestati tradidit.

F 28 Cic. *De or.* 2.203

[SULPICIUS:] deinde qui locus a te praetermissus est in
Caepionem?

F 29 Cic. *De or.* 2.199–201

[ANTONIUS:] tum omnem orationem traduxi et converti in

of an "act of treason"; on this word, according to the *Lex Appuleia* [*Lex Appuleia de maiestate minuta*: *LPPR*, pp. 329–30], that whole case depended. [108] . . . [109] In that case at any rate Sulpicius did no such thing nor did I attempt to do it [to define the term]. For both of us, so far as each of us could, extended with all fluency of speaking what it meant to commit an act of treason.

F 26   Cicero, *On the Orator*

[ANTONIUS:] Arguments are deduced from connected matters as follows: . . . But from a term denoting a class: "If the magistracies ought to be under the control of the Roman People, why are you accusing Norbanus, whose Tribunate was subservient to the will of the community?"

F 27   Cicero, *On the Orator*

[ANTONIUS:] If the matter as a whole is at issue, the general idea has to be made plain by a definition, for example: "If sovereignty is the grandeur and glory of the community, it was violated by the man who delivered up to the enemy an army of the Roman People, not by him who delivered the man who had done that into the power of the Roman People."

F 28   Cicero, *On the Orator*

[SULPICIUS:] Then, what point did you pass over against Caepio [Q. Servilius Caepio (**62**)]? [continued by F 30]

F 29   Cicero, *On the Orator*

[ANTONIUS:] Then I moved my entire speech to another context and turned it into a denunciation of the running

increpandam Caepionis fugam, in deplorandum interitum
exercitus. sic et eorum dolorem, qui lugebant suos, oratione refricabam et animos equitum Romanorum, apud
quos tum iudices causa agebatur, ad Q. Caepionis odium,
a quo erant ipsi propter iudicia abalienati, renovabam atque revocabam. [200] quod ubi sensi me in possessionem
iudicii ac defensionis meae constitisse, quod et populi
benevolentiam mihi conciliaram, cuius ius etiam cum se-
ditionis coniunctione defenderam, et iudicum animos totos vel calamitate civitatis vel luctu ac desiderio propin-
quorum vel odio proprio in Caepionem ad causam nostram
converteram, tum admiscere huic generi orationis vehementi atque atroci genus illud alterum, de quo ante dis-
putavi, lenitatis et mansuetudinis coepi: me pro meo sodali, qui mihi in liberum loco more maiorum esse deberet,
et pro mea omni fama prope fortunisque decernere, nihil
mihi ad existimationem turpius, nihil ad dolorem acerbius
accidere posse quam si is, qui saepe alienissimis a me, sed
meis tamen civibus saluti existimarer fuisse, sodali meo
auxilium ferre non potuissem. [201] petebam a iudicibus,
ut illud aetati meae, ut honoribus, ut rebus gestis, si iusto,
si pio dolore me esse adfectum viderent concederent,
praesertim si in aliis causis intellexissent omnia me semper
pro amicorum periculis, nihil umquam pro me ipso depre-
catum.

away of Caepio [Q. Servilius Caepio (**62**)], into a lament for the destruction of the army. In this way, by my speech I both excited afresh the pain of those who were mourning their own folk and renewed and rekindled the feelings of the Roman knights, by whom as judges the case was then handled, into hatred of Q. Caepio, from whom they had been estranged over [the composition of] the criminal courts [see **62**]. [200] As soon as I felt I had set up a firm hold on the court and on my line of defense, when I had won for me the goodwill of the People, whose claims I had upheld even when involved with civil discord, and had also turned the minds of the judges entirely in favor of our cause, by reason either of the calamity of the community, or of yearning grief for relatives, or of private hatred of Caepio, then I began to blend with this impetuous and violent type of oratory that other type, of which I spoke earlier [Cic. *De or.* 2.183–84], characterized by mildness and gentleness: I said that I was fighting for my comrade, who, for me, should have the place of children according to ancestral tradition, and for all my own fair reputation and general welfare as it were; nothing more disgraceful could happen to my reputation, nothing bitterer for my distress, than if I, who was thought to have often saved complete strangers to myself, though nonetheless my fellow citizens, had been unable to aid my own comrade. [201] I begged the judges, if they saw me affected by justifiable, loyal distress, to excuse this in consideration of my years, my official career, my achievements, particularly if, in other trials, they had realized that I always made my petitions on behalf of friends in danger, never for myself.

F 30 Cic. *De or.* 2.203

[SULPICIUS:] ut tu illa omnia odio, invidia, misericordia miscuisti! neque haec solum in defensione sed etiam in Scauro ceterisque meis testibus, quorum tu testimonia non refellendo, sed ad eundem impetum populi confugiendo refutasti.

On Q. Rex (F 31)

F 31 Cic. *De or.* 2.125
= F 17.

Against the Brothers Cossi (F 32)

F 32 Cic. *De or.* 2.98

[ANTONIUS:] . . . neque vero vester aequalis Curio, patre mea sententia vel eloquentissimo temporibus illis, quemquam mihi magno opere videtur imitari; qui tamen verborum gravitate et elegantia et copia suam quandam expres-

F 30 Cicero, *On the Orator*

[SULPICIUS:] [continued from F 28] How you mixed all this with hatred, ill will, and compassion! And this not only in your speech for the defense, but also with regard to Scaurus [M. Aemilius Scaurus (**43**)] and the rest of my witnesses, whose evidence you refuted not by disproving it, but by taking refuge in that same impetuosity of the People.

On Q. Rex (F 31)

Q. Rex might be Q. Marcius Rex (cos. 118 BC); he must have been referred to in a speech delivered before 91 BC, the dramatic date of the dialogue in which the reference occurs.

F 31 Cicero, *On the Orator*

= F 17.

Against the Brothers Cossi (F 32)

Also before 91 BC, Antonius spoke against the brothers Cossi in the centumviral court (TLRR 360).

F 32 Cicero, *On the Orator*

[ANTONIUS:] . . . indeed, Curio [C. Scribonius Curio (**86**), F 6] too, your contemporary, whose father [C. Scribonius Curio (**47**)], in my view, was even the most eloquent of that time, seems to me to copy no one particularly; still, through the dignity, refinement, and copiousness of his language he has produced, as it were, his own peculiar

417

sit quasi formam figuramque dicendi, quod ego maxime iudicare potui in ea causa quam ille contra me apud centumviros pro fratribus Cossis[1] dixit; in qua nihil illi defuit, quod non modo copiosus, sed etiam sapiens orator habere deberet.

[1] Cossis *vel* Cosiis *codd.*: Cossii *vel* consciis *vel* consociis *codd. rec.*

On Behalf of M. Marius Gratidianus (F 33)

F 33 Cic. *Off.* 3.67

M. Marius Gratidianus, propinquus noster, C. Sergio Oratae vendiderat aedes eas quas ab eodem ipse paucis ante annis emerat. eae {Sergio}[1] serviebant, sed hoc in mancipio Marius non dixerat. adducta res in iudicium est; Oratam Crassus, Gratidianum defendebat Antonius. ius Crassus urgebat: quod vitii venditor non dixisset sciens, id oportere praestari, aequitatem Antonius: quoniam id vitium ignotum Sergio non fuisset, qui illas aedes vendidisset, nihil fuisse necesse dici, nec eum esse deceptum qui id quod emerat quo iure esset teneret.

[1] *del. Balduinus*: sergio *vel* sergio alii *codd.*

form and shape of speaking, as it were; of that I could judge very well in that case in which he spoke against me before the centumviral court, on behalf of the brothers Cossi; in that he lacked nothing that not only a copious orator, but also a wise one, should possess.

On Behalf of M. Marius Gratidianus (F 33)

Antonius supported M. Marius Gratidianus, a son of M. Gratidius (54), against C. Sergius Orata, defended by L. Licinius Crassus (66 F 42) (TLRR 362).

F 33 Cicero, *On Duties*

M. Marius Gratidianus, a kinsman of ours, had sold back to C. Sergius Orata the house that he himself had bought from that same person a few years earlier. It was subject to an easement {to Sergius}, but Marius had not mentioned this in the sale. The matter was carried to the courts; Crassus [L. Licinius Crassus (66), F 42] defended Orata, Antonius Gratidianus. Crassus pleaded the letter of the law: that with regard to a defect the vendor had knowingly not declared there was bound to be responsibility for making good. Antonius laid stress upon equity: since this defect had not been unknown to Sergius, as he had sold that same house, it had in no way been necessary to mention it, and that man had not been deceived, who was aware of the legal status of what he had bought.

On His Own Behalf under Lex Varia *(F 34)*

F 34 Cic. *Tusc.* 2.56–57

[M.:] quid? qui volunt exclamare maius, num satis habent latera, fauces, linguam intendere, e quibus elici vocem et fundi videmus? toto corpore atque omnibus ungulis, ut dicitur, contentioni vocis adserviunt. [57] genu mehercule M. Antonium vidi, cum contente pro se ipse lege Varia diceret, terram tangere.

Unplaced Fragments (F 35–36)

F 35 Cic. *De or.* 2.257

[CAESAR STRABO:] nam in Coelio sane etiam ad causam utile fuit tuum illud, Antoni, cum ille a se pecuniam profectam diceret testis et haberet filium delicatiorem, ab-

---

1 It is uncertain what trial is meant and which Coelius is referred to. The incident is sometimes connected with Antonius being prosecuted for having obtained the office of censor (97 BC)

On His Own Behalf under Lex Varia *(F 34)*

Cases tried under the Lex Varia de maiestate *are dated to 90 BC, when the proposer Q. Varius Hybrida (88) was Tribune of the People (see 88). Antonius spoke on behalf of himself at such a trial (TLRR 108).*

F 34 Cicero, *Tusculan Disputations*

[M.:] What? Those who want to shout louder, don't they find it enough to intensify the effort of sides, throat, and tongue, from which we see the voice is brought forth and poured out? With the entire body and with tooth and nail, as the saying is, they second the straining of the voice. [57] With his knee, by Hercules, have I seen M. Antonius, when he spoke with great exertion on behalf of himself under the *Lex Varia*, touch the ground.

Unplaced Fragments (F 35–36)

These fragments seem to come from verbal exchanges rather than proper speeches.

F 35 Cicero, *On the Orator*

[CAESAR STRABO:] For, doubtless, with regard to Coelius that quotation of yours, Antonius, was even useful for the case, when he said, as a witness,[1] that money had come

by *ambitus* (Cic. *De or.* 2.274), and C. Coelius Caldus (**67A**) is identified as the witness (*TLRR* 83). The comment indicates that Coelius' son managed to get money from his father for his own benefit rather than for the alleged purpose.

eunte iam {aet} a te[1] illo, "sentin senem esse tactum triginta minis?" [*Pall. inc. inc.* 45 R.[2–3]]

[1] {aet} a te *Kumaniecki:* aetate *codd.: om. alii*

F 36 Cic. *De or.* 2.265

[CAESAR STRABO:] trahitur etiam aliquid ex historia, ut cum Sex. Titius[1] se Cassandram esse diceret: "multos" inquit Antonius "possum tuos Aiaces Oileos nominare."

[1] Sex. Titius *vel* Sextius *codd.*

Treatise on the Art of Speaking (F 37–40)

Antonius produced a short work on the art of speaking; thus, according to Quintilian, he was the first Roman after M. Porcius Cato (8) to write on oratory (Quint. Inst. 3.1.19). Cicero has Antonius claim that this piece was just a rough, brief text, which was circulated against his will

F 37 (= 1 *ORF*[4]) Cic. *Brut.* 163

hoc loco BRUTUS: "quando quidem tu istos oratores," inquit, "tanto opere laudas, vellem aliquid Antonio praeter illum de ratione dicendi sane exilem libellum, plura Crasso libuisset scribere: cum enim omnibus memoriam sui tum etiam disciplinam dicendi nobis reliquissent. . . ."

from him and he had a rather wanton son, [you said,] as he was already moving away from you: "Do you notice that the old man has been diddled out of thirty *minae*?" [*Pall. inc. inc.* 45 R.²⁻³]

F 36 Cicero, *On the Orator*

[CAESAR STRABO:] Some material is also derived from stories from the past, as, when Sex. Titius [**67C**] said that he was a Cassandra, Antonius commented: "I can name your Lesser Ajaxes."[1]

[1] Cassandra, since she was not believed; Ajax (son of Oileus, often called "the Lesser"), since he raped Cassandra.

Treatise on the Art of Speaking (F 37–40)

(*F 38, 39*). *While the excerpts relating to this work do not provide practical examples of or information about speeches, they contribute to illustrating Antonius' views on oratory.*

F 37 (= 1 *ORF*⁴) Cicero, *Brutus*

At this point BRUTUS said: "Since you praise those orators so much, I wish that Antonius had cared to write something besides that quite meager little treatise on the art of speaking and Crassus [L. Licinius Crassus (**66**)] to write more; for then they would have left a memorial of themselves for all men and particularly instructions on the art of speaking for us. . . ."

F 38 (= 2 *ORF*⁴) Cic. *De or.* 1.94

[ANTONIUS:] itaque ego hac eadem opinione adductus scripsi etiam illud quodam in libello, qui me imprudente et invito excidit et pervenit in manus hominum, disertos me cognosse nonnullos, eloquentem adhuc neminem, quod eum statuebam disertum, qui posset satis acute atque dilucide apud mediocres homines ex communi quadam opinione hominum dicere, eloquentem vero, qui mirabilius et magnificentius augere posset atque ornare quae vellet, omnisque omnium rerum, quae ad dicendum pertinerent, fontis animo ac memoria contineret.

Cf. Cic. *De or.* 1.206; *Orat.* 18; Quint. *Inst.* 8.pr.13, 12.1.21; Plin. *Ep.* 5.20.5.

F 39 (= 3 *ORF*⁴) Cic. *De or.* 1.208

[ANTONIUS:] neque enim sum de arte dicturus, quam numquam didici, sed de mea consuetudine; ipsaque illa, quae in commentarium meum rettuli, sunt eius modi, non aliqua mihi doctrina tradita, sed in rerum usu causisque tractata; quae si vobis hominibus eruditissimis non probabuntur, vestram iniquitatem accusatote, qui ex me ea quaesieritis quae ego nescirem, meam facilitatem laudatote, cum vobis non meo iudicio sed vestro studio inductus non gravate respondero.

F 40 (= 4 *ORF*⁴) Quint. *Inst.* 3.6.44–45

a plurimis tres sunt facti generales status, quibus et Cicero in Oratore [Cic. *Orat.* 45] utitur et omnia quae aut in con-

F 38 (= 2 *ORF*[4]) Cicero, *On the Orator*

[ANTONIUS:] And so, convinced by this very view [i.e., that nobody could be an eloquent orator who did not know about discussions among eminent philosophers; cf. Cic. *De or.* 2.93], I actually wrote down in some little treatise, which got about without my knowledge or consent and got into the hands of the public, that statement that I had known several accomplished speakers, but so far no one eloquent, since I judged anyone to be an accomplished speaker who was able to speak sufficiently to the point and clearly before an everyday audience and in line with some standard view of men, but that man to be eloquent who was able, in a style more admirable and more splendid, to amplify and adorn any subject he chose, and who encompassed in his mind and memory all the sources of all matters that are relevant to speaking.

F 39 (= 3 *ORF*[4]) Cicero, *On the Orator*

[ANTONIUS:] For I am not going to speak of an art that I have never learned, but of my own practice; and those very things that I have collated in my notebook are of this kind, not conveyed to me by some kind of doctrine, but used in actual affairs and court cases: if these are not approved by you, very learned men, blame your own unfairness as you have asked me for things that I do not know; praise my good nature when I answer you not reluctantly, prompted not by my own judgment, but by your enthusiasm.

F 40 (= 4 *ORF*[4]) Quintilian, *The Orator's Education*

Most writers have assumed three general issues [for court cases]; Cicero too employs these in the *Orator* [Cic. *Orat.*

troversiam aut in contentionem veniant contineri putat: sitne, quid sit, quale sit. . . . [45] . . . tres fecit et M. Antonius his quidem verbis: "paucae res sunt quibus ex rebus omnes orationes nascuntur, factum non factum, ius iniuria, bonum malum." sed quoniam quod iure dicimur fecisse non hunc solum intellectum habet, ut lege, sed illum quoque, ut iuste fecisse videamur, secuti Antonium apertius voluerunt eosdem status distinguere, itaque dixerunt coniecturalem, legalem, iuridicalem . . .

66 L. LICINIUS CRASSUS

*L. Licinius Crassus (140–91 BC; cos. 95, censor 92 BC; RE Licinius 55) was regarded, along with M. Antonius (**65**), as the outstanding orator of his age (T 1–3, 5–7; Cic. Brut. 145, 148, 186, 189, 215: **65** T 6, 333; De or. 3.16: **65** T 2). He did not leave much in writing (T 12; Cic. De or. 2.8; Orat. 132: **80** T 6); but some of his speeches were published and available in Cicero's time (F 18, 22, 34). Crassus is one of the main speakers in Cicero's De oratore.*

*As censor with Cn. Domitius Ahenobarbus (**69**), Crassus issued an edict forbidding the activity of Latin rhetoricians in the city of Rome (Cic. De or. 3.93; Tac. Dial. 35.1; Gell. NA 15.11.2; Suet. Gram. et rhet. 25.2). As a young*

45] and thinks that everything that comes into either dispute or contention is covered thereby: whether it is the case, what it is [i.e., how to define it], what its nature is [i.e., how to assess it]. . . . [45] . . . M. Antonius has also assumed three types, indeed in these words: "There are only a few things from which all speeches are born: done or not done, right or wrong, good or bad."[1] But since, when we are said to have done something rightly, this does not only have the meaning that [it was done] legally, but also that we seem to have done it justly, Antonius' followers wished to distinguish these issues more clearly and therefore spoke of the conjectural, legal, and juridical [issue] . . .

[1] This passage does not include an explicit reference to the treatise, but such a comment is more likely to have been made in this text than in a speech (and Antonius' treatise was known to Quintilian).

66 L. LICINIUS CRASSUS

man, Crassus trained daily, for instance by reading famous orations and rendering them in his own words and later commenting on Greek orations (Cic. De or. 1.154–55; Quint. Inst. 10.5.2). He attended lectures of the Academic Metrodorus, when he was quaestor in Asia (Cic. De or. 2.365, 3.75), and of various other philosophers in Athens (Cic. De or. 1.45), but he pretended to look down on such studies and to prefer Roman scholars (Cic. De or. 2.4: **65 T 8**). Crassus was a friend of the poet Archias (Cic. Arch. 6); he studied law with L. Coelius Antipater, who was also his friend, and was regarded as a legal expert (Cic. De or. 2.54; Brut. 102, 145).

T 1 Cic. *Brut.* 138

= **65** T 5.

T 2 Cic. *Brut.* 143–44 (cf. **65** T 5)

[CICERO:] huic alii parem esse dicebant, alii anteponebant L. Crassum. illud quidem certe omnes ita iudicabant, neminem esse qui horum altero utro patrono cuiusquam ingenium requireret. equidem quamquam Antonio tantum tribuo quantum supra dixi, tamen Crasso nihil statuo fieri potuisse perfectius. erat summa gravitas, erat cum gravitate iunctus facetiarum et urbanitatis oratorius, non scurrilis lepos, Latine loquendi accurata et sine molestia diligens elegantia, in disserendo mira explicatio; cum de iure civili, cum de aequo et bono disputaretur, argumentorum et similitudinum copia. [144] nam ut Antonius coniectura movenda aut sedanda suspicione aut excitanda incredibilem vim habebat, sic in interpretando, in definiendo, in explicanda aequitate nihil erat Crasso copiosius
. . .

T 3 Cic. *Brut.* 158–59

[CICERO:] paratus igitur veniebat Crassus, exspectabatur, audiebatur; a principio statim, quod erat apud eum semper accuratum, exspectatione dignus videbatur. non multa iactatio corporis, non inclinatio vocis, nulla inambulatio, non crebra supplosio pedis; vehemens et interdum irata et

T 1 Cicero, *Brutus*
= **65** T 5.

T 2 Cicero, *Brutus* (cf. **65** T 5)

[CICERO:] Some said that L. Crassus was equal to him [M. Antonius (**65**)], some placed him [Crassus] higher. At any rate all were of the view that there would be nobody who, with either of these two as advocate, required the help of any other man's talent. For my part, though I assign to Antonius all that I have pointed out above, still I declare that nothing could have been more perfect than Crassus. There was the greatest dignity, there was, combined with dignity, a charm consisting of pleasantry and wit, of an orator, not of a buffoon, a meticulous and careful elegance of speaking Latin without creating annoyance, in setting out matters an admirable style of exposition, and, when there were discussions about civil law, about what is fair and right, copiousness of arguments and analogies. [144] For as Antonius possessed incredible skill in creating an inference, in provoking or allaying a suspicion, so in interpreting, in defining, in explaining equity nothing was more resourceful than Crassus . . . [continued by F 29]

T 3 Cicero, *Brutus*

[CICERO:] Crassus, then, came always prepared, he was awaited, he was listened to. Straight from the exordium, which with him was always carefully arranged, he showed himself worthy of the expectation. Not much violent movement of the body, no variation of the voice's pitch, no walking up and down, no frequent stamping of the foot; his language vehement and sometimes angry and filled

plena iusti doloris oratio, multae et cum gravitate facetiae; quodque difficile est, idem et perornatus et perbrevis; iam in altercando invenit parem neminem. [159] versatus est in omni fere genere causarum; mature in locum principum oratorum venit.

T 4 Cic. *Brut.* 162

[Cicero:] in his omnibus inest quidam sine ullo fuco veritatis color; quin etiam comprehensio et ambitus ille verborum, si sic περίοδον appellari placet, erat apud illum contractus et brevis, et in membra quaedam, quae κῶλα Graeci vocant, dispertiebat orationem libentius.

T 5 Cic. *Brut.* 165

= **65** T 5.

T 6 Cic. *Brut.* 296

[Atticus:] . . . venio ad eos in quibus iam perfectam putas esse eloquentiam, quos ego audivi sine controversia magnos oratores, Crassum et Antonium. de horum laudibus tibi prorsus adsentior, sed tamen non isto modo: ut Polycliti Doryphorum sibi Lysippus aiebat, sic tu suasionem legis Serviliae tibi magistram fuisse; haec germana ironia est. cur ita sentiam non dicam, ne me tibi adsentari putes.

with justified distress; much wit but dignified, and, what is difficult, he was at once very ornate and very brief; finally, in altercation he found nobody his equal. [159] He dealt with almost every type of case; early in his career he obtained a position among the first orators.

T 4 Cicero, *Brutus*

[CICERO:] In all these [speeches of Crassus] there is a certain color representing true nature without any makeup; even that grouping and balancing of words, if *periodos* ["period"] may be described in this way, with him was compact and short, and he preferred to break up his language into some sort of sections, which the Greeks call *cola* ["elements of periods"].

T 5 Cicero, *Brutus*

= **65** T 5.

T 6 Cicero, *Brutus*

[ATTICUS:] . . . I come to those in whom you [Cicero] consider that eloquence was finally perfected, whom I have heard, great orators without question, Crassus and Antonius [M. Antonius (**65**)]. As for their merits, I thoroughly agree with you, yet not in that way of yours: as Lysippus [Greek sculptor of 4th cent. BC] used to say that Polyclitus' Doryphorus was a teacher for him, so you said the speech in support of the *Lex Servilia* [F 22–26] was for you; this is pure irony. Why I think so, I shall not say, lest you suspect me of flattering you.

T 7 Cic. *De or.* 2.220

[CAESAR STRABO:] nam id quod tu mihi tribuis, Antoni, Crasso est omnium sententia concedendum. non enim fere quisquam reperietur praeter hunc in utroque genere leporis excellens, et illo quod in perpetuitate sermonis et hoc quod in celeritate atque dicto est.

T 8 Cic. *De or.* 2.228

tum ANTONIUS "ego vero ita fecissem" inquit "nisi interdum in hoc Crasso paulum inviderem. nam esse quamvis facetum atque salsum non nimis est per se ipsum invidendum; sed cum omnium sit venustissimus et urbanissimus, omnium gravissimum et severissimum et esse et videri, quod isti contigit uni, id mihi vix ferendum videbatur."

T 9 Cic. *Orat.* 222–23
= F 51 + 52.

T 10 Tac. *Dial.* 18.2
= **48** T 9.

T 11 Tac. *Dial.* 26.1
= **48** T 10.

T 12 Cic. *Brut.* 163
= **65** F 37.

T 7 Cicero, *On the Orator*

[CAESAR STRABO:] For, what you give me credit for, Antonius [M. Antonius (**65**)], ought, by unanimous verdict, to be yielded to Crassus. For scarcely anyone will be found apart from him who is outstanding in both kinds of humor, both the one that is present all through a continuous discourse and the other that is present in instantaneous puns.

T 8 Cicero, *On the Orator*

Then ANTONIUS said: "I should certainly have done so [i.e., declare Crassus as most accomplished in using witticisms], were I not sometimes a little envious of Crassus in this respect. For to be as witty and shrewd as you like is not by itself something to be overly envied; but that he who is the most graceful and polished of all should both be and be seen as the most impressive and austere of all, that this was granted to him alone, this seemed hardly bearable to me."

T 9 Cicero, *Orator*

= F 51 + 52.

T 10 Tacitus, *Dialogue on Oratory*

= **48** T 9.

T 11 Tacitus, *Dialogue on Oratory*

= **48** T 10.

T 12 Cicero, *Brutus*

= **65** F 37.

Against C. Papirius Carbo (F 13–14)

*Crassus' first major appearance as an orator was the pros-
ecution of the ex-consul C. Papirius Carbo (**35**) in 119 BC
(TLRR 30; Cic. De or. 3.74; Tac. Dial. 34.7: **121** F 15 [age
slightly incorrect]): while he is said to have been somewhat
shy at the start of the first speech, he delivered such an
effective oration at the second hearing that the defendant*

F 13 Cic. *Brut.* 159

[CICERO:] accusavit C. Carbonem eloquentissimum hominem admodum adulescens; summam ingeni non laudem modo sed etiam admirationem est consecutus.

F 14 Cic. *De or.* 2.170

[ANTONIUS:] ex consentaneis et ex praecurrentibus et ex
repugnantibus ut olim Crassus adulescens: "non si Opi-
mium defendisti, Carbo, idcirco te isti bonum civem puta-
bunt. simulasse te et aliquid quaesisse perspicuum est,
quod Ti. Gracchi mortem saepe in contionibus deplorasti,
quod P. Africani necis socius fuisti, quod eam legem in
tribunatu tulisti, quod semper a bonis dissedisti."

---

[1] Carbo's behavior is consistent when he laments the death of
Ti. Sempronius Gracchus (**34**) and was involved in the murder of
P. Cornelius Scipio Aemilianus Africanus minor (**21**), who was
critical of Gracchus. A precondition for this attitude is that Carbo
always disagreed with the loyal men. Such actions, however, con-
tradict Carbo's defense of L. Opimius, responsible for killing C.
Sempronius Gracchus (**48**) and many of his supporters.

Against C. Papirius Carbo (F 13–14)

*avoided the penalty only by killing himself (Cic. De or.
1.40, 1.121; Brut. 103; Verr. 2.3.3; Val. Max. 3.7.6). This
appearance ensured great recognition and admiration for
Crassus (F 13), though he might have been active in the
courts earlier (Cic. De or. 2.365).*

F 13 Cicero, *Brutus*

[CICERO:] When only a young man, he [Crassus] prosecuted C. Carbo, a most eloquent man; he won not only the
highest reputation for his talent, but also great admiration.

F 14 Cicero, *On the Orator*

[ANTONIUS:] [Arguments are developed] from consistent
elements, from preconditions, and from contradictions, as
Crassus once [did] as a young man: "Not just because you
defended Opimius [L. Opimius, cos. 121 BC], Carbo [C.
Papirius Carbo (**35**), F 8–11], for that reason will these
men deem you a loyal citizen. It is clear that you were
pretending and aiming for something, since in your
speeches to the People you frequently lamented the death
of Ti. Gracchus [Ti. Sempronius Gracchus (**34**)], since you
were a party to the murder of P. Africanus [P. Cornelius
Scipio Aemilianus Africanus minor (**21**)], since you
brought in that law [cf. **35** F 7] during your Tribunate [131
or 130 BC] and since you always disagreed with the loyal
men."[1]

On a Colony at Narbo (F 15–17)

F 15 Cic. *Brut.* 160

[CICERO:] voluit adulescens in colonia Narbonensi causae
popularis aliquid adtingere eamque coloniam, ut fecit,
ipse deducere; exstat in eam legem senior, ut ita dicam,
quam aetas illa ferebat oratio.

F 16 Cic. *Clu.* 140–41

= F 46.

F 17 Cic. *Off.* 2.63

atque haec benignitas etiam reipublicae est utilis, redimi
e servitute captos, locupletari tenuiores; quod quidem
vulgo solitum fieri ab ordine nostro in oratione Crassi
scriptum copiose videmus.

On a Colony at Narbo (F 15–17)

*In 118 BC Crassus spoke in favor of a law approving the
foundation of a colony at Narbo and went on to establish
the colony (Cic.* De or. *2.223; Quint.* Inst. *6.3.43–44; Vell.
Pat. 2.7.8).*

F 15 Cicero, *Brutus*

[CICERO:] While a young man, he [Crassus] wished to
ingratiate himself somewhat with the cause of the People
regarding the matter of the colony at Narbo and to establish that colony himself, as he did. The speech on this law
is extant, somewhat older in tone, so to say, than his age at
the time would suggest.

F 16 Cicero, *Pro Cluentio*

= F 46.

F 17 Cicero, *On Duties*

And this form of generosity is a service to the Republic
too, namely ransoming prisoners from servitude and supporting the less wealthy; and that this used to be the common practice of our order we see written in great detail in
an oration of Crassus.[1]

---

[1] Some scholars attribute this reference to the speech about
the colony, presumably because of the mention of support for the
less wealthy; others point out that the comment seems to indicate
praise of the Senate and therefore is more likely an allusion to the
speech on the *Lex Servilia* (see F 16).

On Behalf of the Vestal Virgin Licinia (F 18–19)

F 18 Cic. *Brut.* 160

[CICERO:] defendit postea Liciniam virginem, cum annos XXVII natus esset. in ea ipsa causa fuit eloquentissimus orationisque eius scriptas quasdam partes reliquit.

F 19 *Rhet. Her.* 4.47

distributio est cum ⟨in⟩[1] plures res aut personas negotia quaedam certa dispertiuntur, hoc modo: . . . et: "accusatoris officium est inferre crimina; defensoris diluere et propulsare; testis dicere, quae sciat aut audierit; quaesitoris est unum quemque horum in officio suo continere. quare, L. Cassi,[2] si testem, praeterquam quod sciat aut audierit, argumentari et coniectura prosequi patieris, ius accusatoris cum iure testimonii commiscebis, testis inprobi cupiditatem confirmabis, reo duplicem defensionem parabis."

[1] in *om. codd. plerique*   [2] luci cassi *unus cod*: .l. causis *codd. plerique*

On Behalf of the Vestal Virgin Licinia (F 18–19)

In 113 BC, in the second trial against the Vestal Virgins charged with sexual impurity (cf. **65** *F 13–14), Crassus defended one of the women, Licinia (TLRR 41); yet all of them were eventually found guilty.*

F 18 Cicero, *Brutus*

[CICERO:] Later, when he [Crassus] was twenty-seven, he defended the Virgin Licinia. In that particular case he was most eloquent, and he has left some parts of that speech in writing.

F 19 *Rhetorica ad Herennium*

Distribution occurs when certain specified roles are divided up ⟨among⟩ a number of things or persons, as follows: . . . and: "The duty of the prosecutor is to bring the charges; that of the counsel for the defense to explain them away and rebut them; that of the witness to say what they know or have heard; that of the presiding judge to hold each of these to their duty. Therefore, L. Cassius, if you allow a witness to argue and to attack by means of conjecture, beyond what they know or have heard, you will be confusing the rights of a prosecutor with the rights of a witness statement, you will confirm the desires of a dishonest witness, and you will set up two occasions for defense for the defendant."[1]

[1] Since L. Cassius Longinus Ravilla (cos. 127 BC) was *quaesitor* in the second trial of the Vestal Virgins (cf. **65** F 13), Crassus may have put forward this argument, addressed to the *quaesitor*, as part of the defense.

On C. Memmius (F 20–21)

F 20 Cic. *De or.* 2.239–40

[CAESAR STRABO:] duo sunt enim genera facetiarum, quorum alterum re tractatur alterum dicto. [240] re, si quando quid tamquam aliqua fabella narratur, ut olim tu, Crasse, in Memmium: comedisse eum lacertum Largi, cum esset cum eo Tarracinae de amicula rixatus. salsa ac tamen a te ipso ficta tota narratio; addidisti clausulam tota Tarracina tum omnibus in parietibus inscriptas fuisse litteras L L L M M.[1] cum quaereres id quid esset, senem tibi quendam oppidanum dixisse: "lacerat lacertum Largi mordax Memmius."

1 litteras LLLMM *Schütz*: litteras tria l. l. l. duo m. m. *vel* litteras duo *codd.*: inscripta fuisse tria L duo M *aut* inscriptas fuisse litteras, tria L, duo M *Friedrich*

Cf. Cic. *De or.* 2.264.

F 21 Cic. *De or.* 2.267

[CAESAR STRABO:] etiam illa, quae minuendi aut augendi causa ad incredibilem admirationem efferuntur; velut tu, Crasse, in contione: ita sibi ipsum magnum videri Mem-

On C. Memmius (F 20–21)

*The sarcastic comments on C. Memmius (**60**) probably come from different occasions. One of them (F 21) was made in a speech before the People.*

F 20 Cicero, *On the Orator*

[CAESAR STRABO:] For there are two types of wit, of which one has to do with facts, the other with expression. [240] With facts, whenever something is told, like some anecdote, as you, Crassus, once did, against Memmius: that he had taken a bite out of Largus' [or Largius'] arm, when he had a quarrel with him at Tarracina [modern Terracina] over a girlfriend. A funny story, and yet entirely invented by you; you added this ending: that in the whole of Tarracina on every wall the letters M M L L L¹ were then inscribed, and that, when you asked what they meant, some old inhabitant of the town said to you: "Mordacious Memmius lacerates Largus' [or Largius'] limb."

¹ The order of L L L and M M has been reversed, to enable a similar pun in English as there is in Latin when the abbreviation is resolved.—The Latin expansion of the abbreviation constitutes an iambic senarius.

F 21 Cicero, *On the Orator*

[CAESAR STRABO:] There also those statements that, in order to make something smaller or greater, are exaggerated up to incredible astonishment, such as your statement, Crassus, in a speech before the People: that Memmius thought himself so great an individual that, on his way down into the Forum, he lowered his head in order

mium, ut in forum descendens caput ad fornicem Fabia-
num demitteret.

On Lex Servilia (F 22–26)

In 106 BC Crassus supported a bill of the consul Q. Ser-
vilius Caepio (62), proposing that the law courts should
again be composed of senators rather than of knights or

F 22 Cic. *Brut.* 161

"omnibus quidem aliis," inquam [CICERO], "in magistra-
tibus, sed tribunus anno post fuit eoque in rostris sedente
suasit Serviliam legem Crassus . . . . sed haec Crassi cum
edita oratio est, quam te saepe legisse certo scio, quattuor
et triginta tum habebat annos totidemque annis mihi aetate praestabat. his enim consulibus eam legem suasit quibus nati sumus, cum ipse esset Q. Caepione consule natus
et C. Laelio, triennio ipso minor quam Antonius. . . ."

F 23 Cic. *Brut.* 164

et ego [CICERO]: "mihi quidem a pueritia quasi magistra
fuit," inquam, "illa in legem Caepionis oratio; in qua et
auctoritas ornatur senatus, quo pro ordine illa dicuntur, et
invidia concitatur in iudicum et in accusatorum factionem,
contra quorum potentiam populariter tum dicendum fuit.
multa in illa oratione graviter, multa leniter, multa aspere,

to pass under the Arch of Fabius [built by Q. Fabius Maximus Allobrogicus (**49**) in 121 BC].

On Lex Servilia (*F 22–26*)

senators and knights (Tac. Ann. *12.60.3; Iul. Obs. 41;* Lex Servilia iudiciaria: LPPR, *p. 325).*

F 22 Cicero, *Brutus*

"In all other offices indeed [Scaevola was Crassus' colleague]," I [CICERO] said, "but he [Q. Mucius Scaevola (**67**)] was Tribune a year later [106 BC], and while he was sitting on the Rostra as presiding officer, Crassus argued in favor of the *Lex Servilia* . . . But when this speech of Crassus, which I know for certain you have often read, was published, he was thirty-four years old and by as many years more advanced in age than me. For he argued in favor of that law under those consuls in whose consulship I was born [106 BC], while he himself was born in the consulship of Q. Caepio and C. Laelius [140 BC]; [he was] three years younger than Antonius. . . ."

F 23 Cicero, *Brutus*

And I [CICERO] said: "For me at any rate, from my boyhood, that speech on the law of Caepio was some sort of textbook: in it the dignity of the Senate is adorned, as these things are said on behalf of that order, and hatred is roused toward the party of the judges and the prosecutors, against whose influence it was then necessary to speak in a manner appealing to the People. In that speech much was said

443

multa facete dicta sunt; plura etiam dicta quam scripta, quod ex quibusdam capitibus expositis nec explicatis intellegi potest. . . ."

F 24 Cic. *De or.* 1.225

[Antonius:] quod si ea probarentur in populis atque in civitatibus, quis tibi, Crasse, concessisset clarissimo viro et amplissimo, principi civitatis, ut illa diceres in maxima contione tuorum civium quae dixisti? "eripite nos ex miseriis, eripite ex faucibus eorum, quorum crudelitas nostro sanguine non potest expleri; nolite sinere nos cuiquam servire nisi vobis universis, quibus et possumus et debemus." omitto "miserias" in quibus, ut illi aiunt, vir fortis esse non potest; omitto "fauces" ex quibus te eripi vis, ne iudicio iniquo exsorbeatur sanguis tuus, quod sapienti negant accidere posse; "servire" vero non modo te, sed universum senatum, cuius tum causam agebas, ausus es dicere?

Cf. Cic. *Parad.* 41; *Rhet. Her.* 4.5.

F 25 Prisc., *GL* II, p. 428.16–19

ex quo impersonale est "miseret" et "miseretur." Lucius Crassus in legis Serviliae suasione: "neque me minus vestri quam mei miserebitur." nam a misereor, quod est deponens, nec inchoativum in o desinens nec impersonale posset nasci . . .

earnestly, much gently, much bitterly, much wittily; more was even said than written, as can be discerned from certain headings indicated and not developed. . . ."

F 24 Cicero, *On the Orator*

[ANTONIUS:] But if these [Plato's ideas on the ideal state] were approved among peoples and among communities, who would have allowed you, Crassus, a highly respected and very famous man, a political leader of the community, to say what you said at a very large meeting of your fellow citizens? "Deliver us out of our miseries, deliver us out of the jaws of those whose ferocity cannot be satisfied with our blood; do not let us be slaves to anyone except to all of you, whose slaves we both can and ought to be." I pass over "miseries," in which, as those men [philosophers] say, a brave man cannot be involved; I pass over "jaws," out of which you desire to be delivered, for fear of your blood being sucked out of you by an unjust judgment, a thing that they say cannot befall the wise man; but "to be slaves," did you dare to say that not yourself only, but the entire Senate, whose case you were then arguing, could be slaves?

F 25 Priscian

From this [the verb *misereo*, "I feel pity"] derives the impersonal form *miseret* and *miseretur* [active and passive]. Lucius Crassus in the speech in favor of the *Lex Servilia*: "and there will be a feeling of pity on my part no less for you [pl.] than for myself." For from *misereor*, which is a deponent, neither the inchoative ending in *-o* [*miseresco*] nor the impersonal can be derived . . .

445

F 26 Cic. *Orat.* 219

et quia non ‹ numero solum ›[1] numerosa oratio sed et compositione fit et genere, quod ante dictum est, concinnitatis
(compositione potest intellegi, cum ita structa verba sunt,
ut numerus non quaesitus sed ipse secutus esse videatur,
ut apud Crassum: "nam ubi lubido dominatur, innocentiae
leve praesidium est"; ordo enim verborum efficit numerum sine ulla aperta oratoris industria) . . .

1 numero solum *om. codd. plerique: pro vocab.* numerosa *habet unus cod. rec.*

Cf. Quint. *Inst.* 9.4.109.

On Behalf of Q. Servilius Caepio (F 27)

F 27 Cic. *Brut.* 162

[CICERO:] sed est etiam L. Crassi in consulatu pro Q.
Caepione † defensione iuncta †[1] non brevis ut laudatio, ut
oratio autem brevis . . .

1 defensiuncula *Lange, Krüger*: ‹laudatio cum› defensione
iuncta *Petersen*: defensio non brevis (*om.* iuncta) *Piderit*: defensio
cum laudatione iuncta *Castiglioni*: defensione ‹senatus› iuncta
Sydow: defensione iuncta ‹oratio› *Fuchs*

F 26 Cicero, *Orator*

And since rhythmical prose is created, not <only by rhythm>, but also by the arrangement [of words] and a kind of symmetry, as has been said before [Cic. *Orat.* 149] ("by arrangement" can be taken to mean: when the words are so placed that the rhythm seems not to be planned, but to come naturally, as in Crassus' phrase: "for where lust dominates, there is little protection for innocence";[1] for the order of the words produces a rhythm without any apparent effort on the part of the orator) . . .

[1] This phrase has been transmitted without attribution to any speech; because of its content it has been placed in this context.— Quintilian (*Inst.* 9.4.109) criticizes that the sentence ends like a pentameter. Cicero probably means that the sequence of long and short syllables combined with the natural word accent creates a rhythm.

On Behalf of Q. Servilius Caepio (F 27)

*The intervention on behalf of Q. Servilius Caepio (during Crassus' consulship) probably refers to the son (**85**) of the consul of 106 BC (TLRR 88).*

F 27 Cicero, *Brutus*

[CICERO:] But there is also extant from the consulship of L. Crassus a little defense speech[1] on behalf of Q. Caepio, not brief as an encomium, but brief as an oration . . .

[1] The text is uncertain; the translation is based on the conjecture *defensiuncula* (defended by Douglas 1966, *ad loc.*).

On Behalf of M'. Curius (F 28–33)

After his consulship in 95 BC (F 29), Crassus spoke on behalf of M'. Curius in the centumviral court in an inheritance case (Cic. De or. *1.180, 1.238, 1.242, 2.140–41, 2.220–21: F 45; Caec. 53; Top. 44; Quint.* Inst. *7.6.9–10), while Q. Mucius Scaevola (67 F 4–6) acted for the prosecution, supporting M. Coponius (TLRR 93): M'. Curius had been named as heir in case a posthumous son should*

F 28 Cic. *Caec.* 69

etenim ipse Crassus non ita causam apud centumviros egit ut contra iuris consultos diceret, sed ut hoc doceret, illud quod Scaevola defendebat, non esse iuris, et in eam rem non solum rationes adferret, sed etiam Q. Mucio, socero suo, multisque peritissimis hominibus auctoribus uteretur.

F 29 Cic. *Brut.* 144–45

[Cicero:] . . . sic in interpretando, in definiendo in explicanda aequitate nihil erat Crasso copiosius; idque cum saepe alias tum apud centumviros in M'. Curi causa cognitum est. [145] ita enim multa tum contra scriptum pro aequo et bono dixit, ut hominem acutissimum Q. Scaevolam et in iure, in quo illa causa vertebatur, paratissimum obrueret argumentorum exemplorumque copia; atque ita

On Behalf of M'. Curius (F 28–33)

die before coming of age, but such a son had never been born; therefore, M. Coponius laid claim to the inheritance. The disputed issue thus was whether M'. Curius could still be heir, in other words, whether the will's literal meaning or its apparent intention should be decisive (on these two views see Dugan 2012).

F 28 Cicero, *Pro Caecina*

For Crassus himself did not plead the case before the centumviral court in such a way so as to speak against the legal experts, but so as to demonstrate that the point that Scaevola [Q. Mucius Scaevola (**67**), F 4–6] was maintaining was not law; and for that purpose he not only put forward arguments, but also employed the authority of Q. Mucius [Q. Mucius Scaevola (**50**)], his father-in-law, and many very learned men.

F 29 Cicero, *Brutus*

[CICERO:] [continued from T 2] . . . so in interpreting, in defining, in explaining equity nothing was more resourceful than Crassus; and this could often be noticed on other occasions and particularly in the case of M'. Curius before the centumviral court. [145] For he [Crassus] then said so much on behalf of what is fair and right against the written word that he overwhelmed Q. Scaevola [Q. Mucius Scaevola (**67**), F 4–6], a very keen-witted man and very experienced in the law around which that case revolved, by the wealth of arguments and precedents. And that case was

449

tum ab his patronis aequalibus et iam consularibus causa
illa dicta est, cum uterque ex contraria parte ius civile
defenderet, ut eloquentium iuris peritissimus Crassus,
iuris peritorum eloquentissimus Scaevola putaretur.

F 30 Cic. *Brut.* 197–98

[CICERO:] at vero, ut contra Crassus ab adulescente delicato, qui in litore ambulans scalmum repperisset ob
eamque rem aedificare navem concupivisset, exorsus est,
similiter Scaevolam ex uno scalmo captionis centumvirale
iudicium hereditatis effecisse: hoc {in} ille initio, consecutis[1] multis eiusdem generis sententiis, delectavit animos-
que omnium qui aderant in hilaritatem a severitate tra-
duxit . . . deinde hoc voluisse eum, qui testamentum
fecisset, hoc sensisse, quoquo modo filius non esset, qui in
suam tutelam veniret, sive non natus sive ante mortuus,
Curius heres ut esset; ita scribere plerosque et id valere
et valuisse semper. haec et multa eius modi dicens fidem
faciebat . . . [198] deinde aequum bonum testamentorum
sententias voluntatesque tutatus est: quanta esset in verbis
captio cum in ceteris rebus tum in testamentis, si negle-
gerentur voluntates; quantam sibi potentiam Scaevola
adsumeret, si nemo auderet testamentum facere postea
nisi de illius sententia. haec cum graviter tum[2] ab exemplis

---

¹ hoc {in} ille initio *Madvig*: hoc in illo initio *codd.*: hoc {in}
ille *ed. princ.*   consecutis *vel* consecutus *codd.*: consecutus
ed. princ.   hocce ille initio, consecutis *Stangl*: hoc ille initio
. . . animos{que} . . . aderant et *Madvig*   ² tum *edd.*: cum
codd.

then argued in such a way by these two pleaders of like age and already of consular rank, while each upheld the civil law from opposite points of view, that Crassus was regarded as the best legal expert among the orators, Scaevola as the best orator among the legal experts [cf. **67 T** 1].

F 30 Cicero, *Brutus*

[CICERO:] Crassus, however, in rebuttal, began with a story of a self-indulgent young man, who, walking along the shore, had found a thole pin and because of that matter become eager to build a boat; in a similar manner, he argued, Scaevola [Q. Mucius Scaevola (**67**), F 4–6], from the basis of a single thole pin of fallacious argument had created a case of inheritance for the centumviral court. With this beginning, when many other comments of the same kind had followed, he delighted the minds of all present and turned them from seriousness to a mood of joyfulness . . . Thereupon [he said] that he who had made the will had wanted this, had had this intention: that, if there should be no son who had come of age in whichever way, irrespective of whether he was not born or had died before that time, Curius was to be the heir; that most people wrote their wills in this way, and that this was valid and had always been valid. Saying this and many other things of that kind, he won credence . . . [198] He then defended right and equity, the meaning and intentions of wills: how many snares lay in words, with respect to other things and particularly in wills, if intentions were ignored; what great power Scaevola was assuming for himself if no one hereafter should venture to make a will unless with his approval. Setting forth all this, with earnestness and

copiose, tum varie, tum etiam ridicule et facete[3] explicans
eam admirationem adsensionemque commovit, dixisse ut
contra nemo videretur; . . .

3 facete *edd.*: facile *codd.*

Cf. Cic. *Inv. rhet.* 2.122.

F 31   Cic. *De or.* 1.243

[ANTONIUS:] ac mea quidem sententia—frequens enim te
audivi atque adfui—multo maiorem partem sententiarum
sale tuo et lepore et politissimis facetiis pellexisti, cum et
illud nimium acumen inluderes et admirarere ingenium
Scaevolae, qui excogitasset nasci prius oportere quam
emori; cumque multa conligeres et ex legibus et ex senatus
consultis et ex vita ac sermone communi non modo acute,
sed etiam ridicule et facete, ubi si verba, non rem seque-
remur, confici nihil posset. itaque hilaritatis plenum iudicium ac laetitiae fuit; in quo quid tibi iuris civilis exercita-
tio profuerit non intellego; dicendi vis egregia summa
festivitate et venustate coniuncta profuit.

F 32   Cic. *Brut.* 256

[CICERO:] "at prodest plus imperator." quis negat? sed
tamen . . . malim mihi L. Crassi unam pro M'. Curio dic-

especially with abundant illustration, with variety, even
with humor and pleasantry, he aroused such admiration
and assent that nobody seemed to have spoken on the
other side . . .

F 31 Cicero, *On the Orator*

[Antonius:] And in my opinion, at any rate—for I often
heard you and was present—you [Crassus] have coaxed by
far the greater part of the verdicts by your wit and charm
and highly refined pleasantries, while you were both
mocking that oversubtlety of Scaevola's [Q. Mucius Scaevola (**67**)] and marveling at his cleverness as he had worked
out that it was necessary to be born before dying; and
while you were adducing numerous examples from laws
and from decrees of the Senate and from everyday life and
conversation, not only shrewdly, but also amusingly and
wittily, where nothing could be achieved if we followed the
letter, not the spirit. Thus the court was filled with gaiety
and joy; of what use your proficiency in the civil law was
to you in that I do not understand; your surpassing power
of eloquence, combined with consummate cheerfulness
and grace, was of use.

F 32 Cicero, *Brutus*

[Cicero:] "But a military leader is of more use [i.e., than
a great orator]." [comment by a fictitious interlocutor]
Who denies it? But still . . . I should choose for myself
rather the single speech of L. Crassus on behalf of M'.
Curius than two triumphs over outposts. "But the capture

tionem quam castellanos triumphos duo. "at plus interfuit rei publicae castellum capi Ligurum quam bene defendi causam M'. Curi."

F 33 Cic. *De or.* 2.24

[CRASSUS:] itaque illud ego, quod in causa Curiana Scae-volae dixi, non dixi secus ac sentiebam: "nam si" inquam "Scaevola, nullum erit testamentum recte factum nisi quod tu scripseris, omnes ad te cives cum tabulis venie-mus, omnium testamenta tu scribes unus. quid igitur?" inquam "quando ages negotium publicum? quando ami-corum? quando tuum? quando denique nihil ages?" tum illud addidi: "mihi enim liber esse non videtur qui non aliquando nihil agit."

Against Cn. Domitius Ahenobarbus as Censor
(F 34–40)

Because of the differences in character and way of life of the two censors of 92 BC, Crassus and his colleague Cn. Domitius Ahenobarbus clashed repeatedly. In this dispute Crassus gave a famous speech (F 34–36; CCMR, App. A:

F 34 Cic. *Brut.* 162–164

[CICERO:] . . . postrema censoris oratio, qua anno duode-quinquagesimo usus est. . . . [164] . . . ipsa illa censoria contra Cn. Domitium conlegam non est oratio, sed quasi

---

[1] This marker probably denotes the final item in an enumera-tion of noteworthy speeches by Crassus. Douglas (1966, *ad loc.*)

of an outpost of the Ligurians [a people in northern Italy, fighting against the Romans on several occasions in the 2nd and 1st cent. BC] was of more benefit for the Republic than a successful defense of the case of M'. Curius."

F 33 Cicero, *On the Orator*

[Crassus:] Therefore, as to that point that I made to Scaevola [Q. Mucius Scaevola (**67**)] in the case of Curius, I made it in no way differently from what I thought: "For if, Scaevola," I said, "no will is to be duly made, unless you have written it, all we citizens will come to you with tablets, you alone will write the wills of all. What then?" I said, "When will you conduct public affairs? When those of your friends? When your own? When, finally, will you do nothing?" Then I added the following: "For to my mind he is not a free man who does not sometimes do nothing."

Against Cn. Domitius Ahenobarbus as Censor
(F 34–40)

217); *other sources refer to comments in altercations that need not have consisted of set speeches and may refer to various occasions.*

F 34 Cicero, *Brutus*

[Cicero:] . . . finally,[1] his [Crassus'] speech as censor, which he delivered in his forty-eighth year [92 BC]. . . . [164] . . . That very speech of his censorship, against Cn.

suggests that it indicates the last speech Crassus published, as he delivered further speeches afterward.

capita rerum et orationis commentarium paulo plenius. nulla est enim altercatio clamoribus umquam habita maioribus.

F 35 Cic. *De or.* 2.227

[CAESAR STRABO:] nec enim contentio maior umquam fuit nec apud populum gravior oratio, quam huius contra collegam in censura nuper, neque lepore et festivitate conditior.

F 36 Cic. *De or.* 2.45

[ANTONIUS:] positis enim his rebus quas Crassus in illius orationis suae, quam contra collegam censor habuit, principio dixit: quae natura aut fortuna darentur hominibus in iis rebus se vinci posse animo aequo pati; quae ipsi sibi homines parare possent, in iis rebus se pati non posse vinci; qui laudabit quempiam, intelleget exponenda sibi esse fortunae bona.

F 37 Suet. *Nero* 2.2

in hunc dixit Licinius Crassus orator non esse mirandum, quod aeneam barbam haberet, cui os ferreum, cor plumbeum esset.

F 38 Plin. *HN* 17.1–4

sed prius mirari[1] succurrit, . . . in tanta deliciarum pretia

---

[1] mirari *edd.*: arari *codd.*

Domitius, his colleague, is not an oration, but basically headings of themes and a somewhat fuller outline of a speech. For no dispute was ever conducted amid greater shouting.

F 35 Cicero, *On the Orator*

[CAESAR STRABO:] For there was never a greater effort nor a speech more effective with the People than that of our friend here [Crassus] recently against his colleague in the censorship [92 BC], nor one better seasoned with charm and gaiety.

F 36 Cicero, *On the Orator*

[ANTONIUS:] For when one takes as an example those points that Crassus made in the opening of that famous speech of his that he delivered when censor against his colleague—that he could cheerfully bear to be defeated with respect to those items that are given to men by nature or chance; that he could not bear to be defeated with respect to those items that men may win for themselves—then he who will praise anyone will understand that he has to describe the gifts of fortune.

F 37 Suetonius, *Life of Nero*

About him [Domitius] the orator Licinius Crassus said that it was not surprising that he had a beard of bronze, he who had a face of iron and a heart of lead.

F 38 Pliny the Elder, *Natural History*

But it comes to mind first to wonder that [trees] . . . have come to such a value as articles of luxury, the most famous

venisse, clarissimo, ut equidem arbitror, exemplo L. Crassi
atque Cn. Domiti Ahenobarbi. [2] Crassus orator fuit in
primis nominis Romani. domus ei magnifica, sed aliquanto
praestantior in eodem Palatio Q. Catuli, qui Cimbros cum
C. Mario fudit, multo vero pulcherrima consensu omnium
aetate ea in colle Viminali C. Aquilli, equitis Romani cla-
rioris illa etiam quam iuris civilis scientia, cum tamen[2]
obiecta Crasso sua est. [3] nobilissimarum gentium ambo[3]
censuram post consulatus simul gessere anno conditae
urbis DCLXII frequentem iurgiis propter dissimilitudi-
nem morum. tum Cn. Domitius, ut erat vehemens natura,
praeterea accensus odio, quod ex aemulatione avidissi-
mum est, graviter increpuit tanti censorem habitare, |L̄X̄|
HS[4] pro domo eius identidem promittens, [4] et Crassus,
ut praesens ingenio semper, ut faceto lepore sollers, addi-
cere se respondit exceptis sex arboribus. ac ne uno quidem
denario, si adimerentur, emptam volente Domitio, Crassus: "utrumne igitur ego sum," inquit, "quaeso, Domiti,
exemplo gravis et ipsa mea censura notandus, qui domo,
quae mihi hereditate obvenit, comiter habitem, an tu, qui
sex arbores |L̄X̄|[5] aestimes?"

---

[2] tum tamen *dub. Mayhoff*   [3] Crassus est (*vel* est *om.*)
atque Domitius *codd.* (*post* ambo): *glossema cognovit et del. Ur-*
lichs   [4] |L̄X̄| HS *Mayhoff*: his *vel* tis *vel* is *codd.*: milia num-
morum *vel* sestertium milies *vel* sestertium sexagies *vel* H̄S̄ *vel* M̄
HS *edd.*   [5] |L̄X̄| *Mayhoff*: CX *vel om. codd.*: HS milies *vel*
sestertio sexagies (*ante* sex) *vel* H̄S̄ (*post* aestimes) *vel* M̄ *edd.*

instance, in my judgment at any rate, being that of L. Crassus and Cn. Domitius Ahenobarbus. [2] Crassus was an orator among the first of those at Rome. He owned a splendid mansion, but it was considerably surpassed by another, also on the Palatine Hill, belonging to Q. Catulus, who defeated the Cimbri [Germanic tribe] with C. Marius; but by far the finest [house] in that period was by universal agreement the one on the Viminal Hill belonging to C. Aquillius, a Roman knight, more famous for that property even than for his knowledge of civil law; nevertheless, Crassus was criticized for his [house]. [3] Both men [Crassus and Domitius], from families of the highest distinction, after their consulship, held the censorship together in the 662nd year since the founding of the city; it was filled with quarrels owing to their dissimilarity of character. Then Cn. Domitius, as he was of a hasty temper by nature, moreover inflamed by that hatred that is extremely sour as a result of rivalry, rebuked [Crassus] severely for living on such an expensive scale while censor, repeatedly declaring that he would give six million sesterces for his mansion. [4] And Crassus, as he always had a ready wit, as he was good at clever repartees, replied that he agreed to the deal, with the exception of six trees. When Domitius did not want to buy the place even for a single denarius if these were excluded, Crassus said: "Well then, tell me, pray, Domitius, am I the one who is setting a bad example and deserves a mark of censure from myself, I who live quite unpretentiously in the house that came to me by inheritance, or is it you, who price six trees at six million sesterces?"

F 39 Val. Max. 9.1.4

Cn. Domitius L. Crasso collegae suo altercatione orta obiecit quod columnas Hymettias in porticu domus haberet. quem continuo Crassus quanti ipse domum suam aestimaret interrogavit, atque ut respondit "sexagiens sestertio," "quanto[1] ergo eam" inquit, "minoris fore existimas, si decem arbusculas inde succidero?" "ipso triciens sestertio" Domitius. tunc Crassus: "uter igitur luxuriosior est, egone, qui decem columnas centum milibus nummum emi, an tu, qui decem arbuscularum umbram triciens sestertii[2] summa conpensas?"

[1] quanto *codd. det.*: quo *codd. rel.*   [2] sestertii *Kempf*: sextertium *codd.*: hs xxx *cod. epit.*: sestertium *codd. corr.*

F 40 Ael. *NA* 8.4

τὴν Κράσσου τε τοῦ Ῥωμαίου μύραιναν ᾄδουσιν, ἥπερ οὖν καὶ ἐνωτίοις καὶ ὁρμίσκοις διαλίθοις κεκόσμητο, οἷα δήπου ὡραία κόρη, καὶ καλοῦντος τοῦ Κράσσου τὸ φώνημα ἐγνώριζε, καὶ ἀνενήχετο, καὶ ὀρέγοντος ὁτιοῦν ἥδε ἤσθιε προθύμως καὶ ἑτοίμως λαμβάνουσα. ταύτην τοι καὶ ἔκλαυσεν ὁ Κράσσος, ὡς ἀκούω, τὸν βίον καταστρέψασαν, καὶ ἔθαψε. καί ποτε Δομετίου πρὸς αὐτὸν εἰπόντος "ὦ μῶρέ, μύραιναν ἔκλαυσας τεθνεῶσαν," ὁ δὲ ὑπολαβών, "ἐγὼ θηρίον," ἔφατο, "σὺ δὲ τρεῖς γυναῖκας θάψας οὐκ ἔκλαυσας."

F 39 Valerius Maximus, *Memorable Doings and Sayings*

After a dispute had started, Cn. Domitius reproached his colleague L. Crassus with having columns of Hymettian marble [from Mount Hymettus near Athens] in the portico of his house. Crassus immediately asked him how much he considered his [Crassus'] house to be worth, and when he replied "six million sesterces," he [Crassus] said: "Well then, how much less do you think it will be worth if I cut down ten little trees from there?" "Just three million," [said] Domitius. Then Crassus [said]: "So, which of us is the more extravagant, I who bought ten columns for a hundred thousand sesterces or you who balance the shade of ten small trees with the sum of three million sesterces?"

F 40 Aelian, *Characteristics of Animals*

And they tell of the moray eel belonging to Crassus the Roman, which had been adorned with earrings and small necklaces set with jewels, just like some lovely maiden; and when Crassus called it, it would recognize his voice and come swimming up, and whatever he offered it, it would eagerly and promptly take and eat. When it died, then, Crassus, as I hear, even mourned for its life brought to an end and buried it. And on one occasion, when Domitius said to him "You fool, mourning for a dead moray eel," he [Crassus] took him up, saying: "I mourned for a fish, but you never mourned for the three wives you buried."

On L. Marcius Philippus in the Senate (F 41)

F 41 Cic. *De or.* 3.1–6

[CICERO:] nam illud immortalitate dignum ingenium, illa humanitas, illa virtus L. Crassi morte extincta subita est vix diebus decem post eum diem, qui hoc et superiore libro continetur. [2] ut enim Romam rediit, extremo ludorum scaenicorum die, vehementer commotus oratione ea, quae ferebatur habita esse in contione a Philippo, quem dixisse constabat videndum sibi aliud esse consilium; illo senatu se rem p(ublicam) gerere non posse, mane idibus Septembr(ibus) et ille et senatus frequens vocatu Drusi in curiam venit. ibi cum Drusus multa de Philippo questus esset, rettulit ad senatum de illo ipso, quod in eum ordinem consul tam¹ graviter in contione esset invectus. [3] hic, ut saepe inter homines sapientissimos constare vidi, quamquam hoc Crasso, cum aliquid accuratius dixisset, semper fere contigisset, ut numquam dixisse melius putaretur, tamen omnium consensu sic esse tum iudicatum, ceteros a Crasso semper omnis, illo autem die etiam ipsum

---

¹ tam *vel* tum *codd.*

On L. Marcius Philippus in the Senate (F 41)

Shortly before his death in 91 BC, Crassus delivered an impressive and passionate speech against the behavior and policies of consul L. Marcius Philippus (70) in the Senate.

F 41 Cicero, *On the Orator*

[CICERO:] For that genius so deserving of immortality, that humanity, that virtue of L. Crassus was extinguished by a sudden death just ten days after that day that is described in this and the preceding book. [2] For when he had returned to Rome, on the concluding day of the dramatic festival, deeply moved by that speech that was reported to have been delivered at a meeting of the People by Philippus [L. Marcius Philippus (70)] (who was known to have said that he would have to look for another council, that with the present Senate he was not able to carry on governing), on the morning of the Ides of September [September 13], at the summons of Drusus [M. Livius Drusus (72)], he and many senators came to the Senate house. There, after Drusus had complained much about Philippus [72 F 7], he [Crassus] raised for discussion in the Senate that very issue, namely that a consul had delivered such a violent attack upon this order at a meeting of the People. [3] Hereupon, as I have frequently seen very wise men agree, although, whenever Crassus had delivered anything rather carefully prepared, it had almost always happened that he was believed never to have spoken better, nevertheless, the verdict according to the unanimous view of all then was that all others had always been surpassed by Crassus, but on that day he was even sur-

a se ‹es›se[2] superatum. deploravit enim casum atque orbi-
tatem senatus, cuius ordinis a consule, qui quasi parens
bonus aut tutor fidelis esse deberet, tamquam ab aliquo
nefario praedone diriperetur patrimonium dignitatis; neque vero esse mirandum, si, cum suis consiliis rem
p(ublicam) profligasset, consilium senatus a re p(ublica)
repudiaret. [4] hic cum homini et vehementi et diserto et
in primis forti ad resistendum Philippo quasi quasdam
verborum faces admovisset, non tulit ille et graviter exarsit pigneribusque ablatis[3] Crassum instituit coercere. quo
quidem ipso in loco multa a Crasso divinitus dicta esse
ferebantur,[4] cum sibi illum consulem esse negaret, cui
senator ipse non esset. "an tu, cum omnem auctoritatem
universi ordinis pro pignore putaris eamque in conspectu
populi R(omani) concideris, me his existimas pigneribus
posse terreri? non tibi illa sunt caedenda, si L. Crassum
vis coercere; haec tibi est excidenda lingua, qua vel evolsa
spiritu ipso libidinem tuam libertas mea refutabit." [5]
permulta tum vehementissima contentione animi, ingenii,
virium ab eo dicta esse constabat, sententiamque eam,
quam senatus frequens secutus est, ornatissimis et gravissimis verbis, ut populo R(omano) satis fieret, numquam
senatus neque consilium rei publicae neque fidem defuisse, ab eo dictam, et eundem, id quod in auctoritatibus

---

[2] se ‹es›se *Kumaniecki*: sese *vel* se *codd.*   [3] ablatis *ed.*
Rom. 1469: allatis *codd.*   [4] esse ferebantur *Lambinus*: effe-
rabantur *codd.*: ferebantur *vel* afferebantur *codd. rec.*

passed by himself. For he deplored the bad fortune and the bereavement of the Senate when the inherited dignity of that order was pulled to pieces by a consul, who should be like a good parent or a faithful guardian, as if by some wicked brigand; but that nevertheless it was not a surprise if, after he had crushed the Republic by his policies, he endeavored to oust the counsel of the Senate from public affairs. [4] When he had applied some torches of words, as it were, to Philippus, a headstrong and eloquent man and particularly courageous at resistance, the latter could not bear it and flared up violently and took steps to coerce Crassus by seizing a pledge.[1] At this very point, it was reported, many things were said divinely by Crassus, when he denied that the man for whom he himself was not a senator was a consul for him. "What, when you have regarded all the authority of the entire order as a pledge and destroyed it in the sight of the Roman People, do you imagine that I could be terrified by these pledges? You must not destroy those pledges if you wish to coerce L. Crassus: you must cut out this tongue; even when this has been torn out, my liberty will refute your license just with my breath." [5] Very many things with the strongest energy of spirit, intellect, and force were then said by him, as was universally agreed, and that motion was put forward by him, which the quorate Senate approved, in most polished and most dignified terms, namely that, in order to pay sufficient attention to the Roman People, neither the Senate's advice for the Republic nor its loyalty had ever been lacking; and he personally was present when it was

---

[1] Assets could be seized as security for payments, as a step in imposing a fine, or as elements of magisterial coercion.

perscriptis exstat, scribendo adfuisse. [6] illa tamquam cycnea fuit divini hominis vox et oratio, quam quasi expectantes post eius interitum veniebamus in curiam, ut vestigium illud ipsum, in quo ille postremum institisset, contueremur. namque tum latus ei dicenti condoluisse sudoremque multum consecutum esse audiebamus; ex quo cum cohorruisset, cum febri domum rediit dieque septimo est lateris dolore consumptus.

Cf. Quint. *Inst.* 8.3.89, 11.1.37; Val. Max. 6.2.2.

On Behalf of C. Sergius Orata Against M. Marius Gratidianus (F 42)

F 42 Cic. *De or.* 1.178

[CRASSUS:] quid? nuper, cum ego C. Sergi Oratae[1] contra hunc nostrum Antonium iudicio privato causam defenderem, nonne omnis nostra in iure versata defensio est? cum enim M. Marius Gratidianus aedis Oratae vendidisset neque servire quandam earum aedium partem in mancipi lege dixisset, defendebamus, quicquid fuisset incommodi in mancipio, id si venditor scisset neque declarasset, praestare debere.

[1] Sergi *vel* Sergii *codd.*   Oratae *unus cod. corr., codd. rec.*: Auratae *codd.*

written down, as it appears in the resolutions recorded. [6]
That oration and utterance was the swan song of the divine
man, as it were, which we almost expected to hear when
we used to come into the Senate house after his death in
order to gaze upon that spot in which he had stood for the
last time. For while speaking on that occasion, we used to
be told, he was seized with a violent pain in the side, followed by profuse perspiration; then, after he had trembled
all over, he returned home with a fever and on the seventh
day was carried off by pleurisy.

On Behalf of C. Sergius Orata Against M. Marius Gratidianus (F 42)

*In the case of C. Sergius Orata (RE Sergius 33; cf. F 48)
against M. Marius Gratidianus, son of M. Gratidius (**54**),
Crassus spoke on behalf of C. Sergius Orata while M. Antonius (**65** F 33) represented the other side (TLRR 362).*

F 42 Cicero, *On the Orator*

[CRASSUS:] What? Recently, when I defended the case of
C. Sergius Orata in a private trial against our Antonius
here [M. Antonius (**65**)], was not our entire defense based
on law? For since M. Marius Gratidianus had sold a house
to Orata and had not declared in the conditions of sale that
a certain part of that building was subject to an easement,
we maintained that the vendor must make good any defect
in the property sold, if he had known of this and not disclosed it.

On Behalf of C. Visellius Aculeo (F 43–44)

*C. Visellius Aculeo, an acquaintance of Crassus and a man
learned in the law (Cic. De or. 1.191, 2.2; Brut. 164), was
supported by Crassus when he was prosecuted by M.*

F 43 Cic. *De or.* 2.269

[CAESAR STRABO:] urbana etiam dissimulatio est, cum
alia dicuntur ac sentias, non illo genere, de quo ante dixi,
cum contraria dicas, ut Lamiae Crassus, sed . . .

F 44 Cic. *De or.* 2.262

[CAESAR STRABO:] invertuntur autem verba, ut Crassus
apud M. Perpernam[1] iudicem pro Aculeone cum diceret,
aderat contra Aculeonem Gratidiano[2] L. Aelius Lamia,[3]
deformis, ut nostis; qui cum interpellaret odiose, "audiamus" inquit "pulchellum puerum" Crassus; cum esset
adrisum, "non potui mihi" inquit Lamia "formam ipse fin-
gere, ingenium potui." tum hic "audiamus" inquit "disertum." multo etiam adrisum est vehementius.

1 Perpernam *codd. rec.*: Perpennam *codd.*   2 Gratidiano
vel Gratidano *codd.*   3 Aelius *Pighi*: Helvius *codd.*   Lamia
vel Lania *codd.*

On Behalf of C. Plancus (F 45–47)

On Behalf of C. Visellius Aculeo (F 43–44)

Marius Gratidianus and his advocate L. Aelius Lamia
(TLRR 366).

F 43 Cicero, *On the Orator*

[CAESAR STRABO:] There is also pleasurable irony, when
something is said other than what you think, not in that
way about which I spoke earlier, when you say the opposite, as Crassus did to Lamia [L. Aelius Lamia], but . . .

F 44 Cicero, *On the Orator*

[CAESAR STRABO:] And words are ironically inverted just
as, when Crassus spoke on behalf of Aculeo before M.
Perperna as judge, L. Aelius Lamia, a misshapen person,
as you know, supported Gratidianus against Aculeo; when
he kept on interrupting in an annoying way, Crassus said:
"Let us hear the beautiful little boy." When the laughter
had subsided, Lamia said: "I could not form my bodily
shape myself; my talent I could." Thereupon Crassus said:
"Let us hear the eloquent speaker." The laughter was even
far more uproarious.

On Behalf of C. Plancus (F 45–47)

Crassus defended C. Plancus (different versions of name
transmitted) against M. Iunius Brutus (**56** F 3–5) (TLRR
98; Quint. Inst. 6.3.43–44).

F 45 Cic. *De or.* 2.220–26

[CAESAR STRABO:] quid in omni oratione Crassus vel
apud centumviros contra Scaevolam vel contra accusa-
torem Brutum, cum pro C. Planco diceret?[1] . . . [222] . . .
sic in Bruto quem oderat et quem dignum contumelia
iudicabat, utroque genere pugnavit. [223] quam multa de
balneis, quas nuper ille vendiderat, quam multa de amisso
patrimonio dixit! atque illa brevia, cum ille diceret se sine
causa sudare: "minime mirum" inquit, "modo enim existi
de balneis"—innumerabilia huiuscemodi fuerunt,[2] sed
non minus iucunda illa perpetua. cum enim Brutus duo
lectores excitasset et alteri De colonia Narbonensi Crassi
orationem legendam dedisset, alteri De lege Servilia et
cum contraria inter sese de re publica capita contulisset,
noster hic facetissime tris patris Bruti de iure civili libellos
tribus legendos dedit. [224] ex libro primo: "forte evenit
ut in Privernati essemus." "Brute, testificatur pater se tibi
Privernatem fundum reliquisse." deinde ex libro secundo:
"in Albano eramus ego et Marcus filius." "sapiens videlicet
homo cum primis nostrae civitatis norat hunc gurgitem;
metuebat ne, cum is nihil haberet, nihil esse ei relictum

---

[1] C. Planco diceret *una familia codd.*: *om. altera*   C.
Planco *codd.*: Cn. Plancio *"ex paucis codd. et edd." Ellendt, Wil-*
kins: Cn. Planco *edd. recc.*   [2] huiuscemodi fuerunt *vel* fuerunt *codd.*: fuerunt eiusmodi *ed. Rom. 1469*: talia fuerunt *Halm,*
Firmani, Sutton: alia fuerunt *Reid*

F 45 Cicero, *On the Orator*

[CAESAR STRABO:] What [help from the art of rhetoric could] Crassus [have had], in every speech, be it before the centumviral court [F 28–33] against Scaevola [Q. Mucius Scaevola (**67**), F 4–6], be it against the prosecutor Brutus [M. Iunius Brutus (**56**), F 3–5], when he spoke on behalf of C. Plancus? . . . [222] . . . thus, in the case of Brutus, whom he hated and whom he deemed deserving of invective, he fought with both modes [of humor; cf. T 7]. [223] How much he said about the baths, which the other had recently sold, how much about his wasted inheritance! And those brief remarks, when the other [Brutus] said that he was sweating without any reason, he said: "Not at all surprising; for you have just come from the baths." There were countless comments of this kind, but the continuous vein was no less pleasing. For when Brutus had summoned two readers and handed one of them Crassus' speech on the colony at Narbo [F 15–17] to read out and the other the one on the *Lex Servilia* [F 22–26], and when he had juxtaposed contradictory passages on the political situation, our friend here most humorously delivered to three people for reading out three pamphlets by Brutus' father, on civil law. [224] From the first book: "It chanced that we were on an estate at Privernum." [His comment was:] "Brutus, your father bears witness that he has bequeathed you an estate at Privernum." Next, from the second book: "I and my son Marcus were on an estate at Alba." [His comment was:] "See how a man among the shrewdest in our community had realized the nature of this devouring whirlpool; he was afraid that, when he [the son] had nothing left, it might be thought that nothing had

471

putaretur." tum ex libro tertio . . . "in Tiburti forte adsedimus ego et M. filius." "ubi sunt hi fundi, Brute, quos tibi pater publicis commentariis consignatos reliquit? quod nisi puberem te, inquit, iam haberet, quartum librum composuisset et se etiam in balneis locutum cum filio scriptum reliquisset." [225] quis est igitur qui non fateatur hoc lepore atque his facetiis non minus refutatum esse Brutum quam illis tragoediis quas egit idem, cum casu in eadem causa {cum} funere efferretur[3] anus Iunia. pro di immortales, quae fuit illa, quanta vis! quam inexpectata! quam repentina! cum coniectis oculis, gestu omni ei[4] imminenti, summa gravitate et celeritate verborum: "Brute, quid sedes? quid illam anum patri nuntiare vis tuo? quid illis omnibus quorum imagines vides duci? quid maioribus tuis? quid L. Bruto, qui hunc populum dominatu regio liberavit? quid te agere? cui rei, cui gloriae, cui virtuti studere? patrimonione augendo? at id non est nobilitatis. sed fac esse, nihil superest; libidines totum dissipaverunt. [226] an iuri[5] civili? est paternum. sed dicet te, cum aedis venderes, ne in rutis quidem et caesis solium tibi paternum recepisse. an rei militari? qui numquam castra videris! an eloquentiae? quae neque est in te et, quicquid est vocis ac linguae, omne in istum turpissimum calumniae

---

[3] cum funere *una familia codd.*: *om. altera*: cum *del. Kumaniecki*   efferretur *unus cod. rec., edd.*: ferretur *codd.*   [4] ei *Piderit*: et *una familia codd.*: *om. altera*   [5] iuri *codd. rec.*: iure *vel* in iure *codd.*

---

[1] Minerals already quarried and timber already felled at the time of the sale could be kept by the vendor of an estate (for the technical term see *OLD* s.v. *ruo* 9).

been bequeathed to him." Finally, from the third book . . .
"I and my son Marcus happened to sit down together on
an estate at Tibur." [His comment was:] "Where are these
estates, Brutus, which your father registered in his public
memoirs as bequeathed to you? Had he not already had
you as an adult, he would have put together a fourth book
and left it in writing that he had also spoken with his son
at the baths!" [225] Who, then, is there who would not
admit that Brutus was refuted by this pleasantry and these
witticisms no less than those tragic histrionics that the
same man carried out when, during the same trial, it happened that the aged Iunia was carried forth in funeral
procession? By the immortal gods, what force was that and
how much of it! How unexpected! How sudden! When,
with piercing gaze, with every motion threatening him, in
the severest tone, and in a torrent of words he said: "Brutus, why are you seated? What news would you like that
old lady carry to your father? What to all those whose busts
you see borne along? What to your ancestors? What to L.
Brutus, who freed this community from the tyranny of the
kings? That you are doing what? What affairs, what glorious deeds, what worthy ends you are busy with? Increasing your inheritance? But that is not something for the
nobility. Yet assuming it were, nothing is left; lust has
squandered everything. [226] Or civil law? It is your father's interest. But she will say that, when you sold the
house, you did not even retain the paternal armchair for
yourself, along with the quarried minerals and felled timber.[1] Or a military career? You who have never seen a
camp! Or eloquence? There is nothing of it in you, and
whatever power of intonation and language there is, you
have applied it all to that foulest way of making money,

473

quaestum contulisti! tu lucem aspicere audes? tu hos in-
tueri? tu in foro, tu in urbe, tu in civium esse conspectu?
tu illam mortuam, tu imagines ipsas non perhorrescis?
quibus non modo imitandis sed ne conlocandis quidem
tibi locum ullum reliquisti."

F 46 Cic. *Clu.* 140–41

. . . hominis eloquentissimi et sapientissimi, L. Crassi . . .
qui, cum C.[1] Plancum defenderet, accusante M. Bruto,
homine in dicendo vehementi et callido, cum Brutus duobus recitatoribus constitutis ex duabus eius orationibus
capita alterna inter se contraria recitanda curasset, quod
in dissuasione rogationis eius quae contra coloniam Nar-
bonensem ferebatur quantum potest de auctoritate senatus detrahit, in suasione legis Serviliae summis ornat senatum laudibus, et multa in equites Romanos cum ex ea
oratione asperius dicta recitasset quo animi illorum iudicum in Crassum incenderentur, aliquantum esse commotus dicitur. [141] itaque in respondendo primum exposuit
utriusque rationem temporis ut oratio ex re et ex causa
habita videretur, deinde ut intellegere posset Brutus
quem hominem et non solum qua eloquentia verum etiam
quo lepore et quibus facetiis praeditum lacessisset, tris
ipse excitavit recitatores cum singulis libellis quos M. Brutus, pater illius accusatoris, de iure civili reliquit. eorum

[1] C. *vel* L. *codd.*: C. Cic. *De or.* 2.220 (F 45), Quint. *Inst.*
6.3.43

namely making false accusations! Dare you look upon the
light of day? Or gaze on these men? Or show yourself in
the Forum, in the city, in the sight of the citizens? Don't
you tremble exceedingly at that dead lady, at those very
busts? Not only for emulating them, but even for setting
them up you have left yourself no room."

F 46 Cicero, *Pro Cluentio*

. . . of the very eloquent and very learned man, L. Crassus,
. . . when he [Crassus] was defending C. Plancus, with M.
Brutus [M. Iunius Brutus (**56**), F 3–5], a man forceful and
skillful in speaking, as prosecutor, when Brutus put forward two readers and had them read in turn contradictory
passages taken from two of the other's speeches, since in
the speech against the bill that was proposed against a
colony at Narbo he disparaged the authority of the Senate
as much as he could [F 15–17] while in the speech in support of the *Lex Servilia* he praised the Senate in the highest terms [F 22–26], when from that speech he [Brutus]
had many bitter attacks upon the Roman knights read out,
so as to inflame the minds of those judges against Crassus,
he [Crassus] is said to have been discomforted not a little.
[141] Accordingly, in his reply, he first explained the re-
quirements of either occasion, so that each speech was
seen to have been delivered according to the facts and to
the case; next, so that Brutus could understand what kind
of man he had provoked, and how gifted not only with
eloquence, but also with wit and humor, he in his turn
called forth three readers, each with one of the books on
civil law that M. Brutus, the father of that prosecutor, had
left. When their beginnings were recited, which I suppose

initia cum recitarentur, ea quae vobis nota esse arbitror: "forte evenit ut ruri in Privernati[2] essemus ego et Brutus[3] filius," fundum Privernatem flagitabat; "in Albano eramus ego et Brutus filius," Albanum poscebat; "in Tiburti forte cum adsedissemus[4] ego et Brutus filius," Tiburtem fundum requirebat; Brutum autem, hominem sapientem, quod fili nequitiam videret, quae praedia ei relinqueret testificari voluisse dicebat. quod si potuisset honeste scribere se in balneis cum id aetatis filio fuisse, non praeterisset; eas se tamen ab eo balneas non ex libris patris sed ex tabulis et ex censu quaerere. Crassus tum ita Brutum ultus est ut illum recitationis suae paeniteret . . .

[2] Privernati *Cic. De or., Quint. Inst.*: Privernate *nonnulli codd.* [3] Marcus *Cic. De or. (ita mox)* [4] adsedimus *Cic. De or.*

F 47 Cic. *De or.* 2.242

[CAESAR STRABO:] in re est item ridiculum, quod ex quadam depravata imitatione sumi solet, ut idem Crassus: "per tuam nobilitatem, per vestram familiam!" quid aliud fuit, in quo contio rideret, nisi illa voltus et vocis imitatio? "per tuas statuas!" vero cum dixit et extento bracchio paulum etiam de gestu addidit, vehementius risimus.

are known to you: "It happened that we were at my country place at Privernum, I and my son Brutus," he asked after the estate at Privernum; "we were at the place at Alba, I and my son Brutus," he inquired after the one at Alba; "when we happened to be sitting at the place at Tibur, I and my son Brutus," he asked after the estate at Tibur. And he said that Brutus, a wise man, since he saw his son's profligacy, had wanted to leave a record of what property he was bequeathing to him. Had he been able to write with propriety that he had been in the baths with a son of that age, he would not have omitted it; he said that, nevertheless, he was asking him about these baths not on the basis of his father's books, but of the accounts and the censor's register. Thus did Crassus then avenge himself on Brutus, to make him sorry for what he had read out . . .

F 47 Cicero, *On the Orator*

[CAESAR STRABO:] In facts there can equally be something funny; it is generally derived from some mimicry as caricature, as in this example of the same Crassus: "By your rank, by your lineage!" What else was there at which the assembly laughed, other than that mimicry of facial expression and intonation? "By your statues!" But when he said this and added even a touch of gesture with his arm stretched out, we laughed more heartily.[1]

[1] This fragment is not assigned to a particular speech in the source; the attribution has been suggested because of the excerpt's tone and style. As there is a reference to a *contio* and no mention of a trial, the allocation is uncertain.

On Behalf of C. Sergius Orata Against
Considius (F 48)

F 48 Val. Max. 9.1.1

C. Sergius Orata . . . aedificiis etiam spatiosis et excelsis deserta ad id tempus ora Lucrini lacus pressit, quo recentiore usu conchyliorum frueretur: ubi dum se publicae aquae cupidius immergit, cum Considio publicano iudicium nanctus est. in quo L. Crassus, adversus illum causam agens, errare amicum suum Considium dixit, quod putaret Oratam remotum a lacu cariturum ostreis: namque ea, si inde petere non licuisset, in tegulis reperturum.

To a Witness in the Case of Piso (F 49)

F 49 Cic. *De or.* 2.285

[CAESAR STRABO:] ab hoc vero Crasso nihil facetius; cum laesisset testis Silus Pisonem, quod se in eum audisse

On Behalf of C. Sergius Orata Against Considius (F 48)

Crassus (again) defended C. Sergius Orata (cf. F 42) against Considius, who had charged him with using public water on his private estate (TLRR 365).

F 48 Valerius Maximus, *Memorable Doings and Sayings*

C. Sergius Orata . . . He also loaded the mouth of the Lucrine Lake, deserted up to that time, with spacious and lofty buildings, so as to enjoy a fresher catch of the shellfish. When he plunged himself too greedily into public water there, he ended up with a lawsuit with the contractor Considius. In that L. Crassus, who was pleading the case against the latter, said that his friend Considius was mistaken in thinking that Orata would have no oysters if he were away from the lake; for if he could not get them from there, he would find them among the roof tiles!

To a Witness in the Case of Piso (F 49)

The case of Piso, presumably L. Calpurnius Piso Caesoninus (cos. 112 BC), seems to have been a case of extortion; the information preserved describes the reaction to a witness statement (TLRR 48).

F 49 Cicero, *On the Orator*

[CAESAR STRABO:] From this point of view [effects created by remarks against expectation], however, nothing could be wittier than Crassus; when a witness called Silus had done damage to Piso [i.e., Piso's case], since he [Silus]

479

dixisset: "potest fieri," inquit "Sile, ut is, unde te audisse dicis, iratus dixerit." adnuit Silus. "potest etiam, ut tu non recte intellexeris." id quoque toto capite adnuit, ut se Crasso daret. "potest etiam fieri" inquit "ut omnino, quod te audisse dicis, numquam audieris." hoc ita praeter expectationem accidit, ut testem omnium risus obrueret.

Testimony Against M. Marcellus (F 50)

F 50 Val. Max. 8.5.3

L. quoque Crassus, tantus apud iudices quantus apud patres conscriptos Aemilius Scaurus . . . cum vehementissimum testimonii fulmen in M. Marcellum reum iniecisset, impetu gravis exitu vanus apparuit.

Unplaced Fragments (F 51–52)

F 51 + 52 Cic. *Orat.* 222–23

sin membratim volumus dicere, insistimus atque,[1] cum opus est, ab isto cursu invidioso facile nos et saepe diiun-

---

[1] atque *Stangl*: idque *codd.*

had said that he had heard something against him [Piso], he said: "It may be the case, Silus, that the person whom you say you heard was speaking in anger." Silus nodded assent. "It is also possible that you did not understand him correctly." To this also Silus nodded emphatic assent, so as to show himself obliging to Crassus. "It may also be the case," he said, "that what you say you heard you never heard." This happened so against expectation that the laughter of all overwhelmed the witness.

Testimony Against M. Marcellus (F 50)

The M. Marcellus against whom Crassus gave testimony (Cic. Font. 24) may have been the legate of C. Marius in 102 BC, M. Claudius Marcellus (TLRR 87).

F 50 Valerius Maximus, *Memorable Doings and Sayings*

L. Crassus too, as great among the judges as Aemilius Scaurus [M. Aemilius Scaurus (**43**)] among the senators . . . when he had launched a very violent thunderbolt of testimony against the defendant M. Marcellus, he turned out to be heavy in the onslaught, flimsy in the outcome.

Unplaced Fragments (F 51–52)

F 51 + 52 Cicero, *Orator*

But if we wish to speak in a sequence of *cola* [i.e., not periods], we stop, and, when necessary, turn away easily and frequently from that offending course [i.e., fully rhythmical periods]. But nothing needs to be rhythmical

gimus. sed nihil tam debet esse numerosum quam hoc quod minime apparet et valet plurimum. ex hoc genere illud est Crassi: "missos faciant patronos; ipsi prodeant." nisi intervallo dixisset "ipsi prodeant," sensisset profecto se fudisse[2] senarium. omnino melius caderet "prodeant ipsi"; sed de genere nunc disputo. [223] "cur clandestinis consiliis nos oppugnant? cur de profugis nostris copias comparant contra nos?" prima sunt illa duo, quae κόμματα Graeci vocant, nos incisa dicimus; deinde tertium—κῶλον illi, nos membrum—sequitur non longa—ex duobus enim versibus, id est membris, perfecta est—comprehensio[3] et in spondeos cadit. et Crassus quidem sic plerumque dicebat, idque ipse genus dicendi maxime probo.

[2] profecto se fudisse *codd. rec.*: profecto se fugisse *vel* profectos effugisse *vel* profecto effugisse *codd.*   [3] comprehensio est *codd.*: *transp. Lambinus*

Cf. Quint. *Inst.* 9.4.101; Ruf., *RLM*, p. 579.17–22.

67 Q. MUCIUS SCAEVOLA
PONTIFEX MAXIMUS

Q. Mucius Scaevola (ca. 140–82 BC; cos. 95 BC; RE Mucius 22) was a member of the pontifical college from about 115 BC and pontifex maximus *from about 89 BC (hence the epithet* pontifex maximus *to distinguish him from namesakes). In 97 BC he was proconsul in Asia and ad-*

as much as this that appears so to a very slight extent and has the greatest effect. Of this kind is that phrase of Crassus: "they shall send their pleaders away; they themselves shall come forward." If he had not said "they themselves shall come forward" after a brief pause, he would indeed have recognized that he had pronounced a senarius. On the whole, "they shall come forward themselves" [reverse word order] would give a better clausula; but I am speaking of general principles now. [223] "Why do they attack us with secret plans? Why do they prepare troops of our fugitives against us?"[1] The first two [pieces][2] are what the Greeks call *commata*, we term *incisa*; then, as the third item—they call it *colon*, we *membrum*—there comes a brief period—for it consists of two verses, that is *membra*, and ends in a spondaic clausula.[3] And Crassus indeed mostly spoke in this style, and that style of speaking I myself chiefly favor.

[1] Whether this phrase is also a quotation from Crassus is not made explicit, though it is probable on the basis of the context.   [2] That is, "they shall . . . away; they . . . come forward."   [3] That is, "Why do they attack . . . ? Why do they . . . against us?"

67 Q. MUCIUS SCAEVOLA
PONTIFEX MAXIMUS

ministered the province in an exemplary manner (Val. Max. 8.15.6; Cic. Div. Caec. 57; Verr. 2.2.27, 2.2.34; on his life and works as well as the testimonia and fragments of his legal writings see Ferrary, Schiavone, and Stolfi 2018). In 95 BC Scaevola was consul with his contemporary L.

Licinius Crassus (66), to whom he was also compared with regard to his eloquence and legal knowledge (T 1–2; F 6; Quint. Inst. *12.3.9; Asc. in Cic.* Corn. *[p. 67.20–22 C.]; cf.* **50** *T 6). Scaevola was a legal expert and left a work in eighteen books about civil law (see Ferrary, Schiavone,*

T 1 Cic. *Brut.* 144–45

= F 4.

T 2 Cic. *Brut.* 148

hic ego [CICERO]: "noli," inquam, "Brute, existimare his duobus quicquam fuisse in nostra civitate praestantius. nam ut paulo ante dixi consultorum alterum disertissimum, disertorum alterum consultissimum fuisse, sic in reliquis rebus ita dissimiles erant inter sese, statuere ut tamen non posses utrius te malles similiorem. Crassus erat elegantium parcissimus, Scaevola parcorum elegantissimus; Crassus in summa comitate habebat etiam severitatis satis, Scaevolae multa in severitate non deerat tamen comitas. . . ."

T 3 Cic. *Brut.* 163

[BRUTUS:] nam Scaevolae dicendi elegantiam satis ex eis orationibus, quas reliquit, habemus cognitam.

and Stolfi 2018). He was regarded as having an exemplary moral character, and he was one of Cicero's mentors (Cic. Amic. 1). Some of Scaevola's speeches were extant in Cicero's time (T 3).

T 1 Cicero, *Brutus*

= F 4.

T 2 Cicero, *Brutus*

Then I [CICERO] said: "Do not believe, Brutus, that there has been anything more outstanding in our community than these two men. For as I said a moment ago [cf. **66** F 29] that one [Scaevola] was the ablest speaker of legal experts, the other [L. Licinius Crassus (**66**)] the ablest legal expert of speakers, so in other respects they were different from each other, though in such a way that you could hardly determine which of the two you would rather be more like. Crassus was the most frugal of the elegant, Scaevola the most elegant of the frugal; Crassus, along with the utmost graciousness, had also a certain severity, Scaevola, along with much severity, did not, however, lack graciousness. . . ."

T 3 Cicero, *Brutus*

[BRUTUS:] For, as for Scaevola, we have adequately seen the elegance of his speaking from those speeches that he left.

On Behalf of M. Coponius (F 4–6)

*After his consulship in 95 BC, Scaevola spoke on behalf of M. Coponius against M'. Curius, defended by L. Licinius Crassus (**66** F 28–33), in an inheritance case (TLRR 93): the controversy focused on the question of whether the*

F 4 Cic. *Brut.* 144–145

= **66** F 29.

F 5 Cic. *Brut.* 194–97

[CICERO:] qua re quis ex populo, cum Q. Scaevolam pro M. Coponio dicentem audiret in ea causa, de qua ante dixi, quicquam politius aut elegantius aut omnino melius aut exspectaret aut posse fieri putaret? [195] cum is hoc probare vellet, M'. Curium, cum ita heres institutus esset, si pupillus ante mortuus esset quam in suam tutelam venisset, pupillo non nato heredem esse non posse: quid ille non dixit de testamentorum iure? de antiquis formulis? quem ad modum scribi oportuisset, si etiam filio non nato heres institueretur? [196] quam captiosum esse populo, quod scriptum esse⟨t⟩[1] neglegi et opinione quaeri voluntates et interpretatione disertorum scripta simplicium hominum pervertere? [197] quam ille multa de auctoritate patris sui, qui semper ius illud esse defenderat? quam

---

[1] esse⟨t⟩*Ernesti*: esse *codd.*

---

[1] The reference to a son born posthumously is clarified by other mentions of the case (F 6; **66** F 30). The term used here (*pupillus,* "ward") denotes a son underage in the care of a guard-

On Behalf of M. Coponius (F 4–6)

will's literal meaning or its apparent intention should be
decisive, since M'. Curius had been named as heir in case
a posthumous son should die before coming of age, but
such a son had never been born (see also Dugan 2012).

F 4 Cicero, *Brutus*

= **66** F 29.

F 5 Cicero, *Brutus*

[CICERO:] Thus, what man of the People, when he listened to Q. Scaevola speaking on behalf of M. Coponius
in that case about which I have spoken before [F 4], would
have either expected or thought that there could be anything more finished or more nicely expressed or in any
respect better? [195] Since he wished to prove that M'.
Curius (as he had been named as heir in the event that a
posthumous son should die before he had come of age)[1]
could not be heir because a posthumous son had not been
born: what did he not say about the legal position of wills,
about ancient formulae? How it should have been written
if he were to become heir even if a son were not born?
[196] What a snare was set for the People when what was
written was ignored and intentions determined by guess-
work and the written words of simpleminded people per-
verted by the interpretation of eloquent men? [197] How
much did he say about the authority of his father, who had

ian: the son can claim the inheritance only once he has come of
age.

omnino multa de conservando iure civili? quae quidem
omnia cum perite et scienter item[2] breviter et presse et
satis ornate et pereleganter diceret, quis esset in populo
qui aut exspectaret aut fieri posse quicquam melius putaret?

[2] item *Haupt*: tum ita *codd.*: tum {ita} *Friedrich*: sumpta
Martha

F 6 Cic. *De or.* 1.180

[CRASSUS:] quid vero? clarissima M'. Curii causa Mar-
cique Coponii nuper apud centumviros quo concursu
hominum, qua exspectatione defensa est? cum Q. Scaevola, aequalis et collega meus, homo omnium et disciplina
iuris civilis eruditissimus et ingenio prudentiaque acutis-
simus et oratione maxime limatus atque subtilis atque, ut
ego soleo dicere, iuris peritorum eloquentissimus, eloquentium iuris peritissimus, ex scripto testamentorum
iura defenderet negaretque, nisi postumus et natus et,
antequam in suam tutelam venisset, mortuus esset, heredem eum esse posse, qui esset secundum postumum et
natum et mortuum heres institutus; ego autem defenderem eum hac tum mente fuisse, qui testamentum fecisset,
ut, si filius non esset, qui in suam tutelam veniret, M'.
Curius esset heres, num destitit uterque nostrum in ea
causa in auctoritatibus, in exemplis, in testamentorum formulis, hoc est, in medio iure civili versari?

always upheld that this [i.e., literal interpretation] was the law? How much generally about preserving civil law? When he said all this with mastery and knowledge, equally with brevity and compactness, with sufficient ornament and perfect finish, who was there among the People who would have either expected or thought that there could be anything better?

F 6 Cicero, *On the Orator*

[CRASSUS:] Well then, the very famous case of M'. Curius and Marcus Coponius, not long ago, before the centumviral court, amid what a crowd of people, with what expectation was it defended? Q. Scaevola, my contemporary and colleague, of all men the most learned in the science of civil law, the most sagacious by talent and wisdom, the most highly polished and exquisite in diction, and, as I always say, among lawyers the best orator, among orators the best lawyer, argued the rights of the case on the literal terms of the will and denied that the person who had been nominated heir after a posthumous son, who should both be born and die, could be heir, unless a posthumous son had both been born and died before he had come of age; on the other side I maintained that the person who had made the will then had in mind that M'. Curius should be heir if there was no son who had come of age. In that case were not both of us unceasingly occupied with authoritative views, with precedents, with formulae of wills, that is, right in the heart of civil law?

On Behalf of P. Rutilius Rufus (F 7–8)

F 7 Cic. *Brut.* 115
= **44** F 3.

F 8 Cic. *De or.* 1.229
= **80** F 9.

67A C. COELIUS CALDUS

C. Coelius (or: Caelius) Caldus (cos. 94 BC; RE Coelius 12) reached the consulship despite opposition against him as a homo novus. *As Tribune of the People (106 BC), he prosecuted C. Popillius Laenas (TLRR 59) and put forward the* Lex Caelia tabellaria *on voting practices for deci-*

T 1 Cic. *Brut.* 165

[Cicero:] . . . quod idem de C. Caelio dixerim, industriam in eo summam fuisse summasque virtutes, eloquentiae tantum quod esset in rebus privatis amicis eius, in re publica ipsius dignitati satis.

On Behalf of P. Rutilius Rufus (F 7–8)

*Presumably in 92 BC Scaevola supported P. Rutilius Rufus (accused of extortion): he was also defended by himself (**44** F 3–6) and C. Aurelius Cotta (**80** F 8–9), but had to go into exile after the trial (TLRR 94).*

F 7 Cicero, *Brutus*

= **44** F 3.

F 8 Cicero, *On the Orator*

= **80** F 9.

67A C. COELIUS CALDUS

sions in trials for perduellio *(LPPR, pp. 324–25). As a judge, Coelius acquitted someone who had attacked the poet Lucilius by name on the stage (Rhet. Her. 2.19; TLRR 353).*

T 1 Cicero, *Brutus*

[CICERO:] . . . I could say the same [as about Cn. Domitius Ahenobarbus (**69**); continued from **69** T 1] about C. Caelius: that he had the greatest industry and the highest qualities, that as much as he had of eloquence was adequate in private cases for his friends and in political matters for his own standing.

67B L. (AURELIUS) COTTA

L. (Aurelius) Cotta (tr. pl. 103, praet. before 91 BC; RE
Aurelius 100) is introduced in Cicero as an example of
someone who aspired to be an orator, but was of only

T 1 Cic. *Brut.* 137

[CICERO:] L. etiam Cotta praetorius in mediocrium oratorum numero, dicendi non ita multum laude processerat,
sed de industria cum verbis tum etiam ipso sono quasi
subrustico persequebatur atque imitabatur antiquitatem.
atque ego et in hoc ipso Cotta et in aliis pluribus intellego
me non ita disertos homines et rettulisse in oratorum
numerum et relaturum. est enim propositum conligere
eos qui hoc munere in civitate functi sint, ut tenerent
oratorum locum . . .

T 2 Cic. *Brut.* 259

[ATTICUS:] Cotta, qui{a}[1] se valde dilatandis litteris a simi-
litudine Graecae locutionis abstraxerat sonabatque contrarium Catulo, subagreste quiddam planeque subrusti-
cum, alia quidem quasi inculta et silvestri via ad eandem
laudem pervenerat.

   [1] qui{a} *Ernesti:* quia codd.

T 3 Cic. *De or.* 3.42, 46

[CRASSUS:] est autem vitium, quod nonnulli de industria
consectantur. rustica vox et agrestis quosdam delectat, quo

67B L. (AURELIUS) COTTA

moderate ability (T 1). He was particularly known for his
rustic pronunciation (T 1–3).

T 1 Cicero, *Brutus*

[CICERO:] L. Cotta too, the ex-praetor, among the ranks
of orators of moderate ability, had not advanced very far
in oratorical renown, but in the choice of words and especially also in a somewhat rustic pronunciation he actively
pursued and imitated antiquity. And I am aware that in the
case of this Cotta and many others I have put into the
ranks of orators men who were not particularly eloquent,
and I shall continue to do so. For it is my purpose to put
together those who have made it their business in civic life
to hold a place among the orators . . .

T 2 Cicero, *Brutus*

[ATTICUS:] Cotta, who, by using broad vowels, had removed himself a great deal from resemblance to Greek
pronunciation and, in contrast to Catulus [Q. Lutatius
Catulus (**63**)], pronounced something rural and almost
rustic, by another route, by an untended woodland path,
as it were, attained the same reputation [of speaking pure
Latin].

T 3 Cicero, *On the Orator*

[CRASSUS:] But there is a fault that some people deliber-
ately affect. A rustic and countrified pronunciation pleases

493

magis antiquitatem, si ita sonet, eorum sermo retinere videatur; ut tuus, Catule, sodalis L. Cotta gaudere mihi videtur gravitate linguae sonoque vocis agresti, et illud, quod loquitur, priscum visum iri putat, si plane fuerit rusticanum. . . . [46] quare Cotta noster, cuius tu illa lata, Sulpici, nonnunquam imitaris ut Iota litteram tollas et E plenissimum dicas, non mihi oratores antiquos, sed messores videtur imitari.

67C SEX. TITIUS

Sex. Titius (tr. pl. 99 BC; RE Titius 23) shared the political views of L. Appuleius Saturninus (64A) and proposed an agrarian law in his year as Tribune of the People (Lex Titia de agris dividundis: LPPR, p. 333; cf. Val. Max. 8.1.damn.3). M. Antonius (65), consul in the same year, was opposed to Titius and gave evidence when Titius was

T 1 Cic. *Brut.* 225

[CICERO:] quos Sex. Titius consecutus ‹est›[1] homo loquax sane et satis acutus, sed tam solutus[2] et mollis in gestu ut saltatio quaedam nasceretur cui saltationi Titius nomen esset.

    [1] *add. Jahn*   [2] solutus *vel* dissolutus *codd.*

certain people, so that, if their speech is in this tone, it may
seem to preserve a greater flavor of antiquity; just as your
friend L. Cotta, Catulus [Q. Lutatius Catulus (**63**)], appears to me to delight in his heavy tongue and the coarse
tone of his voice, and thinks that what he says will seem to
have a flavor of former times if it is completely rustic. . . .
[46] Consequently, our Cotta, whose broad [way of speak-
ing] you occasionally imitate, Sulpicius [P. Sulpicius Rufus
(**76**)], in dropping the letter I and pronouncing E at its
fullest length, is, in my view, imitating not the orators of
the past but harvesters.

67C SEX. TITIUS

*taken to court after their year of office (***65*** F 18; TLRR
80). A witty verbal exchange between the two men is attested (F 2). In Cicero's survey of orators, Titius is singled
out because of the way in which he moved his body when
speaking (T 1).*

T 1 Cicero, *Brutus*

[CICERO:] Sex. Titius followed these men [L. Appuleius
Saturninus (**64A**) and C. Servilius Glaucia (**58b**), continued from **58b** T 1], a loquacious individual and certainly
acute, but so languid and lax in his bodily movement that
a kind of dance came into vogue that had the name "Titius."

On M. Antonius (F 2)

F 2 Cic. *De or.* 2.265

= **65** F 36.

68 M. DURONIUS

M. Duronius (tr. pl. 97 BC [or slightly earlier]; RE Du-
ronius 3), when Tribune of the People, argued (CCMR,
App. A: 215) for the abolition of a law limiting luxury at
dinner parties (Lex Licinia sumptuaria: LPPR, pp. 327–
28; Lex Duronia de lege Licinia sumptuaria abroganda:

On the Abolition of a Sumptuary Law (F 1)

F 1 Val. Max. 2.9.5

M. autem Antonius et L. Flaccus censores Duronium senatu moverunt, quod legem de coercendis conviviorum
sumptibus latam tribunus plebi abrogaverat. mirifica notae causa: quam enim impudenter Duronius rostra con-
scendit illa dicturus: "freni sunt iniecti vobis, Quirites,
nullo modo perpetiendi. adligati et constricti estis amaro
vinculo servitutis: lex enim lata est quae vos esse frugi
iubet. abrogemus igitur istud horridae vetustatis rubigine
obsitum imperium: etenim quid opus libertate, si volentibus luxu perire non licet?"

On M. Antonius (F 2)

F 2 Cicero, *On the Orator*
= **65** F 36.

68 M. DURONIUS

LPPR, *pp. 334–35). In response, the censors M. Antonius
(*65*) and L. Valerius Flaccus (97 BC) expelled Duronius
from the Senate. Thereupon, he accused M. Antonius of
ambitus, but without success (*71* F 1A; TLRR 83).*

On the Abolition of a Sumptuary Law (F 1)

F 1 Valerius Maximus, *Memorable Doings and Sayings*

And the censors [97 BC] M. Antonius [**65**] and L. Flaccus
[L. Valerius Flaccus] expelled Duronius from the Senate
because, as Tribune of the Plebs, he had revoked a law
passed to limit money spent on dinner parties. A remarkable reason for a stigma: for how impudently does Duronius ascend the Rostra to speak as follows: "Bridles have
been laid upon you, Romans, in no way tolerable. You have
been bound and tied with a galling chain of slavery: for a
law has been passed that orders you to be frugal. Let us
then revoke that regulation, overlaid with the rust of rug-
ged antiquity. For indeed, what use is liberty if those who
want to are not allowed to go to perdition through luxury?"

69 CN. DOMITIUS AHENOBARBUS

Cn. Domitius Ahenobarbus (cos. 96, censor 92 BC; RE Domitius 21), when Tribune of the People in 104 (or perhaps 103) BC, proposed a law transferring the election of priests from the colleges to the People (Lex Domitia de sacerdotiis: LPPR, p. 329); *he was* pontifex maximus *from 103 BC until his death. When censor with L. Licinius*

T 1 Cic. *Brut.* 165

[Cicero:] hoc loco ipsum Domitium non relinquo. nam etsi non fuit in oratorum numero, tamen pono satis in eo fuisse orationis atque ingeni, quo et magistratus personam et consularem dignitatem tueretur . . .

T 2 Cic. *De or.* 2.230

[Antonius:] erat autem tanta in Domitio gravitas, tanta auctoritas, ut, quod esset ab eo obiectum, lepore magis elevandum quam contentione frangendum videretur.

Against M. Aemilius Scaurus (F 3–4)

*As Tribune of the People, Ahenobarbus spoke against M. Aemilius Scaurus (**43**); he alleged that the latter had not looked after cult practices properly (TLRR 68; Cic.* Deiot.

F 3 Cic. *Scaur.* F I(c)

subiit etiam populi iudicium inquirente Cn. Domitio tribuno plebis.

69 CN. DOMITIUS AHENOBARBUS

Crassus (66), Ahenobarbus issued an edict forbidding the activity of Latin rhetoricians in the city (Cic. De or. 3.93; Tac. Dial. 35.1; Gell. NA 15.11.2; Suet. Gram. et rhet. 25.2). In Cicero, Ahenobarbus is assigned dignity and some ability in speaking (T 1–2).

T 1 Cicero, *Brutus*

[CICERO:] At this point I am not passing over Domitius himself. For even though he was not among the orators, still I assert that he had sufficient eloquence and talent to sustain the role of a magistrate and the rank of a consular . . .

T 2 Cicero, *On the Orator*

[ANTONIUS:] Yet there was such dignity, such distinction about Domitius that it seemed fitting that what had been charged by him should rather be made light of by pleasantry than be shattered by force.

Against M. Aemilius Scaurus (F 3–4)

31; Val. Max. 6.5.5; Cass. Dio 27, F 92; on problems in Asconius' account, see Marshall 1985, 129–33).

F 3 Cicero, *Pro Scauro*

He [Scaurus] also underwent trial before the People when Cn. Domitius, a Tribune of the People, was making judicial inquiries.

F 4 Asc. in Cic. *Scaur.* I.1 (pp. 18–19 KS = 21.3–12 C.)

Cn. Domitius qui consul fuit cum <C.>[1] Cassio, cum esset
tribunus plebis, iratus Scauro quod eum in augurum collegium non cooptaverat, diem ei dixit apud populum et
multam irrogavit, quod eius opera sacra {multa}[2] populi
Romani deminuta esse diceret. crimini dabat sacra publica
populi Romani deum Penatium quae Lavini fierent[3] opera
eius minus recte casteque fieri. quo crimine absolutus est
Scaurus quidem, sed ita ut a tribus tribubus damnaretur,
a XXXII absolveretur, et in eis pauca puncta inter damna-
tionem et absolutionem interessent.

[1] *add. Manutius*   [2] *del. Clark*   [3] fierent *Manutius*:
fuerunt *codd.*

Against M. Iunius Silanus (F 5–6)

F 5 Cic. *Corn.* II, F 7 Puccioni = 7 Crawford

quid? idem Domitius M. Silanum consularem hominem,
quem ad modum tr. pl. vexavit?

F 6 Asc. in Cic. *Corn.* (p. 71 KS = 80.18–25 C.)

M. Silanus quinquennio ante consul fuerat quam Domitius tr. pl. esset, atque ipse quoque adversus Cimbros rem

F 4 Asconius on Cicero, *Pro Scauro*

Cn. Domitius, who was consul with <C.> Cassius [C. Cassius Longinus, 96 BC], when he was Tribune of the People and angry with Scaurus, since he had not co-opted him into the college of augurs, summoned him to trial in front of the People and demanded a fine, since he said that due to his agency the sacred activities of the Roman People had been curtailed. He presented it as a crime that, through his agency, the public rites of the Roman People for the Penates gods, which happened at Lavinium [south of Rome, in Latium], happened less correctly and chastely. Scaurus was found not guilty of this crime, yet in such a way that he was condemned by three tribes and released by thirty-two, and among those there were only few votes between conviction and release.

Against M. Iunius Silanus (F 5–6)

As Tribune of the People, Ahenobarbus spoke against M. Iunius Silanus (cos. 109 BC) because of his unsuccessful fighting against the Cimbri (TLRR 63; Liv. Epit. 65; Vell. Pat. 2.12.2; Flor. 1.38.2–4).

F 5 Cicero, *Pro Cornelio*

What? How did this same Domitius, a Tribune of the People, harass M. Silanus, an ex-consul?

F 6 Asconius on Cicero, *Pro Cornelio*

M. Silanus had been consul five years before Domitius was a Tribune of the People, and he himself had also carried out the war against the Cimbri [Germanic tribe] badly: for

male gesserat: quam ob causam Domitius eum apud populum accusavit. criminabatur rem cum[1] Cimbris iniussu
populi gessisse, idque principium fuisse calamitatum quas
eo bello populus accepisset; ac de eo tabellam quoque
edidit. sed plenissime Silanus absolutus est; nam duae
solae tribus eum, Sergia et Quirina, damnaverunt.

[1] rem cum *Stangl*: eum cum *codd.*: eum bellum *Manutius*:
eum bellum cum *Bücheler*

Against L. Licinius Crassus (F 6A)

*When Ahenobarbus and L. Licinius Crassus (66) were
censors in 92 BC, the two men had frequent arguments;
Ahenobarbus spoke against Crassus, provoking the latter's*

F 6A Cic. *Brut.* 162–64; *De or.* 2.227, 2.45; Suet. *Nero*
2.2; Plin. *HN* 17.1–4; Val. Max. 9.1.4; Ael. *NA* 8.4

= **66** F 34–40.

this reason Domitius accused him before the People. He charged him with the fact that he had carried out the war with the Cimbri without instructions from the People, and that this had been the beginning of the calamities that the People had suffered in that war; and about him he even issued a written record. But Silanus was acquitted by a large majority; for only two tribes, the Sergia and the Quirina, condemned him.

Against L. Licinius Crassus (F 6A)

defense and counteraccusation (66 F 34–40; CCMR, App. A: 217).

F 6A Cicero; Suetonius; Pliny the Elder; Valerius Maximus, Aelian

= **66** F 34–40.